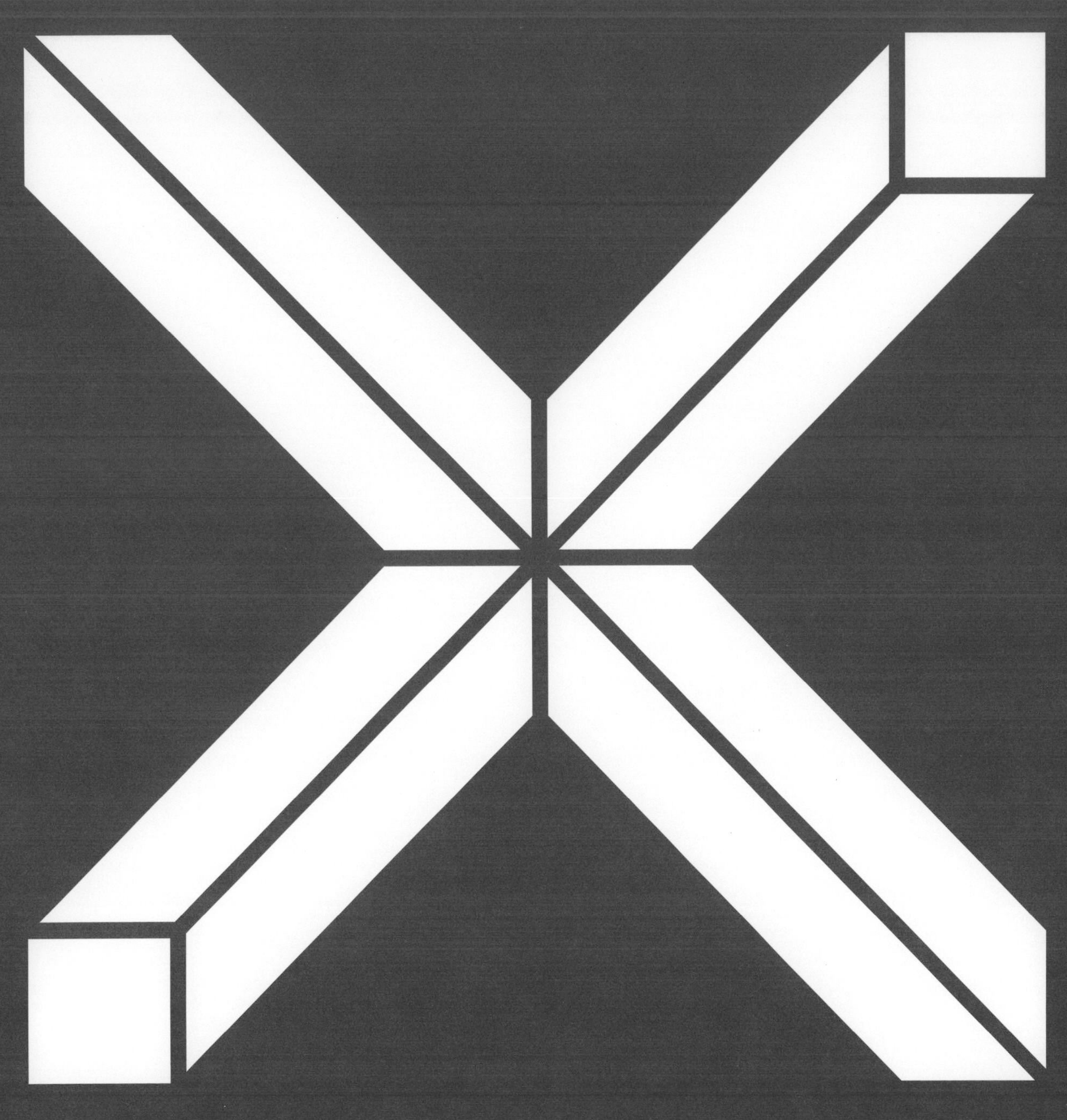

SECOND EDITION

# Explorations in Typography

Carolina de Bartolo

with Stephen Coles and Erik Spiekermann

EXPLORATIONSINTYPOGRAPHY.COM

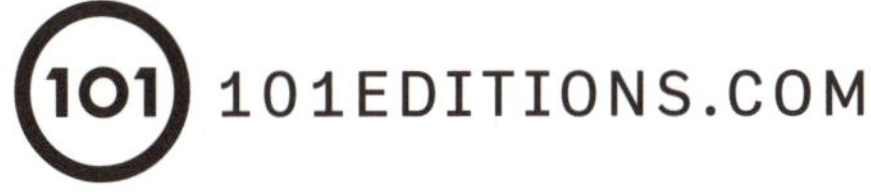

101EDITIONS.COM

TO MY TEACHERS.
TO MY STUDENTS.
TO MY PARENTS.

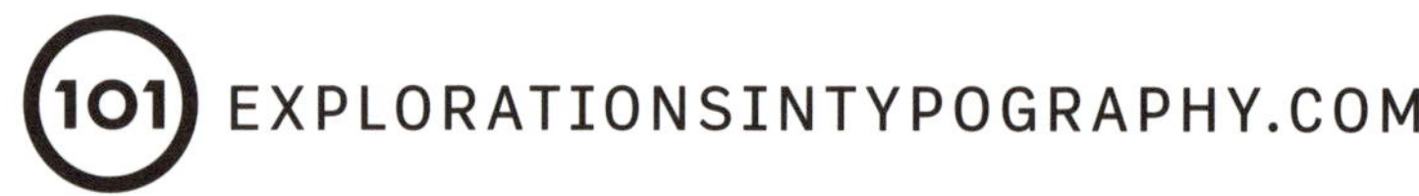



For supplementary resources and teaching materials, or to purchase copies of this book or ebook, please visit the interactive website at *explorationsinsintypography.com.*

Printed in China.

Library of Congress Cataloging-in-Publication Data

de Bartolo, Carolina with Coles, Stephen and Spiekermann, Erik.
Explorations in Typography. Second edition (paperback).
First edition published in 2011 as *Explorations in Typography: Mastering the Art of Fine Typesetting.*

ISBN: 978-0-9843707-0-2



The typeface Output Sans licensed by permission of David Jonathan Ross.

This book would not have been possible without the generous font licensing support from FontShop International and Monotype Imaging, Inc. To purchase any of the FontFont or Monotype fonts shown in this book, visit *monotype.com/fonts, myfonts.com* or *fontshop.com.*

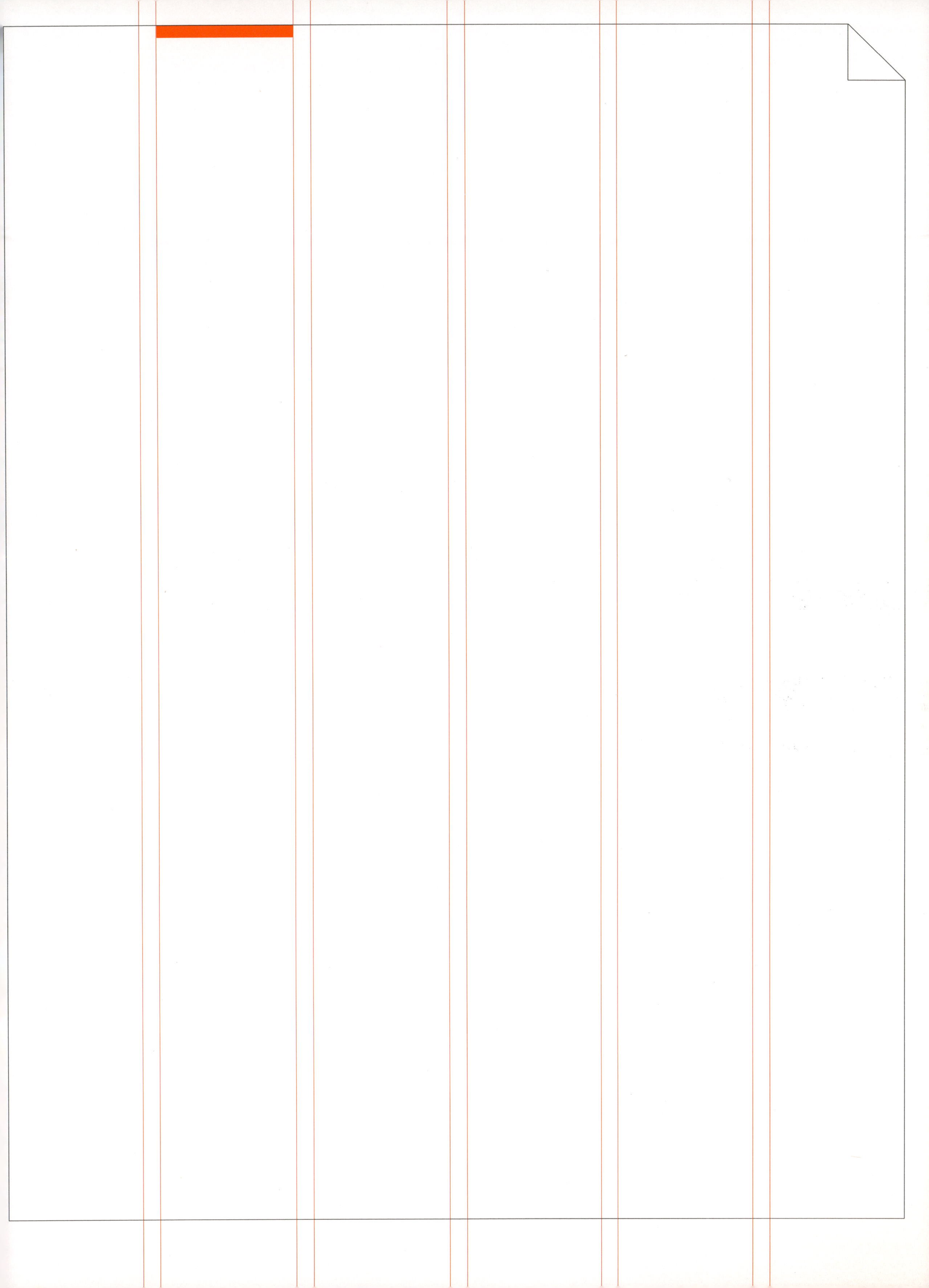

**“Even simple problems benefit from thinking about the problem and careful planning.”**

—Erik Spiekermann

# Contents

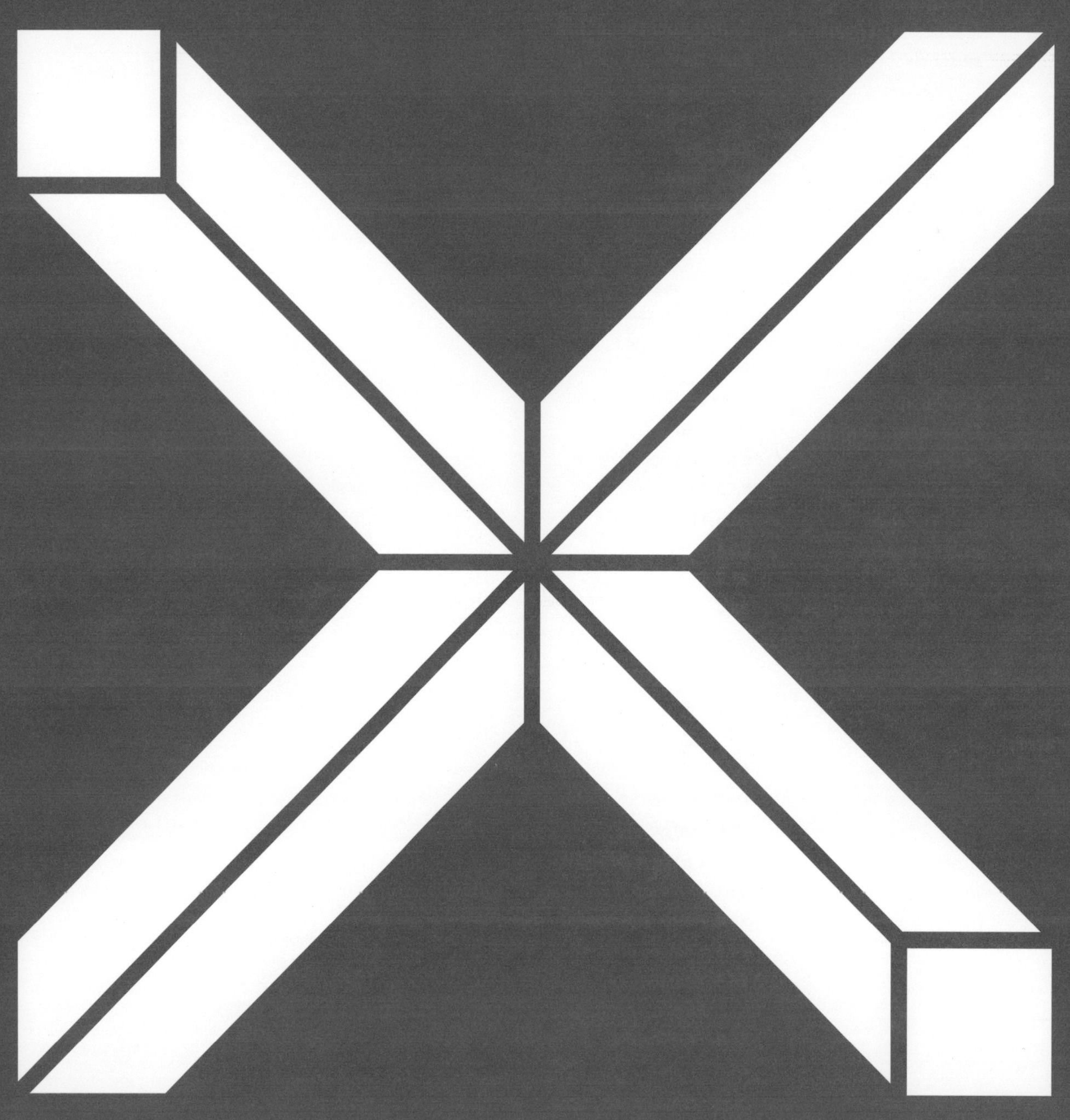

# Introduction

Welcome to the new edition of *Explorations in Typography*! This compendium of typesetting examples can help you learn the art of fine typesetting through careful study and practice of both the art and the craft of typesetting. It can also simply serve as a resource for typographic inspiration and ideas.

The typesetting examples use excerpts from *Stop Stealing Sheep and Find Out How Type Works* by Erik Spiekermann. We call them "Explorations" because you can use them to investigate the variety of ways text type might be composed when you exploit the natural breaks in the language. These breaks occur with each new paragraph of body copy and with hierarchical elements such as heads, bylines, subheads, and footnotes.

Practicing by typesetting the same text over and over is a bit similar to playing scales on a musical instrument. It familiarizes you with your "instrument"—in this case, type on the page. You gain fluency and facility with both the macro- and micro-aesthetics of typography and page composition.

Any text can be composed and typeset on a page in infinite ways, all of them potentially beautiful as well as legible and hierarchical. Some of the less conventional typesetting samples in the later chapters of this book demonstrate the expressive potential of text type. To some degree, all of them are functional as reading material. None are merely aesthetic or conceptual experiments.

The Explorations are shown at full size on a letter-size page outline so that you can easily see, evaluate, and mimic the page composition as well as the point size, leading, tracking, and other features. The details of proportion, spacing, and alignment (micro-aesthetics) most often distinguish extraordinary typesetting from the ordinary kind.

Each page includes type specifications (a colophon), which are composed on the page to complement the layout and in a second typeface that combines well with the primary ones in the sample. This colophon information allows you to re-create the typesetting you see. In another music analogy, the colophon is like the sheet music that instructs you how to play the song: it tells you how to set the type. And, like playing from sheet music, you can follow the instructions precisely or improvise from them a little bit...or a lot.

Numbered design notes with explanations are set in sidebars on each page. These highlight some of the details that make the typesetting and the page design work. When you improvise using these Explorations, the design notes point out qualities that would likely be best to retain. The lower sidebars contain historical and background information about the typefaces in use.

To highlight the importance of page composition, a few grid lines of each Exploration are exposed (using thin orange lines). Miniature versions of all the page layouts are in a section at the back of this book. These can be scaled and used as templates for page composition and typesetting of any content.

Note that because a number of excellent introductory typography texts already exist, this book is geared toward intermediate to advanced typographic study. For that reason, it does not cover material that is customarily included in a collegiate Typography 101 course, such as letterform anatomy, type measurements, and type classifications. See the Further Reading section at the end of this publication for recommended books.

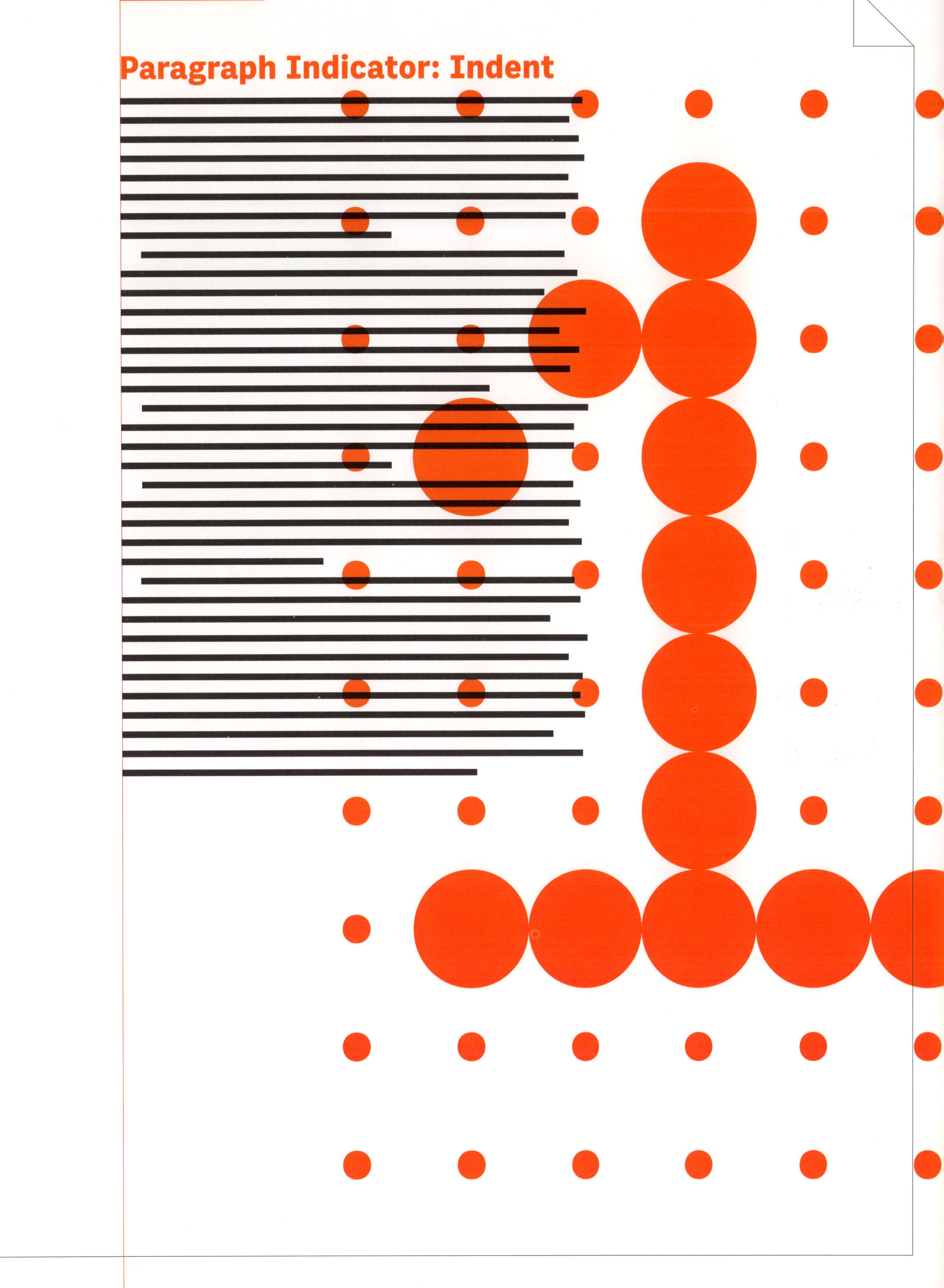
Paragraph Indicator: Indent

# 1 Paragraph Indicator: Indent

The most common way to indicate paragraphs in text type is by indentation. Indents are especially commonplace in continuous-reading text in print. The first paragraph is typically not indented in order to keep a square upper-left corner on the text block. Subheads mark a new beginning, so the first paragraph under a subhead is also not indented.

Indents of 1 em are usually sufficient on narrow (approximately 20–50 characters) to medium (50–80 characters) column widths. Wide columns (80–100 characters) may require 2 ems indent. Generous leading may also necessitate a 2-em indent.

The negative space produced by indentations of 1 or 2 ems forms a harmonious proportion with the type size. Ideally, we always set type in proportional amounts, not in arbitrary amounts.

Two ems is the maximum recommended indent. If you were to indent more than that and the last line of a paragraph above an indent was rather short, those two lines might not overlap, making the linespace between paragraphs appear much larger.

It might seem like 1 or 2 ems is not enough indentation, but indents can be fairly subtle because readers find them so familiar and are quite comfortable reading them.

Exploration 1 ▸ Paragraph Indicator: Indent   text: 8/12 FF Meta Book, tracking +20/1000 em   indent: 1 em

1▸ Ever since people have been writing things down, they have had to consider their audience before actually putting pen to paper: letters would have to look different depending on whether they were to be read by mainly other people (in official documents or inscriptions), just one other person (in a letter), or only the writer (in a notebook or diary). There would be less room for guesswork if letter shapes were made more formal as the diversity of the readership expanded.

Some of the first messages to be read by a large number of people were rendered not by pens but by chisels. Large inscriptions on monuments in ancient Rome were carefully planned, with letters drawn on the stone with a brush before they were chiseled. Even if white-out had existed in those days, it would not have helped to remove mistakes made in stone. A bit of planning was also more important then, since stonemasons were sometimes more expendable than slabs of marble.

2▸ Graphic design and typography are complicated activities, but even the simple projects benefit from thinking about the problem, forming a mental picture of the solution, and then carefully planning the steps between.

Scientists have not been content with just calling the human face “beautiful” if it meets certain ideals, or “ugly” if it doesn’t. They had to go out and measure proportions of nose to jaw, forehead to chin, and so on to establish why some faces are more appealing than others.

Typographers and graphic designers often choose typefaces for the very same reason they might fancy a person: They just like that person. For more scientifically-minded people, however, there are specific measurements, components, details, and proportions to describe various parts of a letter. While these won’t tell you what makes a typeface good, they will at least give you the right words to use when you discuss the benefits of a particular face over another. You can say “I hate the x-height on Such-a-Gothic” or “These descenders just don’t work for me” or “Please, may I see something with a smaller cap height?” and you’ll know what you are talking about.

3▸ While metal letters could be made to any width and height, digital type has to conform to multiples of the smallest unit: the pixel. Every character has to be a certain number of pixels wide and high. This is not a problem when the letters are made up of 600 pixels per inch, as is the case with modern laser printers—those pixels are not discernible to our eyes, and we are happy to believe that we are looking at smooth curves instead of little squares fitted into tight grids.

On most screens, only 72 pixels make up one inch. We could see each and every one of them, if engineers hadn’t already found ways around that. Computer screens, however, are not where we read most of our type these days. Smart phones, computers, and tablets all have high-resolutions screens, but microwave ovens, espresso makers, and all the other gadgets around us all still use small and modest displays. And the type unmistakably consists of bitmaps, which means that an 8-point letter is actually made up of eight pixels. If we allow six pixels above the baseline, including accents, and two below for descenders, that’ll leave only three or four pixels for a lowercase character. In spite of these restrictions, there are hundreds of bitmap fonts, all different from one another by only a few pixels, but enough to prove that typographic variety cannot be suppressed by technological constraints.

Rhythm and contrast keep coming up when discussing good music and good typographic design. They are concepts that also apply to spoken language, as anyone who has had to sit through a monotonous lecture will attest; the same tone, volume and speed of speech will put even the most interested listener into dreamland. Every now and again the audience needs to be shaken, either by a change in voice or pitch, by a question being posed, or by the speaker talking very quietly and then suddenly shouting. An occasional joke also works, just as the use of a funny typeface can liven up a page.

1 The first paragraph of a text is not indented so you have a square corner.

2 One em indent is typically enough on a medium (50–80 characters) column width, or “measure.”

3 Begin new columns with a new paragraph whenever possible. Indent this top paragraph just like the others. Although it is at the top of a column, it is not the first paragraph of the text.

**FF Meta**

In 1991, Erik Spiekermann designed this typeface to be used for small text on West German Post Office forms. The legibility and functionality, combined with a contemporary Humanist look, made it an extremely popular alternative to more conservative corporate typefaces. Its ubiquity made it “the Helvetica of the 1990s.” In 2011, it was enshrined in the MoMA Architecture and Design Collection.

EXP
**1.2**

Ever since people have been writing things down, they have had to consider their audience before actually putting pen to paper: letters would have to look different depending on whether they were to be read by mainly other people (in official documents or inscriptions), just one other person (in a letter), or only the writer (in a notebook or diary). There would be less room for guesswork if letter shapes were made more formal as the diversity of the readership expanded.

1▸ Some of the first messages to be read by a large number of people were rendered not by pens but by chisels. Large inscriptions on monuments in ancient Rome were carefully planned, with letters drawn on the stone with a brush before they were chiseled. Even if white-out had existed in those days, it would not have helped to remove mistakes made in stone. A bit of planning was also more important then, since stonemasons were sometimes more expendable than slabs of marble or granite.

Graphic design and typography are complicated activities, but even the simple projects benefit from thinking about the problem, forming a mental picture of the solution, and then carefully planning the steps between.

Scientists have not been content with just calling the human face "beautiful" if it meets certain ideals, or "ugly" if it doesn't. They had to go out and measure proportions of nose to jaw, forehead to chin, and so on to establish why some faces are more appealing than others.

Typographers and graphic designers often choose typefaces for the very same reason they might fancy a person: They just like that person. For more scientifically-minded people, however, there are specific measurements, components, details, and proportions to describe various parts of a letter. While these won't tell you what makes a typeface good, they will at least give you the right words to use when you discuss the benefits of a particular face over another. You can say "I hate the x-height on Such-a-Gothic" or "These descenders just don't work for me" or "Please, may I see something with a smaller cap height?" ◂2
and you'll know what you are talking about.

While metal letters could be made to any width and height, digital type has to conform to multiples of the smallest unit: the pixel. Every character has to be a certain number of pixels wide and high. This is not a problem when the letters are made up of 600 pixels per inch, as is the case with modern laser printers—those pixels are not discernible to our eyes, and we are happy to believe that we are looking at smooth curves instead of little squares fitted into tight grids.

Exploration 1 :: Paragraph Indicator :: Indent    text: 7/16 ITC Mendoza, tracking +20/1000 em    indent: 2 ems

EXP
1.3

*Ever since people have been writing things down, they have had to consider their audience before actually putting pen to paper: letters would have to look different depending on whether they were to be read by mainly other people (in official documents or inscriptions), just one other person (in a letter), or only the writer (in a notebook or diary). There would be less room for guesswork if letter shapes were made more formal as the diversity of the readership expanded.*

*Some of the first messages to be read by a large number of people were rendered not by pens but by chisels. Large inscriptions on monuments in ancient Rome were carefully planned, with letters drawn on the stone with a brush before they were chiseled. Even if white-out had existed in those days, it would not have helped to remove mistakes made in stone. A bit of planning was also more important then, since stonemasons were sometimes more expendable than slabs of marble or granite.*

*Graphic design and typography are complicated activities, but even the simple projects benefit from thinking about the problem, forming a mental picture of the solution, and then carefully planning the steps between.*

*Scientists have not been content with just calling the human face "beautiful" if it meets certain ideals, or "ugly" if it doesn't. They had to go out and measure proportions of nose to jaw, forehead to chin, and so on to establish why some faces are more appealing than others.*

*Typographers and graphic designers often choose typefaces for the very same reason they might fancy a person: They just like that person. For more scientifically-minded people, however, there are specific measurements, components, details, and proportions to describe various parts of a letter. While these won't tell you what makes a typeface good, they will at least give you the right words to use when you discuss the benefits of a particular face over another. You can say "I hate the x-height on Such-a-Gothic" or "These descenders just don't work for me" or "Please, may I see something with a smaller cap height?" and you'll know what you are talking about.*

*While metal letters could be made to any width and height, digital type has to conform to multiples of the smallest unit: the pixel. Every character has to be a certain number of pixels wide and high. This is not a problem when the letters are made up of 600 pixels per inch, as is the case with modern laser printers—those pixels are not discernible to our eyes, and we are happy to believe that we are looking at smooth curves instead of little squares fitted into tight grids.*

◂3

Exploration 1//Paragraph Indicator: Indent   text: 6.5/11.5 PMN Caecilia 56 Italic, tracking +30/1000 em   indent: 1 em

**Opposite page**

1 On wide columns, indent by 2 ems. The wider the column, the wider the indent. However, if you find you need more than 2 ems indent, you may have too wide a column (more than 100 characters) or too much leading for comfortable reading.

2 With many words per line, wide columns can easily be set justified without the danger of creating rivers.

**This page**

3 The second column is shorter than the first. Uneven column depths activate the page, which is typically a desirable attribute.

**ITC Mendoza**

Most text faces made in the early years of digital typography were poor revivals of metal type, made too spindly for modern printing. ITC Mendoza (1991) is one of the few Oldstyle faces from that era with a low stroke contrast, making it ideal for setting text at small sizes or on coated paper. Its rugged build and sturdy serifs were ahead of their time—around 20 years later these attributes became common in new text faces, but ITC Mendoza was largely forgotten, making it an uncommon and intriguing choice today.

**PMN Caecilia**

Designed in 1990 but still feeling fresh today, Peter Matthias Noordzij's Humanist slab serif has become a contemporary model for readability, earning it many imitators (even decades later). It was the default font for the first Kindle devices.

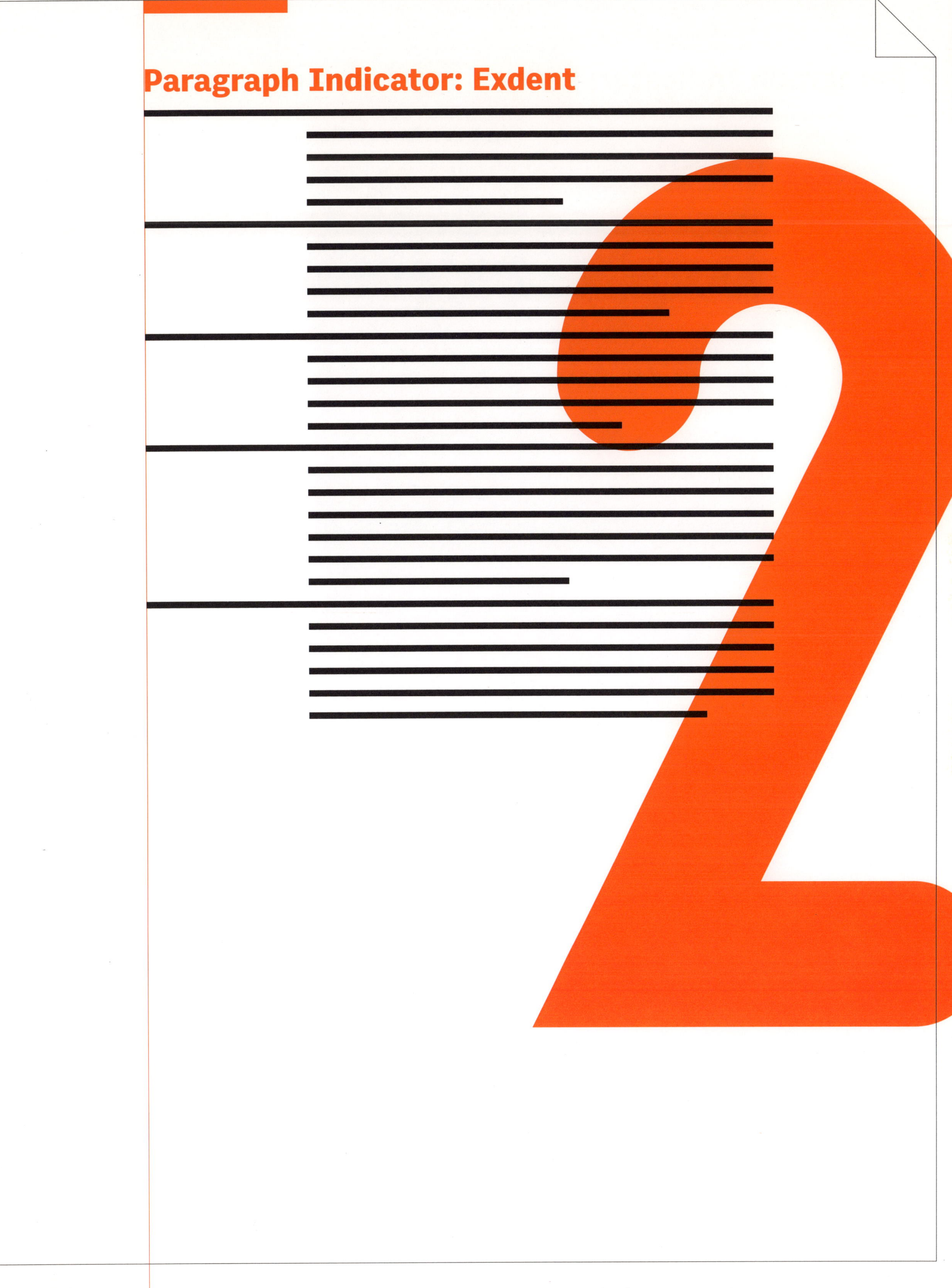
Paragraph Indicator: Exdent
2

# 2 Paragraph Indicator: Exdent

Exdents are also called hanging indents or outdents because the first line of each paragraph is wider than the other lines.

Unlike indents, the first paragraph is exdented just as all the other paragraphs are. In order for an exdent to be noticeable and therefore functional to a reader, the first lines need to hang by at least 2 ems or more.

Exdenting by a number of ems, rather than by any random number, keeps the negative space proportional to the type size.

While they are perfectly acceptable for use on text type in paragraphs, exdents are not frequently used this way. They are more often used for listings such as in an index, phone book, or dictionary.

1 Ever since people have been writing things down, they have had to consider their audience before actually putting pen to paper: letters would have to look different depending on whether they were to be read by mainly other people (in official documents or inscriptions), just one other person (in a letter), or only the writer (in a notebook or diary). There would be less room for guesswork if letter shapes were made more formal as the diversity of the readership expanded.

Some of the first messages to be read by a large number of people were rendered not by pens but by chisels. Large inscriptions on monuments in ancient Rome were carefully planned, with letters drawn on the stone with a brush before they were chiseled. Even if white-out had existed in those days, it would not have helped to remove mistakes made in stone. A bit of planning was also more important then, since stonemasons were sometimes more expendable than slabs of marble or granite.

Graphic design and typography are complicated activities, but even the simple projects benefit from thinking about the problem, forming a mental picture of the solution, and then carefully planning the steps between.

Scientists have not been content with just calling the human face "beautiful" if it meets certain ideals, or "ugly" if it doesn't. They had to go out and measure proportions of nose to jaw, forehead to chin, and so on to establish why some faces are more appealing than others.

Typographers and graphic designers often choose typefaces for the very same reason they might fancy a person: They just like that person. For more scientifically-minded people, however, there are specific measurements, components, details, and proportions to describe various parts of a letter. While these won't tell you what makes a typeface good, they will at least give you the right words to use when you discuss the benefits of a particular face over another. You can say "I hate the x-height on Such-a-Gothic" or "These descenders just don't work for me" or "Please, may I see something with a smaller cap height?" and you'll know what you are talking about.

While metal letters could be made to any width and height, digital type has to conform to multiples of the smallest unit: the pixel. Every character has to be a certain number of pixels wide and high. This is not a problem when the letters are made up of 600 pixels per inch, as is the case with modern laser printers—those pixels are not discernible to our eyes, and we are happy to believe that we are looking at smooth curves instead of little squares fitted into tight grids.

2

*EXPLORATION 2 // Paragraph Indicator: Exdent*

*text: 8/12 ITC Officina Sans, tracking +15/1000 em*

*exdent: 3 ems*

1 Unlike using indents as a paragraph indication, the first paragraph is set with an exdent like all the others.

2 Note that the bulk of the body copy is in this narrower column width, 3 ems narrower than the full measure when you include the width of the exdents.

**ITC Officina Sans**
Erik Spiekermann designed Officina for the low-resolution printing of office documents. His inspiration was the hard-nosed monospaced faces of the Information Age—such as Letter Gothic and Courier—and he retained much of their workaday qualities while reshaping them with a warm, Humanist touch.

**This page**

1 The wider the column, the wider the exdent can be. You can exdent by a lot more than you can indent.

**Opposite page**

2 Two ems is the minimum amount of exdent. Less than 2 ems is too subtle and usually looks like a mistake rather than like a clear paragraph indication.

3 Set narrow columns flush left/rag right rather than justified in order to avoid rivers (i.e., when word space is optically greater than linespace).

**FF QType**

Achaz Reuss's goal of this 1997 release was simply to design a large family based on a square with four different widths and four weights. The family now consists of five subfamilies with five weights each.

**FF BeoSans Hard**

In the late 1980s, designers Just van Rossum and Erik van Blokland found a way to change the programming in fonts so that each point in each letter would move randomly, as it was rendered, giving the letters a shaky, distressed appearance. The resulting typeface was first called RandomFont. The latest version of the face does not dynamically alter its shape as its forebears did, but instead it contains ten randomly generated alternatives for every character.

Ever since people have been writing things down, they have had to consider their audience before actually putting pen to paper: letters would have to look different depending on whether they were to be read by mainly other people (in official documents or inscriptions), just one other person (in a letter), or only the writer (in a notebook or diary). There would be less room for guesswork if letter shapes were made more formal as the diversity of the readership expanded.

Some of the first messages to be read by a large number of people were rendered not by pens but by chisels. Large inscriptions on monuments in ancient Rome were carefully planned, with letters drawn on the stone with a brush before they were chiseled. Even if white-out had existed in those days, it would not have helped to remove mistakes made in stone. A bit of planning was also more important then, since stonemasons were sometimes more expendable than slabs of marble or granite.

1

Graphic design and typography are complicated activities, but even the simple projects benefit from thinking about the problem, forming a mental picture of the solution, and then carefully planning the steps between.

Scientists have not been content with just calling the human face "beautiful" if it meets certain ideals, or "ugly" if it doesn't. They had to go out and measure proportions of nose to jaw, forehead to chin, and so on to establish why some faces are more appealing than others.

Typographers and graphic designers often choose typefaces for the very same reason they might fancy a person: They just like that person. For more scientifically-minded people, however, there are specific measurements, components, details, and proportions to describe various parts of a letter. While these won't tell you what makes a typeface good, they will at least give you the right words to use when you discuss the benefits of a particular face over another. You can say "I hate the x-height on Such-a-Gothic" or "These descenders just don't work for me" or "Please, may I see something with a smaller cap height?" and you'll know what you are talking about.

While metal letters could be made to any width and height, digital type has to conform to multiples of the smallest unit: the pixel. Every character has to be a certain number of pixels wide and high. This is not a problem when the letters are made up of 600 pixels per inch, as is the case with modern laser printers—those pixels are not discernible to our eyes, and we are happy to believe that we are looking at smooth curves instead of little squares fitted into tight grids.

On most screens, only 72 pixels make up one inch. We could see each and every one of them, if engineers hadn't already found ways around that. Computer screens, however, are not where we read most of our type these days. Smart phones, computers, and tablets all have high-resolutions screens, but microwave ovens, espresso makers, and all the other gadgets around us all still use small and modest displays. And the type unmistakably consists of bitmaps, which means that an 8-point letter is actually made up of eight pixels. If we allow six pixels above the baseline, including accents, and two below for descenders, that'll leave only three or four pixels for a lowercase character. In spite of these restrictions, there are hundreds of bitmap fonts, all different from one another by only a few pixels, but enough to prove that typographic variety cannot be suppressed by technological constraints.

EXPLORATION 2 » PARAGRAPH INDICATOR » EXDENT    TEXT:7/14 FF QTYPE CONDENSED BOOK, TRACKING +10/1000 EM    EXDENT:7 EMS

2▸ Ever since people have been writing things down, they have had to consider their audience before actually putting pen to paper: letters would have to look different depending on whether they were to be read by mainly other people (in official documents or inscriptions), just one other person (in a letter), or only the writer (in a notebook or diary). There would be less room for guesswork if letter shapes were made more formal as the diversity of the readership expanded.

Some of the first messages to be read by a large number of people were rendered not by pens but by chisels. Large inscriptions on monuments in ancient Rome were carefully planned, with letters drawn on the stone with a brush before they were chiseled. Even if white-out had existed in those days, it would not have helped to remove mistakes made in stone. A bit of planning was also more important then, since stonemasons were sometimes more expendable than slabs of marble or granite.

Graphic design and typography are complicated activities, but even the simple projects benefit from thinking about the problem, forming a mental picture of the solution, and then carefully planning the steps between.

Scientists have not been content with just calling the human face “beautiful” if it meets certain ideals, or “ugly” if it doesn’t. They had to go out and measure proportions of nose to jaw, forehead to chin, and so on to establish why some faces are more appealing than others.

Typographers and graphic designers often choose typefaces for the very same reason they might fancy a person: They just like that person. For more scientifically-minded people, however, there are specific measurements, components, details, and proportions to describe various parts of a letter. While these won’t tell you what makes a typeface good, they will at least give you the right words to use when you discuss the benefits of a particular face over another. You can say “I hate the x-height on Such-a-Gothic” or “These descenders just don’t work for me” or “Please, may I see something with a smaller cap height?” and you’ll know what you are talking about.

While metal letters could be made to any width and height, digital type has to conform to multiples of the smallest unit: the pixel. Every character has to be a certain number of pixels wide and high. This is not a problem when the letters are made up of 600 pixels per inch, as is the case with modern laser printers—those pixels are not discernible to our eyes, and we are happy to believe that we are looking at smooth curves instead of little squares fitted into tight grids.

On most screens, only 72 pixels make up one inch. We could see each and every one of them, if engineers hadn’t already found ways around that. Computer screens, however, are not where we read most of our type these days. Smart phones, computers, and tablets all have high-resolutions screens, but ◂3 microwave ovens, espresso makers, and all the other gadgets around us all still use small and modest displays. And the type unmistakably consists of bitmaps, which means that an 8-point letter is actually made up of eight pixels. If we allow six pixels above the baseline, including accents, and two below for descenders, that’ll leave only three or four pixels for a lowercase character. In spite of these restrictions, there are hundreds of bitmap fonts, all different from one another by only a few pixels, but enough to prove that typographic variety cannot be suppressed by technological constraints.

**Exploration 2**
*Paragraph Indicator: Exdent*
*text: 7/13 FF BeoSans Hard R20, tracking +45/1000 em*
*exdent: 2 ems*

EXP
**2.4**

Exploration 2 : Paragraph indicator : Exdent    Text : 7/13 FF Engine Light Italic, tracking +5/1000 em    Exdent : 2 ems

1 Ever since people have been writing things down, they have had to consider their audience before actually putting pen to paper: letters would have to look different depending on whether they were to be read by mainly other people (in official documents or inscriptions), just one other person (in a letter), or only the writer (in a notebook or diary).

2▸ Some of the first messages to be read by a large number of people were rendered not by pens but by chisels. Large inscriptions on monuments in ancient Rome were carefully planned, with letters drawn on the stone with a brush before they were chiseled. Even if white-out had existed in those days, it would not have helped to remove mistakes made in stone. A bit of planning was also more important then, since stonemasons were sometimes more expendable than slabs of marble or granite. ◂3

Graphic design and typography are complicated activities, but even the simple projects benefit from thinking about the problem, forming a mental picture of the solution, and then carefully planning the steps between.

Scientists have not been content with just calling the human face "beautiful" if it meets certain ideals, or "ugly" if it doesn't. They had to go out and measure proportions of nose to jaw, forehead to chin, and so on to establish why some faces are more appealing than others.

While metal letters could be made to any width and height, digital type has to conform to multiples of the smallest unit: the pixel. This is not a problem when the letters are made up of 600 pixels per inch, as is the case with modern laser printers—those pixels are not discernible to our eyes, and we are happy to believe that we are looking at smooth curves instead of little squares fitted into tight grids.

On most screens, only 72 pixels make up one inch. We could see each and every one of them, if engineers hadn't already found ways around that. Computer screens, however, are not where we read most of our type these days. Smart phones, computers, and tablets all have high-resolutions screens, but microwave ovens, espresso makers, and all the other gadgets around us all still use small and modest displays. And the type unmistakably consists of bitmaps, which means that an 8-point letter is actually made up of eight pixels.

EXPLORATION 2 PARAGRAPH INDICATOR › EXDENT TEXT: 7.5/13 FF TIBERE, TRACKING +40/1000 EM EXDENT: 12 EMS

Ever since people have been writing things down, they have had to consider their audience before actually putting pen to paper: letters would have to look different depending on whether they were to be read by mainly other people (in official documents or inscriptions), just one other person (in a letter), or only the writer (in a notebook or diary). There would be less room for guesswork if letter shapes were made more formal as the diversity of the readership expanded.

Some of the first messages to be read by a large number of people were rendered not by pens but by chisels. Large inscriptions on monuments in ancient Rome were carefully planned, with letters drawn on the stone with a brush before they were chiseled. Even if white-out had existed in those days, it would not have helped to remove mistakes made in stone. A bit of planning was also more important then, since stonemasons were sometimes more expendable than slabs of marble or granite.

Graphic design and typography are complicated activities, but even the simple projects benefit from thinking about the problem, forming a mental picture of the solution, and then carefully planning the steps between.

Scientists have not been content with just calling the human face "beautiful" if it meets certain ideals, or "ugly" if it doesn't. They had to go out and measure proportions of nose to jaw, forehead to chin, and so on to establish why some faces are more appealing than others.

Typographers and graphic designers often choose typefaces for the very same reason they might fancy a person: They just like that person. For more scientifically-minded people, however, there are specific measurements, components, details, and proportions to describe various parts of a letter. While these won't tell you what makes a typeface good, they will at least give you the right words to use when you discuss the benefits of a particular face over another. You can say "I hate the x-height on Such-a-Gothic" or "These descenders just don't work for me" or "Please, may I see something with a smaller cap height?" and you'll know what you are talking about.

4

**Opposite page**

1 Beginning each column with a new paragraph and staggering the top baselines of each column creates more movement and visual interest.

2 Narrow columns can only be exdented by 2 ems or the bulk of the type will lie in too narrow of a measure for comfortable reading.

3 A single word on a line is not always a widow if it takes up a large part of the width of the column.

**This page**

4 The long exdent activates a wider area of the page yet allows for a more comfortable reading width for the bulk of the text.

**FF Engine**

According to designer Alex Scholing, this face is a monoline in an attempt to "make a good, solid, general purpose typeface with as little effort as possible." The small serif-like bulges at the terminals are intended to enhance legibility.

**FF Tibere**

Typefaces inspired by classic Roman capitals are rarely seen as text faces. In 2003, Albert Boton reconsidered that notion with FF Tibere, which adds a fittingly elegant lowercase and italic. If you were ever looking for a Trajan suited for body copy, you could do far worse than this face.

EXP
2.5

## Paragraph Indicator: Extra Leading

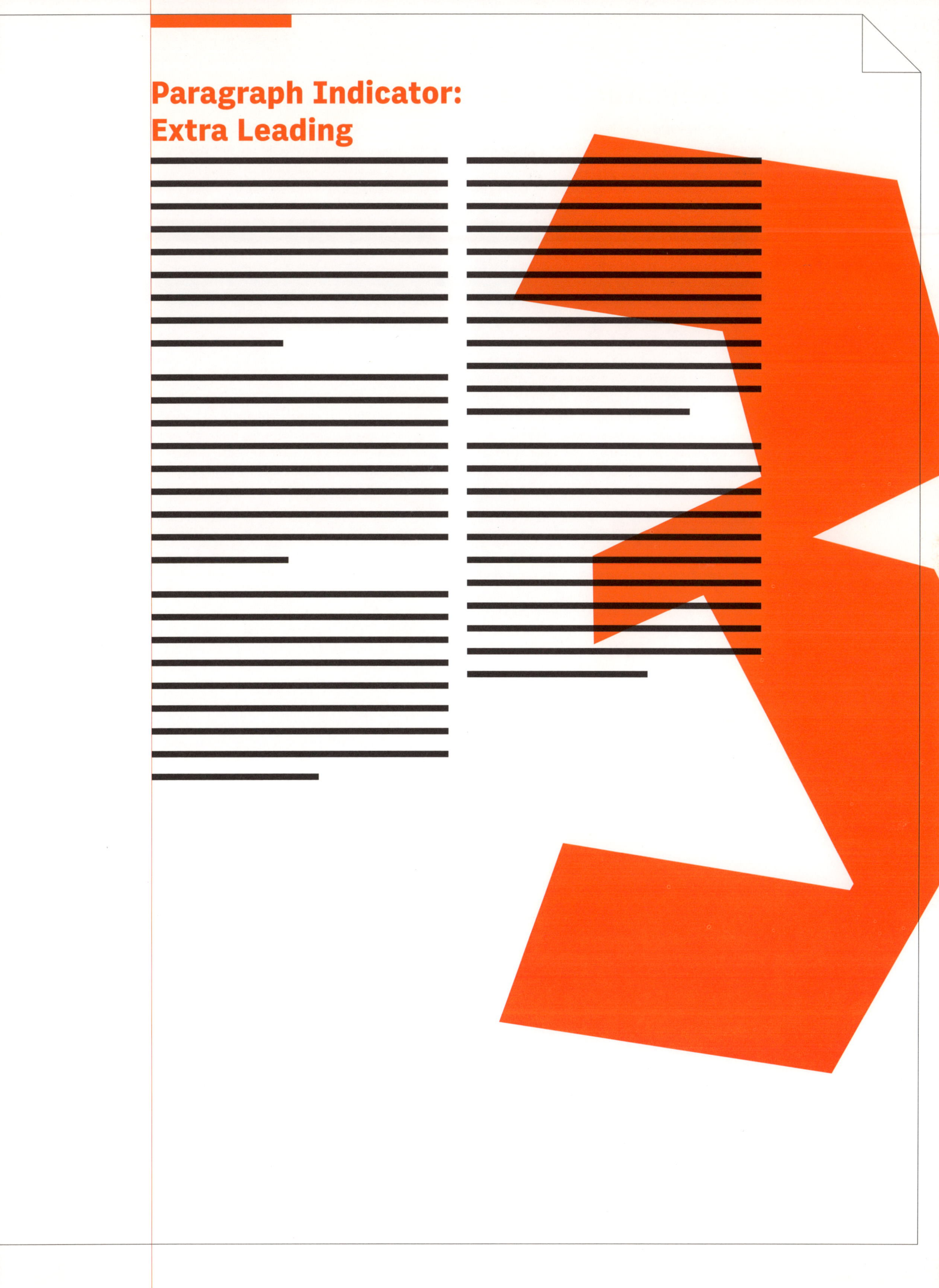

# 3 Paragraph Indicator: Extra Leading

Adding extra leading (linespace) between paragraphs is another common paragraph indicator. Extra leading is a very modern, tidy, and clear way to indicate paragraphs. In digital environments, it is more common as paragraph indication than indentation.

Extra leading of an additional 50% between paragraphs makes an obvious separation, yet it's not so much that it separates the text into visually detached blocks. Using a simple proportion of additional leading makes the negative space between paragraphs coordinate with the leading within the paragraphs.

EXP
**3.1**

EXPLORATION 3 PARAGRAPH INDICATOR: EXTRA LEADING    TEXT: 6.5/12 FF OCR-F LIGHT, TRACKING +5/1000 EM    EXTRA LEADING: 6 PTS

(1) Ever since people have been writing things down, they have had to consider their audience before actually putting pen to paper: letters would have to look different depending on whether they were to be read by mainly other people (in official documents or inscriptions), just one other person (in a letter), or only the writer (in a notebook or diary). There would be less room for guesswork if letter shapes were made more formal as the diversity of the readership expanded.

Some of the first messages to be read by a large number of people were rendered not by pens but by chisels. Large inscriptions on monuments in ancient Rome were carefully planned, with letters drawn on the stone with a brush before they were chiseled. Even if white-out had existed in those days, it would not have helped to remove mistakes made in stone. A bit of planning was also more important then, since stonemasons were sometimes more expendable than slabs of marble or granite.

Graphic design and typography are complicated activities, but even the simple projects benefit from thinking about the problem, forming a mental picture of the solution, and then carefully planning the steps between.

Scientists have not been content with just calling the human face "beautiful" if it meets certain ideals, or "ugly" if it doesn't. They had to go out and measure proportions of nose to jaw, forehead to chin, and so on to establish why some faces are more appealing than others.

Typographers and graphic designers often choose typefaces for the very same reason they might fancy a person: They just like that person. For more scientifically-minded people, however, there are specific measurements, components, details, and proportions to describe various parts of a letter. While these won't tell you what makes a typeface good, they will at least give you the right words to use when you discuss the benefits of a particular face over another. You can say "I hate the x-height on Such-a-Gothic" or "These descenders just don't work for me" or "Please, may I see something with a smaller cap height?" and you'll know what you are talking about.

While metal letters could be made to any width and height, digital type has to conform to multiples of the smallest unit: the pixel. Every character has to be a certain number of pixels wide and high. This is not a problem when the letters are made up of 600 pixels per inch, as is the case with modern laser printers—those pixels are not discernible to our eyes, and we are happy to believe that we are looking at smooth curves instead of little squares fitted into tight grids.

(2) On most screens, only 72 pixels make up one inch. We could see each and every one of them, if engineers hadn't already found ways around that. Computer screens, however, are not where we read most of our type these days. Smart phones, computers, and tablets all have high-resolutions screens, but microwave ovens, espresso makers, and all the other gadgets around us all still use small and modest displays. And the type unmistakably consists of bitmaps, which means that an 8-point letter is actually made up of eight pixels. If we allow six pixels above the baseline, including accents, and two below for descenders, that'll leave only three or four pixels for a lowercase character. In spite of these restrictions, there are hundreds of bitmap fonts, all different from one another by only a few pixels, but enough to prove that typographic variety cannot be suppressed by technological constraints.

Rhythm and contrast keep coming up when discussing good music and good typographic design. They are concepts that also apply to spoken language, as anyone who has had to sit through a monotonous lecture will attest; the same tone, volume and speed of speech will put even the most interested listener into dreamland. Every now and again the audience needs to be shaken, either by a change in voice or pitch, by a question being posed, or by the speaker talking very quietly and then suddenly shouting. An occasional joke also works, just as the use of a funny typeface can liven up a page.

3▸

Ever since people have been writing things down, they have had to consider their audience before actually putting pen to paper: letters would have to look different depending on whether they were to be read by mainly other people (in official documents or inscriptions), just one other person (in a letter), or only the writer (in a notebook or diary). There would be less room for guesswork if letter shapes were made more formal as the diversity of the readership expanded.

Some of the first messages to be read by a large number of people were rendered not by pens but by chisels. Large inscriptions on monuments in ancient Rome were carefully planned, with letters drawn on the stone with a brush before they were chiseled. Even if white-out had existed in those days, it would not have helped to remove mistakes made in stone. A bit of planning was also more important then, since stonemasons were sometimes more expendable than slabs of marble or granite.

Graphic design and typography are complicated activities, but even the simple projects benefit from thinking about the problem, forming a mental picture of the solution, and then carefully planning the steps between.

Scientists have not been content with just calling the human face "beautiful" if it meets certain ideals, or "ugly" if it doesn't. They had to go out and measure proportions of nose to jaw, forehead to chin, and so on to establish why some faces are more appealing than others.

Rhythm and contrast keep coming up when discussing good music and good typographic design. They are concepts that also apply to spoken language, as anyone who has had to sit through a monotonous lecture will attest; the same tone, volume and speed of speech will put even the most interested listener into dreamland. Every now and again the audience needs to be shaken, either by a change in voice or pitch, by a question being posed, or by the speaker talking very quietly and then suddenly shouting. An occasional joke also works, just as the use of a funny typeface can liven up a page.

There's only one thing worse than a badly told joke, and that is a joke told twice. Whatever typographic device you come up with, don't let it turn into a gimmick. A well-coordinated range of fonts will give you the scope for contrast as well as rhythm, and will keep you secure in the bosom of a well-behaved family.

***EXPLORATION 3*** ***Paragraph Indicator: Extra Leading***

***text: 7/11 Bell Centennial, tracking +50/1000 em*** ***extra leading: 5.5 pts***

EXP
**3.2**

**Opposite page**

1. Lighter weights of a typeface set better with more generous tracking. A basic guideline for tracking is: the lighter the weight, the looser the tracking.
2. Note that when 50% extra leading is used as the paragraph indicator, no other paragraph indication, such as indent or exdent, is necessary.

**This page**

3. Beginning each column with a new paragraph is called "clotheslining" and it creates more movement on the page than when all columns are the same depth. Note the tidiness of extra leading when only one column contains a paragraph break here.

**FF OCR-F**

Adrian Frutiger's OCR fonts were produced in 1968 for optical character recognition—type that computers can read. OCR-B has shapes that are more familiar to human readers, and Albert-Jan Pool extended that concept with this design. OCR-F has a monospaced feel but is mostly proportional, allowing for better spacing and readability. This typographic modification of an engineered typeface is a similar approach to his FF DIN, which was completed about the same time.

**Bell Centennial**

Commissioned by AT&T in 1978 to create a new typeface for their phone books, Matthew Carter designed this face to address that environment's tight spaces and poor printing. Its most apparent trait is its deep ink traps: the bits carved out of stroke joints, which compensate for the significant bleeding of ink on porous paper.

The specific proportions of the typeface you are working with (its x-height, ascenders, descenders, etc.) factor into the decision of how much leading to use.

On text type, use at least 4 points more leading than the type size to ensure good legibility. Avoid leading greater than 10 points above the type size so that the body copy holds together as a visual unit. In percentages, these recommendations correspond to no less than 120% leading and no more than 220% leading.

In general, you can use tighter leading on narrow columns and more generous leading on wider columns.

Extra leading between paragraphs is not your best option when space is severely limited because it increases the overall amount of space the text occupies on the page.

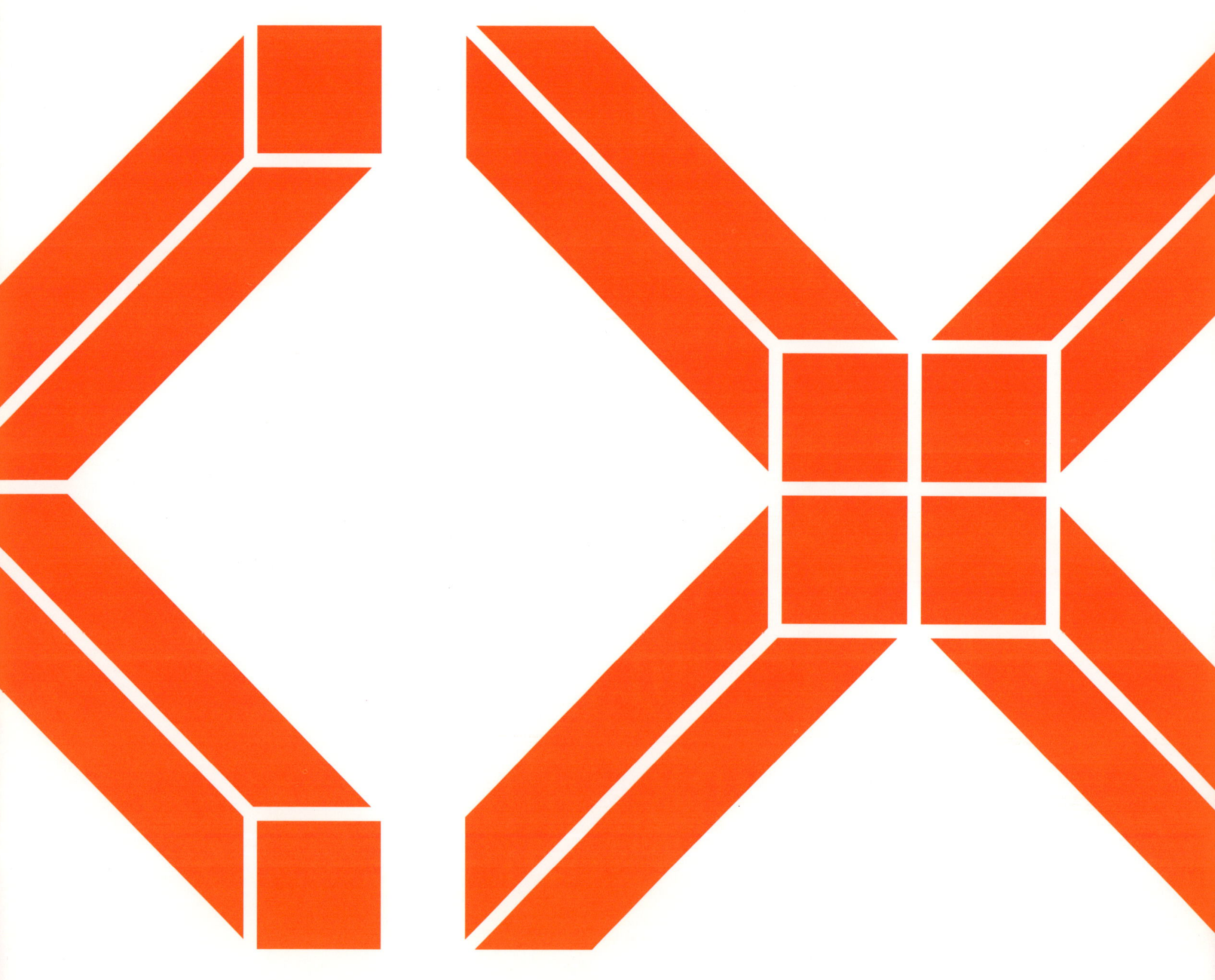

1 The side margin is clearly narrower than the top margin. Unequal page margins help type (and other things) look designed on the page.

2 Generous linespacing (+7 points) allows the type to be justified on a rather narrow column without creating rivers.

**FF Nuvo**
Siegfried Rückel designed this sans serif face in 2008. Its soft, angled stroke endings and dynamic structure give it a lively presence on the page. It's a nice option for informal subject matter.

1

2▸ Ever since people have been writing things down, they have had to consider their audience before actually putting pen to paper: letters would have to look different depending on whether they were to be read by mainly other people (in official documents or inscriptions), just one other person (in a letter), or only the writer (in a notebook or diary). There would be less room for guesswork if letter shapes were made more formal as the diversity of the readership expanded.

Some of the first messages to be read by a large number of people were rendered not by pens but by chisels. Large inscriptions on monuments in ancient Rome were carefully planned, with letters drawn on the stone with a brush before they were chiseled. Even if white-out had existed in those days, it would not have helped to remove mistakes made in stone. A bit of planning was also more important then, since stonemasons were sometimes more expendable than slabs of marble.

Graphic design and typography are complicated activities, but even the simple projects benefit from thinking about the problem, forming a mental picture of the solution, and then carefully planning the steps between. Scientists have not been content with just calling the human face "beautiful" if it meets certain ideals, or "ugly" if it doesn't. They had to go out and measure proportions of nose to jaw, forehead to chin, and so on to establish why some faces are more appealing than others.

Typographers and graphic designers often choose typefaces for the very same reason they might fancy a person: They just like that person. For more scientifically-minded people, however, there are specific measurements, components, details, and proportions to describe various parts of a letter. While these won't tell you what makes a typeface good, they will at least give you the right words to use when you discuss the benefits of a particular face over another. You can say "I hate the x-height on Such-a-Gothic" or "These descenders just don't work for me" or "Please, may I see something with a smaller cap height?" and you'll know what you are talking about.

Rhythm and contrast keep coming up when discussing good music and good typographic design. They are concepts that also apply to spoken language, as anyone who has had to sit through a monotonous lecture will attest; the same tone, volume and speed of speech will put even the most interested listener into dreamland. Every now and again the audience needs to be shaken, either by a change in voice or pitch, by a question being posed, or by the speaker talking very quietly and then suddenly shouting. An occasional joke also works, just as the use of a funny typeface can liven up a page.

Exploration 3

Paragraph Indicator:
Extra Leading

Text:
7/14
FF Nuvo Medium,
tracking
+30/1000 em

Extra Leading:
7 pts

EXP
3.3

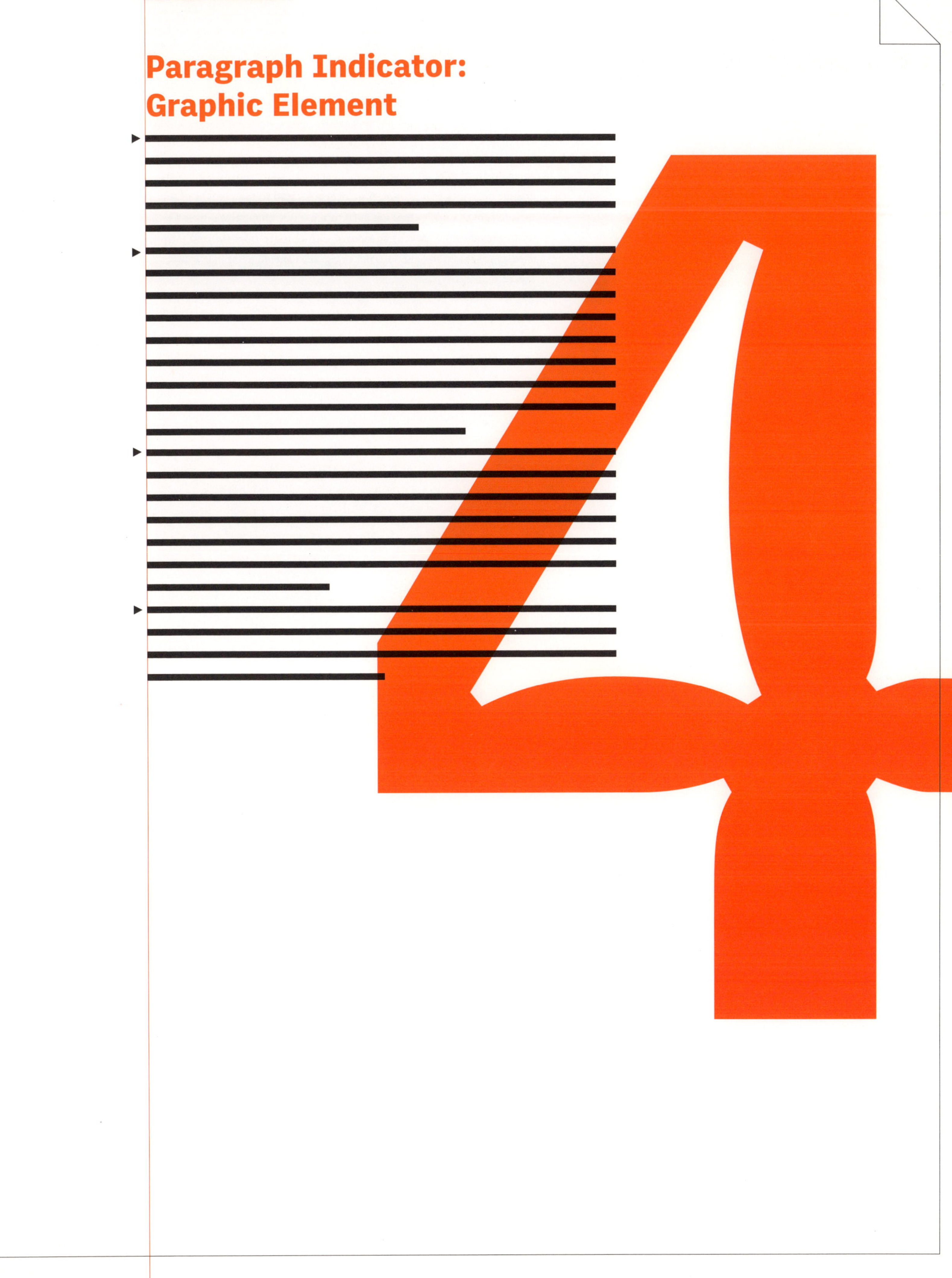
Paragraph Indicator:
Graphic Element

# 4 Paragraph Indicator: Graphic Element

A graphic element such as a bullet, pilcrow, or fleuron between paragraphs can be used either with returns after each paragraph or without them.

Numbers can also be considered graphic elements, particularly if they are typeset in a way that adds visual interest.

The mark you choose to use as a graphic element should go with the typeface your body text is set in. For example, you might choose a simple neutral geometric form to use with a contemporary sans but choose a decorative fleuron to use with a classic serif.

A plain circular bullet is widely disdained for its banality. Luckily, more interesting selections abound. Look for them as special characters within certain faces or as separate dingbat fonts.

Avoid dingbats that add unintended meaning to your typesetting. Choose graphic elements that are either neutral or related to the content of the text. Graphic elements that are solid forms rather than stroke-based forms provide a bold accent and clearly differentiate from the text. Arrows used as graphic elements between paragraphs should point in the direction of reading.

(1) **01** Ever since people have been writing things down, they have had to consider their audience before actually putting pen to paper: letters would have to look different depending on whether they were to be read by mainly other people (in official documents or inscriptions), just one other person (in a letter), or only the writer (in a notebook or diary). There would be less room for guesswork if letter shapes were made more formal as the diversity of the readership expanded.

**02** Some of the first messages to be read by a large number of people were rendered not by pens but by chisels. Large inscriptions on monuments in ancient Rome were carefully planned, with letters drawn on the stone with a brush before they were chiseled. Even if white-out had existed in those days, it would not have helped to remove mistakes made in stone.

(2)

**03** Graphic design and typography are complicated activities, but even the simple projects benefit from thinking about the problem, forming a mental picture of the solution, and then carefully planning the steps between.

**04** Scientists have not been content with just calling the human face "beautiful" if it meets certain ideals, or "ugly" if it doesn't. They had to go out and measure proportions of nose to jaw, forehead to chin, and so on to establish why some faces are more appealing than others.

**05** Typographers and graphic designers often choose typefaces for the very same reason they might fancy a person: They just like that person. For more scientifically-minded people, however, there are specific measurements, components, details, and proportions to describe various parts of a letter. While these won't tell you what makes a typeface good, they will at least give you the right words to use when you discuss the benefits of a particular face over another. You can say "I hate the x-height on Such-a-Gothic" or "These descenders just don't work for me" or "Please, may I see something with a smaller cap height?" and you'll know what you are talking about.

EXPLORATION 4 // PARAGRAPH INDICATOR: GRAPHIC ELEMENT
TEXT: 6/12 FF TRONIC, NO TRACKING
EXTRA LEADING: 3 PTS // GRAPHIC ELEMENT (NUMBER): 6PT FF FOLK

1 Each graphic element (numbers, in this case) hangs outside the column width. Set these just like an exdent, but instead of exdenting by a number of ems, exdent precisely the width of the graphic element plus the space beside it.

2 A few points of extra linespace between paragraphs helps clarify the paragraph breaks, particularly when the last line of a paragraph runs full width.

**FF Tronic**
The letterforms that used to be so common on headers for faxes served as the inspiration for Hyun Cho's FF Tronic, designed in 2003.

**FF Folk**
Illustrator Ben Shahn created his primitive "Folk Alphabet" in 1940 and used some variation of it for many of his signature pieces throughout his career. Maurizio Osti and Jane Patterson adapted this typeface in 1995. The blocky shapes appear to be cut from paper or drawn with rough charcoal, and the family offers two degrees of "roughness." Alternate glyphs in the lowercase slots prevent this all-caps font from too much repetition, maintaining its hand-drawn feel.

EXP
**4.2**

1 →→ Ever since people have been writing things down, they have had to consider their audience before actually putting pen to paper: letters would have to look different depending on whether they were to be read by mainly other people (in official documents or inscriptions), just one other person (in a letter), or only the writer (in a notebook or diary). There would be less room for guesswork if letter shapes were made more formal as the diversity of the readership expanded. → Some of the first messages to be read by a large number of people were rendered not by pens but by chisels. Large inscriptions on monuments in ancient Rome were carefully planned, with letters drawn on the stone with a brush before they were chiseled. Even if white-out had existed in those days, it would not have helped to remove mistakes made in stone. → Graphic design and typography are complicated activities, but even the simple projects benefit from thinking about the problem, forming a mental picture of the solution, and then carefully planning the steps between. → Scientists have not been content with just calling the human face "beautiful" if it meets certain ideals, or "ugly" if it doesn't. They had to go out and measure proportions of nose to jaw, forehead to chin, and so on to establish why some faces are more appealing than others. → Typographers and graphic designers often choose typefaces for the very same reason they might fancy 2
a person: They just like that person. For more scientifically-minded people, however, there are specific measurements, components, details, and proportions to describe various parts of a letter. While these won't tell you what makes a typeface good, they will at least give you the right words to use when you discuss the benefits of a particular face over another. You can say "I hate the x-height on Such-a-Gothic" or "These descenders just don't work for me" or "Please, may I see something with a smaller cap height?" and you'll know what you are talking about. → While metal letters could be made to any width and height, digital type has to conform to multiples of the smallest unit: the pixel. Every character has to be a certain number of pixels wide and high. This is not a problem when the letters are made up of 600 pixels per inch, as is the case with modern laser printers–those pixels are not discernible to our eyes, and we are happy to believe that we are looking at smooth curves instead of little squares fitted into tight grids. ←← 3

EXPLORATION FOUR

PARAGRAPH INDICATOR: GRAPHIC ELEMENT

TEXT: 8/15 FF CUBE LIGHT TRACKING +40/1000 EM

GRAPHIC ELEMENT: 8PT FF DINGBATS 2.0 ARROWS

4▸

:: Ever since people have been writing things down, they have had to consider their audience before actually putting pen to paper: letters would have to look different depending on whether they were to be read by mainly other people (in official documents or inscriptions), just one other person (in a letter), or only the writer (in a notebook or diary). There would be less room for guesswork if letter shapes were made more formal as the diversity of the readership expanded.

:: Some of the first messages to be read by a large number of people were rendered not by pens but by chisels. Large inscriptions on monuments in ancient Rome were carefully planned, with letters drawn on the stone with a brush before they were chiseled. Even if white-out had existed in those days, it would not have helped to remove mistakes made in stone.

:: Graphic design and typography are complicated activities, but even the simple projects benefit from thinking about the problem, forming a mental picture of the solution, and then carefully planning the steps between.

:: Scientists have not been content with just calling the human face "beautiful" if it meets certain ideals, or "ugly" if it doesn't. They had to go out and measure proportions of nose to jaw, forehead to chin, and so on to establish why some faces are more appealing than others.

:: Typographers and graphic designers often choose typefaces for the very same reason they might fancy a person: They just like that person. For more scientifically-minded people, however, there are specific measurements, components, details, and proportions to describe various parts of a letter. While these won't tell you what makes a typeface good, they will at least give you the right words to use when you discuss the benefits of a particular face over another. You can say "I hate the x-height on Such-a-Gothic" or "These descenders just don't work for me" or "Please, may I see something with a smaller cap height?" and you'll know what you are talking about.

*Exploration 4 → Paragraph Indicator: Graphic Element* *text: 7.5/15 FF Zwo Semibold, tracking +40/1000 em* *exdent: 4 ems*

EXP
**4.3**

**Opposite page**

1 Arrows point in the direction of reading. The two initial exdented arrows break the monotony of this dense text block.

2 A justified alignment tends to be best when type is set with graphic elements and no returns between paragraphs. It is also best to avoid having the graphic elements at the beginning or the end of a line.

3 Arrows pointing left signal the end of the text.

**This page**

4 A colon (or double colon) with space after it serves as a subtle graphic element that makes a simple exdented setting a bit more distinctive.

**FF Cube**

Many typefaces wrestle the geometric rectangle into display type, but the concept rarely works for blocks of text. Jan Maack's 2008 face is one of the better attempts because it softens the corners and retains typographic features that improve legibility, such as open apertures, spurred stems ('a,d,m,n,r,u'), and a double-story 'g.' It even has text (Oldstyle) figures.

**FF Zwo**

Jörg Hemker describes this 2002 design as an effort "to combine formal discretion with subtle irony." As a clean, contemporary sans serif—like a sober variation on FF Meta and FF Fago—the result leans toward the first of these two qualities, but some quirks keep it lively, such as the splayed 'M' with raised vertex and the flat-topped binocular 'g.'

# Type BUILDS CHARACTER

× Ever since people have been writing things down, they have had to consider their audience before actually putting pen to paper: letters would have to look different depending on whether they were to be read by mainly other people (in official documents or inscriptions), just one other person (in a letter), or only the writer (in a notebook or diary). There would be less room for guesswork if letter shapes were made more formal as the diversity of the readership expanded.

× Some of the first messages to be read by a large number of people were rendered not by pens but by chisels. Large inscriptions on monuments in ancient Rome were carefully planned, with letters drawn on the stone with a brush before they were chiseled. Even if white-out had existed in those days, it would not have helped to remove mistakes made in stone. A bit of planning was also more important then, since stonemasons were sometimes more expendable than slabs of marble or granite.

× Graphic design and typography are complicated activities, but even the simple projects benefit from thinking about the problem, forming a mental picture of the solution, and then carefully planning the steps between.

× On most screens, only 72 pixels make up one inch. We could see each and every one of them, if engineers hadn't already found ways around that. Computer screens, however, are not where we read most of our type these days. Smart phones, computers, and tablets all have high-resolutions screens, but microwave ovens, espresso makers, and all the other gadgets around us all still use small and modest displays. And the type unmistakably consists of bitmaps, which means that an 8-point letter is actually made up of eight pixels. If we allow six pixels above the baseline, including accents, and two below for descenders, that'll leave only three or four pixels for a lowercase character. In spite of these restrictions, there are hundreds of bitmap fonts, all different from one another by only a few pixels.

× Scientists have not been content with just calling the human face "beautiful" if it meets certain ideals, or "ugly" if it doesn't. They had to go out and measure proportions of nose to jaw, forehead to chin, and so on to establish why some faces are more appealing than others.

× Rhythm and contrast keep coming up when discussing good music and good typographic design. They are concepts that also apply to spoken language, as anyone who has had to sit through a monotonous lecture will attest; the same tone, volume and speed of speech will put even the most interested listener into dreamland. Every now and again the audience needs to be shaken, either by a change in voice or pitch, by a question being posed, or by the speaker talking very quietly and then suddenly shouting. An occasional joke also works, just as the use of a funny typeface can liven up a page.

**EXP 4**
**PARAGRAPH INDICATOR**
Graphic Element

**TITLE**
57pt, 36pt, 22pt
MVB Verdigris
Small Caps

**TEXT**
8.5/13
MVB Verdigris
Regular
tracking
+40/1000 em

**GRAPHIC ELEMENT**
8.5pt
FF Dingbats 2.0
Circles
and
Crosses

EXP
**4.4**

**Type Builds Character** Ever since people have been writing things down, they have had to consider their audience before actually putting pen to paper: letters would have to look different depending on whether they were to be read by mainly other people (in official documents or inscriptions), just one other person (in a letter), or only the writer (in a notebook or diary). There would be less room for guesswork if letter shapes were made more formal as the diversity of the readership expanded. ¶ Some of the first messages to be read by a large number of people were rendered not by pens but by chisels. Large inscriptions on monuments in ancient Rome were carefully planned, with letters drawn on the stone with a brush before they were chiseled. Even if white-out had existed in those days, it would not have helped to remove mistakes made in stone. A bit of planning was also more important then, since stonemasons were sometimes more expendable than slabs of marble or granite. ¶ Graphic design and typography are complicated activities, but even the simple projects benefit from thinking about the problem, forming a mental picture of the solution, and then carefully planning the steps between. ¶ Scientists have not been content with just calling the human face "beautiful" if it meets certain ideals, or "ugly" if it doesn't. They had to go out and measure proportions of nose to jaw, forehead to chin, and so on to establish why some faces are more appealing than others. ¶ Rhythm and contrast keep coming up when discussing good music and good typographic design. They are concepts that also apply to spoken language, as anyone who has had to sit through a monotonous lecture will attest; the same tone, volume and speed of speech will put even the most interested listener into dreamland. Every now and again the audience needs to be shaken, either by a change in voice or pitch, by a question being posed, or by the speaker talking very quietly and then suddenly shouting. An occasional joke also works, just as the use of a funny typeface can liven up a page. ¶ Typographers and graphic designers often choose typefaces for the very same reason they might fancy a person: They just like that person. For more scientifically-minded people, however, there are specific measurements, components, details, and proportions to describe various parts of a letter. While these won't tell you what makes a typeface good, they will at least give you the right words to use when you discuss the benefits of a particular face over another. You can say "I hate the x-height on Such-a-Gothic" or "These descenders just don't work for me" or "Please, may I see something with a smaller cap height?" and you'll know what you are talking about. ¶ While metal letters could be made to any width and height, digital type has to conform to multiples of the smallest unit: the pixel. Every character has to be a certain number of pixels wide and high. This is not a problem when the letters are made up of 600 pixels per inch, as is the case with modern laser printers—those pixels are not discernible to our eyes, and we are happy to believe that we are looking at smooth curves instead of little squares fitted into tight grids. ¶ There's only one thing worse than a badly told joke, and that is a joke told twice. Whatever typographic device you come up with, don't let it turn into a gimmick. A well-coordinated range of fonts will give you the scope for contrast as well as rhythm, and will keep you secure in the bosom of a well-behaved family.

EXPLORATION 4
PARAGRAPH INDICATOR:
GRAPHIC ELEMENT

TEXT:
7.5/14 FF NETTO REGULAR,
TRACKING +25/1000 EM

GRAPHIC ELEMENT:
6PT FF NETTO ICONS

**Opposite page**

1 A combination of small caps and lowercase forms in different sizes creates a custom style for the first word of the headline.

2 A dingbat made up of five circles reflects the circular dots (tittles) on the lowercase 'i' and 'j' in the typeface.

**This page**

3 The pilcrow (¶) used as the graphic element in this setting creates a refreshing juxtaposition of classic and contemporary typographic styles. It is set with a single word space on either side.

4 Quotation marks that fall midway down the column are not hanging to keep a sharper edge on the justified column.

5 The baseline of the colophon type is aligned to the baseline of the last line of the text and flush left to the right edge of the text block above. Aligning one thing to another on the page gives structure to the composition.

**MVB Verdigris**

Garaldes like Garamond, Bembo, and Sabon are the most commonly used typefaces for long text, but digital versions in this class are often poor reproductions of the originals. In 2003, Mark van Bronkhorst sought to remedy that with this design inspired by Robert Granjon. The result is darker and more readable than most Oldstyle revivals.

**FF Netto**

Daniel Utz's 2008 face is an experiment in "removing all historical details yet maintaining the geometric construction" of the alphabet. The result has several distinguishing characteristics: minimal monoline forms without spurs and rounded terminals. It has a look that is at once technical and approachable—a humanized update of the old mechanical classic face Isonorm.

## Paragraph Indicator: Rule

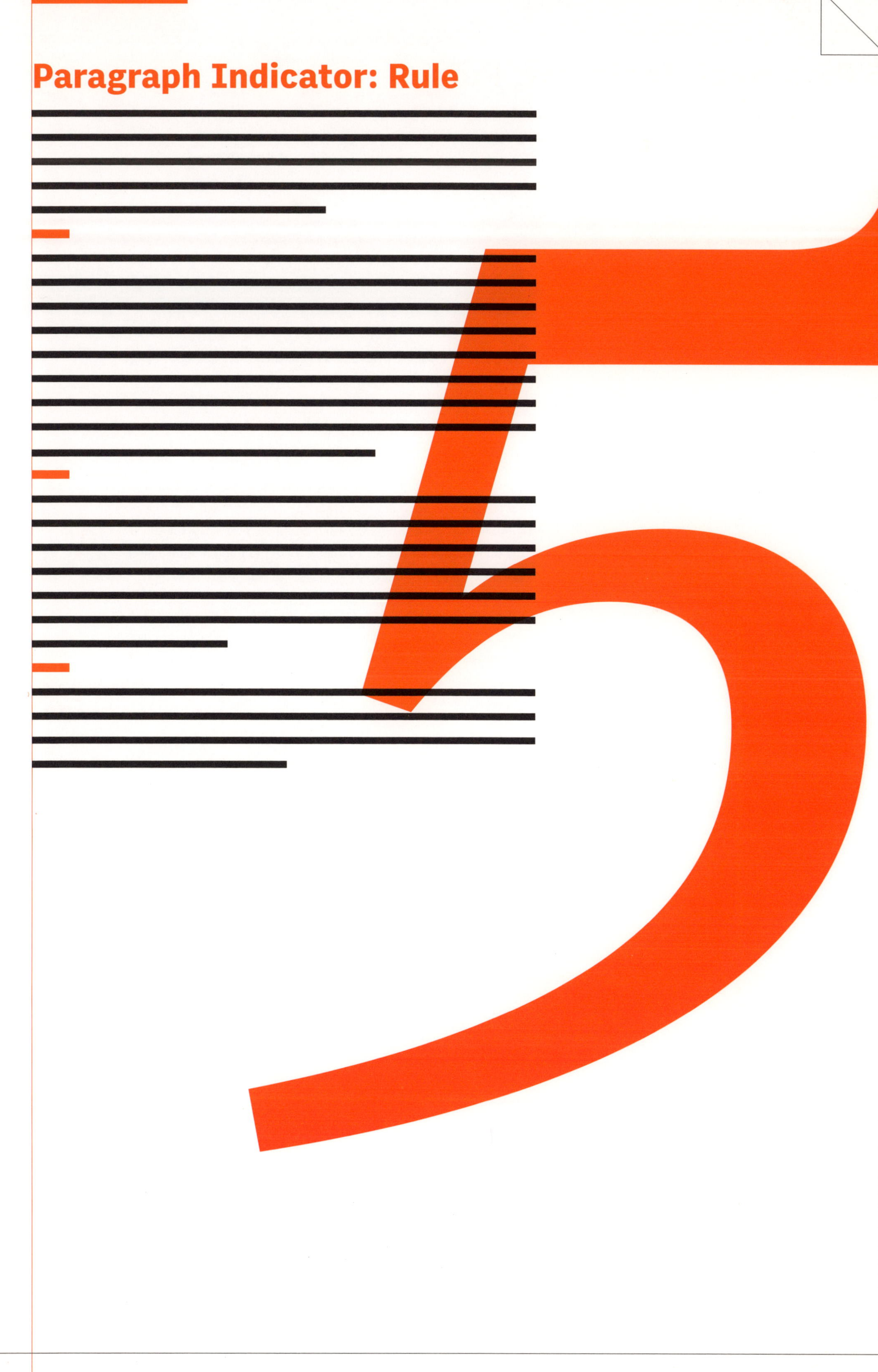

# 5 Paragraph Indicator: Rule

Using a rule between paragraphs is a simple way to create separation. The rule can be long or short, fat or thin, dotted or solid, black or gray. The variety of ways to use a rule as a paragraph indicator is endless.

Add extra leading between paragraphs to account for the width of the rule. Center the rule in the linespace between paragraphs or make it clearly closer to the paragraph above or below.

When the rule is the full column width and your type is set ragged, shorten the rule on the ragged edge a bit so that its length blends in with the rag.

EXP
**5.1**

EXPLORATION 5 **Paragraph Indicator : Rule** text : 7/13 Memphis Light, tracking +50/1000 em extra leading : 9 pts rule : 4 pts

Ever since people have been writing things down, they have had to consider their audience before actually putting pen to paper: letters would have to look different depending on whether they were to be read by mainly other people (in official documents or inscriptions), just one other person (in a letter), or only the writer (in a notebook or diary). There would be less room for guesswork if letter shapes were made more formal as the diversity of the readership expanded.

1▸

Some of the first messages to be read by a large number of people were rendered not by pens but by chisels. Large inscriptions on monuments in ancient Rome were carefully planned, with letters drawn on the stone with a brush before they were chiseled. Even if white-out had existed in those days, it would not have helped to remove mistakes made in stone. A bit of planning was also more important then, since stonemasons were sometimes more expendable than slabs of marble.

Graphic design and typography are complicated activities, but even the simple projects benefit from thinking about the problem, forming a mental picture of the solution, and then carefully planning the steps between. Scientists have not been content with just calling the human face "beautiful" if it meets certain ideals, or "ugly" if it doesn't. They had to go out and measure proportions of nose to jaw, forehead to chin, and so on to establish why some faces are more appealing than others.

Typographers and graphic designers often choose typefaces for the very same reason they might fancy a person: They just like that person. For more scientifically-minded people, however, there are specific measurements, components, details, and proportions to describe various parts of a letter. While these won't tell you what makes a typeface good, they will at least give you the right words to use when you discuss the benefits of a particular face over another. You can say "I hate the x-height on Such-a-Gothic" or "These descenders just don't work for me" or "Please, may I see something with a smaller cap height?" and you'll know what you are talking about.

Rhythm and contrast keep coming up when discussing good music and good typographic design. They are concepts that also apply to spoken language, as anyone who has had to sit through a monotonous lecture will attest; the same tone, volume and speed of speech will put even the most interested listener into dreamland. Every now and again the audience needs to be shaken, either by a change in voice or pitch, by a question being posed, or by the speaker talking very quietly and then suddenly shouting. An occasional joke also works, just as the use of a funny typeface can liven up a page.

Opposite page

1 The short, bold rules have a similar sturdiness to the slab serif letterforms. The leading above and below the rule is optically similar to the leading between lines of text.

This page

2 A bold rule in a light gray contrasts with the texture of the typesetting. It is right-indented a few points from the full width of the column so that its length blends in with the ragged-right edge of the text.

3 Note that there is no rule below the last paragraph. A rule here might make the type look "trapped" on the page.

TypeBuildsCharacter

Ever since people have been writing things down, they have had to consider their audience before actually putting pen to paper: letters would have to look different depending on whether they were to be read by mainly other people (in official documents or inscriptions), just one other person (in a letter), or only the writer (in a notebook or diary). There would be less room for guesswork if letter shapes were made more formal as the diversity of the readership expanded.

2

Some of the first messages to be read by a large number of people were rendered not by pens but by chisels. Large inscriptions on monuments in ancient Rome were carefully planned, with letters drawn on the stone with a brush before they were chiseled. Even if white-out had existed in those days, it would not have helped to remove mistakes made in stone. A bit of planning was also more important then, since stonemasons were sometimes more expendable than slabs of marble or granite.

Graphic design and typography are complicated activities, but even the simple projects benefit from thinking about the problem, forming a mental picture of the solution, and then carefully planning the steps between.

Scientists have not been content with just calling the human face "beautiful" if it meets certain ideals, or "ugly" if it doesn't. They had to go out and measure proportions of nose to jaw, forehead to chin, and so on to establish why some faces are more appealing than others. Typographers and graphic designers often choose typefaces for the very same reason they might fancy a person: They just like that person. For more scientifically-minded people, however, there are specific measurements, components, details, and proportions to describe various parts of a letter.

3

**Exploration 5** Paragraph Indicator: Rule
Title: 14pt FF Prater Script, no tracking
Text: 7/15 Base 9, tracking +30/1000 em
Extra leading: 7.5 pts Rule: 2 pts

Memphis

"Egyptian" slab serifs originated in the early 1800s, but in 1929–30 Rudolf Wolf was among the first to develop a comprehensive geometric slab serif family. Memphis was quickly accepted because of its clarity, similarity to the popular sans serifs of the time, and availability for the Linotype machine. Many like-minded slabs followed (Beton, Rockwell, Karnak, Girder), but none were as successful.

FF Prater Script

This quirky condensed script was designed by Henning Wagenbreth and Steffen Sauerteig for the FontFont library in 2000. They aimed to re-create the unevenness of handwriting by varying line widths, angles, and letterspacing in the font.

Base 9

Zuzana Licko devised the Base fonts primarily for the screen beginning in 1994, so it was the coarse pixel grid that determined the odd proportions, spacing, and details of the design. Emigre revisited Base 9 in 2010 to produce a family better suited for versatile typography: Base 900.

EXP 5.2

## TYPE BUILDS CHARACTER

1▸

Ever since people have been writing things down, they have had to consider their audience before actually putting pen to paper: letters would have to look different depending on whether they were to be read by mainly other people (in official documents or inscriptions), just one other person (in a letter), or only the writer (in a notebook or diary). There would be less room for guesswork if letter shapes were made more formal as the diversity of the readership expanded.

Some of the first messages to be read by a large number of people were rendered not by pens but by chisels. Large inscriptions on monuments in ancient Rome were carefully planned, with letters drawn on the stone with a brush before they were chiseled. Even if white-out had existed in those days, it would not have helped to remove mistakes made in stone. A bit of planning was also more important then, since stonemasons were sometimes more expendable than slabs of marble.

Graphic design and typography are complicated activities, but even the simple projects benefit from thinking about the problem, forming a mental picture of the solution, and then carefully planning the steps between. Scientists have not been content with just calling the human face "beautiful" if it meets certain ideals, or "ugly" if it doesn't. They had to go out and measure proportions of nose to jaw, forehead to chin, and so on to establish why some faces are more appealing than others.

Scientists have not been content with just calling the human face "beautiful" if it meets certain ideals, or "ugly" if it doesn't. They had to go out and measure proportions of nose to jaw, forehead to chin, and so on to establish why some faces are more appealing than others. ◂2

Typographers and graphic designers often choose typefaces for the very same reason they might fancy a person: They just like that person. For more scientifically-minded people, however, there are specific measurements, components, details, and proportions to describe various parts of a letter. While these won't tell you what makes a typeface good, they will at least give you the right words to use when you discuss the benefits of a particular face over another. You can say "I hate the x-height on Such-a-Gothic" or "These descenders just don't work for me" or "Please, may I see something with a smaller cap height?" and you'll know what you are talking about.

Rhythm and contrast keep coming up when discussing good music and good typographic design. They are concepts that also apply to spoken language, as anyone who has had to sit through a monotonous lecture will attest; the same tone, volume and speed of speech will put even the most interested listener into dreamland. Every now and again the audience needs to be shaken, either by a change in voice or pitch, by a question being posed, or by the speaker talking very quietly and then suddenly shouting. An occasional joke also works, just as the use of a funny typeface can liven up a page.

◂3

*EXP 5*
*Paragraph Indicator: Rule*

*Title: 16pt Neutraface Text Demi Small Caps, tracking +50/1000 em*

*Text: 8/17 Rufina Regular, tracking +40/1000 em*

4▸

*Ever since people have been writing things down, they have had to consider their audience before actually putting pen to paper: letters would have to look different depending on whether they were to be read by mainly other people (in official documents or inscriptions), just one other person (in a letter), or only the writer (in a notebook or diary). There would be less room for guesswork if letter shapes were made more formal as the diversity of the readership expanded.*

5▸

*Some of the first messages to be read by a large number of people were rendered not by pens but by chisels. Large inscriptions on monuments in ancient Rome were carefully planned, with letters drawn on the stone with a brush before they were chiseled. Even if white-out had existed in those days, it would not have helped to remove mistakes made in stone.*

*Graphic design and typography are complicated activities, but even the simple projects benefit from thinking about the problem, forming a mental picture of the solution, and then carefully planning the steps between.*

*Scientists have not been content with just calling the human face "beautiful" if it meets certain ideals, or "ugly" if it doesn't. They had to go out and measure proportions of nose to jaw, forehead to chin, and so on to establish why some faces are more appealing than others.*

*Typographers and graphic designers often choose typefaces for the very same reason they might fancy a person: They just like that person. For more scientifically-minded people, however, there are specific measurements, components, details, and proportions to describe various parts of a letter. While these won't tell you what makes a typeface good, they will at least give you the right words to use when you discuss the benefits of a particular face over another. You can say "I hate the x-height on Such-a-Gothic" or "These descenders just don't work for me" or "Please, may I see something with a smaller cap height?" and you'll know what you are talking about.*

*Rhythm and contrast keep coming up when discussing good music and good typographic design. They are concepts that also apply to spoken language, as anyone who has had to sit through a monotonous lecture will attest; the same tone, volume and speed of speech will put even the most interested listener into dreamland. Every now and again the audience needs to be shaken, either by a change in voice or pitch, by a question being posed, or by the speaker talking very quietly and then suddenly shouting. An occasional joke also works, just as the use of a funny typeface can liven up a page.* ◂6

*Exploration 5 / Paragraph Indicator: Rule   Text: 7.5/16 FF Enzo Medium Italic, tracking +60/1000 em   Extra leading: 3 pts   Rule: 1 pt*

**Opposite page**

1 The rules between the paragraphs are slightly exdented from the text.

2 The columns break mid-paragraph so that the rule is always between two lines of type. When you break columns in the middle of a paragraph, keep at least two lines of type at the top and at the bottom of columns.

3 The same rule is used to separate the body copy from the colophon.

**This page**

4 Rules used with exdented settings extend the full width of the column. The dots in the rule are the same shape and similar in size to the tittles and periods in the typeface.

5 A few extra points of leading between paragraphs makes enough room for the rule to fit comfortably.

6 For a single-column text block to look more stable on the page, ideally the last line of the last paragraph fills half the column width or more.

**Neutraface Text**
In 2002, Christian Schwartz combined architect Richard Neutra's uppercase lettering with his own lowercase derived from Geometric sans serifs such as Avenir and Nobel. Neutraface Text is the subfamily intended for smaller settings with a larger x-height and less extreme ascenders.

**Rufina**
Martin Sommaruga's 2014 design has the contrast and stress axis of a Didone but the liveliness of a Humanist face. This gives it an informality and swing that Bodonis and Didots don't have. That demeanor is further enhanced by casual alternates (such as 'a,e,g' and 'y') for each of the family's four styles.

**FF Enzo**
Tobias Kvant's 2008 sans has a friendly feel owing to its large lowercase, short descenders, full bowls, large apertures, and angled endings on the diagonal strokes. It seems intended primarily for display use, but it works surprisingly well for text and became one of the early favorites for approachable body copy on the Web after it arrived on Typekit in 2009.

Ever since people have been writing things down, they have had to consider their audience before actually putting pen to paper: letters would have to look different depending on whether they were to be read by mainly other people (in official documents or inscriptions), just one other person (in a letter), or only the writer (in a notebook or diary). There would be less room for guesswork if letter shapes were made more formal as the diversity of the readership expanded.

1

Some of the first messages to be read by a large number of people were rendered not by pens but by chisels. Large inscriptions on monuments in ancient Rome were carefully planned, with letters drawn on the stone with a brush before they were chiseled. Even if white-out had existed in those days, it would not have helped to remove mistakes made in stone. A bit of planning was also more important then, since stonemasons were sometimes more expendable than slabs of marble or granite.

Graphic design and typography are complicated activities, but even the simple projects benefit from thinking about the problem, forming a mental picture of the solution, and then carefully planning the steps between.

Scientists have not been content with just calling the human face "beautiful" if it meets certain ideals, or "ugly" if it doesn't. They had to go out and measure proportions of nose to jaw, forehead to chin, and so on to establish why some faces are more appealing than others.

Typographers and graphic designers often choose typefaces for the very same reason they might fancy a person: They just like that person. For more scientifically-minded people, however, there are specific measurements, components, details, and proportions to describe various parts of a letter. While these won't tell you what makes a typeface good, they will at least give you the right words to use when you discuss the benefits of a particular face over another. You can say "I hate the x-height on Such-a-Gothic" or "These descenders just don't work for me" or "Please, may I see something with a smaller cap height?" and you'll know what you are talking about.

**EXPLORATION 5**
PARAGRAPH INDICATOR: RULE
(TYPESET BY GLORIA HIEK)

TEXT: 8.5/15 FF ROICE,
TRACKING +25/1000 EM

EXTRA LEADING: 7.5 PTS
RULE: 1 PT

Opposite page

1 The rules between lines of type bleed off the left edge of the page. The rules between paragraphs are stronger than the others. The loosely spaced dots in the dotted lines are similar to the lightness of the typeface.

This page

2 If you use a "default" line weight, it's a good idea to customize the rule in some other way. Here the 1-point rule is exdented with a vertical stroke at the end, as though a half of a bracket is housing each paragraph.

2

Ever since people have been writing things down, they have had to consider their audience before actually putting pen to paper: letters would have to look different depending on whether they were to be read by mainly other people (in official documents or inscriptions), just one other person (in a letter), or only the writer (in a notebook or diary). There would be less room for guesswork if letter shapes were made more formal as the diversity of the readership expanded.

Some of the first messages to be read by a large number of people were rendered not by pens but by chisels. Large inscriptions on monuments in ancient Rome were carefully planned, with letters drawn on the stone with a brush before they were chiseled. Even if white-out had existed in those days, it would not have helped to remove mistakes made in stone. A bit of planning was also more important then, since stonemasons were sometimes more expendable than slabs of marble or granite.

Graphic design and typography are complicated activities, but even the simple projects benefit from thinking about the problem, forming a mental picture of the solution, and then carefully planning the steps between.

Scientists have not been content with just calling the human face "beautiful" if it meets certain ideals, or "ugly" if it doesn't. They had to go out and measure proportions of nose to jaw, forehead to chin, and so on to establish why some faces are more appealing than others.

Typographers and graphic designers often choose typefaces for the very same reason they might fancy a person: They just like that person. For more scientifically-minded people, however, there are specific measurements, components, details, and proportions to describe various parts of a letter. While these won't tell you what makes a typeface good, they will at least give you the right words to use when you discuss the benefits of a particular face over another. You can say "I hate the x-height on Such-a-Gothic" or "These descenders just don't work for me" or "Please, may I see something with a smaller cap height?" and you'll know what you are talking about.

Exploration 5: Paragraph Indicator: Rule
Text: 7/14 Spartan Book Classified, tracking +20/1000 em
Extra Leading: 7 pts * Rule: 1 pt

**FF Roice**
In 1995, Alex Scholing produced the very idiosyncratic FF Engine, a monolinear typeface that appears to be drawn with a round-nibbed pen, not unlike the lettering found in 1920s showcards and silent film intertitles. In 2003, Scholing designed FF Roice, a revision of the style, "more mature, well-mannered and well-balanced." If you want cute text, there may be no better choice.

**Spartan Classified**
Released by Linotype and ATF in the 1930s, Spartan was the American version of Futura. It was essentially a clone, but there were some unique offerings, including this special version cut at very small sizes for tiny text and classified advertising. The spacing is loose, the ascenders are short, the caps are wide, and the descenders are almost nonexistent. It looks very strange at anything above 8-point but performs admirably below that size.

EXP
5.6

**This page**

1 The headline is set in all lowercase without word spaces. Brackets around the middle word are the only separation.

2 A textured rule created from a pattern font is used under the headline as well as between paragraphs.

**Opposite page**

3 Rules vary in length according to the length of the last line of each paragraph.

4 When using rules between paragraphs on multiple columns, break the column mid-paragraph so that no rule falls at the top or bottom of a column.

**Lingua**
Eric Olson's 2003 design combines two rare features: an entirely curveless monolinear construction and nearly 200 unconventional ligatures, making it something of a high-tech upright script. The ligatures are a fun novelty for display use, but Lingua also sets surprisingly readable short passages of text despite its mechanical build.

**TXT101**
Ornament and border fonts are traditionally decorative and naturalistic (i.e., they include fleurons, stars, flowers, leaves). Carolina de Bartolo departed from frilly convention to create a very practical and contemporary set of shapes for building borders and patterns. There are also handy loops and zigzags for striking and greeking text.

**FF Trixie**
Many fonts simulate the impressions of a typewriter; Erik van Blokland's FF Trixie is one of the more thoughtful efforts. The first version, released in 1991, captured the imperfections of the medium in clean and rough variants. In 2008, van Blokland added Trixie HD, which is an even better emulation of typewriters with finer detail.

EXPLORATION 5 / PARAGRAPH INDICATOR: RULE

TITLE: 29PT LINGUA REGULAR

TEXT: 9/15 LINGUA REGULAR, TRACKING +25/1000 EM

RULE: 9PT TXT101 REGULAR

1 

# type{builds}character

2

Ever since people have been writing things down, they have had to consider their audience before actually putting pen to paper: letters would have to look different depending on whether they were to be read by mainly other people (in official documents or inscriptions), just one other person (in a letter), or only the writer (in a notebook or diary). There would be less room for guesswork if letter shapes were made more formal as the diversity of the readership expanded.

Some of the first messages to be read by a large number of people were rendered not by pens but by chisels. Large inscriptions on monuments in ancient Rome were carefully planned, with letters drawn on the stone with a brush before they were chiseled. Even if white-out had existed in those days, it would not have helped to remove mistakes made in stone. A bit of planning was also more important then, since stonemasons were sometimes more expendable than slabs of marble.

Graphic design and typography are complicated activities, but even the simple projects benefit from thinking about the problem, forming a mental picture of the solution, and then carefully planning the steps between. Scientists have not been content with just calling the human face "beautiful" if it meets certain ideals, or "ugly" if it doesn't. They had to go out and measure proportions of nose to jaw, forehead to chin, and so on to establish why some faces are more appealing than others.

Typographers and graphic designers often choose typefaces for the very same reason they might fancy a person: They just like that person. For more scientifically-minded people, however, there are specific measurements, components, details, and proportions to describe various parts of a letter. While these won't tell you what makes a typeface good, they will at least give you the right words to use when you discuss the benefits of a particular face over another. You can say "I hate the x-height on Such-a-Gothic" or "These descenders just don't work for me" or "Please, may I see something with a smaller cap height?" and you'll know what you are talking about.

Rhythm and contrast keep coming up when discussing good music and good typographic design. They are concepts that also apply to spoken language, as anyone who has had to sit through a monotonous lecture will attest; the same tone, volume and speed of speech will put even the most interested listener into dreamland. Every now and again the audience needs to be shaken, either by a change in voice or pitch, by a question being posed, or by the speaker talking very quietly and then suddenly shouting. An occasional joke also works, just as the use of a funny typeface can liven up a page.

EXPLORATION FIVE
PARAGRAPH
INDICATOR: RULE

TEXT: 7.5/14
FF TRIXIE HEAVY

TRACKING
+10/1000 EM

EXTRA LEADING:
7 PTS

RULE: 3 PTS

Ever since people have been writing things down, they have had to consider their audience before actually putting pen to paper: letters would have to look different depending on whether they were to be read by mainly other people (in official documents or inscriptions), just one other person (in a letter), or only the writer (in a notebook or diary). There would be less room for guesswork if letter shapes were made more formal as the diversity of the readership expanded.

3▸

---

Some of the first messages to be read by a large number of people were rendered not by pens but by chisels. Large inscriptions on monuments in ancient Rome were carefully planned, with letters drawn on the stone with a brush before they were chiseled. Even if white-out had existed in those days, it would not have helped to remove mistakes made in stone. A bit of planning was also more important then, since stonemasons were sometimes more expendable than slabs of marble or granite.

4

---

Graphic design and typography are complicated activities, but even the simple projects benefit from thinking about the problem, forming a mental picture of the solution, and then carefully planning the steps between.

---

Scientists have not been content with just calling the human face "beautiful" if it meets certain ideals, or "ugly" if it doesn't. They had to go out and measure proportions of nose to jaw, forehead to chin, and so on to establish why some faces are more appealing than others.

---

Typographers and graphic designers often choose typefaces for the very same reason they might fancy a person: They just like that person. For more scientifically-minded people, however, there are specific measurements, components, details, and proportions to describe various parts of a letter. While these won't tell you what makes a typeface good, they will at least give you the right words to use when you discuss the benefits of a particular face over another. You can say "I hate the x-height on Such-a-Gothic" or "These descenders just don't work for me" or "Please, may I see something with a smaller cap height?" and you'll know what you are talking about.

---

While metal letters could be made to any width and height, digital type has to conform to multiples of the smallest unit: the pixel. Every character has to be a certain number of pixels wide and high. This is not a problem when the letters are made up of 600 pixels per inch, as is the case with modern laser printers—those pixels are not discernible to our eyes, and we are happy to believe that we are looking at smooth curves instead of little squares fitted into tight grids.

## Paragraph Indicator: Initial Capital

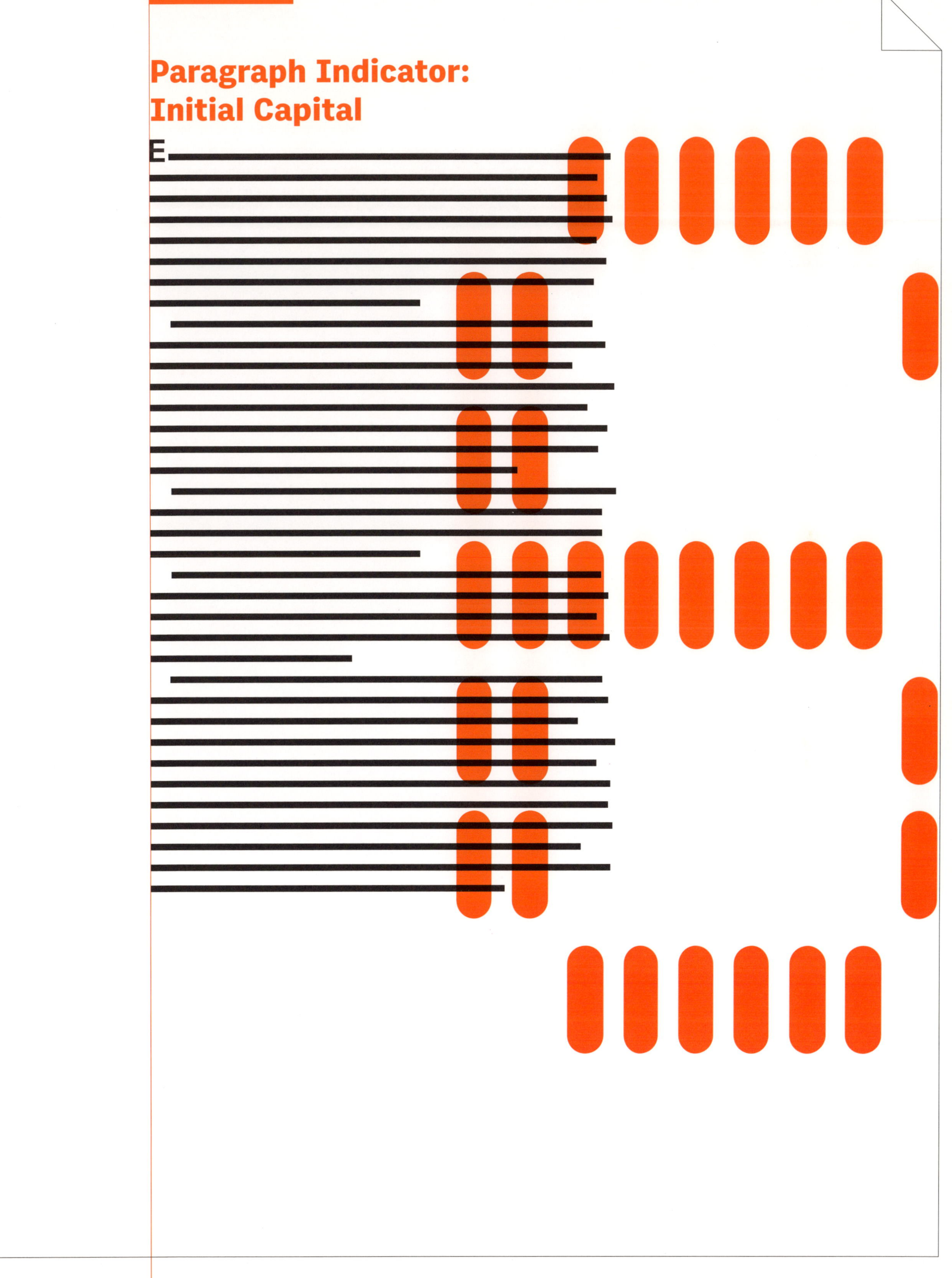

# 6 Paragraph Indicator: Initial Capital

Often used to indicate the beginning of a new section within a text, initial capitals are larger than the text size and set on the same baseline as the first line of the top paragraph.

Initial capitals may be set for the first letter, first word, or first line. Set an initial capital on the first paragraph and use indents or extra leading as the paragraph indication on the remaining paragraphs. To use exdents as paragraph indicators with an initial capital on the first paragraph, you must exdent the initial capital.

To set multiple columns of text with an initial capital in the first column, you need to shift the type in subsequent columns down so that all top baselines align.

Initial capitals tend to have a classic quality, so they often look best with classic typefaces. Initial capitals may be set in the same typeface and weight or in a different typeface or weight than the body text. If you set the capital in another face, select one that differentiates from the text face rather than one that is very similar to it. See the index of typeface combinations at the back of this book for some ideas.

Note: In this Exploration and the following one, paragraphs of the excerpt may be reordered to explore the visual variety of large letterforms.

1▸ ***Typographers*** and graphic designers often choose typefaces for the very same reason they might fancy a person: They just like that person. For more scientifically-minded people, however, there are specific measurements, components, details, and proportions to describe various parts of a letter. While these won't tell you what makes a typeface good, they will at least give you the right words to use when you discuss the benefits of a particular face over another. You can say "I hate the x-height on Such-a-Gothic" or "These descenders just don't work for me" or "Please, may I see something with a smaller cap height?" and you'll know what you are talking about.

2▸ While metal letters could be made to any width and height, digital type has to conform to multiples of the smallest unit: the pixel. Every character has to be a certain number of pixels wide and high. This is not a problem when the letters are made up of 600 pixels per inch, as is the case with modern laser printers—those pixels are not discernible to our eyes, and we are happy to believe that we are looking at smooth curves instead of little squares fitted into tight grids.

On most screens, only 72 pixels make up one inch. We could see each and every one of them, if engineers hadn't already found ways around that. Computer screens, however, are not where we read most of our type these days. Smart phones, computers, and tablets all have high-resolutions screens, but microwave ovens, espresso makers, and all the other gadgets around us all still use small and modest displays. And the type unmistakably consists of bitmaps, which means that an 8-point letter is actually made up of eight pixels. If we allow six pixels above the baseline, including accents, and two below for descenders, that'll leave only three or four pixels for a lowercase character. In spite of these restrictions, there are hundreds of bitmap fonts, all different from one another by only a few pixels, but enough to prove that typographic variety cannot be suppressed by technological constraints.

Rhythm and contrast keep coming up when discussing good music and good typographic design. They are concepts that also apply to spoken language, as anyone who has had to sit through a monotonous lecture will attest; the same tone, volume and speed of speech will put even the most interested listener into dreamland. Every now and again the audience needs to be shaken, either by a change in voice or pitch, by a question being posed, or by the speaker talking very quietly and then suddenly shouting. An occasional joke also works, just as the use of a funny typeface can liven up a page.

*EXPLORATION 6 ▸ Paragraph Indicator: Initial Capital ▸ capital: 19pt Matrix Script Bold, tracking +15/1000 em ▸ text: 9/14 FF Scala Sans, tracking +35/1000 em ▸ indent: 1 em*

1 The first word is sitting on the same baseline as the first line of type. It is set in a larger point size and a different typeface. Both the script and the sans serif in use here make a graceful yet friendly impression. Formally, the two are quite different, yet they evoke a similar feeling—which is an ideal circumstance for making two different faces work well together.

2 All the remaining paragraphs are indicated by simple indentation.

**Matrix Script**
Zuzana Licko's 1992 addition to her Matrix family is essentially an italic but with some cursive forms ('E,Y,f,s') and other unusual details, such as ball terminals and tapering, curled instrokes and tails.

**FF Scala Sans**
In 1993, Majoor added this companion to FF Scala. The very Humanist approach to a sans serif, inspired by Renaissance text faces, is well suited for book typography, supplemented by a variety of weights, Oldstyle figures, and small caps.

**This page**

1 The first letter and the graphic elements between paragraphs are both set in the decorative companion face to the text face.

2 Ideally, very few lines end in punctuation. When type is set justified, it looks best to make a crisp shape. The more lines that end in punctuation, the more the text block appears to have an uneven right edge.

**Opposite page**

3 The first word is set larger and in caps and the first line is exdented the width of the first word plus the space after it.

4 The bar defining the narrow column for the colophon is the same width as the exdent at the top.

**FF Scala Jewel**
This set of four titling styles for FF Scala arrived in 1997. Inspired by the ornamental faces from the 19th century, they work well for classical headlines, title pages, drop caps, and other decorative trimmings.

**FF Scala**
Martin Majoor's design was FontFont's first serious text release and became the epitome of an Oldstyle serif for the digital era. Its squared serifs and low contrast share qualities with Eric Gill's Joanna, but it is otherwise a very contemporary design: a crisp, modern alternative to Garamond and other classical book faces.

**FF Absara**
Like FF Scala, this 2004 face is a contemporary take on the writing and type of the Renaissance. Xavier Dupré reduced the stroke contrast, added heft to the serifs, and emphasized the angularity of the French Humanist pen.

*Exploration 6 // Paragraph Indicator: Initial Capital    capital: 20pt FF Scala Jewel    text: 9/14.5 FF Scala, tracking +40/1000 em    graphic element: 11pt FF Scala Jewel*

1▸ Ever since people have been writing things down, they have had to consider their audience before actually putting pen to paper: letters would have to look different depending on whether they were to be read by mainly other people (in official documents or inscriptions), just one other person (in a letter), or only the writer (in a notebook or diary). There would be less room for guesswork if letter shapes were made more formal as the diversity of the readership expanded. ✲ Some of the first messages to be read by a large number of people were rendered not by pens but by chisels. Large inscriptions on monuments in ancient Rome were carefully planned, with letters drawn on the stone with a brush before they were chiseled. Even if white-out had existed in those days, it would not have helped to remove mistakes made in stone. A bit of planning was also more important then, since stonemasons were sometimes more expendable than slabs of marble or granite. ✲ Graphic design and typography are complicated activities, but even the simple projects benefit from thinking about the problem, forming a mental picture of the solution, and then carefully planning the steps between. ✲ Scientists have not been content with just calling the human face "beautiful" if it meets certain ideals, or "ugly" if it doesn't. They had to go out and measure proportions of nose to jaw, forehead to chin, and so on to establish why some faces are more appealing than others. ✲ Rhythm and contrast keep coming up when discussing good music and good typographic design. They are concepts that also apply to spoken language, as anyone who has had to sit through a monotonous lecture will attest; the same tone, volume and speed of speech will put even the most interested listener into dreamland. Every now and again the audience needs to be shaken, either by a change in voice or pitch, by a question being posed, or by the speaker talking very quietly and then suddenly shouting. An occasional joke also works, just as the use of a funny typeface can liven up a page. ✲ Typographers and graphic designers often choose typefaces for the very same reason they might fancy a person: They just like that person. For more scientifically-minded people, however, there are specific measurements, components, details, and proportions to describe various parts of a letter. While these won't tell you what makes a typeface good, they will at least give you the right words to use when you discuss the benefits of a particular face over another. You can say "I hate the x-height on Such-a-Gothic" or "These descenders just don't work for me" or "Please, may I see something with a smaller cap height?" and you'll know what you are talking about. ✲ While metal letters could be made to any width and height, digital type has to conform to multiples of the smallest unit: the pixel. Every character has to be a certain number of pixels wide and high. This is not a problem when the letters are made up of 600 pixels per inch, as is the case with modern laser printers—those pixels are not discernible to our eyes, and we are happy to believe that we are looking at smooth curves instead of little squares fitted into tight grids.

EXP
6.3

3▸ **TYPOGRAPHERS** and graphic designers often choose typefaces for the very same reason they might fancy a person: They just like that person. For more scientifically-minded people, however, there are specific measurements, components, details, and proportions to describe various parts of a letter. While these won't tell you what makes a typeface good, they will at least give you the right words to use when you discuss the benefits of a particular face over another. You can say "I hate the x-height on Such-a-Gothic" or "These descenders just don't work for me" or "Please, may I see something with a smaller cap height?" and you'll know what you are talking about.

While metal letters could be made to any width and height, digital type has to conform to multiples of the smallest unit: the pixel. Every character has to be a certain number of pixels wide and high. This is not a problem when the letters are made up of 600 pixels per inch, as is the case with modern laser printers—those pixels are not discernible to our eyes, and we are happy to believe that we are looking at smooth curves instead of little squares fitted into tight grids.

On most screens, only 72 pixels make up one inch. We could see each and every one of them, if engineers hadn't already found ways around that. Computer screens, however, are not where we read most of our type these days. Smart phones, computers, and tablets all have high-resolutions screens, but microwave ovens, espresso makers, and all the other gadgets around us all still use small and modest displays. And the type unmistakably consists of bitmaps, which means that an 8-point letter is actually made up of eight pixels. If we allow six pixels above the baseline, including accents, and two below for descenders, that'll leave only three or four pixels for a lowercase character. In spite of these restrictions, there are hundreds of bitmap fonts, all different from one another by only a few pixels, but enough to prove that typographic variety cannot be suppressed by technological constraints.

Rhythm and contrast keep coming up when discussing good music and good typographic design. They are concepts that also apply to spoken language, as anyone who has had to sit through a monotonous lecture will attest; the same tone, volume and speed of speech will put even the most interested listener into dreamland. Every now and again the audience needs to be shaken, either by a change in voice or pitch, by a question being posed, or by the speaker talking very quietly and then suddenly shouting. An occasional joke also works, just as the use of a funny typeface can liven up a page.

EXPLORATION 6
Paragraph Indicator:
Initial Capital

Capitals:
11pt FF Absara
tracking +35/1000 em

Text:
7.5/14 FF Absara
tracking +25/1000 em

**This page**

1. The first lines of each column are set on the same baseline, not hanging from the same capline. Initial caps in the first column are larger, so subsequent columns are baseline-shifted downward to align properly.
2. The body copy typeface has generous sidebearings because it is a font designed for writing code. This is a rare case of text type set with negative tracking for better legibility.

**Opposite page**

3. The first word is set in a contemporary blackletter face. The pen-drawn forms of blackletter have a similarity to Humanist (Venetian) faces.
4. The fleuron used between paragraphs matches the classic decorative style of the typesetting.

**Cholla Unicase**
Sibylle Hagmann's typeface from 1999 is an unusual combination of several concepts: unicase letterforms (caps and lowercase share the same height), modularity, and monospacing (many of the glyphs have the same width). And yet it doesn't rigidly conform to any of these ideas, allowing it to retain a legibility uncommon in similarly experimental type.

**Input Serif**
This 2014 monoline slab serif is part of an extensive coding family conceived and designed by David Jonathan Ross. In a reversal of the usual design process, the font began with 11-pixel bitmaps, and then vector outlines were drawn over the gridded forms afterward.

**Sabbath Black**
This ghostly blackletter designed by Miles Newlyn in 1992 resembles the aged lettering found on a gravestone or monument that has eroded over the years, eliminating the lighter strokes.

**Adobe Jenson**
Various digital versions of Nicolas Jenson's landmark Venetian Oldstyle from the 15th century exist, but Robert Slimbach's 1996 family comes closer than most to capturing its printed essence.

Exploration 6: Initial Capital (typeset by Beth Wong)    Initial Capital: 18pt Cholla Unicase    Text: 7/13 Input Serif Condensed, tracking -10/1000 em    Indent: 1 em

(1) TYPOGRAPHERS and graphic designers often choose typefaces for the very same reason they might fancy a person: They just like that person. For more scientifically-minded people, however, there are specific measurements, components, details, and proportions to describe various parts of a letter. While these won't tell you what makes a typeface good, they will at least give you the right words to use when you discuss the benefits of a particular face over another. You can say "I hate the x-height on Such-a-Gothic" or "These descenders just don't work for me" or "Please, may I see something with a smaller cap height?" and you'll know what you are talking about.

While metal letters could be made to any width and height, digital type has to conform to multiples of the smallest unit: the pixel. Every character has to be a certain number of pixels wide and high. This is not a problem when the letters are made up of 600 pixels per inch, as is the case with modern laser printers—those pixels are not discernible to our eyes, and we are happy to believe that we are looking at smooth curves instead of little squares fitted into tight grids.

On most screens, only 72 pixels make up one inch. We could see each and every one of them, if engineers hadn't already found ways around that. Computer screens, however, are not where we read most of our type these days. Smart phones, computers, and tablets all have high-resolutions screens, but microwave ovens, espresso makers, and all the other gadgets around us all still use small and modest displays. And the type unmistakably consists of bitmaps, which means that an 8-point letter is actually made up of eight pixels. If we allow six pixels above the baseline, including accents, and two below for descenders, that'll leave only three or four pixels for a lowercase character. In spite of these restrictions, there are hundreds of bitmap fonts, all different from one another by only a few pixels, but enough to prove that typographic variety cannot be suppressed by technological constraints.

Graphic design and typography are complicated activities, but even the simple projects benefit from thinking about the problem, forming a mental picture of the solution, and then carefully planning the steps between.

Scientists have not been content with just calling the human face "beautiful" if it meets certain ideals, or "ugly" if it doesn't. They had to go out and measure proportions of nose to jaw, forehead to chin, and so on to establish why some faces are more appealing than others.

Rhythm and contrast (2) keep coming up when discussing good music and good typographic design. They are concepts that also apply to spoken language, as anyone who has had to sit through a monotonous lecture will attest; the same tone, volume and speed of speech will put even the most interested listener into dreamland. Every now and again the audience needs to be shaken, either by a change in voice or pitch, by a question being posed, or by the speaker talking very quietly and then suddenly shouting. An occasional joke also works, just as the use of a funny typeface can liven up a page.

There's only one thing worse than a badly told joke, and that is a joke told twice. Whatever typographic device you come up with, don't let it turn into a gimmick. A well-coordinated range of fonts will give you the scope for contrast as well as rhythm, and will keep you secure in the bosom of a well-behaved family.

EXP **6.4**

3▸ Typographers and graphic designers often choose typefaces for the very same reason they might fancy a person: They just like that person. For more scientifically-minded people, however, there are specific measurements, components, details, and proportions to describe various parts of a letter. While these won't tell you what makes a typeface good, they will at least give you the right words to use when you discuss the benefits of a particular face over another. You can say "I hate the x-height on Such-a-Gothic" or "These descenders just don't work for me" or "Please, may I see something with a smaller cap height?" and you'll know what you are talking about.

4▸ ❧

While metal letters could be made to any width and height, digital type has to conform to multiples of the smallest unit: the pixel. Every character has to be a certain number of pixels wide and high. This is not a problem when the letters are made up of 600 pixels per inch, as is the case with modern laser printers—those pixels are not discernible to our eyes, and we are happy to believe that we are looking at smooth curves instead of little squares fitted into tight grids.

❧

On most screens, only 72 pixels make up one inch. We could see each and every one of them, if engineers hadn't already found ways around that. Computer screens, however, are not where we read most of our type these days. Smart phones, computers, and tablets all have high-resolutions screens, but microwave ovens, espresso makers, and all the other gadgets around us all still use small and modest displays. And the type unmistakably consists of bitmaps, which means that an 8-point letter is actually made up of eight pixels. If we allow six pixels above the baseline, including accents, and two below for descenders, that'll leave only three or four pixels for a lowercase character. In spite of these restrictions, there are hundreds of bitmap fonts, all different from one another by only a few pixels, but enough to prove that typographic variety cannot be suppressed by technological constraints.

❧

Graphic design and typography are complicated activities, but even the simple projects benefit from thinking about the problem, forming a mental picture of the solution, and then carefully planning the steps between.

❧

Rhythm and contrast keep coming up when discussing good music and good typographic design. They are concepts that also apply to spoken language, as anyone who has had to sit through a monotonous lecture will attest; the same tone, volume and speed of speech will put even the most interested listener into dreamland. Every now and again the audience needs to be shaken, either by a change in voice or pitch, by a question being posed, or by the speaker talking very quietly and then suddenly shouting. An occasional joke also works, just as the use of a funny typeface can liven up a page.

❧

There's only one thing worse than a badly told joke, and that is a joke told twice. Whatever typographic device you come up with, don't let it turn into a gimmick. A well-coordinated range of fonts will give you the scope for contrast as well as rhythm, and will keep you secure in the bosom of a well-behaved family.

**Exploration Six: Initial Capital**
**Initial capitals: 18pt Sabbath Black Heavy**
**Text: 7.5/11.5 Adobe Jenson, tracking +50/1000 em**
**Fleuron: 11pt Dalliance Flourishes**

## Paragraph Indicator: Drop Capital

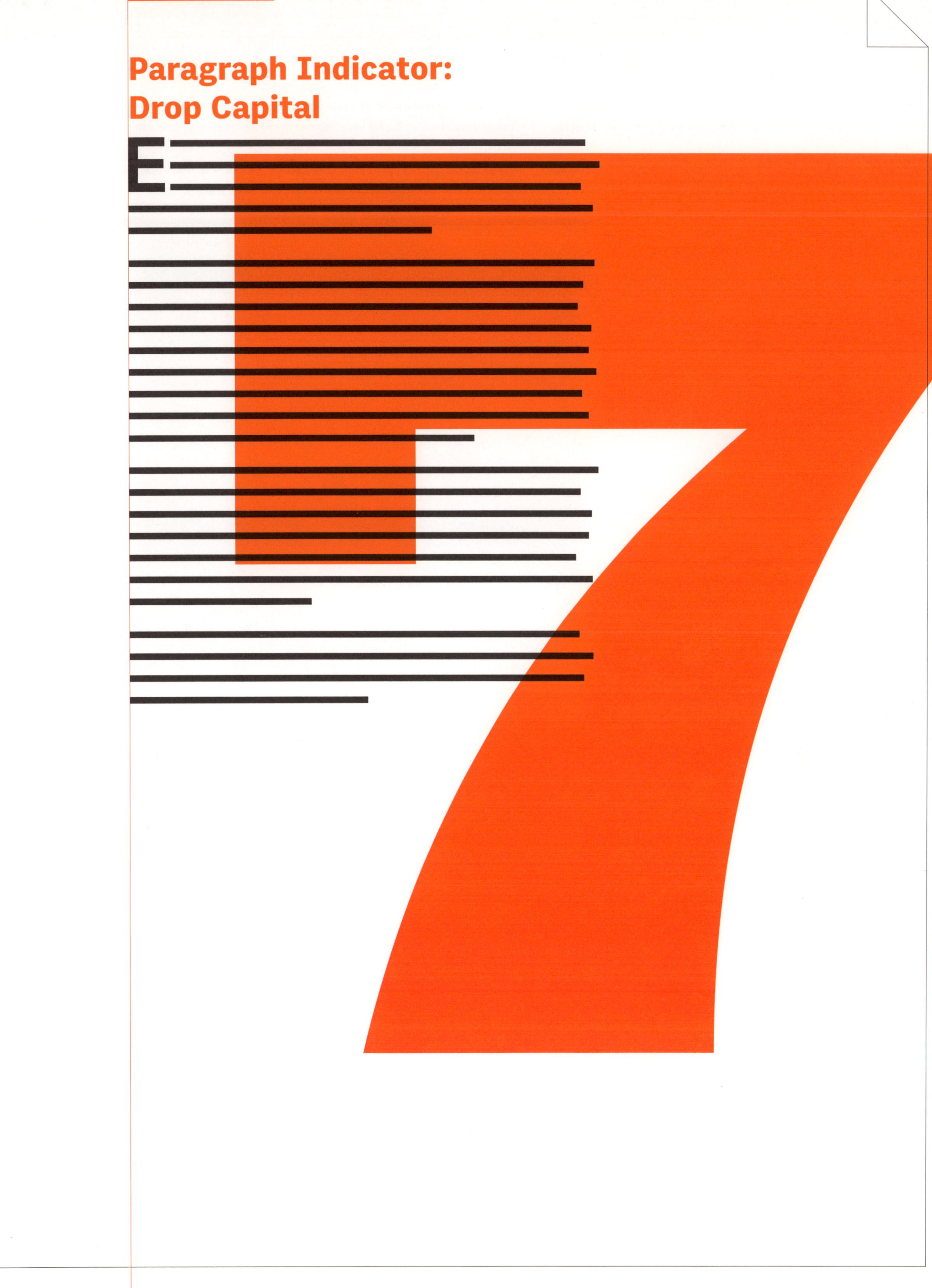

# 7 Paragraph Indicator: Drop Capital

Like initial capitals, drop capitals are often used to indicate the beginning of a new section within a text. Drop capitals are set larger than the text size and on the same baseline as the second, third, or fourth line of the first paragraph. Typically we would avoid setting a drop capital deeper than the number of lines in the first paragraph.

A drop capital may be set for the first letter or first word. Kern the type next to the drop capital so that it reads as continuously as possible. You'll notice that certain letterforms can be composed and read as drop capitals much better than others.

Set a drop capital on the first paragraph and use indent or extra leading as the paragraph indication on the paragraphs after that.

Even more than initial capitals, drop capitals have a traditional look and feel, so they often work best when typeset in classic typefaces. Drop capitals may be set in the same typeface and weight or in a different typeface or weight than the body text. If you set the capital in another face, select one that differentiates from the text face rather than one that is very similar to it. See the typeface combinations at the back of this book for some ideas.

Note: In this Exploration and the previous one, paragraphs of the excerpt may be reordered to explore the visual variety of large letterforms.

1

Ever since people have been writing things down, they have had to consider their audience before actually putting pen to paper: letters would have to look different depending on whether they were to be read by mainly other people (in official documents or inscriptions), just one other person (in a letter), or only the writer (in a notebook or diary). There would be less room for guesswork if letter shapes were made more formal as the diversity of the readership expanded.

Some of the first messages to be read by a large number of people were rendered not by pens but by chisels. Large inscriptions on monuments in ancient Rome were carefully planned, with letters drawn on the stone with a brush before they were chiseled. Even if white-out had existed in those days, it would not have helped to remove mistakes made in stone. A bit of planning was also more important then, since stonemasons were sometimes more expendable than slabs of marble or granite.

Graphic design and typography are complicated activities, but even the simple projects benefit from thinking about the problem, forming a mental picture of the solution, and then carefully planning the steps between.

Scientists have not been content with just calling the human face "beautiful" if it meets certain ideals, or "ugly" if it doesn't. They had to go out and measure proportions of nose to jaw, forehead to chin, and so on to establish why some faces are more appealing than others.

Typographers and graphic designers often choose typefaces for the very same reason they might fancy a person: They just like that person. For more scientifically-minded people, however, there are specific measurements, components, details, and proportions to describe various parts of a letter. While these won't tell you what makes a typeface good, they will at least give you the right words to use when you discuss the benefits of a particular face over another. You can say "I hate the x-height on Such-a-Gothic" or "These descenders just don't work for me" or "Please, may I see something with a smaller cap height?" and you'll know what you are talking about.

While metal letters could be made to any width and height, digital type has to conform to multiples of the smallest unit: the pixel. Every character has to be a certain number of pixels wide and high. This is not a problem when the letters are made up of 600 pixels per inch, as is the case with modern laser printers—those pixels are not discernible to our eyes, and we are happy to believe that we are looking at smooth curves instead of little squares fitted into tight grids.

On most screens, only 72 pixels make up one inch. We could see each and every one of them, if engineers hadn't already found ways around that. Computer screens, however, are not where we read most of our type these days. Smart phones, computers, and tablets all have high-resolutions screens, but microwave ovens, espresso makers, and all the other gadgets around us all still use small and modest displays. And the type unmistakably consists of bitmaps, which means that an 8-point letter is actually made up of eight pixels. If we allow six pixels above the baseline, including accents, and two below for descenders, that'll leave only three or four pixels for a lowercase character. In spite of these restrictions, there are hundreds of bitmap fonts, all different from one another by only a few pixels.

Rhythm and contrast keep coming up when discussing good music and good typographic design. They are concepts that also apply to spoken language, as anyone who has had to sit through a monotonous lecture will attest; the same tone, volume and speed of speech will put even the most interested listener into dreamland. Every now and again the audience needs to be shaken, either by a change in voice or pitch, by a question being posed, or by the speaker talking very quietly and then suddenly shouting. An occasional joke also works, just as the use of a funny typeface can liven up a page.

EXPLORATION 7
DROP CAPITAL

DROP CAPITAL: 3 LINES DEEP
CHARLEMAGNE BOLD

TEXT: 8/13 JOANNA NOVA LIGHT ITALIC
TRACKING +40/1000 EM

EXTRA LEADING: 6.5 PTS

1 The cap is optically aligned to the type below it. As the drop cap gets larger, its sidebearings and serifs also get larger, so accommodate this by exdenting the cap slightly. Make it look aligned flush to the text below and not at all indented. Also be sure the top of the cap looks to be at least as high as or higher than the capline of the text type beside it.

**Charlemagne**
Carol Twombly designed this alternative interpretation of classical Roman inscriptions in 1989, the same year as her Trajan. The exaggerated serifs and simplified strokes make it more of a modern caricature than a revival.

**Joanna Nova**
This 2015 version of Eric Gill's Joanna (originally from 1931) was revived by Ben Jones as a part of Monotype's Eric Gill Series. This lovely yet underused face is notable for its almost upright and narrow italic. This Nova revision equalizes the italic x-height with the roman.

**This page**

1 Although drop caps are a classic style, this example shows how it is possible to use them in less traditional settings and with contemporary typefaces.

2 The small square relates to the cap. It punctuates the text block as a graphic element between paragraphs and as a marker for the very end of the text.

**Opposite page**

3 The large drop cap here has been exdented not only to optically align it with the text below but also to accommodate the descending loop on this particular letterform.

4 The bold rule complements the bold strokes in the blackletter drop cap. Its end aligns with the baseline of the last line of type.

**FF Stealth**
*FUSE*, the influential magazine edited by Neville Brody, enabled designers to experiment with type in an environment free of the typical usability constraints. Malcolm Garrett's contribution, made of straight lines and semicircles, reduced letterforms to their essential strokes.

**FF Hydra**
Silvio Naploeone's family is inspired by the lettering of French poster art from the late 19th and early 20th centuries. Indeed, the chunky irregularities have the look of rough-cut wood type. Large, rounded ink traps add another idiosyncrasy.

**Goudy Text**
This Frederic Goudy design from 1928 has become a standard blackletter. The caps are full and ornate, suitable for drop caps, and the lowercase has the tight verticality of the type from Gutenberg's 42-line Bible.

**FF Parango**
Xavier Dupré has made a habit of distilling French Garaldes into typefaces for modern use. This was his 2001 installment, retaining the somewhat angular structure of a calligraphic roman, but softening the contours.

**EXPLORATION 7** Paragraph Indicator: Drop Capital — Drop Capital: 3 Lines, FF Stealth — Text: 8/17 FF Hydra Text Light, tracking +25/1000 em

(1) Ever since people have been writing things down, they have had to consider their audience before actually putting pen to paper: letters would have to look different depending on whether they were to be read by mainly other people (in official documents or inscriptions), just one other person (in a letter), or only the writer (in a notebook or diary). There would be less room for guesswork if letter shapes were made more formal as the diversity of the readership expanded. ■ Some of the first messages to be read by a large number of people were rendered not by pens but by chisels. Large inscriptions on monuments in ancient Rome were carefully planned, with letters drawn on the stone with a brush before they were chiseled. Even if white-out had existed in those days, it would not have helped to remove mistakes made in stone. A bit of planning was also more important then, since stonemasons were sometimes more expendable than slabs of marble or granite. ■ Graphic design and typography are complicated activities, but even the simple projects benefit from thinking about the problem, forming a mental picture of the solution, and then carefully planning the steps between. ■ Scientists have not been content with just calling the human face "beautiful" if it meets certain ideals, or "ugly" if it doesn't. They had to go out and measure proportions of nose to jaw, forehead to chin, and so on to establish why some faces are more appealing than others. ■ Typographers and graphic designers often choose typefaces for the very same reason they might fancy a person: They just like that person. For more scientifically-minded people, however, there are specific measurements, components, details, and proportions to describe various parts of a letter. While these won't tell you what makes a typeface good, they will at least give you the right words to use when you discuss the benefits of a particular face over another. You can say "I hate the x-height on Such-a-Gothic" or "These descenders just don't work for me" or "Please, may I see something with a smaller cap height?" and you'll know what you are talking about. ■ While metal letters could be made to any width and height, digital type has to conform to multiples of the smallest unit: the pixel. Every character has to be a certain number of pixels wide and high. This is not a problem when the letters are made up of 600 pixels per inch, as is the case with modern laser printers—those pixels are not discernible to our eyes, and we are happy to believe that we are looking at smooth curves instead of little squares fitted into tight grids. ■ (2)

EXP
**7.3**

Some of the first messages to be read by a large number of people were rendered not by pens but by chisels. Large inscriptions on monuments in ancient Rome were carefully planned, with letters drawn on the stone with a brush before they were chiseled. Even if white-out had existed in those days, it would not have helped to remove mistakes made in stone. A bit of planning was also more important then, since stonemasons were sometimes more expendable than slabs of marble or granite. ◆ Graphic design and typography are complicated activities, but even the simple projects benefit from thinking about the problem, forming a mental picture of the solution, and then carefully planning the steps between. ◆ Scientists have not been content with just calling the human face "beautiful" if it meets certain ideals, or "ugly" if it doesn't. They had to go out and measure proportions of nose to jaw, forehead to chin, and so on to establish why some faces are more appealing than others. ◆ Typographers and graphic designers often choose typefaces for the very same reason they might fancy a person: They just like that person. For more scientifically-minded people, however, there are specific measurements, components, details, and proportions to describe various parts of a letter. While these won't tell you what makes a typeface good, they will at least give you the right words to use when you discuss the benefits of a particular face over another. You can say "I hate the x-height on Such-a-Gothic" or "These descenders just don't work for me" or "Please, may I see something with a smaller cap height?" and you'll know what you are talking about. ◆ While metal letters could be made to any width and height, digital type has to conform to multiples of the smallest unit: the pixel. Every character has to be a certain number of pixels wide and high. This is not a problem when the letters are made up of 600 pixels per inch, as is the case with modern laser printers—those pixels are not discernible to our eyes, and we are happy to believe that we are looking at smooth curves instead of little squares fitted into tight grids. ◆ On most screens, only 72 pixels make up one inch. We could see each and every one of them, if engineers hadn't already found ways around that. Computer screens, however, are not where we read most of our type these days. Smart phones, computers, and tablets all have high-resolutions screens, but microwave ovens, espresso makers, and all the other gadgets around us all still use small and modest displays. And the type unmistakably consists of bitmaps, which means that an 8-point letter is actually made up of eight pixels. If we allow six pixels above the baseline, including accents, and two below for descenders, that'll leave only three or four pixels for a lowercase character. In spite of these restrictions, there are hundreds of bitmap fonts, all different from one another by only a few pixels, but enough to prove that typographic variety cannot be suppressed by technological constraints.

3▸ ◂4

EXPLORATION 7
Paragraph Indicator:
Drop Capital
(typeset by Fred Carriedo)

Capital:
4 lines Goudy Text

Text:
7/13 FF Parango
Tracking +25/1000 em

Bullet:
14pt Goudy Text

## Alignment: Flush Left

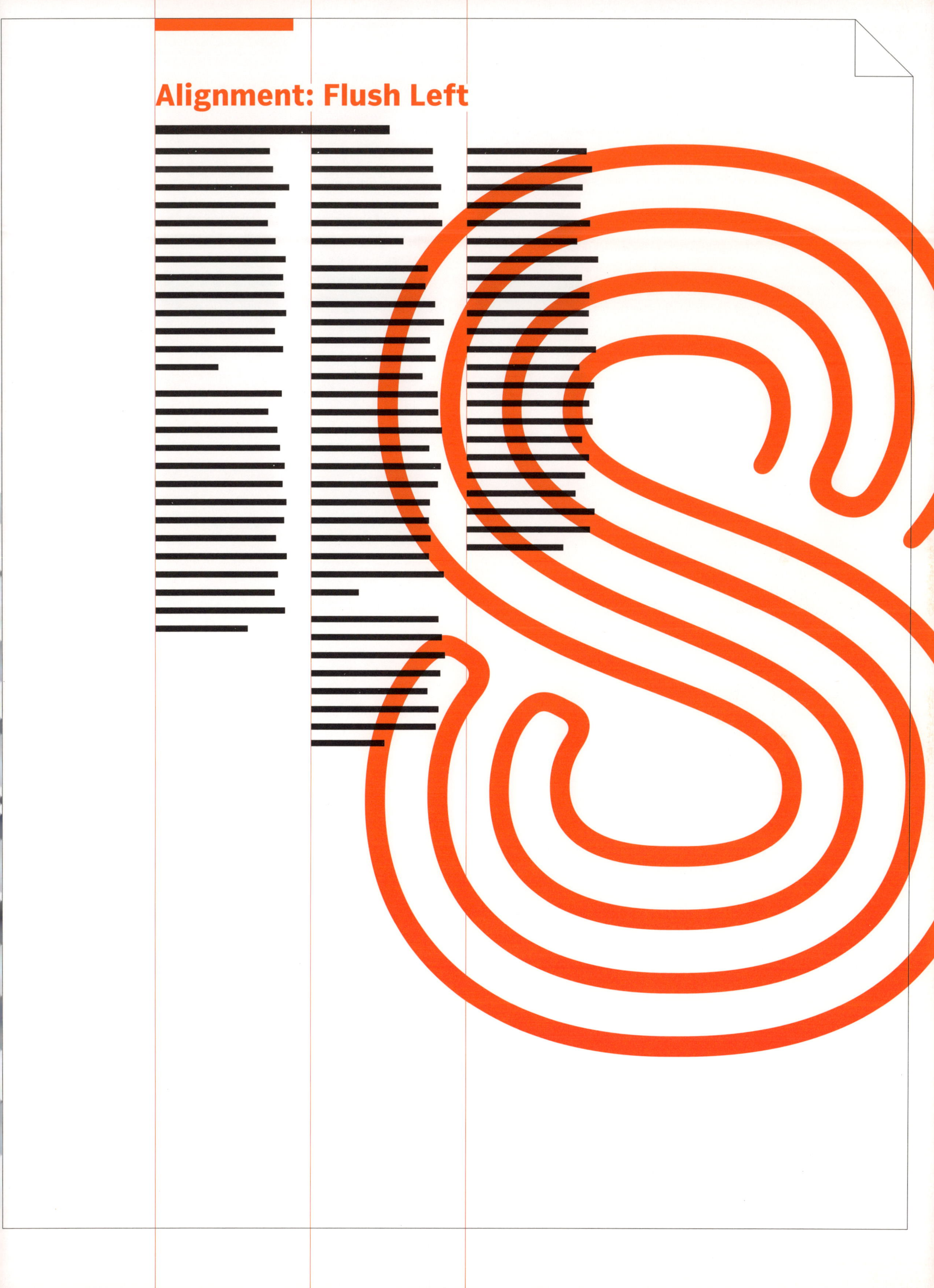

# 8 Alignment: Flush Left

We will now take a typographic interlude from paragraph indications to explore the topic of alignment.

Flush left/rag right (FL/RR) is a versatile alignment and can be used on any column width and in single- or multiple-column layouts.

In flush left/rag right settings, all word spaces are equal; therefore, the overall typographic color of your text is likely to remain even. When setting type flush left/rag right, you have the option of using automatic hyphenation or not. Turning on autohyphenation results in a more subtle ragged edge, whereas keeping it off creates a more dramatic rag.

A ragged edge on text type should look like a torn sheet of paper—in other words, the eye should not notice any strong shapes along any part of the rag. Poor rags might show up in the form of barrel shapes, sharp angles, or flat areas.

For this and the other three alignment Explorations that follow, typeset at least four paragraphs of the text as well as the title of the article. Align title and text the same way rather than mixing multiple kinds of alignments.

Typesetting the byline of the Spiekermann excerpt is optional for the alignment Explorations. If you choose to typeset the byline, note that even though it is the second item in the sequence, it is the least important item in the typographic hierarchy.

It is possible to use any of the paragraph indications from Explorations 1 through 7 with flush left alignments.

# Type Builds Character

Ever since people have been writing things down, they have had to consider their audience before actually putting pen to paper: letters would have to look different depending on whether they were to be read by mainly other people (in official documents or inscriptions), just one other person (in a letter), or only the writer (in a notebook or diary). There would be less room for guesswork if letter shapes were made more formal as the diversity of the readership expanded.

Some of the first messages to be read by a large number of people were rendered not by pens but by chisels. Large inscriptions on monuments in ancient Rome were carefully planned, with letters drawn on the stone with a brush before they were chiseled. Even if white-out had existed in those days, it would not have helped to remove mistakes made in stone. A bit of planning was also more important then, since stonemasons were sometimes more expendable than slabs of marble or granite.

Graphic design and typography are complicated activities, but even the simple projects benefit from thinking about the problem, forming a mental picture of the solution, and then carefully planning the steps between. Scientists have not been content with just calling the human face "beautiful" if it meets certain ideals, or "ugly" if it doesn't. They had to go out and measure proportions of nose to jaw, forehead to chin, and so on to establish why some faces are more appealing than others.

Typographers and graphic designers often choose typefaces for the very same reason they might fancy a person: They just like that person. For more scientifically-minded people, however, there are specific measurements, components, details, and proportions to describe various parts of a letter. While these won't tell you what makes a typeface good, they will at least give you the right words to use when you discuss the benefits of a particular face over another. You can say "I hate the x-height on Such-a-Gothic" or "These descenders just don't work for me" or "Please, may I see something with a smaller cap height?" and you'll know what you are talking about.

Rhythm and contrast keep coming up when discussing good music and good typographic design. They are concepts that also apply to spoken language, as anyone who has had to sit through a monotonous lecture will attest; the same tone, volume and speed of speech will put even the most interested listener into dreamland. Every now and again the audience needs to be shaken, either by a change in voice or pitch, by a question being posed, or by the speaker talking very quietly and then suddenly shouting. An occasional joke also works, just as the use of a funny typeface can liven up a page.

1 The title is set flush left on one long line above all three columns. Note that the width of this top line is not the same width as the first column alone nor of the first and second columns together. Instead, it ends about midway across the second column. This placement helps to make it clear that it is the head for all three columns below.

2 Rules touching the left edges of the text type echo the rule under the title, which is a part of the design of this typeface.

**FF Schulschrift B**
Just van Rossum based this 1992 face on the writing models used by German schools in the 1970s. There are three variations based on different official "norms;" B is the most like the cursive script familiar to English writers. It has special glyphs for starting and ending words, and a variation has ledger lines built into the font.

**FF Profile**
This face designed by Martin Wenzel in 1999 has gently flaring strokes that hint at serifs but that keep it in sans serif territory. The narrow build, tall lowercase, and generous apertures give it a cheerful, informal disposition. It is a clean sans with sway.

EXPLORATION 8 Alignment: Flush Left Title: 30pt FF Schulschrift B LinienEins Text: 8/14 FF Profile Light, tracking +25/1000 em Extra Leading: 9 pts

If you hyphenate, it looks best to avoid hyphenating words shorter than six characters and to keep at least three letters on a line before or after a hyphen.

Hyphens (-), en dashes (–), and em dashes (—) are often confused and misused. A hyphen is the shortest of these, and it is used only for hyphenation, never as a bullet or as a substitute for an em or en dash. Each of these punctuation marks has a very specific and limited use and is not interchangeable with the other two.

EXP
**8.2**

**TYPE BUILDS CHARACTER**

1

Ever since people have been writing things down, they have had to consider their audience before actually putting pen to paper: letters would have to look different depending on whether they were to be read by mainly other people (in official documents or inscriptions), just one other person (in a letter), or only the writer (in a notebook or diary). There would be less room for guesswork if letter shapes were made more formal as the diversity of the readership expanded.

Some of the first messages to be read by a large number of people were rendered not by pens but by chisels. Large inscriptions on monuments in ancient Rome were carefully planned, with letters drawn on the stone with a brush before they were chiseled. Even if white-out had existed in those days, it would not have helped to remove 2
mistakes made in stone. A bit of planning was also more important then, since stonemasons were sometimes more expendable than slabs of marble.

Graphic design and typography are complicated activities, but even the simple projects benefit from thinking about the problem, forming a mental picture of the solution, and then carefully planning the steps between. Scientists have not been content with just calling the human face "beautiful" if it meets certain ideals, or "ugly" if it doesn't. They had to go out and measure proportions of nose to jaw, forehead to chin, and so on to establish why some faces are more appealing than others.

Rhythm and contrast keep coming up when discussing good music and good typographic design. They are concepts that also apply to spoken language, as anyone who has had to sit through a monotonous lecture will attest; the same tone, volume and speed of speech will put even the most interested listener into dreamland. Every now and again the audience needs to be shaken, either by a change in voice or pitch, by a question being posed, or by the speaker talking very quietly and then suddenly shouting. An occasional joke also works, just as the use of a funny typeface can liven up a page.

EXPLORATION 8 : ALIGNMENT: FLUSH LEFT
TITLE: 7PT FF REAL BLACK TRACKING +95/1000 EM
TEXT: 7/15 FF REAL LIGHT TRACKING +25/1000 EM
EXTRA LEADING: 10 PTS /// RULE: 4 PTS

**Opposite page**

1 The length of the rules is the same as the width of the type in the title.

2 Automatic hyphenation has been turned off. The wider the column, the more likely you do not need to hyphenate in order to keep a good rag.

**This page**

3 Because the type in all caps for the title and byline has no descenders, it clearly differentiates from the body text and no extra linespace is added underneath.

**FF Real**

This face began as the voice of Erik Spiekermann for his biography *Hello, I am Erik*. First drawn in just two styles—one for headlines and one for text—the face was expanded into a superfamily by Spiekermann with the help of Ralph du Carrois. It is available in 13 finely graded weights. As a very special feature, Spiekermann not only produced his font digitally, but also had it cut into wood.

**Tarzana**

This pleasant yet peculiar face was designed in 1998 by Zuzana Licko. Her goal was "to balance the neutrality required for a text face with just enough idiosyncrasies to create a slightly unfamiliar design." She designed the roman and italic versions simultaneously, and the face's rather fluid informality derives from the fact that some roman forms were based on the italic.

3▸ ***TYPE BUILDS CHARACTER*** ***BY ERIK SPIEKERMANN***

Ever since people have been writing things down, they have had to consider their audience before actually putting pen to paper: letters would have to look different depending on whether they were to be read by mainly other people (in official documents or inscriptions), just one other person (in a letter), or only the writer (in a notebook or diary). There would be less room for guesswork if letter shapes were made more formal as the diversity of the readership expanded.

Some of the first messages to be read by a large number of people were rendered not by pens but by chisels. Large inscriptions on monuments in ancient Rome were carefully planned, with letters drawn on the stone with a brush before they were chiseled. Even if white-out had existed in those days, it would not have helped to remove mistakes made in stone. A bit of planning was also more important then, since stonemasons were sometimes more expendable than slabs of marble.

Graphic design and typography are complicated activities, but even the simple projects benefit from thinking about the problem, forming a mental picture of the solution, and then carefully planning the steps between. Scientists have not been content with just calling the human face "beautiful" if it meets certain ideals, or "ugly" if it doesn't. They had to go out and measure proportions of nose to jaw, forehead to chin, and so on to establish why some faces are more appealing than others.

Typographers and graphic designers often choose typefaces for the very same reason they might fancy a person: They just like that person. For more scientifically-minded people, however, there are specific measurements, components, details, and proportions to describe various parts of a letter. While these won't tell you what makes a typeface good, they will at least give you the right words to use when you discuss the benefits of a particular face over another. You can say "I hate the x-height on Such-a-Gothic" or "These descenders just don't work for me" or "Please, may I see something with a smaller cap height?" and you'll know what you are talking about.

*EXPLORATION 8*
*ALIGNMENT: FLUSH LEFT*

*TITLE:*
*9PT TARZANA WIDE BOLD ITALIC, TRACKING +30/1000 EM*

*BYLINE:*
*6PT TARZANA WIDE BOLD ITALIC, TRACKING +30/1000 EM*

*TEXT:*
*8/14 TARZANA WIDE, TRACKING +10/1000 EM*

*INDENT:*
*1 EM*

EXP
**8.3**

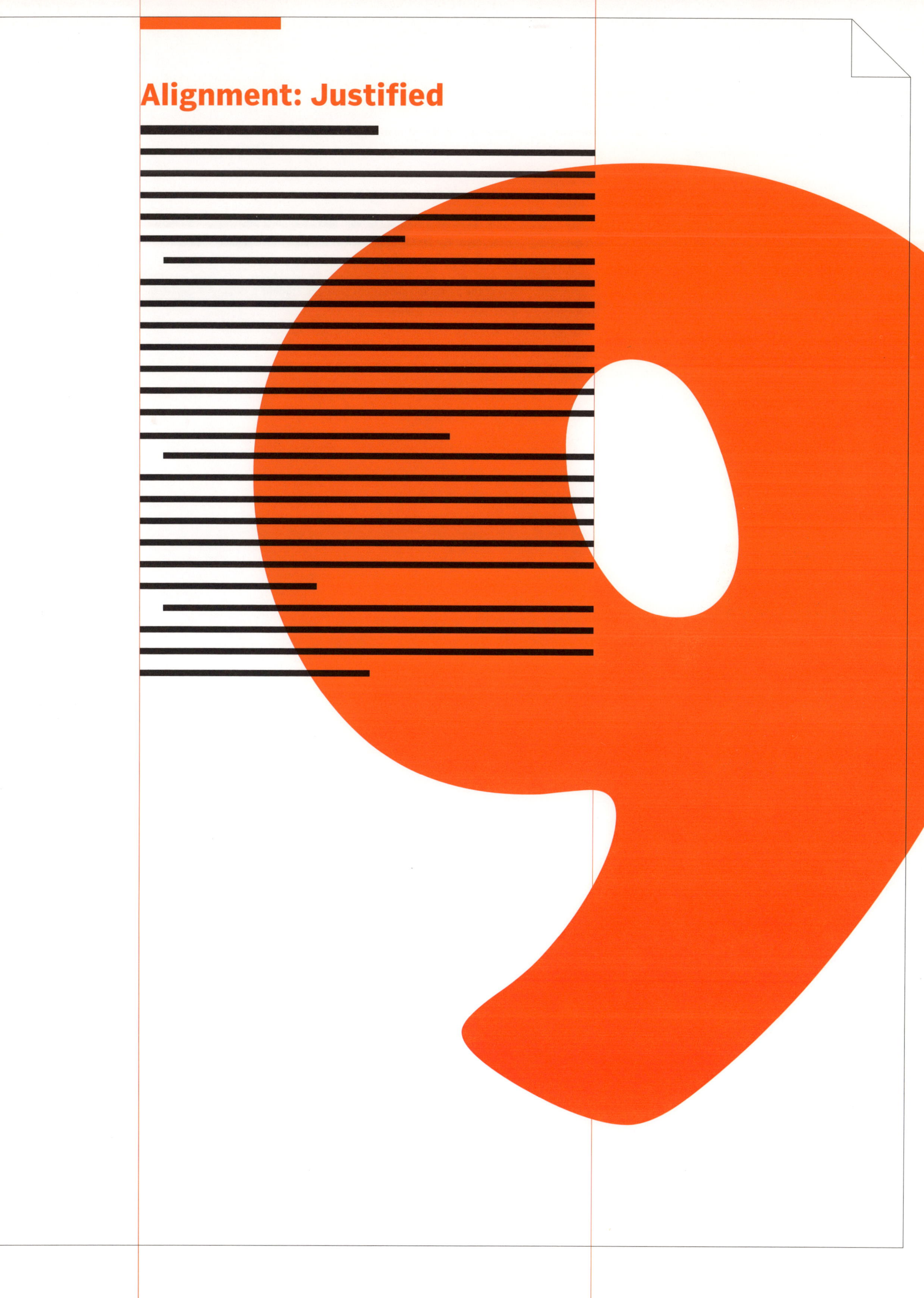
Alignment: Justified

# 9 Alignment: Justified

Justified alignment is best used on medium to wide column widths and can be set in one or more columns per page.

Justified settings are sometimes derided, but when set well (with even typographic color), they can be both appealing and elegant. Justifying type increases the likelihood of creating "rivers"—places where word space has expanded and is optically larger than linespace. Rivers are a form of uneven typographic color, which is a mark of poor typographic craftsmanship.

To reduce the likelihood of rivers when setting justified type, always turn on automatic hyphenation. This helps maintain more even word spacing and therefore more consistent typographic color. Because autohyphen-ation is not reliably controlled in digital environments, justification is best avoided there.

Additionally, it is best to avoid justifying text set in narrow columns. Where there are few words per line, inevitably word spaces on some lines expand noticeably more than others. To steer clear of this problem, set narrow columns ragged instead.

A title set above a justified column may be aligned flush left, flush right, or centered. The last lines of each of the paragraphs usually look best aligned the same way as the title.

Any of the paragraph indications from Explorations 1 through 7 can work with justified alignments.

# 1 TYPE BUILDS CHARACTER

BY ERIK SPIEKERMANN

2 » Ever since people have been writing things down, they have had to consider their audience before actually putting pen to paper: letters would have to look different depending on whether they were to be read by mainly other people (in official documents or inscriptions), just one other person (in a letter), or only the writer (in a notebook or diary). There would be less room for guesswork if letter shapes were made more formal as the diversity of the readership expanded.

» Some of the first messages to be read by a large number of people were rendered not by pens but by chisels. Large inscriptions on monuments in ancient Rome were carefully planned, with letters drawn on the stone with a brush before they were chiseled. Even if white-out had existed in those days, it would not have helped to remove mistakes made in stone. A bit of planning was also more important then, since stonemasons were sometimes more expendable than slabs of marble or granite.

» Graphic design and typography are complicated activities, but even the simple projects benefit from thinking about the problem, forming a mental picture of the solution, and then carefully planning the steps between.

» Scientists have not been content with just calling the human face "beautiful" if it meets certain ideals, or "ugly" if it doesn't. They had to go out and measure proportions of nose to jaw, forehead to chin, and so on to establish why some faces are more appealing than others.

» Typographers and graphic designers often choose typefaces for the very same reason they might fancy a person: They just like that person. For more scientifically-minded people, however, there are specific measurements, components, details, and proportions to describe various parts of a letter. While these won't tell you what makes a typeface good, they will at least give you the right words to use when you discuss the benefits of a particular face over another. You can say "I hate the x-height on Such-a-Gothic" or "These descenders just don't work for me" or "Please, may I see something with a smaller cap height?" and you'll know what you are talking about.

Exploration 9 /
Alignment: Justified
[typeset by
Fred Carriedo]

Title:
20/20 FF Letter Gothic
Text Bold
Tracking +30/1000 em

Byline:
7pt FF Letter Gothic
Text Light
Tracking +75/1000 em

Text:
8/14 FF Letter Gothic
Text Light
Tracking +40/1000 em

1 Whereas the text is justified, the title and byline are set flush left/rag right. Note also that they are aligned to the flush left edge of the text, not to the graphic elements that are hanging.

2 Title, byline, and text are all the same weight of the same typeface. Hierarchy is created by changing point size only. Robert Bringhurst said, "Don't use a font you don't need," reminding us that streamlined typography is a mark of excellence.

**FF Letter Gothic Text**
Like FF OCR-B, this is another text-optimized adaptation of an early technology classic. As an IBM Selectric typewriter font from the 1960s, the original Letter Gothic was monospaced. Albert Pinggera's 1998 reinterpretation adds proportional spacing, additional weights, italics, and text figures.

EXP
9.2

1▸ [ TYPE BUILDS CHARACTER ] ◂2

*by Erik Spiekermann*

Ever since people have been writing things down, they have had to consider their audience before actually putting pen to paper: letters would have to look different depending on whether they were to be read by mainly other people (in official documents or inscriptions), just one other person (in a letter), or only the writer (in a notebook or diary). There would be less room for guesswork if letter shapes were made more formal as the diversity of the readership expanded.

Some of the first messages to be read by a large number of people were rendered not by pens but by chisels. Large inscriptions on monuments in ancient Rome were carefully planned, with letters drawn on the stone with a brush before they were chiseled. Even if white-out had existed in those days, it would not have helped to remove mistakes made in stone. A bit of planning was also more important then, since stonemasons were sometimes more expendable than slabs of marble or granite.

Graphic design and typography are complicated activities, but even the simple projects benefit from thinking about the problem, forming a mental picture of the solution, and then carefully planning the steps between.

Scientists have not been content with just calling the human face "beautiful" if it meets certain ideals, or "ugly" if it doesn't. They had to go out and measure proportions of nose to jaw, forehead to chin, and so on to establish why some faces are more appealing than others.

Typographers and graphic designers often choose typefaces for the very same reason they might fancy a person: They just like that person. For more scientifically-minded people, however, there are specific measurements, components, details, and proportions to describe various parts of a letter. While these won't tell you what makes a typeface good, they will at least give you the right words to use when you discuss the benefits of a particular face over another. You can say "I hate the x-height on Such-a-Gothic" or "These descenders just don't work for me" or "Please, may I see something with a smaller cap height?" and you'll know what you are talking about.

While metal letters could be made to any width and height, digital type has to conform to multiples of the smallest unit: the pixel. Every character has to be a certain number of pixels wide and high. This is not a problem when the letters are made up of 600 pixels per inch, as is the case with modern laser printers—those pixels are not discernible to our eyes, and we are happy to believe that we are looking at smooth curves instead of little squares fitted into tight grids.

On most screens, only 72 pixels make up one inch. We could see each and every one of them, if engineers hadn't already found ways around that. Computer screens, however, are not where we read most of our type these days. Smart phones, computers, and tablets all have high-resolutions screens, but microwave ovens, espresso makers, and all the other gadgets around us all still use small and modest displays. And the type unmistakably consists of bitmaps, which means that an 8-point letter is actually made up of eight pixels. If we allow six pixels above the baseline, including accents, and two below for descenders, that'll leave only three or four pixels for a lowercase character.

Rhythm and contrast keep coming up when discussing good music and good typographic design. They are concepts that also apply to spoken language, as anyone who has had to sit through a monotonous lecture will attest; the same tone, volume and speed of speech will put even the most interested listener into dreamland. Every now and again the audience needs to be shaken, either by a change in voice or pitch, by a question being posed, or by the speaker talking very quietly and then suddenly shouting. An occasional joke also works, just as the use of a funny typeface can liven up a page.

EXPLORATION 9: JUSTIFIED    Title: 8/12 Fournier, tracking +50/1000 em    Byline: 8/12 Fournier Italic, tracking +40/1000 em    Text: 8/12 Fournier, tracking +30/1000 em

EXP
9.3

**TYPE BUILDS CHARACTER** ***BY ERIK SPIEKERMANN***

Ever since people have been writing things down, they have had to consider their audience before actually putting pen to paper: letters would have to look different depending on whether they were to be read by mainly other people (in official documents or inscriptions), just one other person (in a letter), or only the writer (in a notebook or diary). There would be less room for guesswork if letter shapes were made more formal as the diversity of the readership expanded.

(3) Some of the first messages to be read by a large number of people were rendered not by pens but by chisels. Large inscriptions on monuments in ancient Rome were carefully planned, with letters drawn on the stone with a brush before they were chiseled. Even if white-out had existed in those days, it would not have helped to remove mistakes made in stone.

Graphic design and typography are complicated activities, but even the simple projects benefit from thinking about the problem, forming a mental picture of the solution, and then carefully planning the steps between.

Scientists have not been content with just calling the human face "beautiful" if it meets certain ideals, or "ugly" if it doesn't. They had to go out and measure proportions of nose to jaw, forehead to chin, and so on to establish why some faces are more appealing than others.

Typographers and graphic designers often choose typefaces for the very same reason they might fancy a person: They just like that person. For more scientifically-minded people, however, there are specific measurements, components, details, and proportions to describe various parts of a letter. While these won't tell you what makes a typeface good, they will at least give you the right words to use when you discuss the benefits of a particular face over another. You can say "I hate the x-height on Such-a-Gothic" or "These descenders just don't work for me" or "Please, may I see something with a smaller cap height?" and you'll know what you are talking about.

Exploration 9 | Alignment: Justified
Title: 8pt Avenir 95 Black, tracking +80/1000 em
Byline: 6pt Avenir 95 Black Oblique, tracking +80/1000
Text: 7.5/15 Avenir 55 Roman, tracking +45/1000 em
Indent: 2 ems

**Opposite page**

1 Brackets hang and the title and byline are aligned to the exdented first lines of the paragraphs below.

2 Custom-designed brackets around the title help the typesetting in an Oldstyle typeface look a bit more up-to-date.

**This page**

3 Indents are 2 ems because the measure is wide. If you need more than 2 ems to make a clear paragraph indication with indents, it is likely that your column width is too wide or your leading is too loose.

**Fournier**

Pierre Simon Fournier's 1742 original is a classic Transitional roman, sitting between a Humanist, calligraphic Oldstyle and a crisp, constructed Modern. Monotype revived the design in 1928, and the digital version is a fairly lightweight replica of the larger sizes. (It may be too feeble for very small text settings, in which case Source Serif is a sturdier choice.) The bony italic is very distinctive and offers a quaint antique feel to page trimmings.

**Avenir**

In 1988, Adrian Frutiger sought to improve on Futura's strict geometry by infusing Humanist traits, such as a two-story 'a,' curved tails on descenders, and rounds that are less rigid. These features make Avenir more readable than other Geometric faces. Twelve years later, Tobias Frere-Jones would adopt many of these concepts for his über popular Gotham. Avenir Next—bundled with Mac OS X—is a revision with a new italic design and new widths and weights.

**This page**

1 The title and byline are justified along the top line. Because all caps nearly always needs more generous tracking than upper- and lowercase (u/lc), you can open the letterspacing to help fill the measure without leaving too much word space after the title. Track lighter weights looser than bold weights.

**Opposite page**

2 The title and byline are set on either side of the same vertical grid line. Whereas justified settings usually look very stable, the shift of these two short lines gives this page a bit more movement.

**FF DIN**

Devised by the German standards organization at the beginning of the 20th century, the DIN series, intended primarily for road signs, was drawn by engineers with ruler and compass. In 1995, Albert-Jan Pool evolved the letter patterns beyond their cold, technical origins, producing a family of digital fonts with refined lettershapes, additional weights, and other typographic optimizations. The improvements made DIN a versatile typeface and a favorite among designers seeking a clean, modern aesthetic.

**Lo-Res**

This is a culmination and revision of Zuzana Licko's type designs from the 1980s when screens required bitmap fonts. Today this style is linked to early digital technology. Lo-Res is unusual among pixel typefaces because of the family's range of styles: various sizes of sans and serifs in regular and bold, narrow to wide, and the Plus/Minus series with soft corners. There are even small caps and alternate forms.

EXPLORATION 9: ALIGNMENT: JUSTIFIED (Typeset by Matthew Cacciola)

Title: 16pt FF DIN Black, tracking +70/1000 em Byline: 6pt FF DIN Regular, tracking +150/1000 em Text: 8/14 FF DIN Regular, tracking +25/1000 em

1 **TYPE BUILDS CHARACTER** BY ERIK SPIEKERMANN

Ever since people have been writing things down, they have had to consider their audience before actually putting pen to paper: letters would have to look different depending on whether they were to be read by mainly other people (in official documents or inscriptions), just one other person (in a letter), or only the writer (in a notebook or diary). There would be less room for guesswork if letter shapes were made more formal as the diversity of the readership expanded.

Some of the first messages to be read by a large number of people were rendered not by pens but by chisels. Large inscriptions on monuments in ancient Rome were carefully planned, with letters drawn on the stone with a brush before they were chiseled. Even if white-out had existed in those days, it would not have helped to remove mistakes made in stone. A bit of planning was also more important then, since stonemasons were sometimes more expendable than slabs of marble or granite.

Graphic design and typography are complicated activities, but even the simple projects benefit from thinking about the problem, forming a mental picture of the solution, and then carefully planning the steps between.

Scientists have not been content with just calling the human face "beautiful" if it meets certain ideals, or "ugly" if it doesn't. They had to go out and measure proportions of nose to jaw, forehead to chin, and so on to establish why some faces are more appealing than others.

Typographers and graphic designers often choose typefaces for the very same reason they might fancy a person: They just like that person. For more scientifically-minded people, however, there are specific measurements, components, details, and proportions to describe various parts of a letter. While these won't tell you what makes a typeface good, they will at least give you the right words to use when you discuss the benefits of a particular face over another. You can say "I hate the x-height on Such-a-Gothic" or "These descenders just don't work for me" or "Please, may I see something with a smaller cap height?" and you'll know what you are talking about.

Rhythm and contrast keep coming up when discussing good music and good typographic design. They are concepts that also apply to spoken language, as anyone who has had to sit through a monotonous lecture will attest; the same tone, volume and speed of speech will put even the most interested listener into dreamland. Every now and again the audience needs to be shaken, either by a change in voice or pitch, by a question being posed, or by the speaker talking very quietly and then suddenly shouting. An occasional joke also works, just as the use of a funny typeface can liven up a page.

2

## TYPE BUILDS CHARACTER

BY ERIK SPIEKERMANN

Ever since people have been writing things down, they have had to consider their audience before actually putting pen to paper: letters would have to look different depending on whether they were to be read by mainly other people (in official documents or inscriptions), just one other person (in a letter), or only the writer (in a note-book or diary). There would be less room for guesswork if letter shapes were made more formal as the diversity of the readership expanded.

Some of the first messages to be read by a large number of people were rendered not by pens but by chisels. Large inscriptions on monuments in ancient Rome were carefully planned, with letters drawn on the stone with a brush before they were chiseled. Even if white-out had existed in those days, it would not have helped to remove mistakes made in stone. A bit of planning was also more important then, since stonemasons were sometimes more expendable than slabs of marble or granite.

Graphic design and typography are complicated activities, but even the simple projects benefit from thinking about the problem, forming a mental picture of the solution, and then carefully planning the steps between.

Scientists have not been content with just calling the human face "beautiful" if it meets certain ideals, or "ugly" if it doesn't. They had to go out and measure proportions of nose to jaw, forehead to chin, and so on to establish why some faces are more appealing than others.

Typographers and graphic designers often choose typefaces for the very same reason they might fancy a person: They just like that person. For more scientifically-minded people, however, there are specific measurements, components, details, and proportions to describe various parts of a letter. While these won't tell you what makes a typeface good, they will at least give you the right words to use when you discuss the benefits of a particular face over another. You can say "I hate the x-height on Such-a-Gothic" or "These descenders just don't work for me" or "Please, may I see something with a smaller cap height?" and you'll know what you are talking about.

EXPLORATION 9:
JUSTIFIED

TITLE:
13PT LO-RES 12 BOLD
TRACKING
+30/1000 EM

BYLINE:
8PT LO-RES 12 BOLD
TRACKING
+30/1000 EM

TEXT:
9/12 LO-RES 12 BOLD
TRACKING
+30/1000 EM

EXP
9.5

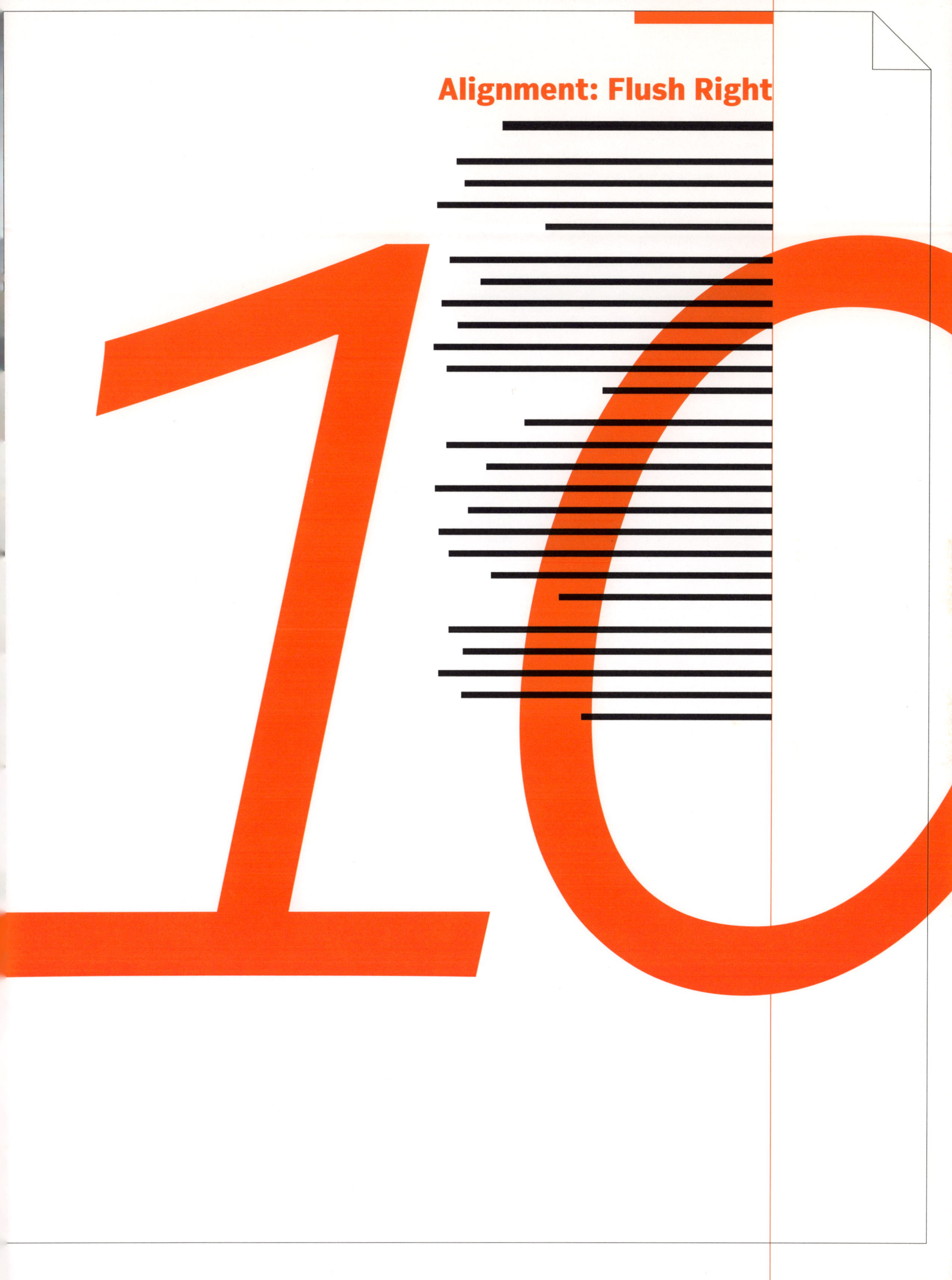
Alignment: Flush Right

# 10 **Alignment: Flush Right**

Because it is lower in readability, flush right is usually used only for small amounts of text such as poems or short articles.

It is best to set flush right/rag left (FR/RL) text type on a single narrow or medium column width.

With flush right alignments, a significant difference in line length makes it easier for the eye to find its way back to the next line on the left edge. Turn off automatic hyphenation to get a dramatic rag with this alignment.

You can also manually add soft returns to make the line lengths on flush right settings more strongly varied. Remember that a rag should ideally have the randomized feel of a torn sheet of paper.

Paragraph indications of indents and exdents don't work with flush right alignments because the left edge already varies. You can use extra leading, graphic elements, or a rule between paragraphs on these settings.

2

# TYPE BUILDS CHARACTER *by Erik Spiekermann*

Ever since people have been writing things down, they have had to consider their audience before actually putting pen to paper: letters would have to look different depending on whether they were to be read by mainly other people (in official 1 documents or inscriptions), just one other person (in a letter), or only the writer (in a notebook or diary). There would be less room for guesswork if letter shapes were made more formal as the diversity of the readership expanded.

3

Some of the first messages to be read by a large number of people were rendered not by pens but by chisels. Large inscriptions on monuments in ancient Rome were carefully planned, with letters drawn on the stone with a brush before they were chiseled. Even if white-out had existed in those days, it would not have helped to remove mistakes made in stone. A bit of planning was also more important then, since stonemasons were sometimes more expendable than slabs of marble or granite.

Graphic design and typography are complicated activities, but even the simple projects benefit from thinking about the problem, forming a mental picture of the solution, and then carefully planning the steps between.

Scientists have not been content with just calling the human face "beautiful" if it meets certain ideals, or "ugly" if it doesn't. They had to go out and measure proportions of nose to jaw, forehead to chin, and so on to establish why some faces are more appealing than others.

Typographers and graphic designers often choose typefaces for the very same reason they might fancy a person: They just like that person. For more scientifically-minded people, however, there are specific measurements, components, details, and proportions to describe various parts of a letter. While these won't tell you what makes a typeface good, they will at least give you the right words to use when you discuss the benefits of a particular face over another.

Rhythm and contrast keep coming up when discussing good music and good typographic design. They are concepts that also apply to spoken language, as anyone who has had to sit through a monotonous lecture will attest; the same tone, volume and speed of speech will put even the most interested listener into dreamland. Every now and again the audience needs to be shaken, either by a change in voice or pitch, by a question being posed, or by the speaker talking very quietly and then suddenly shouting. An occasional joke also works, just as the use of a funny typeface can liven up a page.

 Title: 10pt Perpetua Bold, Tracking +60/1000 em Byline: 7pt Perpetua Italic, Tracking +50/1000 em Text: 7/11 Perpetua, tracking +40/1000 em Fleurons: 7pt P22 Victorian Ornaments

1 When autohyphenation is off, as it should be for flush right settings, line lengths will vary more widely. It is more legible to have a dramatic rag on flush right settings.

2 The top line and the text are aligned on either side of the same vertical grid line to help activate the right side of the page.

3 The decorative fleuron between paragraphs matches the classic style of this serif typeface and is also set flush right.

**Perpetua**

Typographically, Eric Gill is best known for Gill Sans, but his love of the chiseled and engraved is best embodied in Perpetua (1928–36), with its classical forms and sharp details derived from inscription lettering. Perpetua is distinguished by its strong axis angle, long descenders, spurred 'U,' and unusual Oldstyle figures.

**P22 Victorian Ornaments**

Digitized by Richard Kegler and Amy Greenan in 2000, these decorative elements were released in conjunction with the Albright-Knox Art Gallery's exhibition of Victorian-era French artist James Tissot. They include floral motifs commonly used to decorate title pages and ads at the turn of the 20th century. Some of the ornaments can be combined for patterns and frames.

EXP
**10.2**

**Type Builds Character** by Erik Spiekermann

1

Ever since people have been writing things down, they have had to consider their audience before actually putting pen to paper: letters would have to look different depending on whether they were to be read by mainly other people (in official documents or inscriptions), just one other person (in a letter), or only the writer (in a notebook or diary). There would be less room for guesswork if letter shapes were made more formal as the diversity 2 of the readership expanded.

Some of the first messages to be read by a large number of people were rendered not by pens but by chisels. Large inscriptions on monuments in ancient Rome were carefully planned, with letters drawn on the stone with a brush before they were chiseled. Even if white-out had existed in those days, it would not have helped to remove mistakes made in stone. A bit of planning was also more important then, since stonemasons were sometimes more expendable than slabs of marble or granite.

Graphic design and typography are complicated activities, but even the simple projects benefit from thinking about the problem, forming a mental picture of the solution, and then carefully planning the steps between.

Scientists have not been content with just calling the human face “beautiful” if it meets certain ideals, or “ugly” if it doesn’t. They had to go out and measure proportions of nose to jaw, forehead to chin, and so on to establish why some faces are more appealing than others.

Rhythm and contrast keep coming up when discussing good music and good typographic design. They are concepts that also apply to spoken language, as anyone who has had to sit through a monotonous lecture will attest; the same tone, volume and speed of speech will put even the most interested listener into dreamland. Every now and again the audience needs to be shaken, either by a change in voice or pitch, by a question being posed, or by the speaker talking very quietly and then suddenly shouting. An occasional joke also works, just as the use of a funny typeface can liven up a page.

**Exploration 10** Alignment: Flush Right
title: 8pt FF Legato Demibold, tracking +20/1000 em * byline: 6pt FF Legato Light, tracking +30/1000 em
text: 8/17 FF Legato Light, tracking +25/1000 em * extra leading: 6 pts * rule: 2 pts

## TYPE BUILDS CHARACTER ✷ *by Erik Spiekermann*

◂3

Ever since people have been writing things down, they have had to consider
their audience before actually putting pen to paper: letters would have to look
different depending on whether they were to be read by mainly
other people (in official documents or inscriptions), just one other person
(in a letter), or only the writer (in a notebook or diary). There would
be less room for guesswork if letter shapes were made more formal as the
diversity of the readership expanded.

Some of the first messages to be read by a large number of people
were rendered not by pens but by chisels. Large inscriptions on monuments in
ancient Rome were carefully planned, with letters drawn on the stone
with a brush before they were chiseled. Even if white-out had existed in those
days, it would not have helped to remove mistakes made in stone.
A bit of planning was also more important then, since stonemasons were
sometimes more expendable than slabs of marble or granite.

Graphic design and typography are complicated activities, but even the
simple projects benefit from thinking about the problem, forming a mental
picture of the solution, and then carefully planning the steps between.

Scientists have not been content with just calling the human face "beautiful" if
it meets certain ideals, or "ugly" if it doesn't. They had to go out and
measure proportions of nose to jaw, forehead to chin, and so on to establish
why some faces are more appealing than others.

Exploration 10
Alignment: Flush Right
(typeset by Gloria Hiek)

title: 13pt Centaur Small Caps
tracking +60/1000 em

text: 8/14 Centaur
tracking +20/1000 em

extra leading: 7 pts

EXP
**10.3**

**Opposite page**

1 The rules between paragraphs have been set with a left indent to blend in with the dramatic left rag. The thin rules are similar in weight to the strokes in the letterforms.

2 Last lines are short to help more clearly signal the end of paragraphs. You can achieve this by strategically adding a few soft returns within each paragraph while keeping an eye on the shape of the rag.

**This page**

3 The extra leading under the top line is six times the leading between paragraphs. Negative spaces on the page are designed in proportion to each other.

**FF Legato**

Evert Bloemsma was known for departing from convention to produce very original type that was also very useful. This was the culmination of those experiments, completed in 2004, just a year before his death. The design treats counters (interior spaces) and outlines independently to create readable forms that are more sculpted than written.

**Centaur**

In the early 1900s, there was renewed interest in the Renaissance types of Nicolas Jenson. Followers of the Arts and Crafts movement transformed the style into chunky, rough-hewn letters. Bruce Rogers took a different tack with his 1914 design for the Metropolitan Museum. Centaur is much lighter and more calligraphic, faring well when letterpressed on soft paper but too fragile for most modern printing.

# Alignment: Centered

# 11 Alignment: Centered

Like flush right alignments, centered settings are typically used only for small quantities of text. They also tend to look and read best on narrow or medium column widths.

Because centered alignments have an inherent symmetry, it usually works best to compose the page with a single text block (one column) and to center the type on the page. Centered type is rarely used in multi-column layouts owing to its lower readability.

When type is centered, you can turn off automatic hyphenation to get strong variations in line length. The rags on centered text may be made even more dramatic than those on flush right.

When you typeset centered type, you usually must manually add soft returns to create an aesthetically pleasing rag. Whenever possible, add the soft returns to break the lines in a logical place, such as at the end of a phrase or after a comma or a period.

Making the last line of each paragraph rather short when setting centered type gives readers the signal that they've come to the end of a paragraph.

Paragraph indications of indents and exdents don't work with centered alignments because the left edge is already variable. You can use extra leading, graphic elements, or a rule between paragraphs on these settings.

1

# Type Builds Character

*by Erik Spiekermann*

 2

Ever since people have been writing things down, they have had to consider their audience before actually putting pen to paper: letters would have to look different depending on whether they were to be read by mainly other people (in official documents or inscriptions), just one other person (in a letter), or only the writer (in a notebook or diary). There would be less room for guesswork if letter shapes were made more formal as the diversity of the readership expanded.

Some of the first messages to be read by a large number of people were rendered not by pens but by chisels. Large inscriptions on monuments in ancient Rome were carefully planned, with letters drawn on the stone with a brush before they were chiseled. Even if white-out had existed in those days, it would not have helped to remove mistakes made in stone. A bit of planning was also more important then, since stonemasons were sometimes more expendable than slabs of marble or granite.

Graphic design and typography are complicated activities, but even the simple projects benefit from thinking about the problem, forming a mental picture of the solution, and then carefully planning the steps between. Scientists have not been content with just calling the human face "beautiful" if it meets certain ideals, or "ugly" if it doesn't. They had to go out and measure proportions of nose to jaw, forehead to chin, and so on to establish why some faces are more appealing than others.

Typographers and graphic designers often choose typefaces for the very same reason they might fancy a person: They just like that person. For more scientifically-minded people, however, there are specific measurements, components, details, and proportions to describe various parts of a letter. While these won't tell you what makes a typeface good, they will at least give you the right words to use when you discuss the benefits of a particular face over another. You can say "I hate the x-height on Such-a-Gothic" or "These descenders just don't work for me" or "Please, may I see something with a smaller cap height?" and you'll know what you are talking about. 3

EXPLORATION 11
4 ALIGNMENT: CENTERED

TITLE:
10/12 PHOTINA ULTRA BOLD
TRACKING +40/1000 EM

BYLINE:
5/10 PHOTINA ITALIC
TRACKING +40/1000 EM

TEXT:
7/12 PHOTINA REGULAR
TRACKING +40/1000 EM

GRAPHIC ELEMENT:
10PT MAXIME ORNAMENTS

1. Centered type looks best on centered layouts.
2. The same fleuron has been used in between the byline and the text as between paragraphs.
3. Like flush right alignments, last lines are short and rags are generally quite dramatic. You can achieve these qualities with a few strategically placed soft returns within each paragraph.
4. The colophon is centered as well. It is difficult to successfully combine center-aligned type with any other alignment.

**Photina**
Created by Jose Mendoza y Almeida specifically for phototypesetting, Photina has crisp details and long serifs to counteract the softening effect of projection. It's a high-contrast design, yet its hairlines are strong enough to survive coated paper (and, incidentally, LED screens) at medium text sizes. Photina was popular after its release in 1971 but was soon forgotten in the move from photo to digital typesetting. It's a hidden gem ripe for rediscovery. The italics are particularly original.

**Maxime Ornaments**
Designed in 1999 by Éric de Berranger, these decorative elements complement his text face of the same name.

**This page**

1 Rules between paragraphs are one-third of the column width and centered.

**Opposite page**

2 Title and byline are stacked one word per line to stress the centered alignment. Note the omission of the word "by" before the author's name. The change in size and weight suffices to express the proper hierarchy of the byline, even without including the word.

**Maiola**

Begun as a thesis project and released in 2005, Veronika Burian's typeface was an immediate success, winning the TDC competition among other awards. Although a contemporary serif face, it retains strong links to historical models—such as work by Czech designer Oldrich Menhart—in its idiosyncratic Oldstyle features and calligraphic forms. Its sharpness and angularity, particularly in the italic, give the face a dynamic expressive tension.

**FF Quadraat**

Fred Smeijers's goal for this 1992 design was to capture the elegance of Renaissance Garaldes with the economy and function of type like Times and Plantin. Unlike many contemporary book serifs, FF Quadraat has modeled outlines that feel hand rendered rather than mechanical. The roman is fairly soft, without any straight lines, and the italic is sharp and narrow.

## TYPE BUILDS CHARACTER

BY ERIK SPIEKERMANN

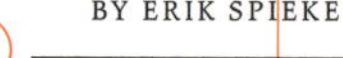

Ever since people have been writing things down, they have had to consider their audience before actually putting pen to paper: letters would have to look different depending on whether they were to be read by mainly other people (in official documents or inscriptions), just one other person (in a letter), or only the writer (in a notebook or diary). There would be less room for guesswork if letter shapes were made more formal as the diversity of the readership expanded.

Some of the first messages to be read by a large number of people were rendered not by pens but by chisels. Large inscriptions on monuments in ancient Rome were carefully planned, with letters drawn on the stone with a brush before they were chiseled. Even if white-out had existed in those days, it would not have helped to remove mistakes made in stone. A bit of planning was also more important then, since stonemasons were sometimes more expendable than slabs of marble or granite.

Graphic design and typography are complicated activities, but even the simple projects benefit from thinking about the problem, forming a mental picture of the solution, and then carefully planning the steps between. Scientists have not been content with just calling the human face "beautiful" if it meets certain ideals, or "ugly" if it doesn't. They had to go out and measure proportions of nose to jaw, forehead to chin, and so on to establish why some faces are more appealing than others.

Typographers and graphic designers often choose typefaces for the very same reason they might fancy a person: They just like that person.
For more scientifically-minded people, however, there are specific measurements, components, details, and proportions to describe various parts of a letter. While these won't tell you what makes a typeface good, they will at least give you the right words to use when you discuss the benefits of a particular face over another. You can say "I hate the x-height on Such-a-Gothic" or "These descenders just don't work for me" or "Please, may I see something with a smaller cap height?" and you'll know what you are talking about.

Exploration 11
Alignment: Centered

Title:
10/14 Maiola Bold
Tracking +120/1000 em

Byline:
6/14 Maiola
Tracking +100/1000 em

Text:
7.5/14 Maiola
Tracking +40/1000 em

Rule:
0.5 pt

# TYPE BUILDS CHARACTER

2▸ ERIK SPIEKERMANN

Ever since people have been writing things down, they have had to consider their audience before actually putting pen to paper: letters would have to look different depending on whether they were to be read by mainly other people (in official documents or inscriptions), just one other person (in a letter), or only the writer (in a notebook or diary). There would be less room for guesswork if letter shapes were made more formal as the diversity of the readership expanded.

Some of the first messages to be read by a large number of people were rendered not by pens but by chisels. Large inscriptions on monuments in ancient Rome were carefully planned, with letter drawn on the stone with a brush before they were chiseled. Even if white-out had existed in those days, it would not have helped to remove mistakes made in stone. A bit of planning was also more important then, since stonemasons were sometimes more expendable than slabs of marble or granite.

Graphic design and typography are complicated activities, but even the simple projects benefit from thinking about the problem, forming a mental picture of the solution, and then carefully planning the steps between. Scientists have not been content with just calling the human face "beautiful" if it meets certain ideals, or "ugly" if it doesn't. They had to go out and measure proportions of nose to jaw, forehead to chin, and so on to establish why some faces are more appealing than others.

Typographers and graphic designers often choose typefaces for the very same reason they might fancy a person: They just like that person. For more scientifically-minded people, however, there are specific measurements, components, details, and proportions to describe various parts of a letter. While these won't tell you what makes a typeface good, they will at least give you the right words to use when you discuss the benefits of a particular face over another.

Exploration 11
Alignment: Centered
(typeset by Gloria Hiek)

Title:
8/12 FF Quadraat Bold
tracking +25/1000 em

Byline:
6/10 FF Quadraat Italic
tracking +50/1000 em

Text:
8/14 FF Quadraat Regular
tracking +25/1000 em

Extra Leading:
7 pts

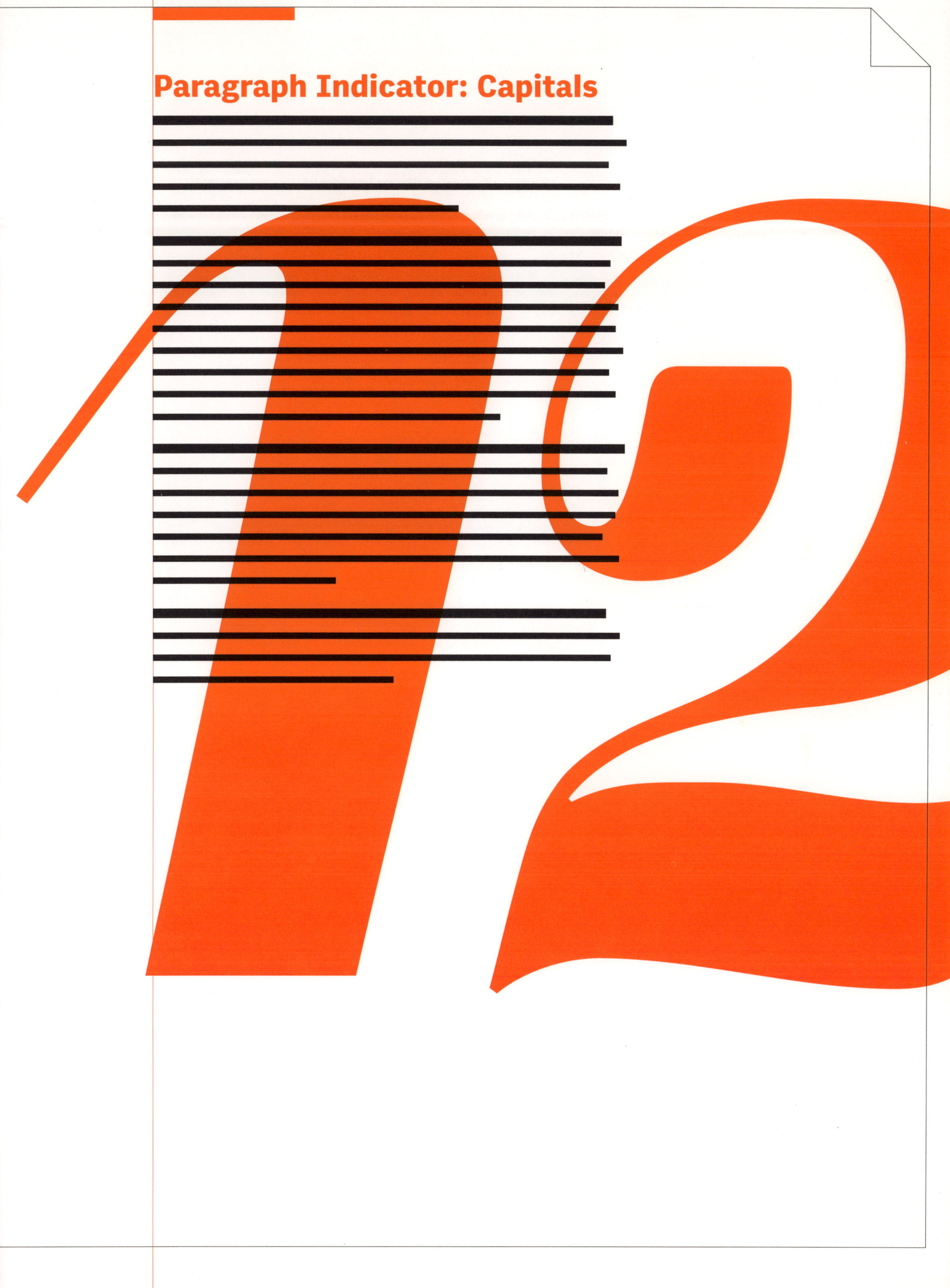
Paragraph Indicator: Capitals

# 12 Paragraph Indicator: Capitals

The Explorations from this point forward nudge the boundaries of some of the conventions of traditional typesetting. Remember, though, even when you push your typesetting to be more expressive, it can and should remain as legible and functional as possible.

Using capitals (or small capitals) as a paragraph indicator is somewhat similar to using a drop or initial capital, but in this case, you do not necessarily need to change the point size of the uppercase letterforms.

Capitals can be used for the first word or first line of each paragraph. Because setting text type in all capitals lowers readability, all caps are not recommended for lengthy texts. On shorter texts, however, readers might even be able to tolerate the entire first paragraph and every other one after it in capitals.

Add more generous tracking to capital letterforms than you use on the same type specification in upper- and lowercase (u/lc).

This style of paragraph indication may be used with or without returns between paragraphs because the difference in overall typographic color and texture between capitals and upper- and lowercase (u/lc) settings is almost always easy to see.

**Exploration 12**
Paragraph Indicator: Capitals
(typeset by Fred Carriedo)

First Words:
7.5pt Serifa Bold
Tracking +90/1000 em

Text:
7.5/13.5 Serifa Light
Tracking +70/1000 em

**EVER** since people have been writing things down, they have had to consider their audience before actually putting pen to paper: letters would have to look different depending on whether they were to be read by mainly other people (in official documents or inscriptions), just one other person (in a letter), or only the writer (in a notebook or diary). There would be less room for guesswork if letter shapes were made more formal as the diversity of the readership expanded. **SOME** of the first messages to be read by a large number of people were rendered not by pens but by chisels. Large inscriptions on monuments in ancient Rome were carefully planned, with letters drawn on the stone with a brush before they were chiseled. Even if white-out had existed in those days, it would not have helped to remove mistakes made in stone. A bit of planning was also more important then, since stonemasons were sometimes more expendable than slabs of marble or granite. **GRAPHIC** design and typography are complicated activities, but even the simple projects benefit from thinking about the problem, forming a mental picture of the solution, and then carefully planning the steps between. **SCIENTISTS** have not been content with just calling the human face "beautiful" if it meets certain ideals, or "ugly" if it doesn't. They had to go out and measure proportions of nose to jaw, forehead to chin, and so on to establish why some faces are more appealing than others. **TYPOGRAPHERS** and graphic designers often choose typefaces for the very same reason they might fancy a person: They just like that person. For more scientifically-minded people, however, there are specific measurements, components, details, and proportions to describe various parts of a letter. While these won't tell you what makes a typeface good, they will at least give you the right words to use when you discuss the benefits of a particular face over another. You can say "I hate the x-height on Such-a-Gothic" or "These descenders just don't work for me" or "Please, may I see something with a smaller cap height?" and you'll know what you are talking about.

1 Although the first word of each paragraph is set in caps and bolder, the rules help direct the eye to the beginning of each new paragraph in this unusual and creative setting.

2 The last line of the text is wider than half the column width so the whole text block feels stable, not teetering on a stubby bottom line.

**Serifa**
Designed in 1967, Adrian Frutiger's Grotesque-style slab serif is loosely based on his Univers, with which it pairs quite well. It has a fairly wide stance and bookish proportions suitable for long text. For display settings, see the narrower Glypha, released about ten years later.

1
# TYPE BUILDS CHARACTER

2

**EVER** since people have been writing things down, they have had to consider their audience before actually putting pen to paper: letters would have to look different depending on whether they were to be read by mainly other people (in official documents or inscriptions), just one other person (in a letter), or only the writer (in a notebook or diary). There would be less room for guesswork if letter shapes were made more formal as the diversity of the readership expanded. **SOME** of the first messages to be read by a large number of people were rendered not by pens but by chisels. Large inscriptions on monuments in ancient Rome were carefully planned, with letters drawn on the stone with a brush before they were chiseled. Even if white-out had existed in those days, it would not have helped to remove mistakes made in stone. A bit of planning was also more important then, since stonemasons were sometimes more expendable than slabs of marble or granite. **GRAPHIC** design and typography are complicated activities, but even the simple projects benefit from thinking about the problem, forming a mental picture of the solution, and then carefully planning the steps between. **SCIENTISTS** have not been content with just calling the human face "beautiful" if it meets certain ideals, or "ugly" if it doesn't. They had to go out and measure proportions of nose to jaw, forehead to chin, and so on to establish why some faces are more appealing than others. **TYPOGRAPHERS** and graphic designers often choose typefaces for the very same reason they might fancy a person: They just like that person. For more scientifically-minded people, however, there are specific measurements, components, details, and proportions to describe various parts of a letter. While these won't tell you what makes a typeface good, they will at least give you the right words to use when you discuss the benefits of a particular face over another. You can say "I hate the x-height on Such-a-Gothic" or "These descenders just don't work for me" or "Please, may I see something with a smaller cap height?" and you'll know what you are talking about. **WHILE** metal letters could be made to any width and height, digital type has to conform to multiples of the smallest unit: the pixel. Every character has to be a certain number of pixels wide and high. This is not a problem when the letters are made up of 600 pixels per inch, as is the case with modern laser printers—those pixels are not discernible to our eyes, and we are happy to believe that we are looking at smooth curves instead of little squares fitted into tight grids. **ON MOST** screens, only 72 pixels make up one inch. We could see each and every one of them, if engineers hadn't already found ways around that. Computer screens, however, are not where we read most of our type these days. Smart phones, computers, and tablets all have high-resolutions screens, but microwave ovens, espresso makers, and all the other gadgets around us all still use small and modest displays. And the type unmistakably consists of bitmaps, which means that an 8-point letter is actually made up of eight pixels. If we allow six pixels above the baseline, including accents, and two below for descenders, that'll leave only three or four pixels for a lowercase character.

EXPLORATION 12: CAPITALS ■ TITLE: 21PT AND 23PT LE CORBUSIER, TRACKING +20/1000 EM ■ FIRST WORDS: 14PT LE CORBUSIER, TRACKING +20/1000 EM ■ TEXT: 8.5/18 FAKT MEDIUM, TRACKING +30/1000 EM 3

4▸ Typographers and graphic designers often choose typefaces for the very same reason they might fancy a person: They just like that person. For more scientifically-minded people, however, there are specific measurements, components, details, and proportions to describe various parts of a letter. While these won't tell you what makes a typeface good, they will at least give you the right words to use when you discuss the benefits of a particular face over another. You can say "I hate the x-height on Such-a-Gothic" or "These descenders just don't work for me" or "Please, may I see something with a smaller cap height?" and you'll know what you are talking about.

5▸ While metal letters could be made to any width and height, digital type has to conform to multiples of the smallest unit: the pixel. Every character has to be a certain number of pixels wide and high. This is not a problem when the letters are made up of 600 pixels per inch, as is the case with modern laser printers—those pixels are not discernible to our eyes, and we are happy to believe that we are looking at smooth curves instead of little squares fitted into tight grids.

On most screens, only 72 pixels make up one inch. We could see each and every one of them, if engineers hadn't already found ways around that. Computer screens, however, are not where we read most of our type these days. Smart phones, computers, and tablets all have high-resolutions screens, but microwave ovens, espresso makers, and all the other gadgets around us all still use small and modest displays. And the type unmistakably consists of bitmaps, which means that an 8-point letter is actually made up of eight pixels. If we allow six pixels above the baseline, including accents, and two below for descenders, that'll leave only three or four pixels for a lowercase character. In spite of these restrictions, there are hundreds of bitmap fonts, all different from one another by only a few pixels, but enough to prove that typographic variety cannot be suppressed by technological constraints.

Rhythm and contrast keep coming up when discussing good music and good typographic design. They are concepts that also apply to spoken language, as anyone who has had to sit through a monotonous lecture will attest; the same tone, volume and speed of speech will put even the most interested listener into dreamland. Every now and again the audience needs to be shaken, either by a change in voice or pitch, by a question being posed, or by the speaker talking very quietly and then suddenly shouting. An occasional joke also works, just as the use of a funny typeface can liven up a page.

**Exploration 12**
Paragraph Indicator: Capitals

First Lines:
8/16 Eidetic Neo Omni
Tracking +40/1000 em

Text:
8/16 EideticNeo
Tracking +25/1000 em

Extra leading:
4 pts

**Opposite page**

1 The words of the title are set on two lines in two sizes to make a justified block. The baseline of the lower line is aligned to the baseline of the first line of the body text.

2 Unlike most examples in this book, side margins on this page are equal.

3 Variable lengths of black bars between items in the colophon help to justify this small block of type.

**This page**

4 First lines are set in the same point size as the text, but they appear quite a bit larger because of being set in caps. In this setting, the caps are set in the unicase version of the typeface.

5 A few points of extra lead between paragraphs helps make the distinction clearer. You don't need 50% extra leading between paragraphs because the first lines are in caps. Only an extra 25% of leading has been added here.

**Le Corbusier**
No one is quite sure where this stencil lettering style originated, but it's been used for labeling of all sorts in France for at least a century. It is also associated with architect and designer Le Corbusier, who frequently used it in his work. Lineto's font is one of many interpretations.

**Fakt**
Thomas Thiemich's 2010 design is a contemporary reimagining of the "neutral" Neo-Grotesque style initiated by Helvetica and Univers. What separates it from those models is a set of stylistic alternates that can turn it into more of a Geometric or Humanist sans. Fakt also benefits from the versatility of 60 styles and a companion Slab family.

**Eidetic Neo**
This unique contemporary serif was designed in 2000 by Rodrigo Xavier Cavazos in collaboration with Zuzana Licko. With its long, sharp, asymmetrical serifs, a script-like italic, and an unusual unicase called "Omni," the face is unlike any other. In many ways it is the embodiment of a postmodern text family.

EXP
**12.4**

Exploration 12 :: Paragraph Indicator: Capitals (typeset by Candice Cheung)
First paragraph: 8/20 Greta Text (small caps), tracking +40/1000 em :: Alternate paragraphs: 8/20 Greta Text, tracking +30/1000 em :: Graphic Element: 10pt FF Eureka Arrows

TYPOGRAPHERS AND GRAPHIC DESIGNERS OFTEN CHOOSE TYPEFACES FOR THE VERY SAME REASON THEY MIGHT FANCY A PERSON: THEY JUST LIKE THAT PERSON. FOR MORE SCIENTIFICALLY-MINDED PEOPLE, HOWEVER, THERE ARE SPECIFIC MEASUREMENTS, COMPONENTS, DETAILS, AND PROPORTIONS TO DESCRIBE VARIOUS PARTS OF A LETTER. WHILE THESE WON'T TELL YOU WHAT MAKES A TYPEFACE GOOD, THEY WILL AT LEAST GIVE YOU THE RIGHT WORDS TO USE WHEN YOU DISCUSS THE BENEFITS OF A PARTICULAR FACE OVER ANOTHER. YOU CAN SAY "I HATE THE X-HEIGHT ON SUCH-A-GOTHIC" OR "THESE DESCENDERS JUST DON'T WORK FOR ME" OR "PLEASE, MAY I SEE SOMETHING WITH A SMALLER CAP HEIGHT?" AND YOU'LL KNOW WHAT YOU ARE TALKING ABOUT. ⇕ While metal letters could be made to any width and height, digital type has to conform to multiples of the smallest unit: the pixel. Every character has to be a certain number of pixels wide and high. This is not a problem when the letters are made up of 600 pixels per inch, as is the case with modern laser printers—those pixels are not discernible to our eyes, and we are happy to believe that we are looking at smooth curves instead of little squares fitted into tight grids. ⇕ ON MOST SCREENS, ONLY 72 PIXELS MAKE UP ONE INCH. WE COULD SEE EACH AND EVERY ONE OF THEM, IF ENGINEERS HADN'T ALREADY FOUND WAYS AROUND THAT. COMPUTER SCREENS, HOWEVER, ARE NOT WHERE WE READ MOST OF OUR TYPE THESE DAYS. SMART PHONES, COMPUTERS, AND TABLETS ALL HAVE HIGH-RESOLUTIONS SCREENS, BUT MICROWAVE OVENS, ESPRESSO MAKERS, AND ALL THE OTHER GADGETS AROUND US ALL STILL USE SMALL AND MODEST DISPLAYS. AND THE TYPE UNMISTAKABLY CONSISTS OF BITMAPS, WHICH MEANS THAT AN 8-POINT LETTER IS ACTUALLY MADE UP OF EIGHT PIXELS. IF WE ALLOW SIX PIXELS ABOVE THE BASELINE, INCLUDING ACCENTS, AND TWO BELOW FOR DESCENDERS, THAT'LL LEAVE ONLY THREE OR FOUR PIXELS FOR A LOWERCASE CHARACTER. IN SPITE OF THESE RESTRICTIONS, THERE ARE HUNDREDS OF BITMAP FONTS, ALL DIFFERENT FROM ONE ANOTHER BY ONLY A FEW PIXELS, BUT ENOUGH TO PROVE THAT TYPOGRAPHIC VARIETY CANNOT BE SUPPRESSED BY TECHNOLOGICAL CONSTRAINTS. ⇕ Rhythm and contrast keep coming up when discussing good music and good typographic design. They are concepts that also apply to spoken language, as anyone who has had to sit through a monotonous lecture will attest; the same tone, volume and speed of speech will put even the most interested listener into dreamland. Every now and again the audience needs to be shaken, either by a change in voice or pitch, by a question being posed, or by the speaker talking very quietly and then suddenly shouting. An occasional joke also works, just as the use of a funny typeface can liven up a page.

◂1

# Type Builds Character ☺

**EVER SINCE PEOPLE HAVE BEEN WRITING THINGS DOWN, THEY HAVE HAD TO CONSIDER** their audience before actually putting pen to paper: letters would have to look different depending on whether they were to be read by mainly other people (in official documents or inscriptions), just one other person (in a letter), or only the writer (in a notebook or diary). There would be less room for guesswork if letter shapes were made more formal as the diversity of the readership expanded. ◆ **SOME OF THE FIRST MESSAGES TO BE READ BY A LARGE** number of people were rendered not by pens but by chisels. Large inscriptions on monuments in ancient Rome were carefully planned, with letters drawn on the stone with a brush before they were chiseled. Even if white-out had existed in those days, it would not have helped to remove mistakes made in stone. A bit of planning was also more important then, since stonemasons were sometimes more expendable than slabs of marble or granite. ◆ **GRAPHIC DESIGN** and typography are complicated activities, but even the simple projects benefit from thinking about the problem, forming a mental picture of the solution, and then carefully planning the steps between. ◆ **SCIENTISTS HAVE NOT BEEN CONTENT WITH JUST CALLING THE HUMAN** face "beautiful" if it meets certain ideals, or "ugly" if it doesn't. They had to go out and measure proportions of nose to jaw, forehead to chin, and so on to establish why some faces are more appealing than others. ◆ **TYPOGRAPHERS AND GRAPHIC DESIGNERS OFTEN CHOOSE TYPE**faces for the very same reason they might fancy a person: They just like that person. For more scientifically-minded people, however, there are specific measurements, components, details, and proportions to describe various parts of a letter. While these won't tell you what makes a typeface good, they will at least give you the right words to use when you discuss the benefits of a particular face over another. You can say "I hate the x-height on Such-a-Gothic" or "These descenders just don't work for me" or "Please, may I see something with a smaller cap height?" and you'll know what you are talking about. ◆ **RHYTHM AND CONTRAST KEEP COMING UP** when discussing good music and good typographic design. They are concepts that also apply to spoken language, as anyone who has had to sit through a monotonous lecture will attest; the same tone, volume and speed of speech will put even the most interested listener into dreamland. Every now and again the audience needs to be shaken, either by a change in voice or pitch, by a question being posed, or by the speaker talking very quietly and then suddenly shouting. An occasional joke also works, just as the use of a funny typeface can liven up a page.

◂2

Exploration 12 // Paragraph Indicator: Capitals  Title: 36pt Suomi Hand Script, no tracking
First lines: 7/12 FF Absara Sans Bold (caps), tracking +25/1000 em  Text: 7/12 FF Absara Sans Regular, tracking +15/1000 em

EXP
12.5

**Opposite page**

1 The entire paragraph is set in all lowercase small caps. Very generous leading is used to offset the low legibility of so much text set in caps. Note the difference in texture from paragraph to paragraph.

**This page**

2 Returns between paragraphs have been eliminated and bold caps are set from the first word of each new paragraph to the end of the line.

**Greta Text**

Recognized by the TDC in 2007, this face was designed by Peter Biľak to directly respond to the special demands of printing in newspapers. It is highly space-efficient with large counters to improve legibility in lower-quality printing and at very small sizes.

**Suomi Hand Script**

This 2010 handwriting font by Finnish designer Tomi Haaparanta includes a heart, star, arrows, and even some little faces. It's one of a recent wave of convincing informal scripts. With more than 700 ligatures, you can "fake it" very, very well without ever lifting a pen.

**FF Absara Sans**

In 2005, Xavier Dupré designed this companion to FF Absara. The occasional lively angles on some letterforms strike a healthy balance between old and new and give it a memorable Humanist quality.

## Paragraph Indicator: Weight

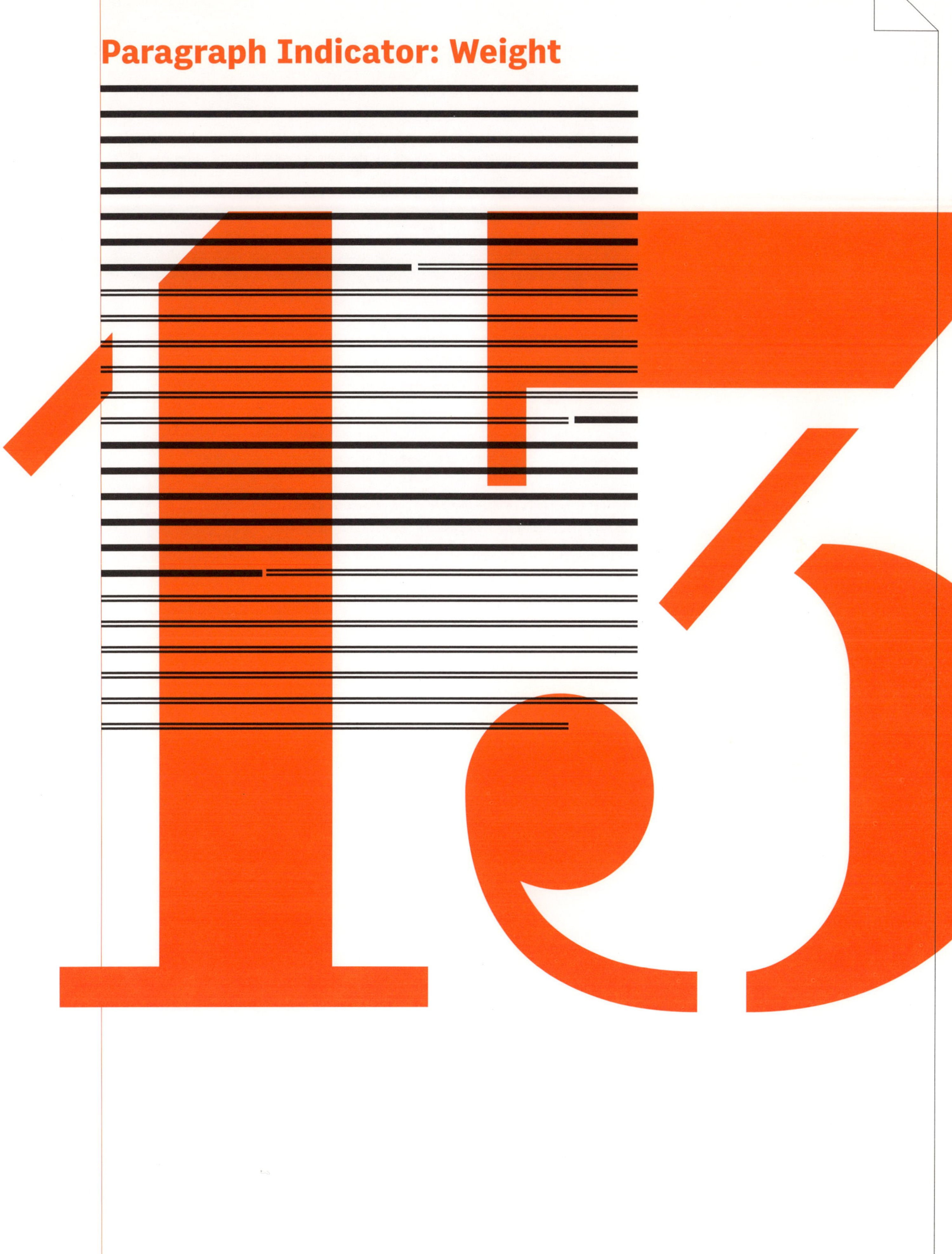

# 13 Paragraph Indicator: Weight

Changing the weight of the type from paragraph to paragraph or for the first lines of each new paragraph can be done with bold or italic. Begin with the stronger of the two weights for the first line or first paragraph and alternate from there.

When using bold in a typeface that has a wide range of weights, it is typically necessary to change weights by two steps to show a clear visual difference. This idea extends into all matters of design: visual elements must be exactly, optically the same or clearly different. Otherwise, it looks like a mistake.

EXP
**13.1**

Exploration 13 » Paragraph Indicator: Weight (typeset by Priscilla Peña)
First lines » 7/14 FF Sanuk Medium, tracking +20/1000 em   Text » 7/14 FF Sanuk Light Italic, tracking +25/1000 em

**Ever since people have been writing things down, they have had to consider their** *audience before actually putting pen to paper: letters would have to look different depending on whether they were to be read by mainly other people (in official documents or inscriptions), just one other person (in a letter), or only the writer (in a notebook or diary). There would be less room for guess-work if letter shapes were made more formal as the diversity of the reader-ship expanded.*

1▸ **Some of the first messages to be read by a large number of people were rendered** *not by pens but by chisels. Large inscriptions on monuments in ancient Rome were carefully planned, with letters drawn on the stone with a brush before they were chiseled. Even if white-out had existed in those days, it would not have helped to remove mistakes made in stone. A bit of planning was also more important then, since stonemasons were sometimes more expendable than slabs of marble or granite.*

**Graphic design and typography are complicated activities, but even the simple** *projects benefit from thinking about the problem, forming a mental picture of the solution, and then carefully planning the steps between.*

**Scientists have not been content with just calling the human face "beautiful" if it** *meets certain ideals, or "ugly" if it doesn't. They had to go out and measure proportions of nose to jaw, forehead to chin, and so on to establish why some faces are more appealing than others.*

**Typographers and graphic designers often choose typefaces for the very same** *reason they might fancy a person: They just like that person. For more scientifically-minded people, however, there are specific measurements, components, details, and proportions to describe various parts of a letter. While these won't tell you what makes a typeface good, they will at least give you the right words to use when you discuss the benefits of a particular face over another. You can say "I hate the x-height on Such-a-Gothic" or "These descenders just don't work for me" or "Please, may I see something with a smaller cap height?" and you'll know what you are talking about.*

EXP
13.2

2▸ Ever since people have been writing things down, they have had to consider their audience before actually putting pen to paper: letters would have to look different depending on whether they were to be read by mainly other people (in official documents or inscriptions), just one other person (in a letter), or only the writer (in a notebook or diary). There would be less room for guesswork if letter shapes were made more formal as the diversity of the readership expanded. ➤ *Some of the first messages to be read by a large number of people were rendered not by pens but by chisels. Large inscriptions on monuments in ancient Rome were carefully planned, with letters drawn on the stone with a brush before they were chiseled. Even if white-out had existed in those days, it would not have helped to remove mistakes made in stone. A bit of planning was also more important then, since stonemasons were sometimes more expendable than slabs of marble or granite.* ➤ Graphic design and typography are complicated activities, but even the simple projects benefit from thinking about the problem, forming a mental picture of the solution, and then carefully planning the steps between. ➤ *Scientists have not been content with just calling the human face "beautiful" if it meets certain ideals, or "ugly" if it doesn't. They had to go out and measure proportions of nose to jaw, forehead to chin, and so on to establish why some faces are more appealing than others.* ➤ Typographers and graphic designers often choose typefaces for the very same reason they might fancy a person: They just like that person. For more scientifically-minded people, however, there are specific measurements, components, details, and proportions to describe various parts of a letter. While these won't tell you what makes a typeface good, they will at least give you the right words to use when you discuss the benefits of a particular face over another. You can say "I hate the x-height on Such-a-Gothic" or "These descenders just don't work for me" or "Please, may I see something with a smaller cap height?" and you'll know what you are talking about.

**Exploration 13** Paragraph Indicator » Weight » First: 7/15 Filosofia, tracking +20/1000 em » Alternate: 7/15 Filosofia italic, tracking +50/1000 em

**Opposite page**

1 Bold first lines are also exdented. Although one indicator would suffice in this case, using both gives the setting a bit more textural contrast.

**This page**

2 The roman looks stronger than the italic, so it is set for the first paragraph. Alternating paragraphs are set in italic. Note that the italic must be set with more generous tracking than the roman for it to look like the same amount of space is between the letters.

**FF Sanuk**

Xavier Dupré designed this face in 2006. The italic is slanted only 5%, keeping it nearly as legible as the roman. As a genuine italic, many lowercase characters differ from the upright versions. It comes in an ample range of weights from hairline to fat.

**Filosofia**

Zuzana Licko's 1996 design seeks to emulate the letterpress impression of a Bodoni, rather than the face of the original metal type. This results in a lower-contrast design and heavier serifs with soft endings. These changes make Filosofia better suited for modern text environments than most Didones. Other options in the family include Unicase and Grande, a higher-contrast version for large sizes.

1▸ **TYPE BUILDS CHARACTER**

**Ever since people have been writing things down, they have had to consider their audience before actually putting pen to paper: letters would have to look different depending on whether they were to be read by mainly other people (in official documents or inscriptions), just one other person (in a letter), or only the writer (in a notebook or diary). There would be less room for guesswork if letter shapes were made more formal as the diversity of the readership expanded.**

Some of the first messages to be read by a large number of people were rendered not by pens but by chisels. Large inscriptions on monuments in ancient Rome were carefully planned, with letters drawn on the stone with a brush before they were chiseled. Even if white-out had existed in those days, it would not have helped to remove mistakes made in stone. A bit of planning was also more important then, since stonemasons were sometimes more expendable than slabs of marble or granite.

**Graphic design and typography are complicated activities, but even the simple projects benefit from thinking about the problem, forming a mental picture of the solution, and then carefully planning the steps between. Scientists have not been content with just calling the human face "beautiful" if it meets certain ideals, or "ugly" if it doesn't. They had to go out and measure proportions of nose to jaw, forehead to chin, and so on to establish why some faces are more appealing than others.**

Typographers and graphic designers often choose typefaces for the very same reason they might fancy a person: They just like that person. For more scientifically-minded people, however, there are specific measurements, components, details, and proportions to describe various parts of a letter. While these won't tell you what makes a typeface good, they will at least give you the right words to use when you discuss the benefits of a particular face over another. You can say "I hate the x-height on Such-a-Gothic" or "These descenders just don't work for me" or "Please, may I see something with a smaller cap height?" and you'll know what you are talking about. ◂2

**Rhythm and contrast keep coming up when dis-cussing good music and good typographic design. They are concepts that also apply to spoken language, as anyone who has had to sit through a monotonous lecture will attest; the same tone, volume and speed of speech will put even the most interested listener into dreamland. Every now and again the audience needs to be shaken, either by a change in voice or pitch, by a question being posed, or by the speaker talking very quietly and then suddenly shouting. An occasional joke also works, just as the use of a funny typeface can liven up a page.**

*Exploration 13 › Weight*

*title: 10pt FF Fago Extra Bold › tracking +10/1000 em*
*first paragraph: 7/16 Chaparral Bold › tracking +15/1000 em*
*alternate paragraphs: 7/16 Chaparral › tracking +20/1000 em*

## Type Builds Character ▸ *by Erik Spiekermann*

3

**Ever since people have been writing things down, they have had to consider their audience** before actually putting pen to paper: letters would have to look different depending on whether they were to be read by mainly other people (in official documents or inscriptions), just one other person (in a letter), or only the writer (in a notebook or diary). There would be less room for guesswork if letter shapes were made more formal as the diversity of the readership expanded.

**Some of the first messages to be read by a large number of people were rendered not by** pens but by chisels. Large inscriptions on monuments in ancient Rome were carefully planned, with letters drawn on the stone with a brush before they were chiseled. Even if white-out had existed in those days, it would not have helped to remove mistakes made in stone. A bit of planning was also more important then, since stonemasons were sometimes more expendable than slabs of marble or granite.

**Graphic design and typography are complicated activities, but even the simple projects** benefit from thinking about the problem, forming a mental picture of the solution, and then carefully planning the steps between.

**Typographers and graphic designers often choose typefaces for the very same reason** they might fancy a person: They just like that person. For more scientifically-minded people, however, there are specific measurements, components, details, and proportions to describe various parts of a letter. While these won't tell you what makes a typeface good, they will at least give you the right words to use when you discuss the benefits of a particular face over another. You can say "I hate the x-height on Such-a-Gothic" or "These descenders just don't work for me" or "Please, may I see something with a smaller cap height?" and you'll know what you are talking about.

**While metal letters could be made to any width and height, digital type has to conform** to multiples of the smallest unit: the pixel. Every character has to be a certain number of pixels wide and high. This is not a problem when the letters are made up of 600 pixels per inch, as is the case with modern laser printers—those pixels are not discernible to our eyes, and we are happy to believe that we are looking at smooth curves instead of little squares fitted into tight grids.

**Exploration 13** Paragraph Indicator: Weight
title: 9pt ITC Officina Serif Bold, tracking +5/1000 em
byline: 6pt ITC Officina Serif Bold Italic, tracking +10/1000 em
first lines: 7/12 ITC Officina Serif Bold, tracking +20/1000 em
text: 7/12 ITC Officina Serif Book, tracking +20/1000 em
extra leading: 3 pts

**Opposite page**

1 The exdented title sits on the same baseline as the top lines of text.

2 The first column begins with the bolder weight and the second column begins with the lighter weight, creating a checkerboard pattern of typographic textures.

**This page**

3 The bold rule is indented from the right to blend in with the rag. It is the same shade of gray as the arrow between the title and the byline.

**FF Fago**
Ole Schäfer created FF Fago in 2000 at the crest of a new wave in type design: the contemporary sans serif, led in part by FF Meta, optimized for clarity and legibility in corporate design. Type in this category has a moderate stroke contrast, compact proportions, fairly loose spacing, large x-height, and wide-open apertures. FF Fago takes these traits to their functional extreme without going too far. The large family includes five weights in three widths.

**Chaparral**
Throughout her stellar career at Adobe, Carol Twombly established a reputation for effortlessly combining utility and elegance. There is perhaps no better exemplar of that legacy than this sturdy slab serif built on the graceful proportions of Renaissance book type. Chaparral has optical sizes, a rarity when it was released in 2000 and still uncommon among slabs today.

**ITC Officina Serif**
In 1988, under the working title "ITC Correspondence," this face was conceived of for use as a replacement typewriter face for office documents produced on low-resolution printers. Today it serves a similar purpose for clear, economical, straightforward copy on websites and other screen-based content.

## Paragraph Indicator: Typeface

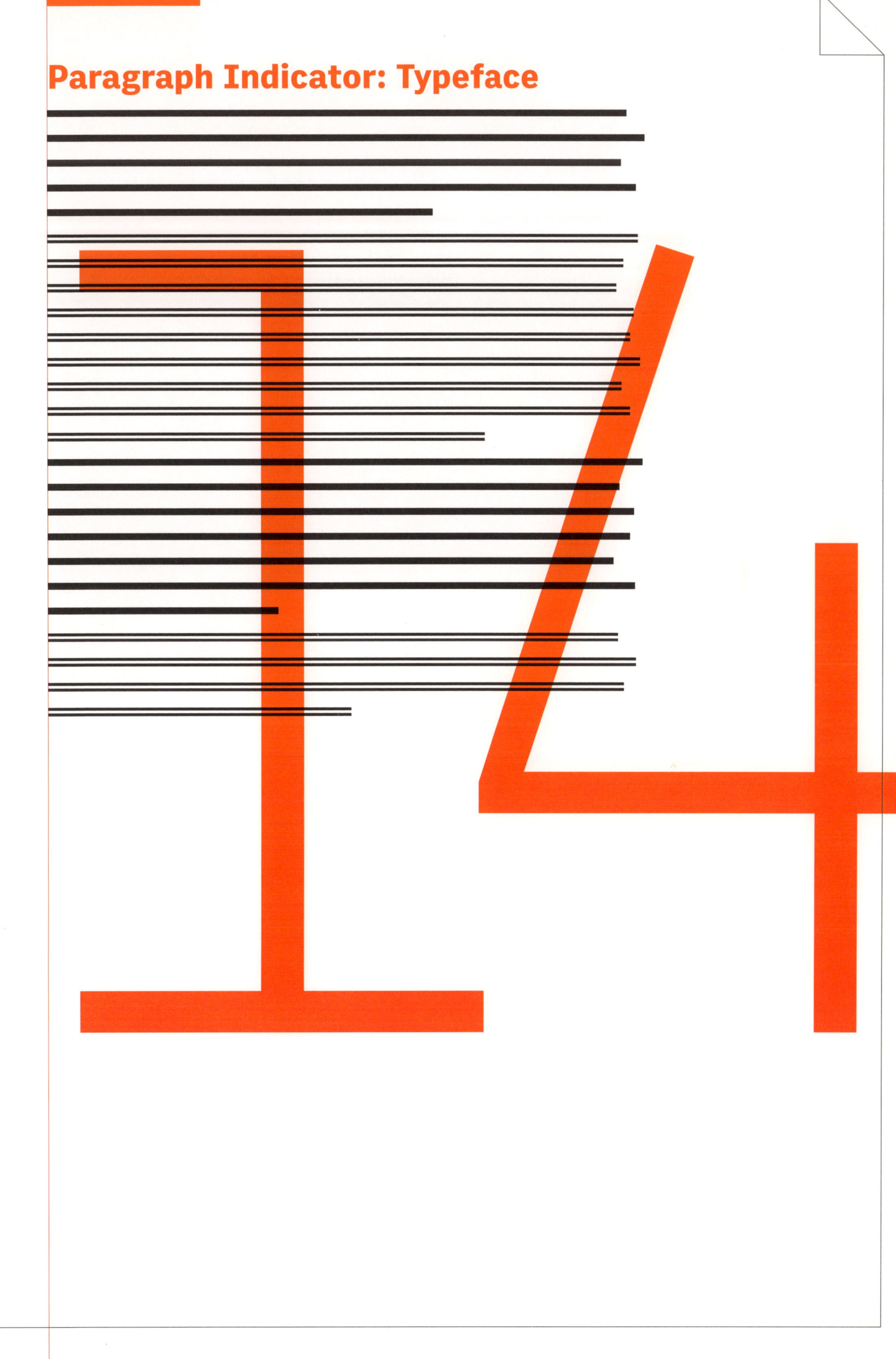

# 14 Paragraph Indicator: Typeface

Changing the typeface for the first line of each paragraph or for every other paragraph can be used alone or in conjunction with a second paragraph indication such as a graphic element or a change in weight.

Begin with the stronger typeface (the one with a bolder stroke weight or larger x-height) of the two for the first line or first paragraph and alternate from there.

Often type set in two different typefaces does not look like the same point size, even though the two typefaces are in fact set at the same size. Sometimes this works to your advantage. Other times, you need the two typefaces to look like they are the same size because they are intended to express the same hierarchy. To make two faces appear to be optically the same size, simply use slightly different point sizes for each face to make their x-heights match.

Choosing two or more typefaces to use together is an important typographic decision. Theoretically, any two typefaces can be used together; the choice only depends on exactly how and why they are used. Realistically, however, some typefaces just don't look very good together.

To familiarize yourself with how to combine typefaces, begin by using the following guidelines: (1) Select a serif and a sans that (2) have similar shapes. To find typefaces with similar shapes, look for ones designed by the same designer or ones from the same time period.

For a list of all the typefaces used together in the Explorations, see the Typeface Combinations section at the back of this book.

1 TYPE BUILDS CHARACTER BY ERIK SPIEKERMANN

ever since people have been writing things down, they have had to consider their audience before actually putting pen to paper: letters would have to look different depending on whether they were to be read by mainly other people (in official documents or inscriptions), just one other person (in a letter), or only the writer (in a notebook or diary). There would be less room for guesswork if letter shapes were made more formal as the diversity of the readership expanded.

some of the first messages to be read by a large number of people were rendered not by pens but by chisels. Large inscriptions on monuments in ancient Rome were carefully planned, with letters drawn on the stone with a brush before they were chiseled. Even if white-out had existed in those days, it would not have helped to remove mistakes made in stone. A bit of planning was also more important then, since stonemasons were sometimes more expendable than slabs of marble or granite.

graphic design and typography are complicated activities, but even the simple projects benefit from thinking about the problem, forming a mental picture of the solution, and then carefully planning the steps between.

scientists have not been content with just calling the human face "beautiful" if it meets certain ideals, or "ugly" if it doesn't. They had to go out and measure proportions of nose to jaw, forehead to chin, and so on to establish why some faces are more appealing than others. ◂2

typographers and graphic designers often choose typefaces for the very same reason they might fancy a person: They just like that person. For more scientifically-minded people, however, there are specific measurements, components, details, and proportions to describe various parts of a letter. While these won't tell you what makes a typeface good, they will at least give you the right words to use when you discuss the benefits of a particular face over another.

rhythm and contrast keep coming up when discussing good music and good typographic design. They are concepts that also apply to spoken language, as anyone who has had to sit through a monotonous lecture will attest; the same tone, volume and speed of speech will put even the most interested listener into dreamland. Every now and again the audience needs to be shaken, either by a change in voice or pitch, by a question being posed, or by the speaker talking very quietly and then suddenly shouting. An occasional joke also works, just as the use of a funny typeface can liven up a page.

EXPLORATION 14
TYPEFACE

TITLE:
9PT FF SPEAK AND
14PT DEMOCRATICA
TRACKING +200/1000 EM

FIRST LINES:
10.5PT DEMOCRATICA
TRACKING +50/1000 EM

TEXT:
9/15.5 FF SPEAK
TRACKING +40/1000 EM

1 The title is set vertically in the gutter and higher than both columns to signify its importance. Letterforms in this line are randomly set in both of the typefaces used in the text.

2 The two columns are not clotheslined but randomly staggered, the second column lower than the first and the title higher than both. The lack of a hangline alignment at the top creates a bit of movement on the page.

**FF Speak**
With primitive forms, curved strokes, and rounded ends, Jan Maack's 2007 face is casual almost to the point of being childlike. Yet, like most FontFonts, this is a professional family with four weights, true italics, and extended language support. Still, a set of playful ligatures prevents FF Speak from being labeled "corporate." In the end, this is a typeface meant for branding and packaging, not serious text.

**Democratica**
This 1991 release is typical of Emigre's postmodern heyday. Miles Newlyn described his design as "a synthesis of the connections I saw between the crude struggle for democracy in the former USSR" and the crudeness of many cut-and-paste designs of the early digital era. The second source of inspiration is easier to spot. Bits and pieces of traditional serif type are combined without regard to the calligraphic model that produced traditional letterforms. The sum is a fascinating and sometimes beautiful jumble.

EXP
**14.2**

1▸ **Ever since people have been writing things down, they have had to consider their audience before actually putting pen to paper: letters would have to look different depending on whether they were to be read by mainly other people (in official documents or inscriptions), just one other person (in a letter), or only the writer (in a notebook or diary). There would be less room for guesswork if letter shapes were made more formal as the diversity of the readership expanded.** ✸ Some of the first messages to be read by a large number of people were rendered not by pens but by chisels. Large inscriptions on monuments in ancient Rome were carefully planned, with letters drawn on the stone with a brush before they were chiseled. Even if white-out had existed in those days, it would not have helped to remove mistakes made in stone. A bit of planning was also more important then, since stonemasons were sometimes more expendable than slabs of marble or granite. ✸ **Graphic design and typography are complicated activities, but even the simple projects benefit from thinking about the problem, forming a mental picture of the solution, and then carefully planning the steps between.** ✸ Scientists have not been content with just calling the human face "beautiful" if it meets certain ideals, or "ugly" if it doesn't. They had to go out and measure proportions of nose to jaw, forehead to chin, and so on to establish why some faces are more appealing than others. ✸ **Typographers and graphic designers often choose typefaces for the very same reason they might fancy a person: They just like that person. For more scientifically-minded people, however, there are specific measurements, components, details, and proportions to describe various parts of a letter. While these won't tell you what makes a typeface good, they will at least give you the right words to use when you discuss the benefits of a particular face over another. You can say "I hate the x-height on Such-a-Gothic" or "These descenders just don't work for me" or "Please, may I see something with a smaller cap height?" and you'll know what you are talking about.** ✸ While metal letters could be made to any width and height, digital type has to conform to multiples of the smallest unit: the pixel. Every character has to be a certain number of pixels wide and high. This is not a problem when the letters are made up of 600 pixels per inch, as is the case with modern laser printers–those pixels are not discernible to our eyes, and we are happy to believe that we are looking at smooth curves instead of little squares fitted into tight grids.

*Exploration 14 :: Paragraph Indicator: Typeface (typeset by Fred Carriedo) :: Initial Cap: 46pt Modula Round Ribbed :: Bullet: 21pt Modula Round Ribbed*
*First Paragraph: 8/14 FF Zine Serif Medium, tracking +30/1000 em :: Alternate Paragraphs: 8/14 FF Zine Sans Regular, tracking +30/1000 em*

Ever since people have been writing things down, they have had to consider their audience before actually putting pen to paper: letters would have to look different depending on whether they were to be read by mainly other people (in official documents or inscriptions), just one other person (in a letter), or only the writer (in a notebook or diary). There would be less room for guesswork if letter shapes were made more formal as the diversity of the readership expanded. Some of the first messages to be read by a large number of people were rendered not by pens but by chisels. Large inscriptions on monuments in ancient Rome were carefully planned, with letters drawn on the stone with a brush before they were chiseled. Even if white-out had existed in those days, it would not have helped to remove mistakes made in stone. A bit of planning was also more important then, since stonemasons were sometimes more expendable than slabs of marble or granite. Graphic design and typography are complicated activities, but even the simple projects benefit from thinking about the problem, forming a mental picture of the solution, and then carefully planning the steps between. Scientists have not been content with just calling the human face "beautiful" if it meets certain ideals, or "ugly" if it doesn't. They had to go out and measure proportions of nose to jaw, forehead to chin, and so on to establish why some faces are more appealing than others. Typographers and graphic designers often choose typefaces for the very same reason they might fancy a person: They just like that person. For more scientifically-minded people, however, there are specific measurements, components, details, and proportions to describe various parts of a letter. While these won't tell you what makes a typeface good, they will at least give you the right words to use when you discuss the benefits of a particular face over another. You can say "I hate the x-height on Such-a-Gothic" or "These descenders just don't work for me" or "Please, may I see something with a smaller cap height?" and you'll know what you are talking about.

**EXPLORATION 14: TYPEFACE**

**FIRST PARAGRAPH:**
**7/15 NEUE HELVETICA REGULAR**
**TRACKING +50/1000 EM**

**ALTERNATE PARAGRAPHS:**
**7.5/15 CLARENDON**
**TRACKING +40/1000 EM**

EXP
**14.3**

**Opposite page**

1 The two faces are a serif and sans from the same family, so they appear quite similar in texture. To help make the paragraph indications clearer, the first paragraph is set in a bolder weight and a dingbat is added between paragraphs.

**This page**

2 Even though both are set at the same point size, the sans serif face looks both larger and bolder than the serif, so it is set first. Sans serifs generally tend to have a larger x-height, making them appear larger than serif faces at the same size. Their low contrast (little to no stroke modulation) is what makes them look bolder.

**Modula**

Initially introduced in 1986, the extra condensed Modula was one of the earliest digital fonts from a digital pioneer, Zuzana Licko. Emigre experimented with it over the years, culminating in Outlined, Round, and Ribbed styles that extrapolate an unassuming type concept into the obscene and amusing. The ridged contours are possible because of the typeface's inherently modular nature.

**FF Zine Serif and FF Zine Sans**

Zine was originally designed by Ole Schäfer as a headline font for a German newspaper (*Sächsische Zeitung*) in 1996. Later, the serif, sans serif, and slab serif versions were all redrawn together for complete integration of the family.

**Neue Helvetica**

In 1957, Max Miedinger changed design history with this idealization of the sans typeface. It is spartan, uniform, and just about as neutral as type can be. Neue Helvetica is a 1983 revision with 51 harmonized weights and widths.

**Clarendon**

Based on "Ionic" and "Antique" type from earlier in the 19th century, Benjamin Fox's 1845 face is the prototype for the "Clarendon" classification. These slab serifs have moderate contrast and bracketed serifs. Clarendon has become a standard for bold, muscular clarity.

**This page**

1 Every other column starts with the alternate typeface to create a checkerboard effect.

2 Although the point size of the serif type is 1 point larger, note that it appears slightly smaller than the sans. To make two faces with different x-heights appear to be the same size, use two different point sizes to make the faces look equally important.

**Opposite page**

3 A bold underscore is set to look like a cursor at the beginning of each new paragraph. It has rounded terminals to echo the face's terminals.

**Myriad**
Carol Twombly based her 1992 design on the ultimate model of spare legibility: Frutiger. Myriad is a warmer take, with round dots, a Humanist italic, and strokes that end naturally rather than sheared vertically. If Helvetica is the neutral sans of the 20th century, Myriad has a shot at that title for the 21st. In part because it's a default in Adobe apps and it's a legitimate standby for plain, readable text.

**FF Atma Serif**
Alan Dague-Greene's 2001 face has the proportions of a classical French Modern, with long descenders and a moderately low x-height. This could make it feel antique, but the low contrast keeps it fresh and enables it to set text at sizes where most Didones cannot. Also handy are the three sizes of small caps, which can serve various purposes, whether for acronyms or titling.

**FF Alega and FF Alega Serif**
Most techno typefaces are made for display purposes, but in 2002 Siegfried Rückel sought "to create a face with a technical look that was still very readable and suitable for headlines as well as body text." He was serious about this goal, giving FF Alega small caps and a true italic, and then following it up in 2003 with a serif companion.

*Exploration 14: Paragraph Indicator: Typeface // First Paragraph: 7/13 Myriad, tracking +40/1000 em // Alternate Paragraphs: 8/13 FF Atma Serif, tracking +50/1000 em*

1▸ Ever since people have been writing things down, they have had to consider their audience before actually putting pen to paper: letters would have to look different depending on whether they were to be read by mainly other people (in official documents or inscriptions), just one other person (in a letter), or only the writer (in a notebook or diary). There would be less room for guesswork if letter shapes were made more formal as the diversity of the readership expanded.

2▸ Some of the first messages to be read by a large number of people were rendered not by pens but by chisels. Large inscriptions on monuments in ancient Rome were carefully planned, with letters drawn on the stone with a brush before they were chiseled. Even if white-out had existed in those days, it would not have helped to remove mistakes made in stone. A bit of planning was also more important then, since stonemasons were sometimes more expendable than slabs of marble or granite.

Graphic design and typography are complicated activities, but even the simple projects benefit from thinking about the problem, forming a mental picture of the solution, and then carefully planning the steps between.

Scientists have not been content with just calling the human face "beautiful" if it meets certain ideals, or "ugly" if it doesn't. They had to go out and measure proportions of nose to jaw, forehead to chin, and so on to establish why some faces are more appealing than others.

Typographers and graphic designers often choose typefaces for the very same reason they might fancy a person: They just like that person. For more scientifically-minded people, however, there are specific measurements, components, details, and proportions to describe various parts of a letter. While these won't tell you what makes a typeface good, they will at least give you the right words to use when you discuss the benefits of a particular face over another. You can say "I hate the x-height on Such-a-Gothic" or "These descenders just don't work for me" or "Please, may I see something with a smaller cap height?" and you'll know what you are talking about.

While metal letters could be made to any width and height, digital type has to conform to multiples of the smallest unit: the pixel. Every character has to be a certain number of pixels wide and high. This is not a problem when the letters are made up of 600 pixels per inch, as is the case with modern laser printers—those pixels are not discernible to our eyes, and we are happy to believe that we are looking at smooth curves instead of little squares fitted into tight grids.

On most screens, only 72 pixels make up one inch. We could see each and every one of them, if engineers hadn't already found ways around that. Computer screens, however, are not where we read most of our type these days. Smart phones, computers, and tablets all have high-resolutions screens, but microwave ovens, espresso makers, and all the other gadgets around us all still use small and modest displays. And the type unmistakably consists of bitmaps, which means that an 8-point letter is actually made up of eight pixels. If we allow six pixels above the baseline, including accents, and two below for descenders, that'll leave only three or four pixels for a lowercase character.

Rhythm and contrast keep coming up when discussing good music and good typographic design. They are concepts that also apply to spoken language, as anyone who has had to sit through a monotonous lecture will attest; the same tone, volume and speed of speech will put even the most interested listener into dreamland. Every now and again the audience needs to be shaken, either by a change in voice or pitch, by a question being posed, or by the speaker talking very quietly and then suddenly shouting. An occasional joke also works, just as the use of a funny typeface can liven up a page.

EXP **14.4**

EXP
**14.5**

_Ever since people have been writing things down, they have had to consider their audience before actually putting pen to paper: letters would have to look different depending on whether they were to be read by mainly other people (in official documents or inscriptions), just one other person (in a letter), or only the writer (in a notebook or diary). There would be less room for guesswork if letter shapes were made more formal as the diversity of the readership expanded.

3 _Some of the first messages to be read by a large number of people were rendered not by pens but by chisels. Large inscriptions on monuments in ancient Rome were carefully planned, with letters drawn on the stone with a brush before they were chiseled. Even if white-out had existed in those days, it would not have helped to remove mistakes made in stone. A bit of planning was also more important then, since stonemasons were sometimes more expendable than slabs of marble or granite.

_Graphic design and typography are complicated activities, but even the simple projects benefit from thinking about the problem, forming a mental picture of the solution, and then carefully planning the steps between.

_Scientists have not been content with just calling the human face "beautiful" if it meets certain ideals, or "ugly" if it doesn't. They had to go out and measure proportions of nose to jaw, forehead to chin, and so on to establish why some faces are more appealing than others.

_Typographers and graphic designers often choose typefaces for the very same reason they might fancy a person: They just like that person. For more scientifically-minded people, however, there are specific measurements, components, details, and proportions to describe various parts of a letter. While these won't tell you what makes a typeface good, they will at least give you the right words to use when you discuss the benefits of a particular face over another. You can say "I hate the x-height on Such-a-Gothic" or "These descenders just don't work for me" or "Please, may I see something with a smaller cap height?" and you'll know what you are talking about.

EXPLORATION 14: PARAGRAPH INDICATOR: TYPEFACE FIRST: 8/16 FF ALEGA BOLD, TRACKING +50/1000 EM // ALTERNATE: 8/16 FF ALEGA SERIF, TRACKING +50/1000 EM

## Paragraph Indicator: Point Size

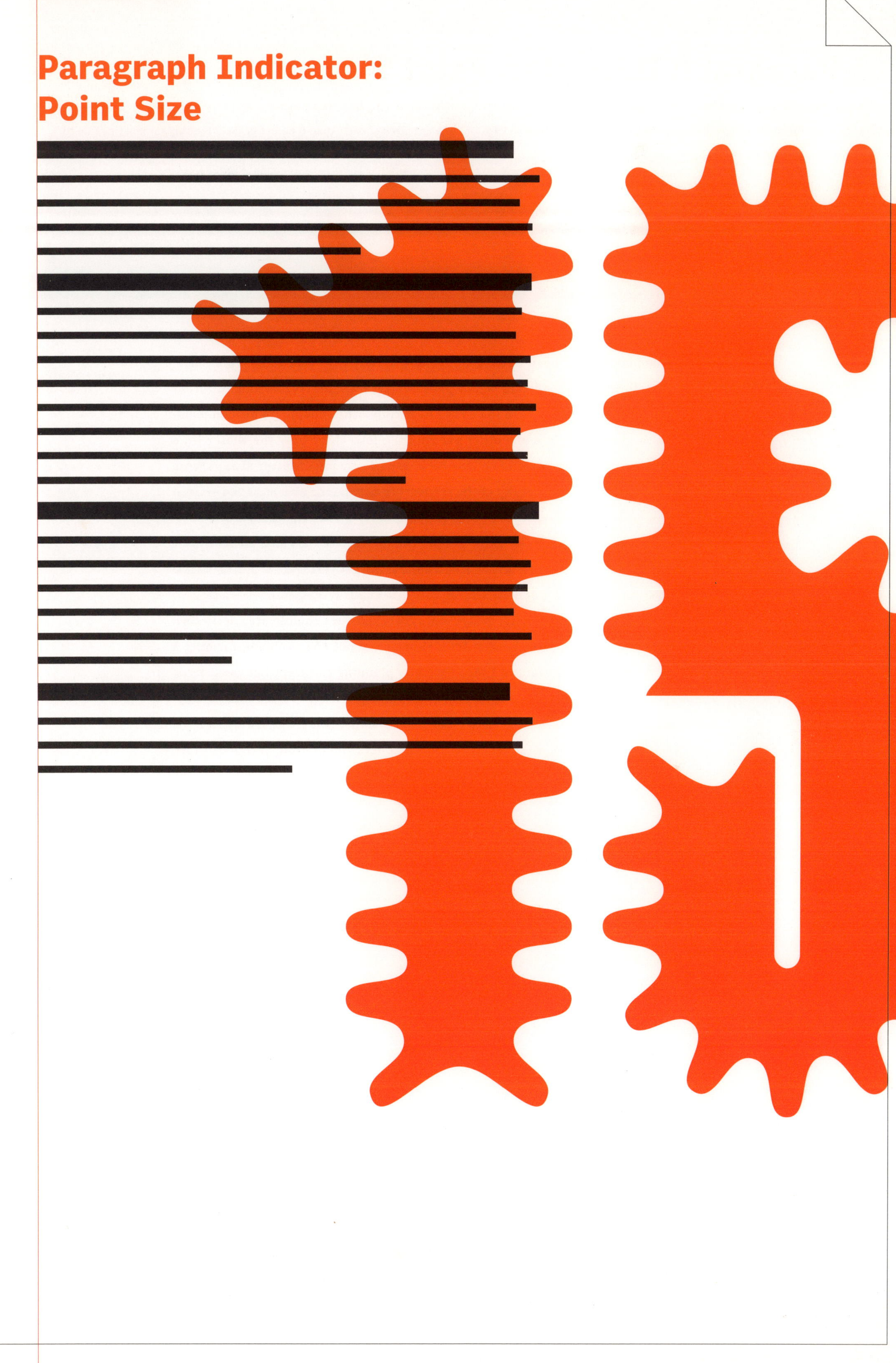

# 15 Paragraph Indicator: Point Size

To use point size as a paragraph indication, begin with the larger point size of the two for the first line or first paragraph and alternate with the smaller point size from there.

When choosing the point size of a headline, make it large enough to create a clear difference in size from the body copy. As a guideline, the larger setting usually needs to be at least 1.25 times larger when both point sizes are in the same weight.

Type set at 12 points and smaller is text size and used for body copy. Type in point sizes smaller than 6 points is likely too tiny for most people to read. Type set at 13 points and larger is called "display" type. Display type is typically used for titles and headlines rather than body copy.

EXP
**15.1**

1▸

Ever since people have been writing things down, they have had to consider their audience before actually putting pen to paper: letters would have to look different depending on whether they were to be read by mainly other people (in official documents or inscriptions), just one other person (in a letter), or only the writer (in a notebook or diary). There would be less room for guesswork if letter shapes were made more formal as the diversity of the readership expanded. Some of the first messages to be read by a large number of people were rendered not by pens but by chisels. Large inscriptions on monuments in ancient Rome were carefully planned, with letters drawn on the stone with a brush before they were chiseled. Even if white-out had existed in those days, it would not have helped to remove mistakes made in stone. A bit of planning was also more important then, since stonemasons were sometimes more expendable than slabs of marble or granite. Graphic design and typography are complicated activities, but even the simple projects benefit from thinking about the problem, forming a mental picture of the solution, and then carefully planning the steps between. Scientists have not been content with just calling the human face "beautiful" if it meets certain ideals, or "ugly" if it doesn't. They had to go out and measure proportions of nose to jaw, forehead to chin, and so on to establish why some faces are more appealing than others. Typographers and graphic designers often choose typefaces for the very same reason they might fancy a person: They just like that person. For more scientifically-minded people, however, there are specific measurements, components, details, and proportions to describe various parts of a letter. While these won't tell you what makes a typeface good, they will at least give you the right words to use when you discuss the benefits of a particular face over another. You can say "I hate the x-height on Such-a-Gothic" or "These descenders just don't work for me" or "Please, may I see something with a smaller cap height?" and you'll know what you are talking about. ◂2

**EXPLORATION 15**
PARAGRAPH INDICATOR: POINT SIZE
(TYPESET BY CANDICE CHEUNG)

FIRST: 8.5/15 FF HERTZ
TRACKING +30/1000 EM

ALTERNATE: 6.5/15 FF HERTZ
TRACKING +40/1000 EM

FRAME: 12PT TXT101 LIGHT

EXPLORATION 15 >> PARAGRAPH INDICATOR: POINT SIZE >> TEXT: 8/14 FF SUB VARIO DRY, NO TRACKING >> FIRST LINES: 10PT FF ARCHIAN NIGHT, TRACKING +25/1000 EM

EVER SINCE PEOPLE HAVE BEEN WRITING THINGS DOWN, they have had to consider their audience before actually putting pen to paper: letters would have to look different depending on whether they were to be read by mainly other people (in official documents or inscriptions), just one other person (in a letter), or only the writer (in a notebook or diary). There would be less room for guesswork if letter shapes were made more formal as the diversity of the readership expanded. ◂3

SOME OF THE FIRST MESSAGES TO BE READ BY A LARGE number of people were rendered not by pens but by chisels. Large inscriptions on monuments in ancient Rome were carefully planned, with letters drawn on the stone with a brush before they were chiseled. Even if white-out had existed in those days, it would not have helped to remove mistakes made in stone. A bit of planning was also more important then, since stonemasons were sometimes more expendable than slabs of marble or granite.

GRAPHIC DESIGN AND TYPOGRAPHY ARE COMPLICATED activities, but even the simple projects benefit from thinking about the problem, forming a mental picture of the solution, and then carefully planning the steps between.

TYPOGRAPHERS AND GRAPHIC DESIGNERS OFTEN CHOOSE typefaces for the very same reason they might fancy a person: They just like that person. For more scientifically-minded people, however, there are specific measurements, components, details, and proportions to describe various parts of a letter. While these won't tell you what makes a typeface good, they will at least give you the right words to use when you discuss the benefits of a particular face over another. You can say "I hate the x-height on Such-a-Gothic" or "These descenders just don't work for me" or "Please, may I see something with a smaller cap height?" and you'll know what you are talking about.

EXP
15.2

**Opposite page**

1 The entire text block is set within a decorative border to accentuate its square format.

2 A change in point size of just 2 points on alternating paragraphs makes a clear difference. Although there are no returns between paragraphs, two word spaces are set between them.

**This page**

3 Because the point size of first lines is considerably larger, this type can be set in a display face. The change in typographic texture of the first lines is creating the paragraph indication. While "even color" is your highest typographic priority within a continuous setting of text, note that a purposeful change in color can create hierarchy and separation.

**FF Hertz**
Jens Kutilek's 2015 design is a uniwidth font, meaning that each letter occupies the same horizontal space in all its finely graded weights. A workhorse that holds up in a variety of outputs from print to screen, it has a number of inspirations, including 1970s typewriter forms and the lettering on old German maps.

**FF Archian**
György Szönyei's typeface made only of horizontal and vertical lines could be rather dull, but this Constructivist-inspired design takes many unexpected turns with semi-serif endings and a broad range of variations, from multiline or stencil to faceted or labyrinthine. The family initially was released in 1999 and was extended in 2010.

**FF SubVario Dry**
Surprisingly legible for a pixel font, this bitmapped design was created by Kai Vermehr in 1998. The family was optimized for 24-point type at a screen resolution of 72 dots per inch.

Two typefaces that are typeset at the same point size may appear to be different sizes because their x-heights are not the same. Sans serifs tend to have larger x-heights, so they often appear larger than serif faces when set at the same point size. To make two faces appear to be optically the same size, simply use slightly different point sizes for each face until their x-heights match.

Some typefaces are specially designed with subtle variations for use in a wide range of point sizes. These are called "optical sizes," and they ensure that a typeface has the same look and feel no matter how small or large it is typeset.

Optical sizes designed for text type may have lower stroke contrast and more generous letterspacing. By contrast, optical sizes for display type may have more details and greater stroke contrast. Be sure to use the correct optical size when a typeface has these size-specific adjustments.

2

1▸ TYPE BUILDS CHARACTER Ever since people have been writing things down, they have had to consider their audience before actually putting pen to paper: letters would have to look different depending on whether they were to be read by mainly other people (in official documents or inscriptions), just one other person (in a letter), or only the writer (in a notebook or diary). There would be less room for guesswork if letter shapes were made more formal as the diversity of the readership expanded. Some of the first messages to be read by a large number of people were rendered not by pens but by chisels. Large inscriptions on monuments in ancient Rome were carefully planned, with letters drawn on the stone with a brush before they were chiseled. Even if white-out had existed in those days, it would not have helped to remove mistakes made in stone. A bit of planning was also more important then, since stonemasons were sometimes more expendable than slabs of marble or granite. Graphic design and typography are complicated activities, but even the simple projects benefit from thinking about the problem, forming a mental picture of the solution, and then carefully planning the steps between. Scientists have not been content with just calling the human face "beautiful" if it meets certain ideals, or "ugly" if it doesn't. They had to go out and measure proportions of nose to jaw, ◂3
forehead to chin, and so on to establish why some faces are more appealing than others. Typographers and graphic designers often choose typefaces for the very same reason they might fancy a person: They just like that person. For more scientifically-minded people, however, there are specific measurements, components, details, and proportions to describe various parts of a letter. While these won't tell you what makes a typeface good, they will at least give you the right words to use when you discuss the benefits of a particular face over another. While metal letters could be made to any width and height, digital type has to conform to multiples of the smallest unit: the pixel. Every character has to be a certain number of pixels wide and high. This is not a problem when the letters are made up of 600 pixels per inch, as is the case with modern laser printers—those pixels are not discernible to our eyes, and we are happy to believe that we are looking at smooth curves instead of little squares fitted into tight grids.

EXP 15 :: PARAGRAPH INDICATOR :: POINT SIZE
TITLE: 11PT BELL GOTHIC, TRACKING +50/1000 EM
TEXT: 11/21 BELL GOTHIC, TRACKING +20/1000 EM
AND 7/21 BELL GOTHIC, TRACKING +30/1000 EM

EXP
**15.3**

**EXPLORATION 15 Paragraph Indicator: Point Size [typeset by Beth Wong]**
**Title and First Words: 16pt Baskerville Regular, tracking +25/1000 em Text: 9/19 Baskerville Regular, tracking +30/1000 em Fleuron: 8.5pt FF Dingbats 2.0 Stars and Flowers**

Type Builds Character ✤ Ever since people have been writing things down, they have had to consider their audience before actually putting pen to paper: letters would have to look different depending on whether they were to be read by mainly other people (in official documents or inscriptions), just one other person (in a letter), or only the writer (in a notebook or diary). There would be less room for guesswork if letter shapes were made more formal as the diversity of the readership expanded. Some of the first messages to be read by a large number of people were rendered not by pens but by chisels. Large inscriptions on monuments in ancient Rome were carefully planned, with letters drawn on the stone with a brush before they were chiseled. Even if white-out had existed in those days, it would not have helped to remove mistakes made in stone. A bit of planning was also more important then, since stonemasons were sometimes more expendable than slabs of marble or granite. Graphic design and typography are complicated activities, but even the simple projects benefit from thinking about the problem, forming a mental picture of the solution, and then carefully planning the steps between. Scientists have not been content with just calling the human face "beautiful" if it meets certain ideals, or "ugly" if it doesn't. They had to go out and measure proportions of nose to jaw, forehead to chin, and so on to establish why some faces are more appealing than others. Typographers and graphic designers often choose typefaces for the very same reason they might fancy a person: They just like that person. For more scientifically-minded people, however, there are specific measurements, components, details, and proportions to describe various parts of a letter. While these won't tell you what makes a typeface good, they will at least give you the right words to use when you discuss the benefits of a particular face over another. ✤ (4)

**Opposite page**

1 The title is set as a run-in head, a head without a return after it. If all other typographic variables are equal, run-in heads will subordinate to heads with a return after them.

2 A thin rule is used as a gutter between columns.

3 The top lines of the columns being different point sizes not only creates a checkerboard effect but also helps separate the two tightly packed columns.

**This page**

4 The same graphic element that is used after the title is used again to signal the end of the text.

**Bell Gothic**
In 1938, Bell Telephone commissioned Chauncey H. Griffith to design compact type for the company's phone books. Bell Gothic uses minimal contrast, loose spacing, pinched joints, and highly distinguishable lettershapes to achieve legibility at very small sizes in poor printing conditions. It was used for 40 years until it was replaced with Matthew Carter's groundbreaking Bell Centennial, which is even more spatially economical.

**Baskerville**
In the mid-18th century, John Baskerville cut type that defined a new genre now known as Transitional. His letterforms had higher contrast, vertical stress, and a less calligraphic structure than the romans that came before it. Most digital versions of this classic face are too delicate to be suitable for very small type.

EXP
**15.4**

## Paragraph Indicator: Leading

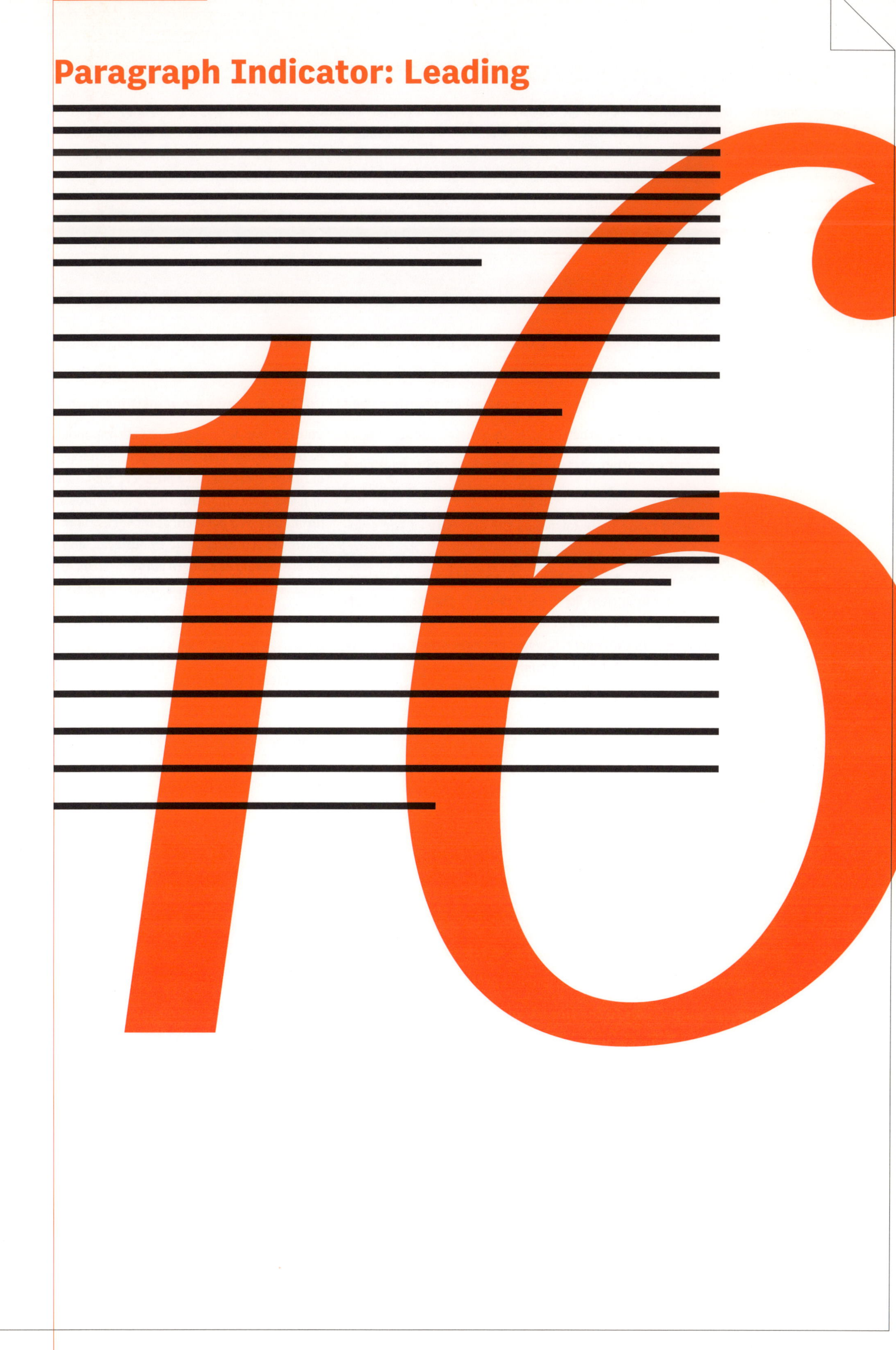

# 16 Paragraph Indicator: Leading

Using 2 points extra leading (e.g., 10/12) had long been the standard for setting text type. Now we recommend a minimum of 4 points extra leading (e.g., 10/14). An extra 4 points ensures legibility on narrow- or medium-width columns of text. As columns get wider, however, leading must get even more generous.

When word space is optically greater than linespace, it creates "rivers," or uneven typographic color. Rivers are more likely to occur on justified type when software expands word spaces to fill the line. Remember that "even color" is one of the hallmarks of fine typesetting.

EXP
**16.1**

Ever since people have been writing things down, they have had to consider their audience before actually putting pen to paper: letters would have to look different depending on whether they were to be read by mainly other people (in official documents or inscriptions), just one other person (in a letter), or only the writer (in a notebook or diary). There would be less room for guesswork if letter shapes were made more formal as the diversity of the readership expanded. ✚ *Some of the first messages to be read by a large*
1▸ *number of people were rendered not by pens but by chisels. Large inscriptions on monuments in ancient Rome were carefully planned, with letters drawn on the stone with a brush before they were chiseled. Even if white-out had existed in those days, it would not have helped to remove mistakes made in stone. A bit of planning was also more important then, since stonemasons were sometimes more expendable than slabs of marble.* ✚ Graphic design and typography are complicated activities, but even the simple projects benefit from thinking about the problem, forming a mental picture of the solution, and then carefully planning the steps between. ✚ *Scientists have not been content with just calling the human face "beautiful" if it meets certain ideals, or "ugly" if it doesn't. They had to go out and measure proportions of nose to jaw, forehead to chin, and so on to establish why some faces are more appealing than others.* ✚ Typographers and graphic designers often choose typefaces for the very same reason they might fancy a person: They just like that person. For more scientifically-minded people, however, there are specific measurements, components, details, and proportions to describe various parts of a letter. While these won't tell you what makes a typeface good, they will at least give you the right words to use when you discuss the benefits of a particular face over another. You can say "I hate the x-heigh on Such-a-Gothic" or "These descenders just don't work for me" or "Please, may I see something with a smaller cap height?" an you'll know what you are talking about. ✚ *While metal letters coul be made to any width and height, digital type has to conform to multiple of the smallest unit: the pixel. Every character has to be a certain numbe of pixels wide and high. This is not a problem when the letters are mad up of 600 pixels per inch, as is the case with modern laser printers—thos pixels are not discernible to our eyes, and we are happy to believe tha we are looking at smooth curves instead of little squares fitted into tigh grids.* ✚ On most screens, only 72 pixels make up one inch. We coul see each and every one of them, if engineers hadn't already foun ways around that. Computer screens, however, are not where w read most of our type these days. Smart phones, computers, an tablets all have high-resolutions screens, but microwave ovens espresso makers, and all the other gadgets around us all still us small and modest displays. And the type unmistakably consists o bitmaps, which means that an 8-point letter is actually made u of eight pixels. If we allow six pixels above the baseline, includin accents, and two below for descenders, that'll leave only three o four pixels for a lowercase character. In spite of these restrictions there are hundreds of bitmap fonts, all different from one anothe by only a few pixels, but enough to prove that typographic variety cannot be suppressed by technological constraints. ✚✚

EXPLORATION 16 — PARAGRAPH INDICATOR:
FIRST PARAGRAPH: 8/18 ANTITHESIS REGULAR
ALTERNATE PARAGRAPHS: ANTITHESIS ITALIC
GRAPHIC ELEMENT: 12PT ANTITHESIS BOLD

## (2) TYPE BUILDS CHARACTER

(3) Ever since people have been writing things down, they have had to consider their audience before actually putting pen to paper: letters would have to look different depending on whether they were to be read by mainly other people (in official documents or inscriptions), just one other person (in a letter), or only the writer (in a notebook or diary). There would be less room for guesswork if letter shapes were made more formal as the diversity of the readership expanded.

Some of the first messages to be read by a large number of people were rendered not by pens but by chisels. Large inscriptions on monuments in ancient Rome were carefully planned, with letters drawn on the stone with a brush before they were chiseled. Even if white-out had existed in those days, it would not have helped to remove mistakes made in stone. A bit of planning was also more important then, since stonemasons were sometimes more expendable than slabs of marble or granite.

Graphic design and typography are complicated activities, but even the simple projects benefit from thinking about the problem, forming a mental picture of the solution, and then carefully planning the steps between.

Scientists have not been content with just calling the human face "beautiful" if it meets certain ideals, or "ugly" if it doesn't. They had to go out and measure proportions of nose to jaw, forehead to chin, and so on to establish why some faces are more appealing than others.

Typographers and graphic designers often choose typefaces for the very same reason they might fancy a person: They just like that person. For more scientifically-minded people, however, there are specific measurements, components, details, and proportions to describe various parts of a letter. While these won't tell you what makes a typeface good, they will at least give you the right words to use when you discuss the benefits of a particular face over another.

(4)

**EXPLORATION 16:PARAGRAPH INDICATOR:LEADING TITLE:12PT FUTURA BLACK:TRACKING +300/1000 EM 7/12 FF SUPER GROTESK:TRACKING +35/1000 EM + 9/24 FF SUPER GROTESK:TRACKING +35/1000 EM**

EXP
**16.2**

**Opposite page**

1 Graphic elements and a change of weight without returns between paragraphs indicate new paragraphs. The change of leading starts with the second line of each paragraph.

**This page**

2 The title and last lines of each paragraph are centered in the justified column of text. Centered type relates to the symmetrical structure of justified text.

3 The looser linespacing is used on the paragraphs set in a larger point size.

4 A double rule separates the text from the colophon. The space between the two rules is optically equivalent to the space from the rule to the type in the text block.

**FF Antithesis**
Jan "Yanone" Gerner gave this design a rugged, hand-cut look and an unusual family structure: rather than the expected set of weights and italics, Antithesis is three styles: Regular (serif), Bold (sans), and Italic (script). It picks up on the naturalistic DIY aesthetic without seeming amateur or twee.

**Futura Black**
Two years after releasing his groundbreaking sans serif, Paul Renner followed up with this stencil in 1929. The design has no formal relationship to Futura but likely was named to capitalize on its success. It is geometric in its own way; the reduction of letters to basic, modular shapes was popular in 1920s Modernism.

**FF Super Grotesk**
In the late 1920s and early 1930s, nearly every type foundry scrambled to develop a geometric sans to capitalize on the success of trendsetters like Futura and Erbar. Super-Grotesk was Schriftguss AG's effort, designed by Arno Drescher. FontFont's 1999 version comes from Svend Smital and includes three weights in two widths. Distinguishing marks include the angled terminals on 'E,F,T,' and 't.'

EXP
**16.3**

1▸ **TYPE BUILDS CHARACTER** Ever since people have been writing things down, they have had to consider their audience before actually putting pen to paper: letters would have to look different depending on whether they were to be read by mainly other people (in official documents or inscriptions), just one other person (in a letter), or only the writer (in a notebook or diary). There would be less room for guesswork if letter shapes were made more formal as the diversity of the readership expanded.

2▸

Some of the first messages to be read by a large number of people were rendered not by pens but by chisels. Large inscriptions on monuments in ancient Rome were carefully planned, with letters drawn on the stone with a brush before they were chiseled. Even if white-out had existed in those days, it would not have helped to remove mistakes made in stone. A bit of planning was also more important then, since stonemasons were sometimes more expendable than slabs of marble or granite.

Graphic design and typography are complicated activities, but even the simple projects benefit from thinking about the problem, forming a mental picture of the solution, and then carefully planning the steps between.

Scientists have not been content with just calling the human face "beautiful" if it meets certain ideals, or "ugly" if it doesn't. They had to go out and measure proportions of nose to jaw, forehead to chin, and so on to establish why some faces are more appealing than others.

Typographers and graphic designers often choose typefaces for the very same reason they might fancy a person: They just like that person. For more scientifically-minded people, however, there are specific measurements, components, details, and proportions to describe various parts of a letter. While these won't tell you what makes a typeface good, they will at least give you the right words to use when you discuss the benefits of a particular face over another. You can say "I hate the x-height on Such-a-Gothic" or "These descenders just don't work for me" or "Please, may I see something with a smaller cap height?" and you'll know what you are talking about.

-------------
EXPLORATION 16
PARAGRAPH INDICATOR: LEADING
-------------
TITLE
12PT FF MAGDA CLEAN MONO BLACK
-------------
FIRST PARAGRAPH
8/12 FF MAGDA CLEAN MONO
NO TRACKING
-------------
ALTERNATE PARAGRAPHS
8/22 FF MAGDA CLEAN MONO
NO TRACKING
-------------

EXP 16.4

# TYPE BUILDS CHARACTER

3▸

Ever since people have been writing things down, they have had to consider their audience before actually putting pen to paper: letters would have to look different depending on whether they were to be read by mainly other people (in official documents or inscriptions), just one other person (in a letter), or only the writer (in a notebook or diary). There would be less room for guesswork if letter shapes were made more formal as the diversity of the readership expanded.

Some of the first messages to be read by a large number of people were rendered not by pens but by chisels. Large inscriptions on monuments in ancient Rome were carefully planned, with letters drawn on the stone with a brush before they were chiseled. Even if white-out had existed in those days, it would not have helped to remove mistakes made in stone. A bit of planning was also more important then, since stonemasons were sometimes more expendable than slabs of marble or granite.

Graphic design and typography are complicated activities, but even the simple projects benefit from thinking about the problem, forming a mental picture of the solution, and then carefully planning the steps between.

Scientists have not been content with just calling the human face "beautiful" if it meets certain ideals, or "ugly" if it doesn't. They had to go out and measure proportions of nose to jaw, forehead to chin, and so on to establish why some faces are more appealing than others.

Typographers and graphic designers often choose typefaces for the very same reason they might fancy a person: They just like that person. For more scientifically-minded people, however, there are specific measurements, components, details, and proportions to describe various parts of a letter. While these won't tell you what makes a typeface good, they will at least give you the right words to use when you discuss the benefits of a particular face over another. You can say "I hate the x-height on Such-a-Gothic" or "These descenders just don't work for me" or "Please, may I see something with a smaller cap height?" and you'll know what you are talking about.

While metal letters could be made to any width and height, digital type has to conform to multiples of the smallest unit: the pixel. Every character has to be a certain number of pixels wide and high. This is not a problem when the letters are made up of 600 pixels per inch, as is the case with modern laser printers—those pixels are not discernible to our eyes, and we are happy to believe that we are looking at smooth curves instead of little squares fitted into tight grids.

On most screens, only 72 pixels make up one inch. We could see each and every one of them, if engineers ◂4 hadn't already found ways around that. Computer screens, however, are not where we read most of our type these days. Smart phones, computers, and tablets all have high-resolutions screens, but microwave ovens, espresso makers, and all the other gadgets around us all still use small and modest displays. And the type unmistakably consists of bitmaps, which means that an 8-point letter is actually made up of eight pixels. If we allow six pixels above the baseline, including accents, and two below for descenders, that'll leave only three or four pixels for a lowercase character.

Rhythm and contrast keep coming up when discussing good music and good typographic design. They are concepts that also apply to spoken language, as anyone who has had to sit through a monotonous lecture will attest; the same tone, volume and speed of speech will put even the most interested listener into dreamland. Every now and again the audience needs to be shaken, either by a change in voice or pitch, by a question being posed, or by the speaker talking very quietly and then suddenly shouting. An occasional joke also works, just as the use of a funny typeface can liven up a page.

**EXPLORATION 16**
**Paragraph Indicator: Leading**

**Title:**
13pt Eskapade Fraktur Black, tracking +220/1000 em

**First paragraph:**
8/12 FF Quadraat Sans Italic, tracking +55/1000 em

**Alternate paragraphs:**
8/18 FF Quadraat Sans Italic, tracking +55/1000 em

**Opposite page**

1. The title is set as a run-in head. Each word is reversed out of a black bar, which is, like the typeface, reminiscent of tape label makers.
2. The extra leading between paragraphs is the same as the looser leading used on every other paragraph.

**This page**

3. The title is set in loosely tracked caps running vertically bottom to top of page, leading the eye toward the first word of the first paragraph.
4. Every other column begins with the alternative leading, making a checkerboard effect. The change in linespace makes a noticeable difference in typographic color and therefore a clear visual separation between paragraphs.

**FF Magda Clean**
Based on 20th-century typewriters and tape label makers, the original FF Magda of 1995 was described by its Swiss designer Cornel Windlin "as a less nostalgic typewriter face for designers with an appetite for banal everyday typography." Three years later, Windlin followed up the grungy original with this face, which reduces the design to its bare, mechanical structure.

**Eskapade Fraktur**
This contemporary take on the fractured old Roman and German forms of blackletter type was designed by Alisa Nowak in 2012. These upright condensed letters are a unique blend of sharp corners with the rounded arcs. Eskapade Roman is a text companion face.

**FF Quadraat Sans**
This sans serif companion to FF Quadraat was designed by Fred Smeijers in 1998. Sans typefaces can look very much alike, particularly in their bold weights, but like many sans faces of the late 20th century, this one has a rather distinctive Humanist character all its own, such as the angled terminals on its stems; the protruding diagonals on 'A,M,N,' and 'W;' and the unusually narrow and calligraphic italic.

## Paragraph Indicator: Tracking

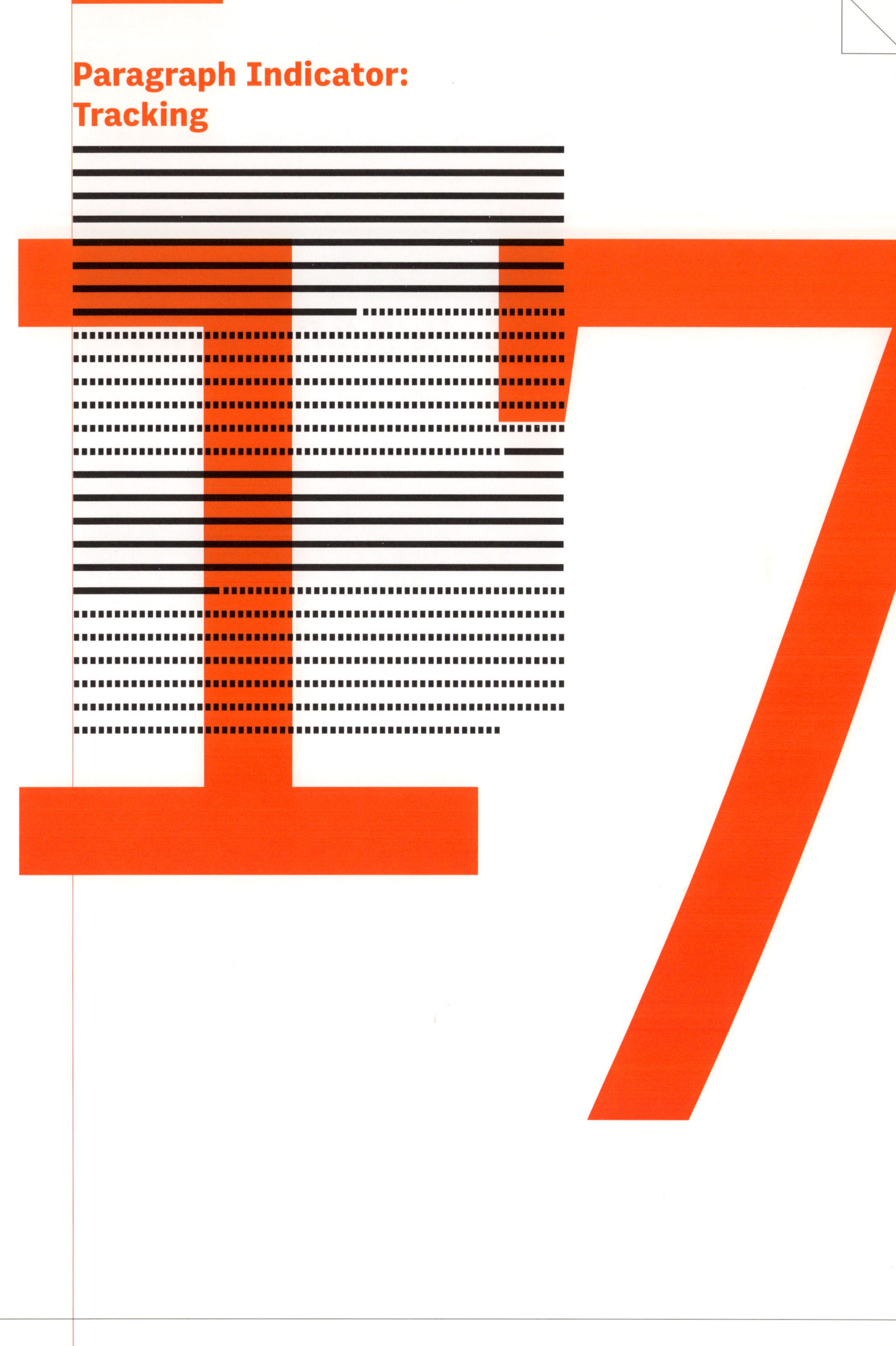

# 17 Paragraph Indicator: Tracking

**In most typefaces, text size type is too tightly letterspaced for comfortable reading unless you add some tracking (letterspacing). Although "even color" is a prized attribute in typography and is typically created by consistent tracking, you can use the unevenness created by a change in tracking as a visual signal for a paragraph indication.**

**The width of sidebearings (horizontal body clearance) in a typeface varies, so the optimal amount of tracking for each face also varies. (Check out the colophon for each Exploration to find out how much tracking has been used on each type specification.)**

EXP
**17.1**

EXPLORATION 17 / Paragraph Indicator » Tracking (typeset by Priscilla Peña)
title: 26pt Fluidum Bold, tracking −20/1000 em
first paragraph: 6.5/14 FF Clan Thin, tracking +40/1000 em
alternate paragraphs: 6.5/14 FF Clan Thin, tracking +170/1000 em

## TypeBuildsCharacter

1▸ Ever since people have been writing things down, they have had to consider their audience before actually putting pen to paper: letters would have to look different depending on whether they were to be read by mainly other people (in official documents or inscriptions), just one other person (in a letter), or only the writer (in a notebook or diary). There would be less room for guesswork if letter shapes were made more formal as the diversity of the readership expanded.

Some of the first messages to be read by a large number of people were rendered not by pens but by chisels. Large inscriptions on monuments in ancient Rome were carefully planned, with letters drawn on the stone ◂2 with a brush before they were chiseled. Even if white-out had existed in those days, it would not have helped to remove mistakes made in stone. A bit of planning was also more important then, since stonemasons were sometimes more expendable than slabs of marble or granite.

Graphic design and typography are complicated activities, but even the simple projects benefit from thinking about the problem, forming a mental picture of the solution, and then carefully planning the steps between.

Scientists have not been content with just calling the human face "beautiful" if it meets certain ideals, or "ugly" if it doesn't. They had to go out and measure proportions of nose to jaw, forehead to chin, and so on to establish why some faces are more appealing than others.

Typographers and graphic designers often choose typefaces for the very same reason they might fancy a person: They just like that person. For more scientifically-minded people, however, there are specific measurements, components, details, and proportions to describe various parts of a letter. While these won't tell you what makes a typeface good, they will at least give you the right words to use when you discuss the benefits of a particular face over another. You can say "I hate the x-height on Such-a-Gothic" or "These descenders just don't work for me" or "Please, may I see something with a smaller cap height?" and you'll know what you are talking about.

While metal letters could be made to any width and height, digital type has to conform to multiples of the smallest unit: the pixel. Every character has to be a certain number of pixels wide and high. This is not a problem when the letters are made up of 600 pixels per inch, as is the case with modern laser printers—those pixels are not discernible to our eyes, and we are happy to believe that we are looking at smooth curves instead of little squares fitted into tight grids.

EXPLORATION 17 PARAGRAPH INDICATOR: TRACKING FIRST PARAGRAPH: 7.5/15 FF TICKET BOLD, TRACKING +10/1000 EM ALTERNATE PARAGRAPHS: 7.5/15 FF TICKET BOLD, TRACKING +190/1000 EM

Ever since people have been writing things down, they have had to consider their audience before actually putting pen to paper: letters would have to look different depending on whether they were to be read by mainly other people (in official documents or inscriptions), just one other person (in a letter), or only the writer (in a notebook or diary). There would be less room for guesswork if letter shapes were made more formal as the diversity of the readership expanded.

Some of the first messages to be read by a large number of people were rendered not by pens but by chisels. Large inscriptions on monuments in ancient Rome were carefully planned, with letters drawn on the stone with a brush before they were chiseled. Even if white-out had existed in those days, it would not have helped to remove mistakes made in stone. A bit of planning was also more important then, since stonemasons were sometimes more expendable than slabs of marble or granite.

Graphic design and typography are complicated activities, but even the simple projects benefit from thinking about the problem, forming a mental picture of the solution, and then carefully planning the steps between.

Scientists (◂3) have not been content with just calling the human face "beautiful" if it meets certain ideals, or "ugly" if it doesn't. They had to go out and measure proportions of nose to jaw, forehead to chin, and so on to establish why some faces are more appealing than others.

Typographers and graphic designers often choose typefaces for the very same reason they might fancy a person: They just like that person. For more scientifically-minded people, however, there are specific measurements, components, details, and proportions to describe various parts of a letter. While these won't tell you what makes a typeface good, they will at least give you the right words to use when you discuss the benefits of a particular face over another. You can say "I hate the x-height on Such-a-Gothic" or "These descenders just don't work for me" or "Please, may I see something with a smaller cap height?" and you'll know what you are talking about.

EXP
**17.2**

**Opposite page**

1 The first paragraph is set in the tighter tracking. Because its tracking is tighter, its overall typographic color is darker and it appears to be the stronger of the two alternating settings.

2 Using a light weight helps the paragraphs with very loose tracking be a bit more legible. Because you must set enough extra tracking to make a clear color change in the text, extraordinary legibility is not a top priority in settings like these.

**This page**

3 Unlikely text faces go with the more unusual styles of paragraph indications. Monospaced and bitmap types look nearly "normal" with very loose tracking.

**Fluidum**
Alessandro Butti's showy script by has an appropriate name: its curvy strokes, undulating in a constant rhythm, have a wave-like quality. It was released by the Italian foundry Nebiolo in 1951 and fits in well with the advertising and branding lettering of the era. Monotype digitized only the heavy weight of its two styles, regular and Nera (Black), and Ralph M. Unger revived both as "Butti."

**FF Clan**
Completed in 2006, this is an extensive family of seven weights in six widths from self-taught designer Łukasz Dziedzic of Poland. It has an engaging, distinctive personality, yet it remains a truly legible face.

**FF Ticket**
Designed by Daniel Fritz in 2000, this charming modular face re-creates the look of thermal printer type that used to be so common on tickets and luggage tags.

Text type set with tracking that is a bit too loose is harder to read than text set with tracking that is just a bit too tight. When in doubt, err on the side of too little rather than too much tracking.

In paragraphs set with loose tracking in this chapter, this typographic variable has been used for stylistic effect at some expenditure of optimal legibility. More typically, changes in tracking would be imperceptible to a reader and used only to improve readability or to produce better paragraph settings (good rags, lack of widows, etc.).

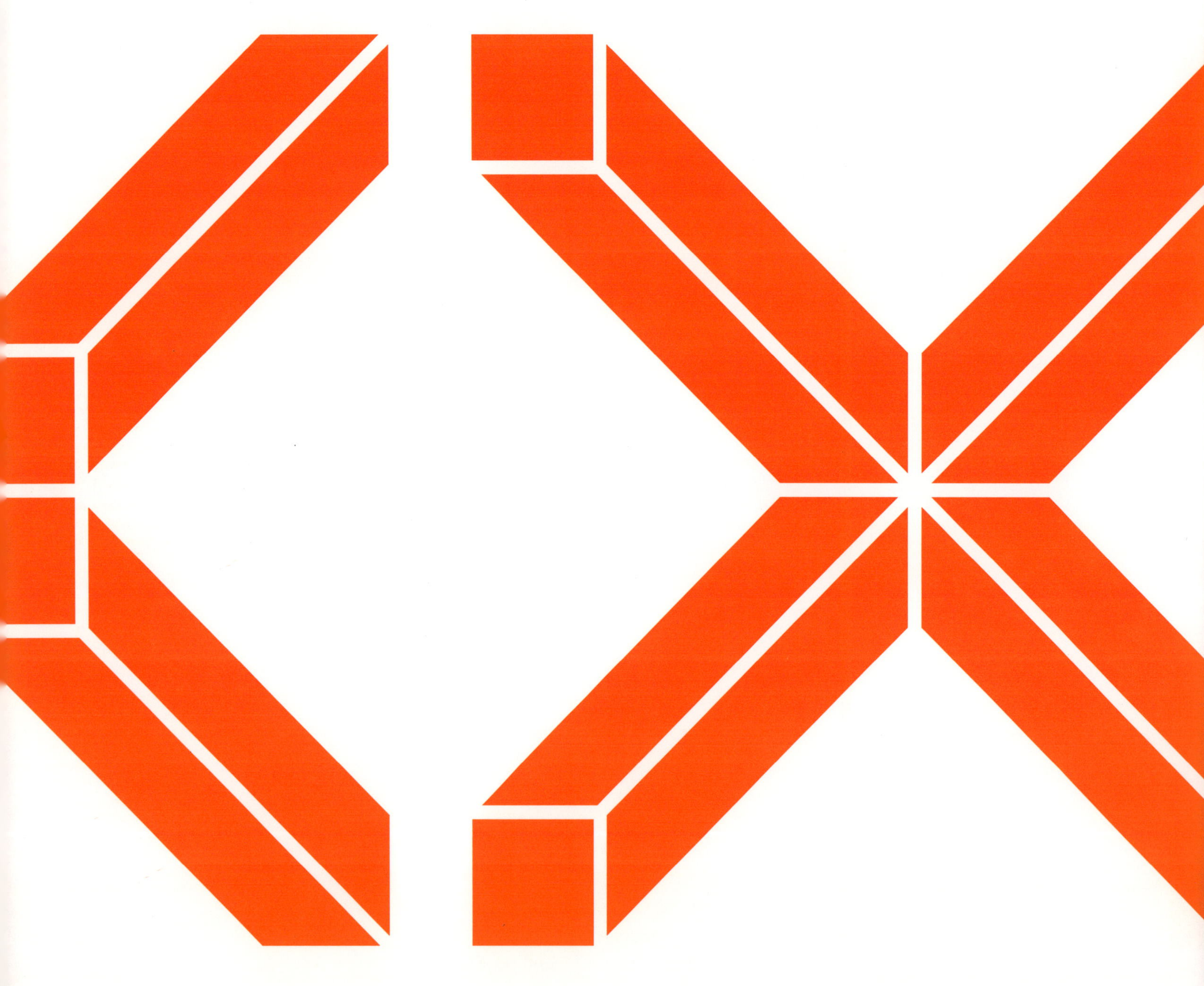

1 TYPE BUILDS CHARACTER

Erik Spiekermann

Ever since people have been writing things down, they have had to consider their audience before actually putting pen to paper: letters would have to look different depending on whether they were to be read by mainly other people (in official documents or inscriptions), just one other person (in a letter), or only the writer (in a notebook or diary). There would be less room for guesswork if letter shapes were made more formal as the diversity of the readership expanded.

Some of the first messages to be read by a large number of people were rendered not by pens but by chisels. Large inscriptions on monuments in ancient Rome were carefully planned, with letters drawn on the stone with a brush before they were chiseled. Even if whiteout had existed in those days, it would not have helped to remove mistakes made in stone. A bit of planning was also more important then, since stonemasons were sometimes more expendable than slabs of marble or granite.

Graphic design and typography are complicated activities, but even the simple projects benefit from thinking about the problem, forming a mental picture of the solution, and then carefully planning the steps between.

Scientists have not been content with just calling the human face "beautiful" if it meets certain ideals, or "ugly" if it doesn't. They had to go out and measure proportions of nose to jaw, forehead to chin, and so on to establish why some faces are more appealing than others. 2

EXPLORATION SEVENTEEN

PARAGRAPH INDICATOR: TRACKING

TITLE: 8/16 OCR-B, TRACKING +260/1000 EM

BYLINE AND FIRST PARAGRAPH: 7.5/16.5 OCR-B, TRACKING -50/1000 EM

ALTERNATE PARAGRAPHS: 7.5/16.5 OCR-B, TRACKING +120/1000 EM

1 The title is set with loose tracking and the byline is set with tight tracking. Monospaced type can sometimes be set with negative tracking and remain quite legible.

2 The three columns of text get progressively shorter in depth. Putting the colophon in the third column under the last paragraph balances the clotheslined columns and creates a better page composition. When clothselining text, the depths of the columns should appear to vary at random, much like a ragged edge.

**OCR-B**

This monospaced face was designed by Adrian Frutiger in 1968 for optical character recognition technology. While OCR-A was intended to be "read" only by electronic devices, this face was designed to be scanned by electronic devices as well as read by people. Compared to OCR-A, this successor is easier for the human eye to read and it has a less technical look and feel.

## Paragraph Indicator: Margin

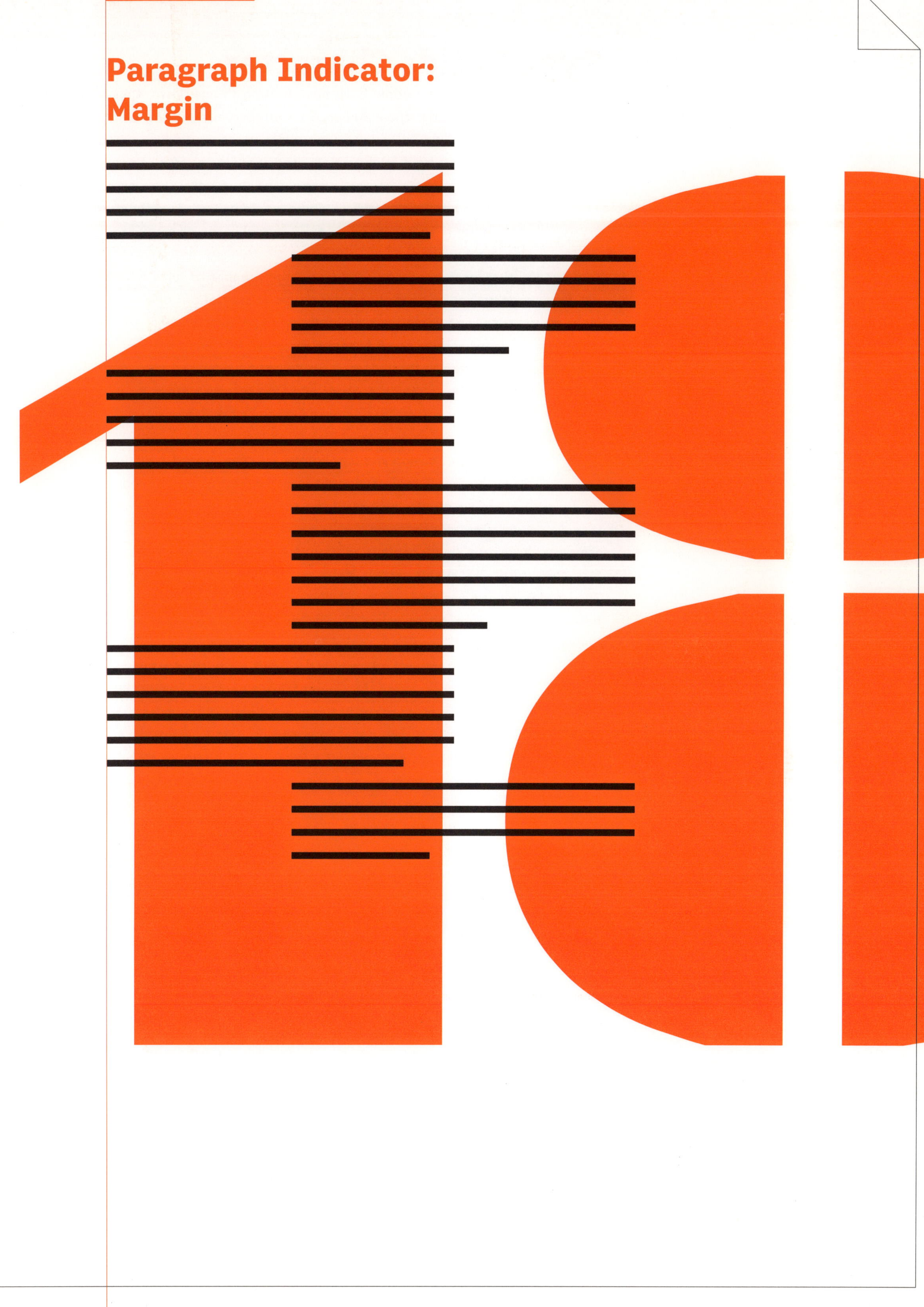

This page
1 The title aligns to the same vertical grid line as the second and fourth paragraphs.
2 The measure (column width) of each paragraph is the same, only every other paragraph is shifting in relation to the edge of the page. In other words, margins vary, but column width stays the same.

Opposite page
3 Every other paragraph begins at the same left vertical grid line.
4 Top lines of the bold paragraphs begin on the same baseline and two word spaces after the last word of each roman paragraph.

**Doko**
Ondrej Jób designed this face in 2011 to be a sort of typographic representation of the casual hand-lettering found in comics and illustration. It dances on the line between expressiveness and functionality, display type and text type. With its swashes and sway, its display qualities are obvious, but its readability and pragmatic features equip it for practical text as well. It is equally at home on a jolly package of chips or filling the pages of a novel.

**Frutiger**
Adrian Frutiger designed this face in 1975 for the signage at the Charles de Gaulle airport in Paris. Although Univers was available for this project, he aimed to avoid letterforms that were "too clinically constructed." Although the two faces share many features, Frutiger is rather warm and friendly compared to Univers—demonstrating that very small shifts in design create quite large differences in overall effect.

**FF Meta Serif**
It took 3 years (2005–2008) and three designers to develop this seriffed version of FF Meta. Erik Spiekermann, Christian Schwartz, and Kris Sowersby worked as a team to create a companion face that retains the general spirit of the sans but has a newsy, authoritative voice of its own.

1 # Type Builds Character BY ERIK SPIEKERMANN

Ever since people have been writing things down, they have had to consider their audience before actually putting pen to paper: letters would have to look different depending on whether they were to be read by mainly other people (in official documents or inscriptions), just one other person (in a letter), or only the writer (in a notebook or diary). There would be less room for guesswork if letter shapes were made more formal as the diversity of the readership expanded.

2 *Some of the first messages to be read by a large number of people were rendered not by pens but by chisels. Large inscriptions on monuments in ancient Rome were carefully planned, with letters drawn on the stone with a brush before they were chiseled. Even if white-out had existed in those days, it would not have helped to remove mistakes made in stone. A bit of planning was also more important then, since stonemasons were sometimes more expendable than slabs of marble or granite.*

Graphic design and typography are complicated activities, but even the simple projects benefit from thinking about the problem, forming a mental picture of the solution, and then carefully planning the steps between.

*Scientists have not been content with just calling the human face "beautiful" if it meets certain ideals, or "ugly" if it doesn't. They had to go out and measure proportions of nose to jaw, forehead to chin, and so on to establish why some faces are more appealing than others.*

Typographers and graphic designers often choose typefaces for the very same reason they might fancy a person: They just like that person. For more scientifically-minded people, however, there are specific measurements, components, details, and proportions to describe various parts of a letter. While these won't tell you what makes a typeface good, they will at least give you the right words to use when you discuss the benefits of a particular face over another. You can say "I hate the x-height on Such-a-Gothic" or "These descenders just don't work for me" or "Please, may I see something with a smaller cap height?" and you'll know what you are talking about.

**EXPLORATION 18** × MARGIN (typeset by Beth Wong)
Title: 24pt Doko Bold, tracking +40/1000 em × Byline: 8pt Doko Book, tracking +130/1000 em
First Paragraph: 8.5/14 Frutiger Roman, tracking +25/1000 em
Alternate Paragraphs: 8.5/14 Frutiger Italic, tracking +25/1000 em

3▸ Ever since people have been writing things down, they have had to consider their audience before actually putting pen to paper: letters would have to look different depending on whether they were to be read by mainly other people (in official documents or inscriptions), just one other person (in a letter), or only the writer (in a notebook or diary). There would be less room for guesswork if letter shapes were made more formal as the diversity of the readership expanded. **Some of the first messages to be read by a large number of people were rendered not by pens but by chisels. Large inscriptions on monuments in ancient Rome were carefully planned, with letters drawn on the stone with a brush before they were chiseled. Even if white-out had existed in those days, it would not have helped to remove mistakes made in stone. A bit of planning was also more important then, since stonemasons were sometimes more expendable than slabs of marble or granite.**

Graphic design and typography are complicated activities, but even the simple projects benefit from thinking about the problem, forming a mental picture of the solution, and then carefully planning the steps between. **Scientists have not been content with just calling the human face "beautiful" if it meets certain ideals, or "ugly" if it doesn't. They had to go out and measure proportions of nose to jaw, forehead to chin, and so on to establish why some faces are more appealing than others.**

Typographers and graphic designers often choose typefaces for the very same reason they might fancy a person: They just like that person. For more scientifically-minded people, however, there are specific measurements, components, details, and proportions to describe various parts of a letter. While these won't tell you what makes a typeface good, they will at least give you the right words to use when you discuss the benefits of a particular face over another. You can say "I hate the x-height on Such-a-Gothic" or "These descenders just don't work for me" or "Please, may I see something with a smaller cap height?" and you'll know what you are talking about. **While metal letters could be made to any width and height, digital type has to conform to multiples of the smallest unit: the pixel. Every character has to be a certain number of pixels wide and high. This is not a problem when the letters are made up of 600 pixels per inch, as is the case with modern laser printers—those pixels are not discernible to our eyes, and we are happy to believe that we are looking at smooth curves instead of little squares fitted into tight grids.** ◂4

**Exploration 18**
Paragraph indicator: Margin
(typeset by Chiharu Tanaka)

First paragraph:
7/12 FF Meta Serif Book
Tracking +40/1000 em

Alternate paragraphs:
7/12 FF Meta Serif Bold
Tracking +35/1000 em

**This page**

1 Title is set to align along the angle created by the text type below.

2 With the right side being flush and the left angled, this setting is akin to a flush right/rag left alignment, so autohyphenation is turned off.

**Opposite page**

3 Three em spaces are set at the end of each paragraph. This makes an intentional "river" in the text that then functions as paragraph indication. Each paragraph is bold from its first word to the end of its first line.

4 Each paragraph is progressively shifted to the right on the page, making a stair-step shape on the left edge of the text block.

**FF Kievit**

In 2001, Mike Abbink created FF Kievit, which takes the forms and proportions of Oldstyle serifs and translates them into a nearly monolinear sans serif. This follows the Humanist Sans tradition, which began with faces like Syntax, but FF Kievit is a calmer, less dynamic design.

**FF Nexus Sans and FF Nexus Mix**

In the early 1990s, FF Scala and FF Scala Sans capitalized on what Martin Majoor called "two typefaces, one form principle." It is common now, but the idea of using the same skeleton for multiple members of a superfamily was rare at the time. Majoor expanded on the idea in 2004 with FF Nexus, which borrows some of its structure from Scala but adds the slab FF Nexus Mix and monospaced FF Nexus Typewriter.

1 **TYPE BUILDS CHARACTER**

*BY ERIK SPIEKERMANN*

Ever since people have been writing things down, they have had to consider their audience before actually putting pen to paper: letters would have to look different depending on whether they were to be read by mainly other people (in official documents or inscriptions), just one other person (in a letter), or only the writer (in a notebook or diary).

There would be less room for guesswork if letter shapes were made more formal as the diversity of the readership expanded. Some of the first messages to be read by a large number of people were rendered not by pens but by chisels. Large inscriptions on monuments in ancient Rome were carefully planned, with letters drawn on the stone with a brush before they were chiseled. Even if white-out had existed in those days, it would not have helped to remove mistakes made in stone. A bit of planning was also more important then, since masons were sometimes more expendable than slabs of marble or granite.

Graphic design and typography are complicated activities, but even the simple projects benefit from thinking about the problem, forming a mental picture of the solution, and then carefully planning the 2 steps between. Scientists have not been content with just calling the human face "beautiful" if it meets certain ideals, or "ugly" if it doesn't. They had to go out and measure proportions of nose to jaw, forehead to chin, and so on to establish why some faces are more appealing than others.

Typographers and graphic designers often choose typefaces for the very same reason they might fancy a person: They just like that person. For more scientifically-minded people, however, there are specific measurements, components, details, and proportions to describe various parts of a letter. While these won't tell you what makes a typeface good, they will at least give you the right words to use when you discuss the benefits of a particular face over another. You can say "I hate the x-height on Such-a-Gothic" or "These descenders just don't work for me" or "Please, may I see something with a smaller cap height?" and you'll know what you are talking about.

While metal letters could be made to any width and height, digital type has to conform to multiples of the smallest unit: the pixel. Every character has to be a certain number of pixels wide and high. This is not a problem when the letters are made up of 600 pixels per inch, as is the case with modern laser printers—those pixels are not discernible to our eyes, and we are happy to believe that we are looking at smooth curves instead of little squares fitted into tight grids.

**EXPLORATION 18** Paragraph Indicator • Margin (typeset by Priscilla Peña) Title: 12pt FF Kievit Bold, tracking +50/1000 em Byline: 7pt FF Kievit Italic, tracking +80/1000 em Text: 7/13 FF Kievit, tracking +20/1000 em

EXPLORATION 18 >> PARAGRAPH INDICATOR: MARGIN (TYPESET BY FRED CARRIEDO)
TITLE: 8PT FF NEXUS SANS BOLD, TRACKING +60/1000 EM
FIRST LINES: 7/13 FF NEXUS SANS REGULAR, TRACKING +60/1000 EM
TEXT: 7/13 FF NEXUS MIX REGULAR, TRACKING +60/1000 EM

## TYPE BUILDS CHARACTER

**Ever since people have been writing things down, they have had to consider their** audience before actually putting pen to paper: letters would have to look different depending on whether they were to be read by mainly other people (in official documents or inscriptions), just one other person (in a letter), or only the writer (in a notebook or diary). There would be less room for guesswork if letter shapes were made more formal as the diversity of the readership expanded. (3)

**Some of the first messages to be read by a** large number of people were rendered not by pens but by chisels. Large inscriptions on monuments in ancient Rome were carefully planned, with letters drawn on the stone with a brush before they were chiseled. Even if white-out had existed in those days, it would not have helped to remove mistakes made in stone. A bit of planning was also more important then, since stonemasons were sometimes more expendable than slabs of marble or granite.

**Graphic design and typography are complicated activities, but** (4) even the simple projects benefit from thinking about the problem, forming a mental picture of the solution, and then carefully planning the steps between.

**Scientists** have not been content with just calling the human face "beautiful" if it meets certain ideals, or "ugly" if it doesn't. They had to go out and measure proportions of nose to jaw, forehead to chin, and so on to establish why some faces are more appealing than others.

**Typographers and graphic designers often choose typefaces for the very** same reason they might fancy a person: They just like that person. For more scientifically-minded people, however, there are specific measurements, components, details, and proportions to describe various parts of a letter. While these won't tell you what makes a typeface good, they will at least give you the right words to use when you discuss the benefits of a particular face over another. You can say "I hate the x-height on Such-a-Gothic" or "These descenders just don't work for me" or "Please, may I see something with a smaller cap height?" and you'll know what you are talking about.

**While metal** letters could be made to any width and height, digital type has to conform to multiples of the smallest unit: the pixel. Every character has to be a certain number of pixels wide and high. This is not a problem when the letters are made up of 600 pixels per inch, as is the case with modern laser printers—those pixels are not discernible to our eyes, and we are happy to believe that we are looking at smooth curves instead of little squares fitted into tight grids.

## Paragraph Indicator: Column Width

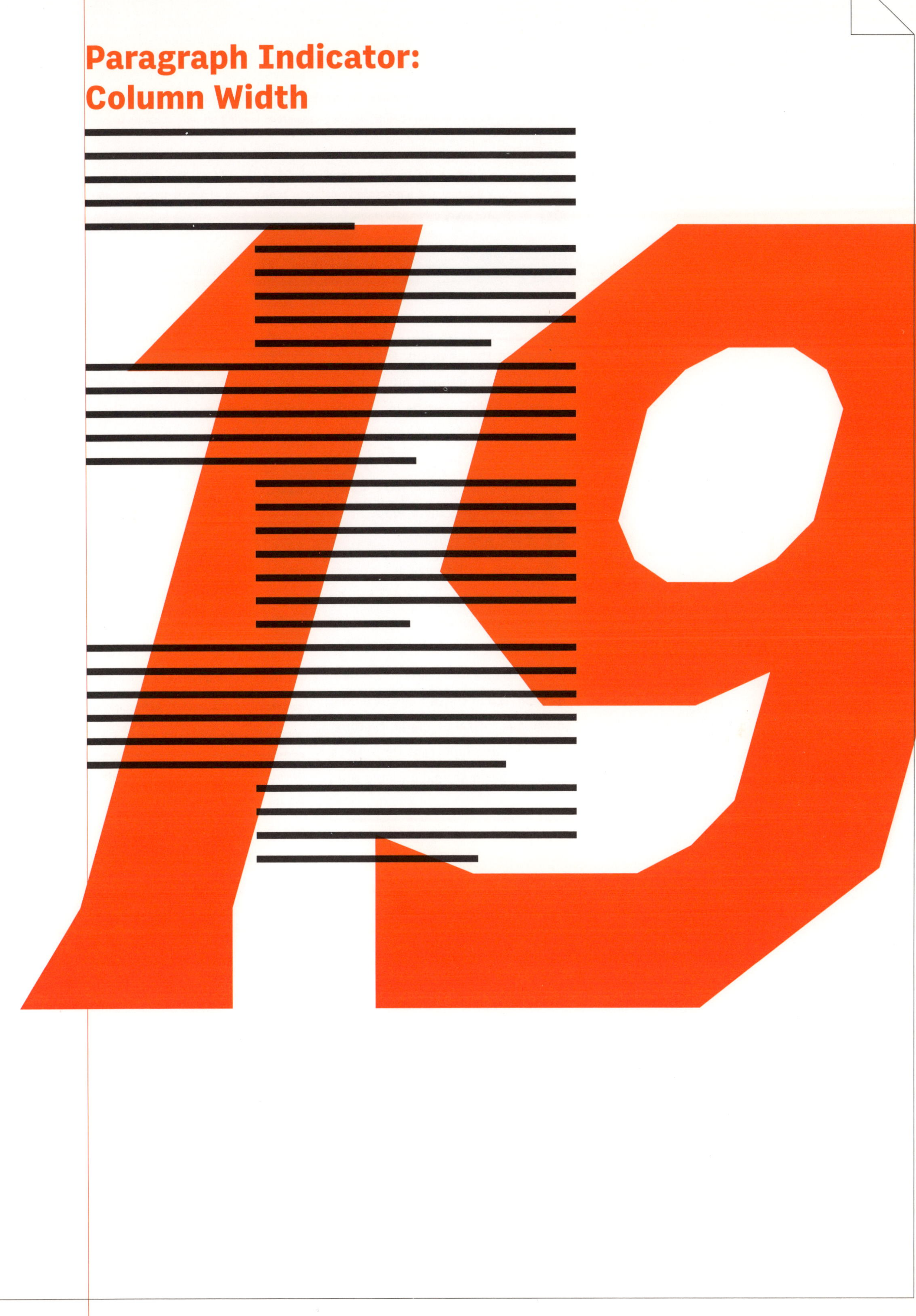

# 19 Paragraph Indicator: Column Width

Text typeset in a medium column width (measure) of 60–80 characters is the most comfortable and legible to read. Narrow columns should not be less than 20 characters; wide columns not more than 100. (Include punctuation and word spaces in the character count.)

The wider the measure, the harder it is for the eye to find its way back to the next line below. Use more generous leading on wide columns to improve ease of reading.

To use column width as a paragraph indication, you can vary the width randomly, use a progressive pattern, or alternate wide and narrow columns for every other paragraph.

EXP **19.1**

Ever since people have been writing things down, they have had to consider their audience before actually putting pen to paper: letters would have to look different depending on whether they were to be read by mainly other people (in official documents or inscriptions), just one other person (in a letter), or only the writer (in a notebook or diary). There would be less room for guesswork if letter shapes were made more formal as the diversity of the readership expanded. (3)

(1▸) Some of the first messages to be read by a large number of people were rendered not by pens but by chisels. Large inscriptions on monuments in ancient Rome were carefully planned, with letters drawn on the stone with a brush before they were chiseled. Even if white-out had existed in those days, it would not have helped to remove mistakes made in stone. A bit of planning was also more important then, since stonemasons were sometimes more expendable than slabs of marble.

Graphic design and typography are complicated activities, but even the simple projects benefit from thinking about the problem, forming a mental picture of the solution, and then carefully planning the steps between.

While metal letters could be made to any width and height, digital type has to conform to multiples of the smallest unit: the pixel. Every character has to be a certain number of pixels wide and high. This is not a problem when the letters are made up of 600 pixels per inch, as is the case with modern laser printers—those pixels are not discernible to our eyes, and we are happy to believe that we are looking at smooth curves instead of little squares fitted into tight grids. (3)

Typographers and graphic designers often choose typefaces for the very same reason they might fancy a person: They just like that person. For more scientifically-minded people, however, there are specific measurements, components, details, and proportions to describe various parts of a letter. While these won't tell you what makes a typeface good, they will at least give you the right words to use when you discuss the benefits of a particular face over another. You can say "I hate the x-height on Such-a-Gothic" or "These descenders just don't work for me" or "Please, may I see something with a smaller cap height?" and you'll know what you are talking about. (◂2)

Scientists have not been content with just calling the human face "beautiful" if it meets certain ideals, or "ugly" if it doesn't. They had to go out and measure proportions of nose to jaw, forehead to chin, and so on to establish why some faces are more appealing than others.

*EXPLORATION 19* PARAGRAPH INDICATOR » COLUMN WIDTH
Column 1 » 9/15.5 FF ThreeSix Regular : Tracking +30/1000 em
Column 2 » 7/16 FF ThreeSix Medium : Tracking +30/1000 em
Space Between » 4 pts Rule » 2 pt

## Opposite page

1 In the first column, every other paragraph is narrower by 4 ems. The second paragraph is narrowed on the left, the fourth on the right.

2 Text in the second column is the same column width, but the colophon below is wider. This allows the two columns to interlock with each other.

3 Gutter widths are the same at top and bottom.

## This page

4 The title is nestled into the text, aligning to the same two vertical grid lines used for the text blocks below.

5 Every other paragraph is set in italic and in a narrower column width. Note that italic text type often needs a bit more tracking than roman.

4▸

# TYPE BUILDS CHARACTER

Typographers and graphic designers often choose typefaces for the very same reason they might fancy a person: They just like that person. For more scientifically-minded people, however, there are specific measurements, components, details, and proportions to describe various parts of a letter. While these won't tell you what makes a typeface good, they will at least give you the right words to use when you discuss the benefits of a particular face over another. You can say "I hate the x-height on Such-a-Gothic" or "These descenders just don't work for me" or "Please, may I see something with a smaller cap height?" and you'll know what you are talking about.

5▸ *While metal letters could be made to any width and height, digital type has to conform to multiples of the smallest unit: the pixel. Every character has to be a certain number of pixels wide and high. This is not a problem when the letters are made up of 600 pixels per inch, as is the case with modern laser printers—those pixels are not discernible to our eyes, and we are happy to believe that we are looking at smooth curves instead of little squares fitted into tight grids.*

On most screens, only 72 pixels make up one inch. We could see each and every one of them, if engineers hadn't already found ways around that. Computer screens, however, are not where we read most of our type these days. Smart phones, computers, and tablets all have high-resolutions screens, but microwave ovens, espresso makers, and all the other gadgets around us all still use small and modest displays. And the type unmistakably consists of bitmaps, which means that an 8-point letter is actually made up of eight pixels. If we allow six pixels above the baseline, including accents, and two below for descenders, that'll leave only three or four pixels for a lowercase character. In spite of these restrictions, there are hundreds of bitmap fonts, all different from one another by only a few pixels, but enough to prove that typographic variety cannot be suppressed by technological constraints.

*Rhythm and contrast keep coming up when discussing good music and good typographic design. They are concepts that also apply to spoken language, as anyone who has had to sit through a monotonous lecture will attest; the same tone, volume and speed of speech will put even the most interested listener into dreamland. Every now and again the audience needs to be shaken, either by a change in voice or pitch, by a question being posed, or by the speaker talking very quietly and then suddenly shouting. An occasional joke also works, just as the use of a funny typeface can liven up a page.*

There's only one thing worse than a badly told joke, and that is a joke told twice. Whatever typographic device you come up with, don't let it turn into a gimmick. A well-coordinated range of fonts will give you the scope for contrast as well as rhythm, and will keep you secure in the bosom of a well-behaved family.

EXPLORATION 19
PARAGRAPH INDICATOR: COLUMN WIDTH
(TYPESET BY CANDICE CHEUNG)

TITLE:
24PT SAUNA AND 26PT SAUNA, NO TRACKING

FIRST PARAGRAPH:
7/14 FF CLIFFORD, TRACKING +40/1000 EM

ALTERNATE PARAGRAPHS:
7/14 FF CLIFFORD ITALIC, TRACKING +45/1000 EM

EXP
19.2

## FF ThreeSix

Bitmapped type goes back to the personal computer's beginnings, and then, even after the pixel grid wasn't a technical limitation, many retro typefaces relived that age, with all sorts of fonts based on rigid geometric systems. So, the idea isn't new, but this family, carefully planned by esteemed designers Paul McNeil and Hamish Muir in 2011, exceeds other attempts in its sheer number of variations and surprising readability.

## Sauna

Designed in 2002 at the Amsterdam-based collective Underware, this warm, relaxed face lives up to its name. It comes with a large set of swashes and ligatures inspired by ornamental calligraphy but true to its informality. Sauna went on to win multiple awards and set a long-running trend for soft-ended sanses.

## FF Clifford

In 1994, Akira Kobayashi began to draw what could be seen as a reaction to the many feeble text faces of that period. Whereas other digital serifs were anemic facsimiles unsuited for modern printing, this was based on sturdy Scottish and English type of the 1700s, redrawn with contemporary presses and paper in mind. The lack of bold is a nod to its prime purpose as a book face.

**This page**

1 Measures vary randomly and two of the paragraphs are set with more generous leading than the others.

2 The title is nestled into the negative space created by the changes in column widths.

3 The amount of leading between paragraphs is the same as the leading on the paragraph below.

**Opposite page**

4 Starting in the second paragraph, the text is exdented to the width of the column above it and each paragraph sits in a progressively narrower measure.

5 The top baseline of the colophon aligns with the last baseline of the text. Although text in the colophon is flush left/rag right, the rules between sections give it a boxy feel that echoes the blocky text type above.

**Iwan Stencil**
Like Futura Black from the same year, Jan Tschichold's 1929 design uses a kit of parts to build an alphabet, but where Futura Black is bold and brash Iwan Stencil is almost airy and delicate. There are more curves here and the negative spaces between shapes (called "bridges") are much wider.

**FF Strada**
With low contrast, open apertures, and short extenders, Albert Pinggera's 2002 face ushered in an era of fresh sans serif families meant for contemporary corporate communication. It is capable of delivering serious financial data, but it also has a friendly, customer-facing personality hiding in its soft corners and lively italic.

**FF Dax**
In 1983, Hans Reichel designed Barmeno, a Humanist sans serif with an unusual postmodern feature: it had no spurs (the parts of the stem that extend beyond bowls). He returned to the idea in 1995 with FF Dax, a minimalist reinterpretation with less stroke contrast and no rounded ends. The new face became so popular for branding and packaging it sparked a spurless trend with many followers.

Ever since people have been writing things down, they have had to consider their audience before actually putting pen to paper: letters would have to look different depending on whether they were to be read by mainly other people (in official documents or inscriptions), just one other person (in a letter), or only the writer (in a notebook or diary). There would be less room for guesswork if letter shapes were made more formal as the diversity of the readership expanded.

(1▸) Some of the first messages to be read by a large number of people were rendered not by pens but by chisels. Large inscriptions on monuments in ancient Rome were carefully planned, with letters drawn on the stone with a brush before they were chiseled. Even if white-out had existed in those days, it would not have helped to remove mistakes made in stone. A bit of planning was also more important then, since stonemasons were sometimes more expendable than slabs of marble or granite.

# (2▸) TYPE BUILDS CHARACTER

Graphic design and typography are complicated activities, but even the simple projects benefit from thinking about the problem, forming a mental picture of the solution, and then carefully planning the steps between.

Scientists have not been content with just calling the human face "beautiful" if it meets certain ideals, or "ugly" if it doesn't. They had to go out and measure proportions of nose to jaw, forehead to chin, and so on to establish why some faces are more appealing than others.

(3▸)

Typographers and graphic designers often choose typefaces for the very same reason they might fancy a person: They just like that person. For more scientifically-minded people, however, there are specific measurements, components, details, and proportions to describe various parts of a letter. While these won't tell you what makes a typeface good, they will at least give you the right words to use when you discuss the benefits of a particular face over another. You can say "I hate the x-height on Such-a-Gothic" or "These descenders just don't work for me" or "Please, may I see something with a smaller cap height?" and you'll know what you are talking about.

EXPLORATION NINETEEN // Column Width (typeset by Vincent Lo) Title: 32/29 Iwan Stencil // Text: 8/14 FF Strada, tracking +35/1000 em and 8/20 FF Strada, tracking +35/1000 em

EXP **19.3**

**Ever since people have been writing things down, they have had to consider their audience before actually putting pen to paper: letters would have to look different depending on whether they were to be read by mainly other people (in official documents or inscriptions), just one other person (in a letter), or only the writer (in a notebook or diary). There would be less room for guesswork if letter shapes were made more formal as the diversity of the readership expanded.**

4▸ Some of the first messages to be read by a large number of people were rendered not by pens but by chisels. Large inscriptions on monuments in ancient Rome were carefully planned, with letters drawn on the stone with a brush before they were chiseled. Even if white-out had existed in those days, it would not have helped to remove mistakes made in stone. A bit of planning was also more important then, since stonemasons were sometimes more expendable than slabs of marble or granite.

Graphic design and typography are complicated activities, but even the simple projects benefit from thinking about the problem, forming a mental picture of the solution, and then carefully planning the steps between.

Scientists have not been content with just calling the human face "beautiful" if it meets certain ideals, or "ugly" if it doesn't. They had to go out and measure proportions of nose to jaw, forehead to chin, and so on to establish why some faces are more appealing than others.

Typographers and graphic designers often choose typefaces for the very same reason they might fancy a person: They just like that person. For more scientifically-minded people, however, there are specific measurements, components, details, and proportions to describe various parts of a letter. While these won't tell you what makes a typeface good, they will at least give you the right words to use when you discuss the benefits of a particular face over another. You can say "I hate the x-height on Such-a-Gothic" or "These descenders just don't work for me" or "Please, may I see something with a smaller cap height?" and you'll know what you are talking about.

EXPLORATION 19 ◂5

PARAGRAPH INDICATOR
COLUMN WIDTH (TYPESET BY CHIHARU TANAKA)

7/12 FF DAX WIDE BLACK
TRACKING +45/1000 EM

7/12 FF DAX BOLD
TRACKING +45/1000 EM

7/12 FF DAX WIDE MEDIUM
TRACKING +45/1000 EM

7/12 FF DAX REGULAR
TRACKING +45/1000 EM

7/12 FF DAX CONDENSED LIGHT
TRACKING +45/1000 EM

## Paragraph Indicator: Interlock

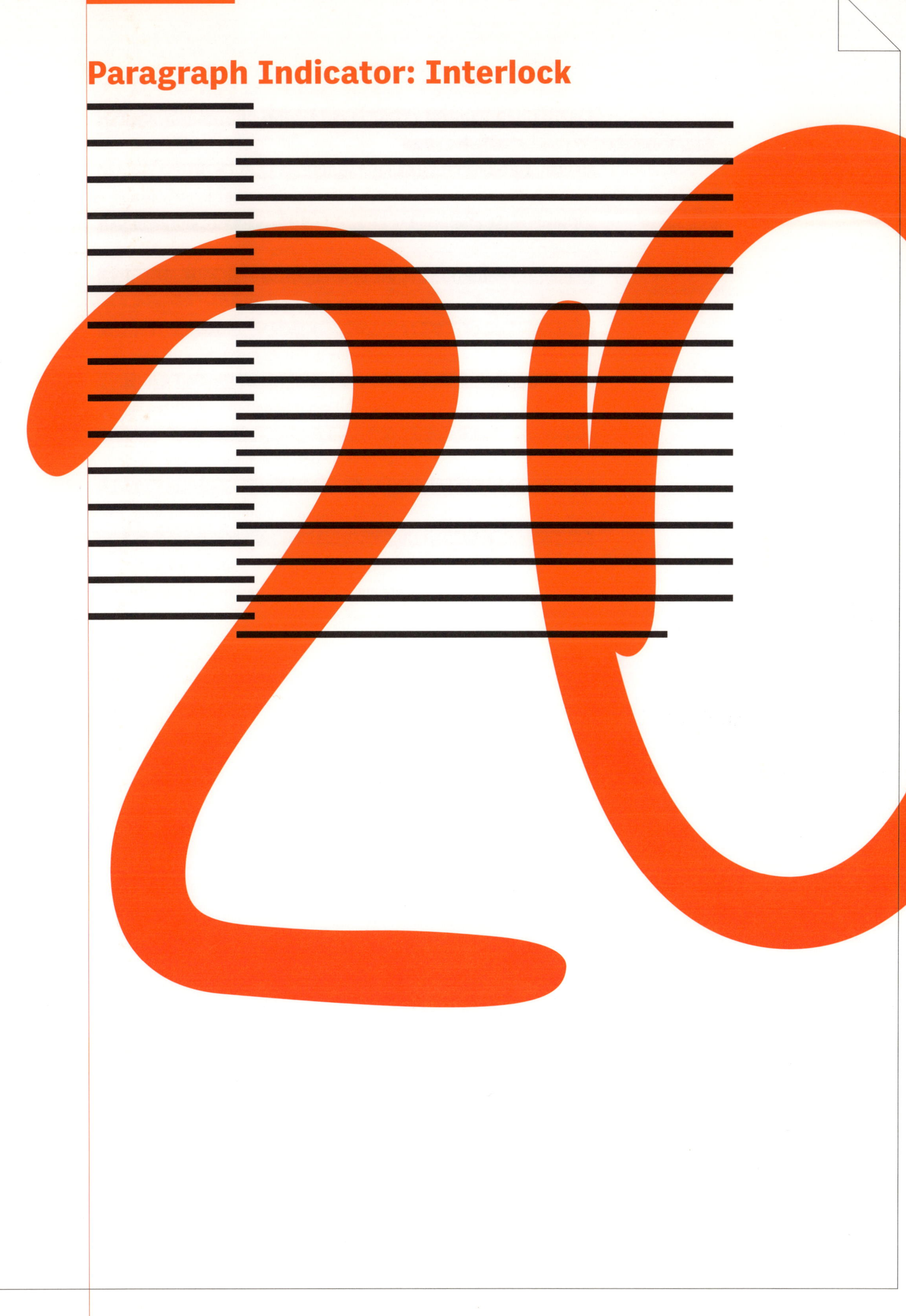

**This page**

1 The title is set to the width of the first column.

2 The byline is reversed out of a black bar and exdented to differentiate it from the similarly set type in the first paragraph.

3 The black bar on the last line of the first paragraph is extended to the width of the interlocking column.

**Opposite page**

4 The same graphic element is set at the same size and used between paragraphs in both columns.

5 Leading is quite loose so that lines can interlock comfortably. Using the same leading on both columns allows you to interlock lines like a zipper. Although legibility is compromised in the interest of visual expression and creativity here, the strong contrast of typographic color in the two columns helps a reader more easily follow the text.

**Ohm**

There have been attempts to bend the continuous shapes of pipes or tubing into letterforms, but most don't make great typefaces. Ohm, by Tal Leming in 2009, is the most successful design in this genre since ITC Neon and Elektrik of the 1970s. So successful, in fact, that it's been used to make real neon signs.

**Locator**

This face designed by Eric Olson in 2003 gets its name from attributes that are well tuned for wayfinding systems: clean, clear shapes, open apertures, and a generous width and x-height. But it's not just a sign font. Locator's six weights with italics offer a lot of flexibility.

**FF Typestar**

This face comes from Steffen Sauerteig of the irreverent design studio eBoy. A playful take on the letters from mid-20th-century typewriters and computers, it somehow seems to be both rigid and animated at once. The monospaced OCR subfamily is closer to its references but retains Sauerteig's amiable spirit.

# 1 TYPE **BUILDS** CHARACTER

2 BY ERIK SPIEKERMANN

**EVER SINCE PEOPLE HAVE BEEN WRITING THINGS DOWN, THEY HAVE HAD TO CONSIDER THEIR AUDIENCE BEFORE ACTUALLY PUTTING PEN TO PAPER: LETTERS WOULD HAVE TO LOOK DIFFERENT DEPENDING ON WHETHER THEY WERE TO BE READ BY MAINLY OTHER PEOPLE (IN OFFICIAL DOCUMENTS OR INSCRIPTIONS), JUST ONE OTHER PERSON (IN A LETTER), OR ONLY THE WRITER (IN A NOTEBOOK OR DIARY). THERE WOULD BE LESS ROOM FOR GUESSWORK IF LETTER SHAPES WERE MADE MORE FORMAL AS THE DIVERSITY OF READERSHIP EXPANDED.** 3

Some of the first messages to be read by a large number of people were rendered not by pens but by chisels. Large inscriptions on monuments in ancient Rome were carefully planned, with letters drawn on the stone with a brush before they were chiseled. Even if white-out had existed in those days, it would not have helped to remove mistakes made in stone. A bit of planning was also more important then, since stonemasons were sometimes more expendable than slabs of marble or granite. ❖ Graphic design and typography are complicated activities, but even the simple projects benefit from thinking about the problem, forming a mental picture of the solution, and then carefully planning the steps between. ❖ While metal letters could be made to any width and height, digital type has to conform to multiples of the smallest unit: the pixel. Every character has to be a certain number of pixels wide and high. This is not a problem when the letters are made up of 600 pixels per inch, as is the case with modern laser printers—those pixels are not discernible to our eyes, and we are happy to believe that we are looking at smooth curves instead of little squares fitted into tight grids. ❖

EXPLORATION 20

**INTERLOCK**

**TITLE**
27.5pt Ohm Light
27.5pt Ohm Bold
tracking +70/1000 em

**BYLINE**
6pt Locator Bold
tracking +100/1000 em

**PARAGRAPH 1**
8/32 Locator Bold
tracking +80/1000 em

**PARAGRAPH 2**
8.5/32 Locator Medium
tracking +40/1000 em

**TEXT + GRAPHIC ELEMENT**
8.5/16 Locator Medium
tracking +40/1000 em

**Ever since people have been writing things down, they have had to con-
sider their audience before actually putting pen to paper: letters would
have to look different depending on whether they were to be read by
mainly other people (in official documents or inscriptions), just one
other person (in a letter), or only the writer (in a notebook or diary).
There would be less room for guesswork if letter shapes were made more
4 formal as the diversity of the readership expanded. ■ Some of the first
messages to be read by a large number of people were rendered not by
pens but by chisels. Large inscriptions on monuments in ancient Rome
were carefully planned, with letters drawn on the stone with a brush
before they were chiseled. Even if white-out had existed in those days, it
would not have helped to remove mistakes made in stone. A bit of planning was also more important then, since stonemasons were sometimes
more expendable than slabs of marble or granite. ■ Graphic design and
typography are complicated activities, but even the simple projects benefit from thinking about the problem, forming a mental picture of the
solution, and then carefully planning the steps between.**

Typographers and graphic designers often choose typefaces for the very same reason they 5
might fancy a person: They just like that person. For more scientifically-minded people, however, there are specific measurements, components, details, and proportions to describe various parts of a letter. While these won't tell you what makes a typeface good, they will at least give you the right words to use when you discuss the benefits of a particular face over another. You can say "I hate the x-height on Such-a-Gothic" or "These descenders just don't work for me" or "Please, may I see something with a smaller cap height?" and you'll know what you are talking about. ■ While metal letters could be made to any width and height, digital type has to conform to multiples of the smallest unit: the pixel. Every character has to be a certain number of pixels wide and high. This is not a problem when the letters are made up of 600 pixels per inch, as is the case with modern laser printers—those pixels are not discernible to our eyes, and we are happy to believe that we are looking at smooth curves instead of little squares fitted into tight grids.

EXPLORATION 20 :: PARAGRAPH INDICATOR: INTERLOCK :: 8/24 FF TYPESTAR BLACK, TRACKING +40/1000 EM :: 7/24 FF TYPESTAR NORMAL, TRACKING +50/1000 EM

EXP
**20.3**

**This page**

1. The first paragraph is set all alone in the first column. The bold lowercase small caps and its top line being higher than the second column signal it as the starting point for a reader.
2. The tiny amount of interlocking, only at the very edges of each column, makes for easier reading.

**Opposite page**

3. On this rather active composition, the title pops forward because of its exdent. Its baseline is aligned to the second baseline of the text in the first paragraph.
4. The order of reading is revealed to some extent by progressive changes in size and weight.

**FF Seria Sans**
Released in 2000 along with FF Seria, Martin Majoor's elegant sans is unusual amid its serifless contemporaries, which are commonly corporate faces boasting a large lowercase and "neutral" voice. FF Seria Sans is thus an ideal pick for modern, poetic content that has room to breathe.

**FF Seria**
With FF Scala, Martin Majoor adapted Oldstyle type to the digital age. In 1996, he returned to the same drawing board but allowed the letters to stretch out, Renaissance style, with a low x-height and long extenders. FF Seria was released in 2000 and was awarded by the ISTD and ATypI typographic organizations.

**FF Max**
Danish designer Morten Olsen began this work by looking at Eurostile, but only the squareness of Aldo Novarese's face remained. Not retro in any way, FF Max is a 21st-century design with a look entirely its own: a stout stance, taut curves, and many unique forms, including the spurless 'a,m,n,r.' It was released in 2003 and followed by a Demi Serif a year later.

EXPLORATION 20 :: PARAGRAPH INDICATOR: INTERLOCK

FIRST PARAGRAPH: 7/20 FF SERIA SANS BOLD. TRACKING +85/1000 EM :: TEXT: 8/20 FF SERIA. TRACKING +45/1000 EM

EVER SINCE PEOPLE HAVE BEEN WRITING THINGS DOWN, THEY HAVE HAD TO CONSIDER THEIR AUDIENCE BEFORE ACTUALLY PUTTING PEN TO PAPER: LETTERS WOULD HAVE TO LOOK DIFFERENT DEPENDING ON WHETHER THEY WERE TO BE READ BY MAINLY OTHER PEOPLE (IN OFFICIAL DOCUMENTS OR INSCRIPTIONS), JUST ONE OTHER PERSON (IN A LETTER), OR ONLY THE WRITER (IN A NOTEBOOK OR DIARY). THERE WOULD BE LESS ROOM FOR GUESSWORK IF LETTER SHAPES WERE MADE MORE FORMAL AS THE DIVERSITY OF THE READERSHIP EXPANDED.

Some of the first messages to be read by a large number of people were rendered not by pens but by chisels. Large inscriptions on monuments in ancient Rome were carefully planned, with letters drawn on the stone with a brush before they were chiseled. Even if white-out had existed in those days, it would not have helped to remove mistakes made in stone. A bit of planning was also more important then, since stonemasons were sometimes more expendable than slabs of marble or granite. ✚ Graphic design and typography are complicated activities, but even the simple projects benefit from thinking about the problem, forming a mental picture of the solution, and then carefully planning the steps between. ✚ Typographers and graphic designers often choose typefaces for the very same reason they might fancy a person: They just like that person. For more scientifically-minded people, however, there are specific measurements, components, details, and proportions to describe various parts of a letter. While these won't tell you what makes a typeface good, they will at least give you the right words to use when you discuss the benefits of a particular face over another. You can say "I hate the x-height on Such-a-Gothic" or "These descenders just don't work for me" or "Please, may I see something with a smaller cap height?" and you'll know what you are talking about.

2

## 3▸ TYPE BUILDS CHARACTER

Ever since people have been writing things down, they have had to consider their audience before actually putting pen to paper: letters would have to look different depending on whether they were to be read by mainly other people (in official documents or inscriptions), just one other person (in a letter), or only the writer (in a notebook or diary). There would be less room for guesswork if letter shapes were made more formal as the diversity of the readership expanded.

***Some of the first messages to be read by a large number of people were rendered not by pens but by chisels. Large inscriptions on monuments in ancient Rome were carefully planned, with letters drawn on the stone with a brush before they were chiseled. Even if white-out had existed in those days, it would not have helped to remove mistakes made in stone. A bit of planning was also more important then, since stonemasons were sometimes more expendable than slabs of marble or granite.***

Graphic design and typography are complicated activities, but even the simple projects benefit from thinking about the problem, forming a mental picture of the solution, and then carefully planning the steps between.

*Scientists have not been content with just calling the human face "beautiful" if it meets certain ideals, or "ugly" if it doesn't. They had to go out and measure proportions of nose to jaw, forehead to chin, and so on to establish why some faces are more appealing than others.* ◂4

**[Exploration 20] Interlock**
► title: 10/27 FF Max Fat Italic, tracking +40/1000 em
► first paragraph: 10/27 FF Max Extra Light, tracking +40/1000 em
► second paragraph: 7/27 FF Max Black Italic, tracking +40/1000 em
► third paragraph: 7/27 FF Max Regular, tracking +40/1000 em
► fourth paragraph: 7/27 FF Max Extra Light Italic, tracking +40/1000 em

## Paragraph Indicator: Overlap

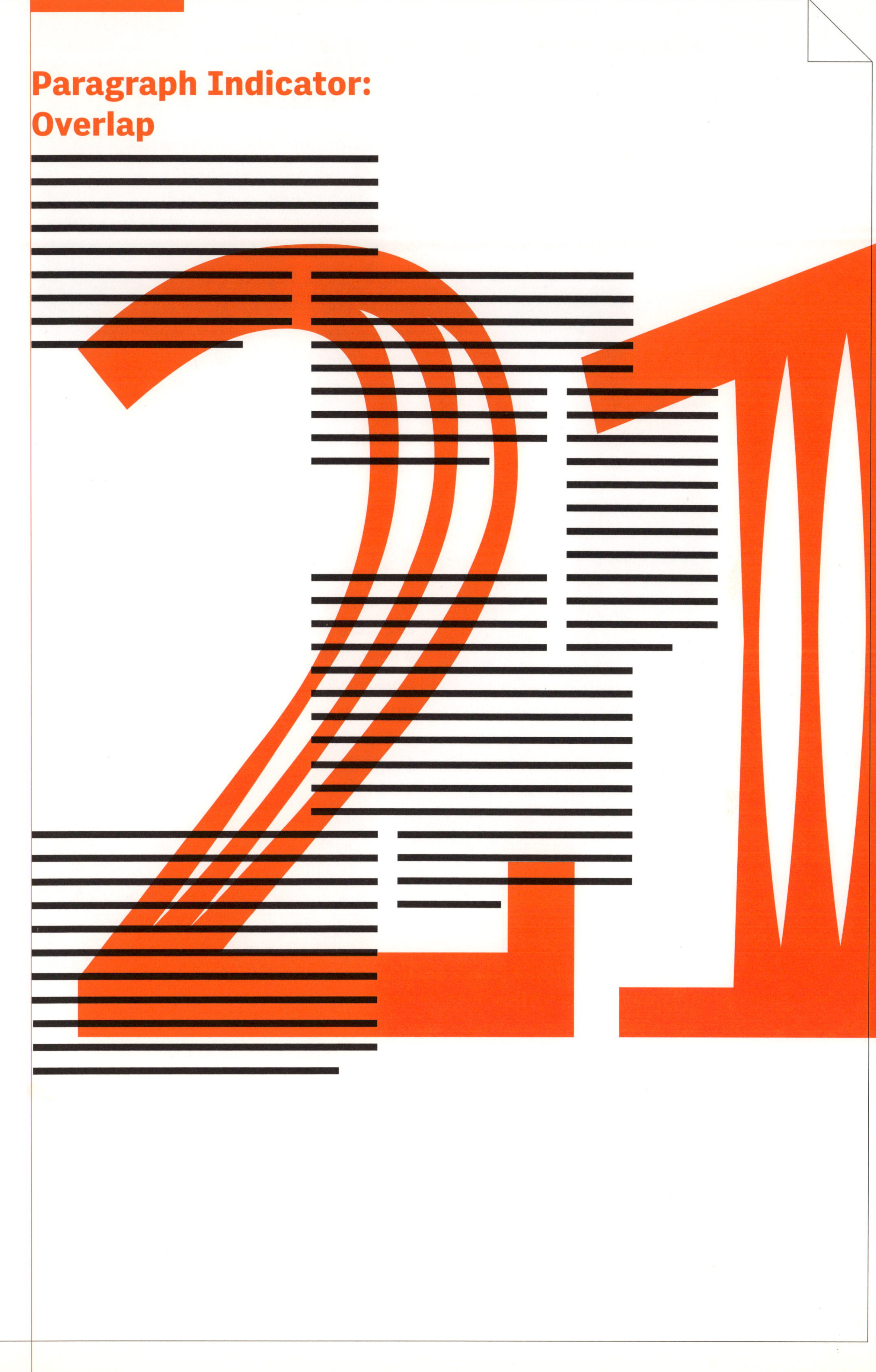

1▸

# TYPE *builds* CHARACTER

2▸ ■ Ever since people have been writing things down, they have had to consider their audience before actually putting pen to paper: letters would have to look different depending on whether they were to be read by mainly other people (in official documents or inscriptions), just one other person (in a letter), or only the writer (in a notebook or diary). There would be less room for guesswork if letter shapes were made more formal as the diversity of the readership expanded. ■ Some of the first messages to be read by a large number of people were rendered not by pens but by chisels. Large inscriptions on monuments in ancient Rome were carefully planned, with letters drawn on the stone with a brush before they were chiseled. Even if white-out had existed in those days, it would not have helped to remove mistakes made in stone. A bit of planning was also more important then, since stonemasons were sometimes more expendable than slabs of marble or granite. ■ Graphic design and typography are complicated activities, but even the simple projects benefit from thinking about the problem, forming a mental picture of the solution, and then carefully planning the steps between. ■ Scientists have not been content with just calling the human face "beautiful" if it meets certain ideals, or "ugly" if it doesn't. They had to go out and measure proportions of nose to jaw, forehead to chin, and so on to establish why some faces are more appealing than others. ■ Typographers and graphic designers often choose typefaces for the very same reason they might fancy a person: They just like that person. For more scientifically-minded people, however, there are specific measurements, components, details, and proportions to describe various parts of a letter. While these won't tell you what makes a typeface good, they will at least give you the right words to use when you discuss the benefits of a particular face over another. You can say "I hate the x-height on Such-a-Gothic" or "These descenders just don't work for me" or "Please, may I see something with a smaller cap height?" and you'll know what you are talking about.

***■■ Rhythm and contrast keep coming up when discussing good music and good typographic design. They are concepts that also apply to spoken language, as anyone who has had to sit through a monotonous lecture will attest; the same tone, volume and speed of speech will put even the most interested listener into dreamland. Every now and again the audience needs to be shaken, either by a change in voice or pitch, by a question being posed, or by the speaker talking very quietly and then suddenly shouting. An occasional joke also works, just as the use of a funny typeface can liven up a page. ■■ There's only one thing worse than a badly told joke, and that is a joke told twice. Whatever typographic device you come up with, don't let it turn into a gimmick. A well-coordinated range of fonts will give you the scope for contrast as well as rhythm, and will keep you secure in the bosom of a well-behaved family.*** ◂4

3

■■■ *1* The official Roman alphabet, as seen on the Trajan Column in Rome, has never gone out of fashion. ■■■ *2* When communications became more international, typefaces that were more universal were in demand. Today fraktur, gothic and similar styles are only used to evoke the feeling of a bygone era, for example on the banner of newspapers such as *The New York Times*. ■■■ *3* Many digital typefaces evoke the timeless beauty of ancient inscriptions and early printing types. Trajan, designed by Carol Twombly in 1990, is a good example.

3

**EXPLORATION 21 PARAGRAPH INDICATOR: OVERLAP ■■■■ TITLE: 60PT AND 25PT HARRIET DISPLAY BLACK (ALL CAPS), 25PT HARRIET DISPLAY BLACK ITALIC ■■■■ FIRST COLUMN: 8/15 HARRIET TEXT LIGHT, TRACKING +65/1000 EM ■■■■ SECOND COLUMN: 10/16 HARRIET TEXT ITALIC, TRACKING +50/1000 EM ■■■■ THIRD COLUMN: 6.5/16 HARRIET TEXT REGULAR, TRACKING +40/1000 EM**

(5) # TYPE BUILDS CHARACTER

Erik Spiekermann

**Ever since people have been writing things down, they have had to consider their audience before actually putting pen to paper: letters would have to look different depending on whether they were to be read by mainly other people (in official documents or inscriptions), just one other person (in a letter), or only the writer (in a notebook or diary). There would be less room for guesswork if letter shapes were made more formal as the diversity of the readership expanded.**

Some of the first messages to be read by a large number of people were rendered not by pens but by chisels. Large inscriptions on monuments in ancient Rome were carefully planned, with letters drawn on the stone with a brush before they were chiseled. Even if white-out had existed in those days, it would not have helped to remove mistakes made in stone. A bit of planning was also more important then, since stonemasons were sometimes more expendable than slabs of marble or
(6) granite. ⌘ Graphic design and typography are complicated activities, but even the simple projects benefit from thinking about the problem, forming a mental picture of the solution, and then carefully planning the steps between. ⌘ Scientists have not been content with just calling the human face "beautiful" if it meets certain ideals, or "ugly" if it doesn't. They had to go out and measure proportions of nose to jaw, forehead to chin, and so on to establish why some faces are more appealing than others. ⌘ Typographers and graphic designers often choose typefaces for the very same reason they might fancy a person: They just like that person. For more scientifically-minded people, however, there are specific measurements, components, details, and proportions to describe various parts of a letter. While these won't tell you what makes a typeface good, they will at least give you the right words to use when you discuss the benefits of a particular face over another. You can say "I hate the x-height on Such-a-Gothic" or "These descenders just don't work for me" or "Please, may I see something with a smaller cap height?" and you'll know what you are talking about. ⌘ While metal letters could be made to any width and height, digital type has to conform to multiples of the smallest unit: the pixel. Every character has to be a certain number of pixels wide and high. This is not a problem when the letters are made up of 600 pixels per inch, as is the case with modern
laser printers—those pixels (7)
are not discernible to our eyes, and we are happy to believe that we are looking at smooth curves instead of little squares fitted into tight grids. ⌘ On most screens, only 72 pixels make up one inch. We could see each and every one of them, if engineers hadn't already found ways around that. Computer screens, however, are not where we read most of our type these days. Smart phones, computers, and tablets all have high-resolutions screens, but microwave ovens, espresso makers, and all the other gadgets around us all still use small and modest displays. And the type unmistakably consists of bitmaps, which means that an 8-point letter is actually made up of eight pixels. If we allow six pixels above the baseline, including accents, and two below for descenders, that'll leave only three or four pixels for a lowercase character.

EXPLORATION 21: OVERLAP

TITLE: 19PT FF COCON, TRACKING +40/1000 EM

BYLINE: 7/11 SASSOON PRIMARY, TRACKING +30/1000 EM

FIRST PARAGRAPH: 8/13.5 FF COCON, TRACKING +25/1000 EM

TEXT: 7/11 SASSOON PRIMARY, TRACKING +30/1000 EM

**Opposite page**

1 To look aligned, the large capital T "hangs" beyond the flush left edge of the text block. Any display size letter whose side is a point (such as T or W) or an arc (O or C) requires optical alignment.

2 Paragraphs are indicated by a single square bullet in the first text block, two bullets in the second, and three in the third.

3 The space below each column is the same.

4 The last line in each block fills the full measure for a neat appearance.

**This page**

5 The title and first paragraph are set in a bolder face. The first paragraph overlaps the columns and its size and boldness signal that it is where a reader should start.

6 Perfectly custom-shaped text blocks can best be achieved by using graphic elements between paragraphs without returns.

7 An em dash is used for a break in thought within a sentence. Proper use of punctuation is a mark of typographic excellence. When in doubt, consult an authoritative style guide such as *The Chicago Manual of Style*.

**Harriet**
Released in 2012, Jackson Cavanaugh's family draws inspiration from Baskerville and Century. With optical sizes as well as many weights and a full character set, it is a highly versatile type family.

**Sassoon Primary**
Rosemary Sassoon did pioneering research into the best methods for teaching children reading and writing. This face, with its simple curves and gentle slant inspired by her handwriting models, is the core of a range of fonts designed with Adrian Williams from 1988 to 1998.

**FF Cocon**
Evert Bloemsma is known for his unconventional methods for serious text faces, such as FF Avance and FF Balance. This face (1998) isn't typical either, but it's far less serious. Its soft strokes are downright cozy and have predictably appeared on packaging for tissues and sweets.

**This page**

1 Although this column is higher on the page, it's also farther to the right and in a lighter weight, both signals that it is not the first paragraph of the text.

2 While the rest of the text is in justified blocks, this last paragraph is set in a very narrow column flush left/rag right.

**Opposite page**

3 Changes in weight, tracking, and overlapping are all combined to create this expressive and unconventional setting.

4 Each line is set to a custom length using soft returns.

**FF Plus Sans**
Much like FF Unit and Apex Sans, also released in 2003, the goal of Jürgen Huber's FF Plus Sans is a gothic for the 21st century: modern, clean, stripped of frills and overt personality while remaining approachable to contemporary readers. In the FontFont sans serif tradition, it also delivers small caps and multiple figure styles for text setting.

**Maxime**
This serif, designed by Éric de Berranger in 1999, has roots in French Oldstyles that are different from the Garamond model that is more commonly used. The lowercase is larger, counters are more open, contrast is lower, and serifs are more blunt and sculpted. All of this makes Maxime more of a small-size specialist but also better suited for screen use. It includes dozens of mildly decorative ligatures and swash alternates for starting and ending sentences with a bit of flair.

**FF Chambers Sans**
Verena Gerlach was inspired by two different sources during the development of FF Chambers Sans: a 17th-century engraved roman and a simplified gothic found on enamel street signs in Basel. This amalgam produced a peculiar form all its own, a monolinear, squared sans with swashes and ligatures usually reserved for calligraphic serifs.

**Ever since people have been writing things down, they have had to consider their audience before actually putting pen to paper: letters would have to look different depending on whether they were to be read by mainly other people (in official documents or inscriptions), just one other person (in a letter), or only the writer (in a notebook or diary). There would be less room for guesswork if letter shapes were made more formal as the diversity of the readership expanded.** Some of the first messages to be read by a large number of people were rendered not by pens but by chisels. Large inscriptions on monuments in ancient Rome were carefully planned, with letters drawn on the stone with a brush before they were chiseled. Even if white-out had existed in those days, it would not have helped to remove mistakes made in stone. A bit of planning was also more important then, since stonemasons were sometimes more expendable than slabs of marble or granite. **Graphic design and typography are complicated activities, but even the simple projects benefit from thinking about the problem, forming a mental picture of the solution, and then carefully planning the steps between. Scientists have not been content with just calling the human face "beautiful" if it meets certain ideals, or "ugly" if it doesn't. They had to go out and measure proportions of nose to jaw, forehead to chin, and so on to establish why some faces are more appealing than others.**

(1) Typographers and graphic designers often choose typefaces for the very same reason they might fancy a person: They just like that person. For more scientifically-minded people, however, there are specific measurements, components, details, and proportions to describe various parts of a letter. While these won't tell you what makes a typeface good, they will at least give you the right words to use when you discuss the benefits of a particular face over another. You can say "I hate the x-height on Such-a-Gothic" or "These descenders just don't work for me" or "Please, may I see something with a smaller cap height?" and you'll know what you are talking about. **While metal letters could be made to any width and height, digital type has to conform to multiples of the smallest unit: the pixel. Every character has to be a certain number of pixels wide and high. This is not a problem when the letters are made up of 600 pixels per inch, as is the case with modern laser printers—those pixels are not discernible to our eyes, and we are happy to believe that we are looking at smooth curves instead of little squares fitted into tight grids.**

***On most screens, only 72 pixels make up one inch. We could see each and every one of them, if engineers hadn't already found ways around that. Computer screens, however, are not where we read most of our type these days. Smart phones, computers, and tablets all have high-resolutions screens, but microwave ovens, espresso makers, and all the other gadgets around us all still use small and modest displays. And the type unmistakably consists of bitmaps, which means that an 8-point letter is actually made up of eight pixels.*** (2)

*Exploration 21: Overlap*

*First Paragraph: 8/15 FF Plus Sans Extra Bold, tracking +30/1000 em*

*Alternate Paragraphs: 8/15 Maxime, tracking +25/1000 em*

*Last Paragraph: 7/15 FF Plus Sans Extra Bold Italic, tracking +30/1000 em*

EXP **21.3**

3▸ Graphic design and typography are complicated activities, but even the simple projects benefit from thinking about the problem, forming a mental picture of the solution, and then carefully planning the steps between.

*Scientists have not been content with just calling the human face "beautiful" if it meets certain ideals, or "ugly" if it doesn't. They had to go out and measure proportions of nose to jaw, forehead to chin, and so on to establish why some faces are more appealing than others.*

**Typographers and graphic designers often choose typefaces for the very same reason they might fancy a person: They just like that person. For more scientifically-minded people, however, there are specific measurements, components, details, and proportions to describe various parts of a letter. While these will not tell you what makes a typeface good, they will at least give you the right words to use when you discuss the benefits of a particular face over another. You can say "I hate the x-height on Such-a-Gothic" or "These descenders just don't work for me" or "Please, may I see something with a smaller cap height?" and you'll know what you are talking about.**

Ever since people have been writing things down, they have had to consider their audience before actually putting pen to paper: letters would have to look different depending on whether they were to be read by mainly other people (in official documents or inscriptions), just one other person (in a letter), or only the writer (in a notebook or diary). ◂4 There would be less room for guesswork if letter shapes were made more formal as the diversity of the readership expanded.

**Some of the first messages to be read by a large number of people were rendered not by pens but by chisels. Large inscriptions on monuments in ancient Rome were carefully planned, with letter drawn on the stone with a brush before they were chiseled.**

**T Y P E B U I L D S C H A R A C T E R**

b y E r i k S p i e k e r m a n n

**Even if white-out had existed in those days, it would not have helped to remove mistakes made in stone. A bit of planning was also more important then, since stonemasons were sometimes more expendable than slabs of marble or granite.**

While metal letters could be made to any width and height, digital type has to conform to multiples of the smallest unit: the pixel. Every character has to be a certain number of pixels wide and high. This is not a problem when the letters are made up of 600 pixels per inch, as is the case with modern laser printers—those pixels are not discernible to our eyes, and we are happy to believe that we are looking at smooth curves instead of little squares fitted into tight grids.

**EXPLORATION 21 Overlap**

**TITLE:** 7/32 FF Chambers Sans Black, tracking +800/1000 em

**BYLINE:** 7/32 FF Chambers Sans, tracking +800/1000 em

**PARAGRAPH 1:** 7/11 FF Chambers Sans, tracking +300/1000 em

**PARAGRAPH 2:** 7/11 FF Chambers Sans Bold, tracking +200/1000 em

**PARAGRAPH 3:** 7/11 FF Chambers Sans Black, tracking +450/1000 em

**PARAGRAPH 4:** 7/11 FF Chambers Sans, tracking +70/1000 em

**PARAGRAPH 5:** 7/11 FF Chambers Sans Medium Italic, tracking +30/1000 em

**PARAGRAPH 6:** 7/11 FF Chambers Sans Bold, tracking +20/1000 em

**PARAGRAPH 7:** 7/11 FF Chambers Sans, tracking +250/1000 em

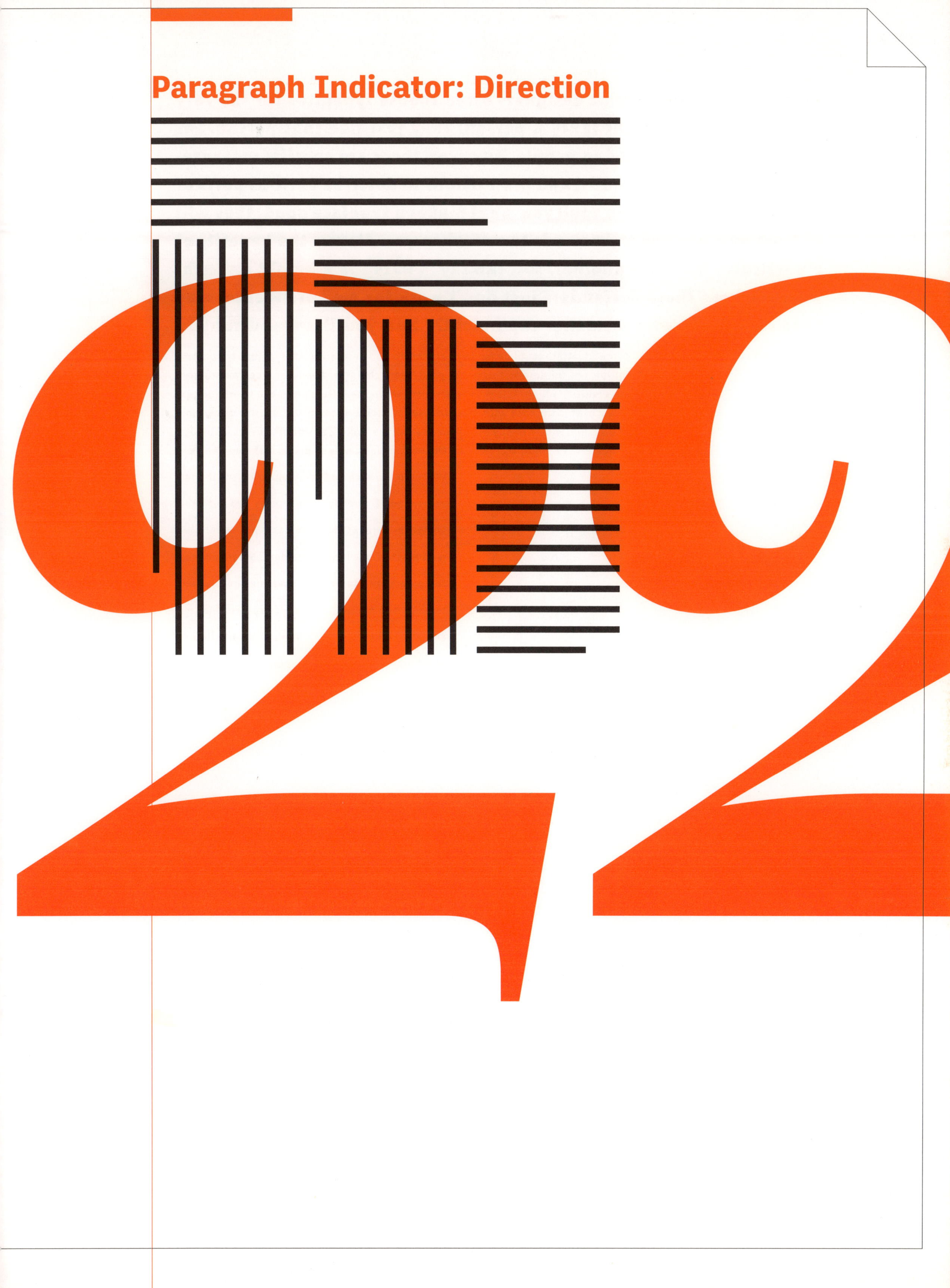
Paragraph Indicator: Direction
22

**Typographers and graphic designers often choose typefaces for the very same reason they might fancy a person: They just like that person. For more scientifically-minded people, however, there are specific measurements, components, details, and proportions to describe various parts of a letter. While these won't tell you what makes a typeface good, they will at least give you the right words to use when you discuss the benefits of a particular face over another. You can say "I hate the x-height on Such-a-Gothic" or "These descenders just don't work for me" or "Please, may I see something with a smaller cap height?" and you'll know what you**

1▸ **are talking about.** While metal letters could be made to any width and height, digital type has to conform to multiples of the smallest unit: the pixel. Every character has to be a certain number of pixels wide and high. This is not a problem when the letters are made up of 600 pixels per inch, as is the case with modern laser printers—those pixels are not discernible to our eyes, and we are happy to believe that we are looking at smooth curves instead of little squares fitted into tight grids. **On most screens, only 72 pixels make up one inch. We could see each and every one of them, if engineers hadn't already found ways around that. Computer screens, however, are not where we read most of our type these days. Smart phones, computers, and tablets all have high-resolutions screens, but microwave ovens, espresso makers, and all the other gadgets around us all still use small and modest displays. And the type unmistakably consists of bitmaps, which means that an 8-point letter is actually made up of eight pixels. If we allow six pixels above the baseline, including accents, and two below for descenders, that'll leave only three or four pixels for a lowercase character. In spite of these restrictions, there are hundreds of bitmap fonts, all different from one another by only a few pixels, but enough to prove that typographic variety cannot be suppressed by technological constraints.**

2▸ Rhythm and contrast keep coming up when discussing good music and good typographic design. They are concepts that also apply to spoken language, as anyone who has had to sit through a monotonous lecture will attest; the same tone, volume and speed of speech will put even the most interested listener into dreamland. Every now and again the audience needs to be shaken, either by a change in voice or pitch, by a question being posed, or by the speaker talking very quietly and then suddenly shouting. An occasional joke also works, just as the use of a funny typeface can liven up a page.

EXPLORATION 22 ▸
Paragraph Indicator: Direction

Paragraph 1:
12/18 TheMix Black, tracking +40/1000 em

Paragraph 2:
7.5/12 TheSans, tracking +50/1000 em

Paragraph 3:
7.5/17 TheSans Bold, tracking +45/1000 em

Paragraph 4:
7.5/16 TheSerif, tracking +60/1000 em

Typographers and graphic designers often choose typefaces for the very same reason they might fancy a person: They just like that person. For more scientifically-minded people, however, there are specific measurements, components, details, and proportions to describe various parts of a letter. While these won't tell you what makes a typeface good, they will at least give you the right words to use when you discuss the benefits of a particular face over another. You can say "I hate the x-height on Such-a-Gothic" or "These descenders just don't work for me" or "Please, may I see something with a smaller cap height?" and you'll know what you are talking about.

3▸ While metal letters could be made to any width and height, digital type has to conform to multiples of the smallest unit: the pixel. Every character has to be a certain number of pixels wide and high. This is not a problem when the letters are made up of 600 pixels per inch, as is the case with modern laser printers—those pixels are not discernible to our eyes, and we are happy to believe that we are looking at smooth curves instead of little squares fitted into tight grids.

On most screens, only 72 pixels make up one inch. We could see each and every one of them, if engineers hadn't already found ways around that. Computer screens, however, are not where we read most of our type these days. Smart phones, computers, and tablets all have high-resolutions screens, but microwave ovens, espresso makers, and all the other gadgets around us all still use small and modest displays. And the type unmistakably consists of bitmaps, which means that an 8-point letter is actually made up of eight pixels. If we allow six pixels above the baseline, including accents, and two below for descenders, that'll leave only three or four pixels for a lowercase character. In spite of these restrictions, there are hundreds of bitmap fonts, all different from one another by only a few pixels.

Rhythm and contrast keep coming up when discussing good music and good typographic design. They are concepts that also apply to spoken language, as anyone who has had to sit through a monotonous lecture will attest; the same tone, volume and speed of speech will put even the most interested listener into dreamland. Every now and again the audience needs to be shaken, either by a change in voice or pitch, or by a question being posed, or by the speaker talking very quietly and then suddenly shouting. An occasional joke also works, just as the use of a funny typeface can liven up a page. ◂4

EXPLORATION 22 >> PARAGRAPH INDICATOR: DIRECTION TEXT: 8/15 FF BAU REGULAR. TRACKING +25/1000 EM RULE: 6 PTS

**Opposite page**

1 Top line of the second paragraph is on the same baseline as last line of the first paragraph. Second and third paragraphs are also aligned in this way.

2 The last paragraph runs vertically and is nestled into the negative space created by the other paragraphs. Its top edge is aligned to the capline of the horizontal line of bold sans type beside it.

**This page**

3 Every other paragraph is set in the opposite direction on the page.

4 Bold bars fill in the negative spaces at the ends of each paragraph, creating a very solid text block.

**Thesis**

TheMix was the starting point of the Thesis superfamily that Luc(as) de Groot released in 1994. Thesis was ambitiously conceived of as a versatile typographic system with three compatible styles (TheSans, TheMix, TheSerif) in an optically harmonious range of eight weights, each of which has a true italic.

**FF Bau**

The 19th-century "Grotesk" from German foundry Schelter & Giesecke was a favorite of the Bauhaus and other Modernists throughout Continental Europe. It can be seen as the antecedent of classics like Akzidenz Grotesk and Helvetica. Christian Schwartz drew this revival in 2002. Common among "families" of the time, each weight differs distinctly, climaxing with a Super that is deliciously bold and broad.

1▸ ❶ **Typographers and graphic designers often choose typefaces for the very same reason they might fancy a person:** They just like that person. For more scientifically-minded people, however, there are specific measurements, components, details, and proportions to describe various parts of a letter. While these won't tell you what makes a typeface good, they will at least give you the right words to use when you discuss the benefits of a particular face over another. You can say "I hate the x-height on Such-a-Gothic" or "These descenders just don't work for me" or "Please, may I see something with a smaller cap height?" and you'll know what you are talking about.

❷ **On screens, however, only 72 pixels make up one inch. We could see each and every** one of them, if engineers hadn't already found ways around that. Computer screens, however, are not where we read most of our type these days. Smart phones, computers, and tablets all have high-resolutions screens, but microwave ovens, espresso makers, and all the other gadgets around us all still use small and modest displays. And the type unmistakably consists of bitmaps, which means that an 8-point letter is actually made up of eight pixels. If we allow six pixels above the baseline, including accents, and two below for descenders, that'll leave only three or four pixels for a lowercase character. In spite of these restrictions, there are hundreds of bitmap fonts, all different from one another by only a few pixels, but enough to prove that typographic variety cannot be suppressed by technological constraints.

❸ **Rhythm and contrast keep coming up** when discussing good music and good typographic design. They are concepts that also apply to spoken language, as anyone who has had to sit through a monotonous lecture will attest; the same tone, volume and speed of speech will put even the most interested listener into dreamland. Every now and again the audience needs to be shaken, either by a change in voice or pitch, by a question being posed, or by the speaker talking very quietly and then suddenly shouting. An occasional joke also works, just as the use of a funny typeface can liven up a page.

❹ **While metal letters could be made to any width and** height, digital type has to conform to multiples of the smallest unit: the pixel. Every character has to be a certain number of pixels wide and high. This is not a problem when the letters are made up of 600 pixels per inch, as is the case with modern laser printers—those pixels are not discernible to our eyes, and we are happy to believe that we are looking at smooth curves instead of little squares fitted into tight grids.

❺ **There's only one thing worse than a badly told joke, and that is a joke told twice. Whatever typographic device** you come up with, don't let it turn into a gimmick. A well-coordinated range of fonts will give you the scope for contrast as well as rhythm, and will keep you secure in the bosom of a well-behaved family.

***Exploration 22***
*Paragraph Indicator: Direction*

*Numbers:*
*8pt FF Dingbats 2.0 Numbers*

*First lines:*
*8/14 Klavika Bold, tracking +30/1000 em*

*Text:*
*8/14 Klavika Regular, tracking +30/1000 em*

Ever since people have been writing things down, they have had to consider their audience before actually putting pen to paper: letters would have to look different depending on whether they were to be read by mainly other people (in official documents or inscriptions), just one other person (in a letter), or only the writer (in a notebook or diary). There would be less room for guesswork if letter shapes were made more formal as the diversity of the readership expanded.

Some of the first messages to be read by a large number of people were rendered not by pens but by chisels. Large inscriptions on monuments in ancient Rome were carefully planned, with letters drawn on the stone with a brush before they were chiseled. Even if whiteout had existed in those days, it would not have helped to remove mistakes made in stone. A bit of planning was also more important then, since stonemasons were sometimes more expendable than slabs of marble or granite.

Graphic design and typography are complicated activities, but even the simple projects benefit from thinking about the problem, forming a mental picture of the solution, and then carefully planning the steps between. Scientists have not been content with just calling the human face "beautiful" if it meets certain ideals, or "ugly" if it doesn't. They had to go out and measure proportions of nose to jaw, forehead to chin, and so on to establish why some faces are more appealing than others.

While metal letters could be made to any width and height, digital type has to conform to multiples of the smallest unit: the pixel. Every character has to be a certain number of pixels wide and high. This is not a problem when the letters are made up of 600 pixels per inch, as is the case with modern laser printers–those pixels are not discernible to our eyes, and we are happy to believe that we are looking at smooth curves instead of little squares fitted into tight grids. ◂2

3▸ Typographers and graphic designers often choose typefaces for the very same reason they might fancy a person: They just like that person. For more scientifically-minded people, however, there are specific measurements, components, details, and proportions to describe various parts of a letter. While these won't tell you what makes a typeface good, they will at least give you the right words to use when you discuss the benefits of a particular face over another. You can say "I hate the x-height on Such-a-Gothic" or "These descenders just don't work for me" or "Please, may I see something with a smaller cap height?" and you'll know what you are talking about.

EXPLORATION 22 > DIRECTION > TEXT: 8.5/12 FF GOOD CONDENSED BOOK > TRACKING +45/1000 EM (TYPESET BY BETH WONG)

**Opposite page**

1 Paragraphs are numbered in order of reading. When using change of direction, reading order can be difficult to discern. Numbering the paragraphs is a simple way to guide a reader. The circular reversed-out numbers also provide a striking bold accent.

**This page**

2 The top baseline of the third paragraph aligns to the baseline of the last line in the paragraph above it. Because neither size nor weight changes from paragraph to paragraph, a generous horizontal space is set between them.

3 This example combines change of margin with change of direction. All paragraphs are set on the same measure in both horizontal and vertical reading directions.

**Klavika**

In 2004, Eric Olson's Klavika defined a new genre of geometric sans serif based on open-ended square shapes (as opposed to the circles and triangles of Futura-style geometry). The straight-sided sans became a trend for at least a decade. After voicing high-profile brands like Facebook and ESPN, Klavika continues to be a common pick for technical or athletic moods.

**FF Good**

Łukasz Dziedzic's decades of experience in the Polish publishing scene before he became a type designer gave him insight into the kind of tools that magazines and newspapers require. A sturdy, condensed, straight gothic is often on their list. First issued in a few weights in 2007, FF Good has grown to a staggering 196 styles—from Compressed to Wide, Light to Ultra, with fine gradations in between—thus responding to another publication industry need: versatile type systems.

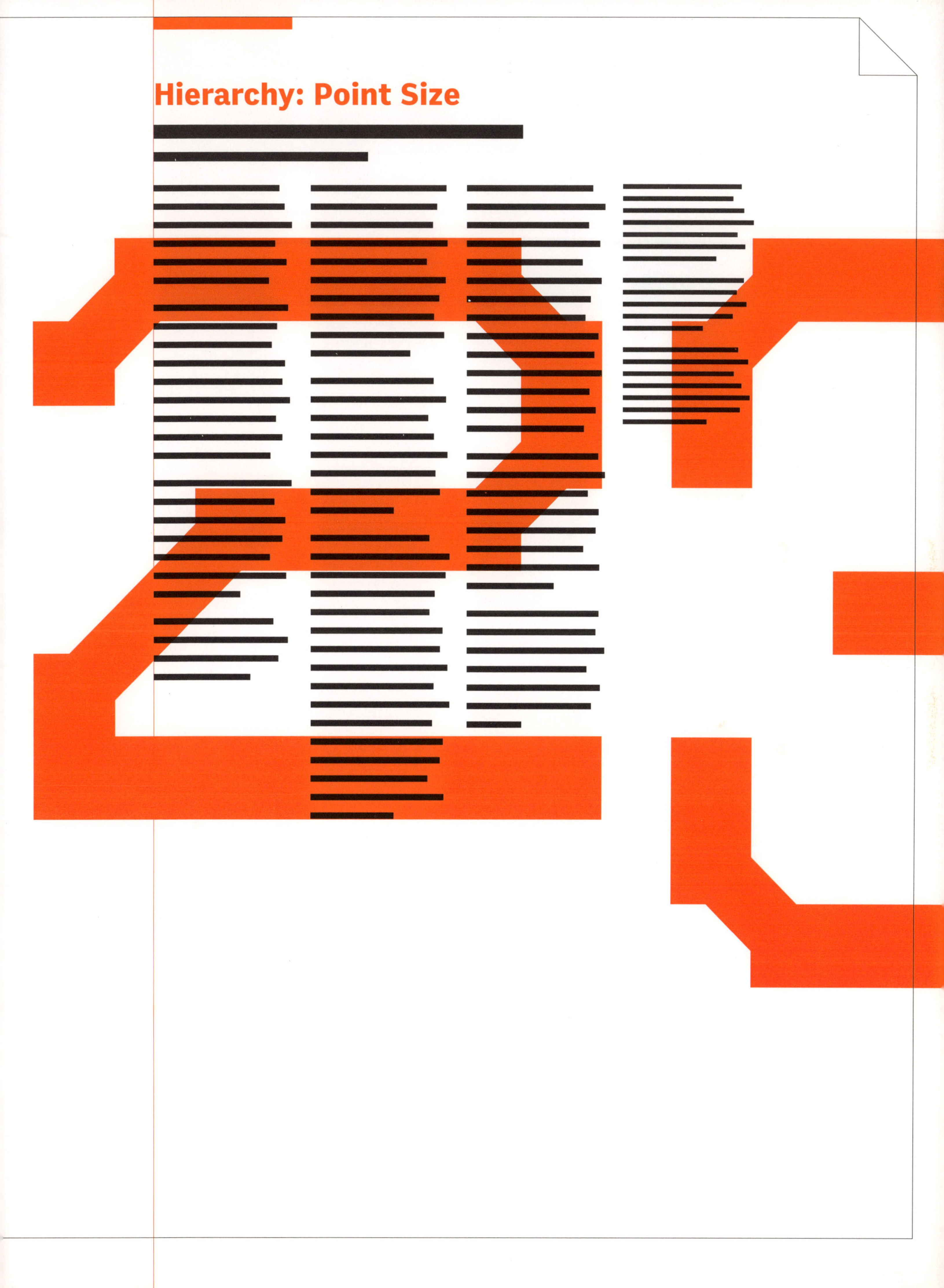
Hierarchy: Point Size

# 23 Hierarchy: Point Size

Creating proper typographic hierarchy is a matter of visually expressing the relative importance of various parts of a text. You must read the text you intend to set in order to understand the hierarchy that is contained within it.

To set type with clear hierarchy, you need to show (1) contrast between disparate elements and (2) association between related elements. Objects that are closer to each other on the page or ones set in the same way will associate. Items that are farther apart on the page or set in different sizes or styles will separate.

Because good typography is economical, minimizing the typographic variables you use to create multiple levels of hierarchy is an admirable achievement. You can create several levels of typographic hierarchy using only changes in point size. Set elements that express the same level of hierarchy in the same point size to create parallels for a reader.

These last two typesetting exercises (Explorations 23 and 24) are more complex and consolidate a number of typographic and compositional skills. Experiment with any of the paragraph indications from previous Explorations and combine them with each other and your own ideas. Always think of the reader and maintain as much legibility as possible as you explore ways to create typographic hierarchy.

1▸ # TYPE BUILDS CHARACTER

BY ERIK SPIEKERMANN

Ever since people have been writing things down, they have had to consider their audience before actually putting pen to paper: letters would have to look different depending on whether they were to be read by mainly other people (in official documents or inscriptions), just one other person (in a letter), or only the writer (in a notebook or diary). There would be less room for guesswork if letter shapes were made more formal as the diversity of the readership expanded.

Some of the first messages to be read by a large number of people were rendered not by pens but by chisels.[1] Large inscriptions on monuments in ancient Rome were carefully planned, with letters drawn on the stone with a brush before they were chiseled.[2] Even if white-out had existed in those days, it would not have helped to remove mistakes made in stone. A bit of planning was also more important then, since stonemasons were sometimes more expendable than slabs of marble or granite.

2▸ 1 → The official Roman alphabet, as seen on the Trajan Column in Rome, has never gone out of fashion.

2 → When communications became more international, typefaces that were more universal were in demand. Today fraktur, gothic and similar styles are only used to evoke the feeling of a bygone era, for example on the banner of newspapers such as 3▸ The New York Times.

Graphic design and typography are complicated activities, but even the simple projects benefit from thinking about the problem, forming a mental picture of the solution, and then carefully planning the steps between.

Scientists have not been content with just calling the human face "beautiful" if it meets certain ideals, or "ugly" if it doesn't. They had to go out and measure proportions of nose to jaw, forehead to chin, and so on to establish why some faces are more appealing than others.[3]

3 → Many digital typefaces evoke the timeless beauty of ancient inscriptions and early printing types. Trajan, designed by Carol Twombly in 1990, is a good example.

Typographers and graphic designers often choose typefaces for the very same reason they might fancy a person: They just like that person. For more scientifically-minded people, however, there are specific measurements, components, details, and proportions to describe various parts of a letter. While these won't tell you what makes a typeface good, they will at least give you the right words to use when you discuss the benefits of a particular face over another. You can say "I hate the x-height on Such-a-Gothic" or "These descenders just don't work for me" or "Please, may I see something with a smaller cap height?" and you'll know what you are talking about.

While metal letters could be made to any width and height, digital type has to conform to multiples of the smallest unit: the pixel. Every character has to be a certain number of pixels wide and high. This is not a problem when the letters are made up of 600 pixels per inch, as is the case with modern laser printers—those pixels are not discernible to our eyes, and we are happy to believe that we are looking at smooth curves instead of little squares fitted into tight grids.

EXPLORATION 23
Hierarchy >> Size

TITLE
4▸ 18pt FF Karbid,
tracking +140/1000 em

BYLINE
8pt FF Karbid,
tracking +180/1000 em

TEXT
7/11 FF Karbid,
tracking +40/1000 em

FOOTNOTES
5/8 FF Karbid,
tracking +40/1000 em

1 Paragraphs are set with change of margin; the title is set to overlap with the first paragraph.

2 Each footnote is set flush right on the same baseline alongside the line of text where it is referenced.

3 Like book titles, names of newspapers are italicized; however, this face has no italic, so italic is indicated with an underline instead. Being consistent is more important than following all the "rules." Design a typographic solution, apply it across the board, and readers will catch on to the system as they read.

4 Four levels of hierarchy are created using only the roman (regular) weight of the typeface set in four different sizes.

**FF Karbid**
Inspired by the lettering on German storefronts from the 1930s, Verena Gerlach designed this informal sans in 1999. In 2011, she expanded the design into a large superfamily, adding a display version with more Deco-style alternatives, a slab serif, and a pared-back cut for text. The superfamily offers lots of variation for speaking with different voices within the same publication, campaign, or corporate identity.

**This page**

1 The byline is set in the same point size as the footnotes, but in all caps. Reusing point sizes is economical. And good typography is economical.

2 The reference numbers for the three footnotes are set as superscripts within the text. Usually a point or two smaller, they are baseline shifted and often kerned to associate clearly with the word before them.

3 Footnotes overlap the last paragraph and are set on a measure equal to the amount of the exdent. Note that the reference numbers in the footnotes themselves are not superscript.

**Opposite page**

4 The title and byline are the same weight in two sizes. The gray vertical slash between them further clarifies the hierarchical difference.

5 Every other paragraph is set with a light gray behind the text. The use of gray is echoed in the numbers for the superscripts within the body and the numbers of the footnotes.

**Interstate**

In 1994, Tobias Frere-Jones rethought the official letter templates used by the US Federal Highway Administration for road signs. He took the simple, clear shapes drawn by engineers and repurposed them for graphic design, adding new weights, styles, and typographic features. Its legibility and everyday familiarity made Interstate one of the most popular typefaces of the 1990s.

**FF Balance**

Released in 1993 after 10 years of development, Evert Bloemsma's first face lacks a single straight line. It also has "reversed contrast:" more weight in the horizontal strokes than in the vertical strokes. Bloemsma theorized that a horizontal emphasis could improve readability. Although this has yet to be proven, the visual effect is novel. FF Balance is fresher than older faces, such as Antique Olive, that have a more exaggerated inverse stress.

TYPE BUILDS CHARACTER » BY ERIK SPIEKERMANN 

Ever since people have been writing things down, they have had to consider their audience before actually putting pen to paper: letters would have to look different depending on whether they were to be read by mainly other people (in official documents or inscriptions), just one other person (in a letter), or only the writer (in a notebook or diary). There would be less room for guesswork if letter shapes were made more formal as the diversity of the readership expanded.

Some of the first messages to be read by a large number of people were rendered not by pens but by chisels.[1] Large inscriptions on monuments in ancient Rome were carefully planned, with letters drawn on the stone with a brush before they were chiseled.[2] Even if white-out had existed in those days, it would not have helped to remove mistakes made in stone. A bit of planning was also more important then, since stonemasons were sometimes more expendable than slabs of marble or granite.

Graphic design and typography are complicated activities, but even the simple projects benefit from thinking about the problem, forming a mental picture of the solution, and then carefully planning the steps between. Scientists have not been content with just calling the human face "beautiful" if it meets certain ideals, or "ugly" if it doesn't. They had to go out and measure proportions of nose to jaw, forehead to chin, and so on to establish why some faces are more appealing than others.[3] ◂2

Typographers and graphic designers often choose typefaces for the very same reason they might fancy a person: They just like that person. For more scientifically-minded people, however, there are specific measurements, components, details, and proportions to describe various parts of a letter. While these won't tell you what makes a typeface good, they will at least give you the right words to use when you discuss the benefits of a particular face over another. You can say "I hate the x-height on Such-a-Gothic" or "These descenders just don't work for me" or "Please, may I see something with a smaller cap height?" and you'll know what you are talking about.

Rhythm and contrast keep coming up when discussing good music and good typographic design. They are concepts that also apply to spoken language, as anyone who has had to sit through a monotonous lecture will attest; the same tone, volume and speed of speech will put even the most interested listener into dreamland. Every now and again the audience needs to be shaken, either by a change in voice or pitch, by a question being posed, or by the speaker talking very quietly and then suddenly shouting. An occasional joke also works, just as the use of a funny typeface can liven up a page.

There's only one thing worse than a badly told joke, and that is a joke told twice. Whatever typographic device you come up with, don't let it turn into a gimmick. A well-coordinated range of fonts will give you the scope for contrast as well as rhythm, and will keep you secure in the bosom of a well-behaved family.

1] The official Roman alphabet, as seen on the Trajan Column, has never gone out of fashion. 2] When communications became more international, typefaces that were more universal were in demand. Today fraktur, gothic and similar styles are only used to evoke the feeling of a bygone era, for example on the banner of newspapers such as The New York Times. 3] Many digital typefaces evoke the timeless beauty of ancient inscriptions and early printing types. Trajan, designed by Carol Twombly in 1990, is a good example. ◂3

EXPLORATION 23 ▸ Hierarchy: Point Size

Title: 8pt Interstate Roman, tracking +50/1000 em
Byline: 5pt Interstate Roman, tracking +70/1000 em
Text: 6/14 Interstate Roman, tracking +15/1000 em
Footnotes: 5/10 Interstate Roman, tracking +10/1000 em
Exdent: 15 ems

# Type Builds Character | Erik Spiekermann

Ever since people have been writing things down, they have had to consider their audience before actually putting pen to paper: letters would have to look different depending on whether they were to be read by mainly other people (in official documents or inscriptions), just one other person (in a letter), or only the writer (in a notebook or diary). There would be less room for guesswork if letter shapes were made more formal as the diversity of the readership expanded. Some of the first messages to be read by a large number of people were rendered not by pens but by chisels.[1] Large inscriptions on monuments in ancient Rome were carefully planned, with letter drawn on the stone with a brush before they were chiseled.[2] Even if white-out had existed in those days, it would not have helped to remove mistakes made in stone. A bit of planning was also more important then, since stonemasons were sometimes more expendable than slabs of marble or granite. Graphic design and typography are complicated activities, but even the simple projects benefit from thinking about the problem, forming a mental picture of the solution, and then carefully planning the steps between. Scientists have not been content with just calling the human face "beautiful" if it meets certain ideals, or "ugly" if it doesn't. They had to go out and measure proportions of nose to jaw, forehead to chin, and so on to establish why some faces are more appealing than others.[3] Typographers and graphic designers often choose typefaces for the very same reason they might fancy a person: They just like that person. For more scientifically-minded people, however, there are specific measurements, components, details, and proportions to describe various parts of a letter. While these won't tell you what makes a typeface good, they will at least give you the right words to use when you discuss the benefits of a particular face over another. You can say "I hate the x-height on Such-a-Gothic" or "These descenders just don't work for me" or "Please, may I see something with a smaller cap height?" and you'll know what you are talking about. While metal letters could be made to any width and height, digital type has to conform to multiples of the smallest unit: the pixel. Every character has to be a certain number of pixels wide and high. This is not a problem when the letters are made up of 600 pixels per inch, as is the case with modern laser printers—those pixels are not discernible to our eyes, and we are happy to believe that we are looking at smooth curves instead of little squares fitted into tight grids.

1 The official Roman alphabet, as seen on the Trajan Column in Rome, has never gone out of fashion.

2 When communications became more international, typefaces that were more universal were in demand. Today fraktur, gothic and similar styles are only used to evoke the feeling of a bygone era, for example on the banner of newspapers such as *The New York Times*.

3 Many digital typefaces evoke the timeless beauty of ancient inscriptions and early printing types. Trajan, designed by Carol Twombly in 1990, is a good example.

*Exploration 23: Hierarchy: Size (typeset by Vincent Lo) Title: 18pt FF Balance, tracking +30/1000 em Byline: 10pt FF Balance, tracking +40/1000 em Text: 7.5/12 FF Balance, tracking +20/1000 em*

EXP
**23.4**

**This page**

1 All four levels of hierarchy are created using just two point sizes, set in all caps and u/lc. This setting is very streamlined and minimal, much like the face it is set in.

2 Bold gray rules under the type reinforce the no-frills quality of the face, making it appear almost as though it was typeset on old-fashioned lined paper. They also help this monospaced type look a little more even in overall typographic color.

**Opposite page**

3 The title and byline are set vertically, reading from bottom to top, leading the eye to the first word of the text. Note the looseness of the tracking on the capitals.

4 On very narrow columns, a single word alone on the last line of a paragraph is not necessarily a widow if it is a long word.

5 Footnotes are given a subhead. The bold half bracket separating them from the text is the same as the one under the title.

**OCR-A**
Designed in 1968 by Adrian Frutiger in collaboration with the European Computer Manufacturers Association, this face fused the strict mathematical criteria for optical character recognition (OCR) technology of that era with typographic tradition. The resulting face was made a world standard for OCR technology in 1973.

**FF Celeste**
Chris Burke designed this modern Humanist face in 1999 to be a mix of the static and the dynamic principles of letter construction. It has triangular serifs and less pronounced contrast than traditional Didones.

1▸ TYPE BUILDS CHARACTER / BY ERIK SPIEKERMANN

2▸ Ever since people have been writing things down, they have had to consider their audience before actually putting pen to paper: letters would have to look different depending on whether they were to be read by mainly other people (in official documents or inscriptions), just one other person (in a letter), or only the writer (in a notebook or diary). There would be less room for guesswork if letter shapes were made more formal as the diversity of the readership expanded.

Some of the first messages to be read by a large number of people were rendered not by pens but by chisels.[1] Large inscriptions on monuments in ancient Rome were carefully planned, with letters drawn on the stone with a brush before they were chiseled.[2] Even if white-out had existed in those days, it would not have helped to remove mistakes made in stone. A bit of planning was also more important then, since stonemasons were sometimes more expendable than slabs of marble or granite.

Graphic design and typography are complicated activities, but even the simple projects benefit from thinking about the problem, forming a mental picture of the solution, and then carefully planning the steps between.

Scientists have not been content with just calling the human face "beautiful" if it meets certain ideals, or "ugly" if it doesn't. They had to go out and measure proportions of nose to jaw, forehead to chin, and so on to establish why some faces are more appealing than others.[3]

Rhythm and contrast keep coming up when discussing good music and good typographic design. They are concepts that also apply to spoken language, as anyone who has had to sit through a monotonous lecture will attest; the same tone, volume and speed of speech will put even the most interested listener into dreamland. Every now and again the audience needs to be shaken, either by a change in voice or pitch, by a question being posed, or by the speaker talking very quietly and then suddenly shouting. An occasional joke also works, just as the use of a funny typeface can liven up a page.

1/ The official Roman alphabet, as seen on the Trajan Column in Rome, has never gone out of fashion.

2/ When communications became more international, typefaces that were more universal were in demand. Today fraktur, gothic and similar styles are only used to evoke the feeling of a bygone era, for example on the banner of newspapers such as The New York Times.

3/ Many digital typefaces evoke the timeless beauty of ancient inscriptions and early printing types. Trajan, designed by Carol Twombly in 1990, is a good example.

EXPLORATION 23 // Hierarchy: Point Size Title + text: 7/13 OCR-A, tracking +20/1000 em Footnotes: 5/10 OCR-A, tracking +20/1000 em Extra leading: 6.5 pts

# TYPE BUILDS CHARACTER

BY ERIK SPIEKERMANN

Ever since people have been writing things down, they have had to consider their audience before actually putting pen to paper: letters would have to look different depending on whether they were to be read by mainly other people (in official documents or inscriptions), just one other person (in a letter), or only the writer (in a notebook or diary). There would be less room for guesswork if letter shapes were made more formal as the diversity of the readership expanded.

Some of the first messages to be read by a large number of people were rendered not by pens but by chisels.[1] Large inscriptions on monuments in ancient Rome were carefully planned, with letters drawn on the stone with a brush before they were chiseled.[2] Even if white-out had existed in those days, it would not have helped to remove mistakes made in stone. A bit of planning was also more important then, since stonemasons were sometimes more expendable than slabs of marble or granite.

Graphic design and typography are complicated activities, but even the simple projects benefit from thinking about the problem, forming a mental picture of the solution, and then carefully planning the steps between.

Scientists have not been content with just calling the human face "beautiful" if it meets certain ideals, or "ugly" if it doesn't. They had to go out and measure proportions of nose to jaw, forehead to chin, and so on to establish why some faces are more appealing than others.[3]

Rhythm and contrast keep coming up when discussing good music and good typographic design. They are concepts that also apply to spoken language, as anyone who has had to sit through a monotonous lecture will attest; the same tone, volume and speed of speech will put even the most interested listener into dreamland. Every now and again the audience needs to be shaken, either by a change in voice or pitch, by a question being posed, or by the speaker talking very quietly and then suddenly shouting. An occasional joke also works, just as the use of a funny typeface can liven up a page.

Typographers and graphic designers often choose typefaces for the very same reason they might fancy a person: They just like that person. For more scientifically-minded people, however, there are specific measurements, components, details, and proportions to describe various parts of a letter. While these won't tell you what makes a typeface good, they will at least give you the right words to use when you discuss the benefits of a particular face over another.

While metal letters could be made to any width and height, digital type has to conform to multiples of the smallest unit: the pixel. Every character has to be a certain number of pixels wide and high. This is not a problem when the letters are made up of 600 pixels per inch, as is the case with modern laser printers—those pixels are not discernible to our eyes, and we are happy to believe that we are looking at smooth curves instead of little squares fitted into tight grids.

On most screens, only 72 pixels make up one inch. We could see each and every one of them, if engineers hadn't already found ways around that. Computer screens, however, are not where we read most of our type these days. Smart phones, computers, and tablets all have high-resolutions screens, but microwave ovens, espresso makers, and all the other gadgets around us all still use small and modest displays. And the type unmistakably consists of bitmaps, which means that an 8-point letter is actually made up of eight pixels. If we allow six pixels above the baseline, including accents, and two below for descenders, that'll leave only three or four pixels for a lowercase character.

NOTES

1 The official Roman alphabet, as seen on the Trajan Column in Rome, has never gone out of fashion.

2 When communications became more international, typefaces that were more universal were in demand. Today fraktur, gothic and similar styles are only used to evoke the feeling of a bygone era, for example on the banner of newspapers such as *The New York Times*.

3 Many digital typefaces evoke the timeless beauty of ancient inscriptions and early printing types. Trajan, designed by Carol Twombly in 1990, is a good example.

**Exploration 23**
**Hierarchy :: Point Size**

Title: 9pt FF Celeste, tracking +200/1000 em

Byline: 6pt FF Celeste, tracking +200/1000 em

Text: 7/12 FF Celeste, tracking +30/1000 em

Extra Leading: 6 pts

Footnotes: 5.5/9.5 FF Celeste, tracking +30/1000 em

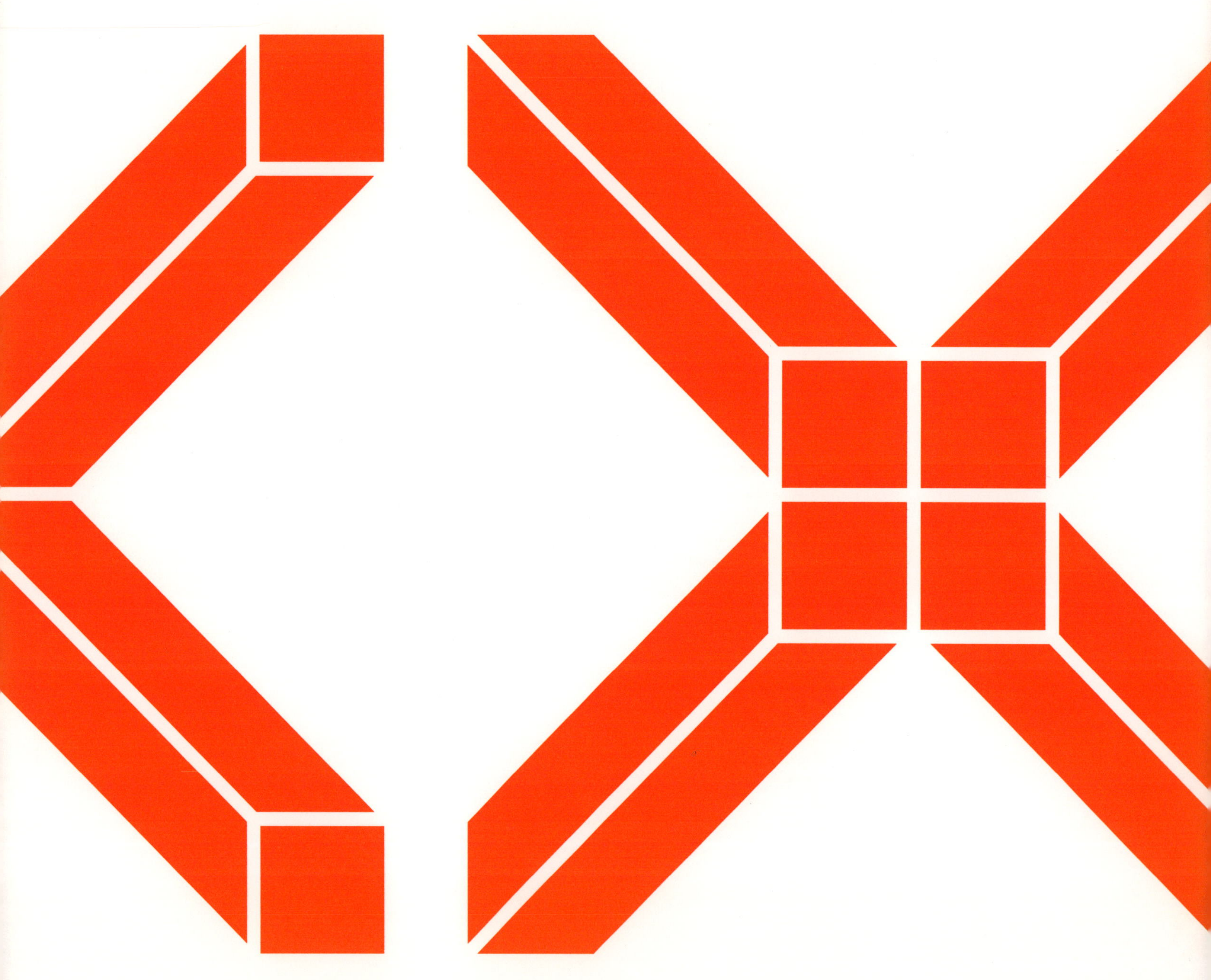

Exploration 23 Hierarchy: Point Size (typeset by Anne Tsuei)

Title: 14pt FF Avance, tracking +125/1000 em and 34pt FF Mister K, no tracking Byline: 8pt FF Avance, tracking +125/1000 em Text: 8/14 FF Avance, tracking +25/1000 em Footnotes: 6/10 FF Avance, tracking +30/1000 em

# TYPE *builds* CHARACTER

1 BY ERIK SPIEKERMANN ▸ EVER SINCE PEOPLE HAVE BEEN WRITING THINGS DOWN, THEY HAVE HAD TO consider their audience before actually putting pen to paper: letters would have to look different depending on whether they were to be read by mainly other people (in official documents or inscriptions), just one other person (in a letter), or only the writer (in a notebook or diary). There would be less room for guesswork if letter shapes were made more formal as the diversity of the readership expanded.

SOME OF THE FIRST MESSAGES TO BE READ BY A LARGE NUMBER OF PEOPLE were rendered not by pens but by chisels.[1] Large inscriptions on monuments in ancient Rome were carefully planned, with letters drawn on the stone with a brush before they were chiseled.[2] Even if white-out had existed in those days, it would not have helped to remove mistakes made in stone. A bit of planning was also more important then, since stonemasons were sometimes more expendable than slabs of marble or granite.

GRAPHIC DESIGN AND TYPOGRAPHY ARE COMPLICATED ACTIVITIES, BUT EVEN the simple projects benefit from thinking about the problem, forming a mental picture of the solution, and then carefully planning the steps between.

SCIENTISTS HAVE NOT BEEN CONTENT WITH JUST CALLING THE HUMAN FACE "beautiful" if it meets certain ideals, or "ugly" if it doesn't. They had to go out and measure proportions of nose to jaw, forehead to chin, and so on to establish why some faces are more appealing than others.[3]

TYPOGRAPHERS AND GRAPHIC DESIGNERS OFTEN CHOOSE TYPEFACES FOR THE very same reason they might fancy a person: They just like that person. For more scientifically-minded people, however, there are specific measurements, components, details, and proportions to describe various parts of a letter. While these won't tell you what makes a typeface good, they will at least give you the right words to use when you discuss the benefits of a particular face over another. You can say "I hate the x-height on Such-a-Gothic" or "These descenders just don't work for me" or "Please, may I see something with a smaller cap height?" and you'll know what you are talking about.

WHILE METAL LETTERS COULD BE MADE TO ANY WIDTH AND HEIGHT, DIGITAL type has to conform to multiples of the smallest unit: the pixel. Every character has to be a certain number of pixels wide and high. This is not a problem when the letters are made up of 600 pixels per inch, as is the case with modern laser printers—those pixels are not discernible to our eyes, and we are happy to believe that we are looking at smooth curves instead of little squares fitted into tight grids.

## NOTES

2 1 The official Roman alphabet, as seen on the Trajan Column in Rome, has never gone out of fashion.

2 When communications became more international, typefaces that were more universal were in demand. Today fraktur, gothic and similar styles are only used to evoke the feeling of a bygone era, for example on the banner of newspapers such as *The New York Times*.

3 Many digital typefaces evoke the timeless beauty of ancient inscriptions and early printing types. Trajan, designed by Carol Twombly in 1990, is a good example.

1 Although the byline and the first lines of each paragraph are the same specification (loosely tracked all lowercase small caps), a graphic element after the byline clearly separates it from the first word of the text. Dingbats, punctuation, and rules can assist you in being economical with your typesetting.

2 When numbers hang in a list, there is no need for any form of punctuation after them. Fewer punctuation marks creates a cleaner, less-cluttered setting, which is especially important when type is very small.

**FF Avance**
Designed in 2000, the most striking characteristic of this face from Dutch type designer Evert Bloemsma is its asymmetrical serifs. He explains: "Symmetry is found in all kinds of shapes. Often it seems to express balance, security and certainty. This static monumentality does not really belong in our present world."

**FF Mister K**
Finnish type designer Julia Sysmäläinen designed this calligraphic script in 2008 based on the handwriting of the Austro-Hungarian author Franz Kafka. With an extensive set of two- and three-character ligatures along with scribbles, cross-outs and hundreds of alternate forms, it produces an impressive likeness to the real thing.

## Hierarchy: Point Size + Weight

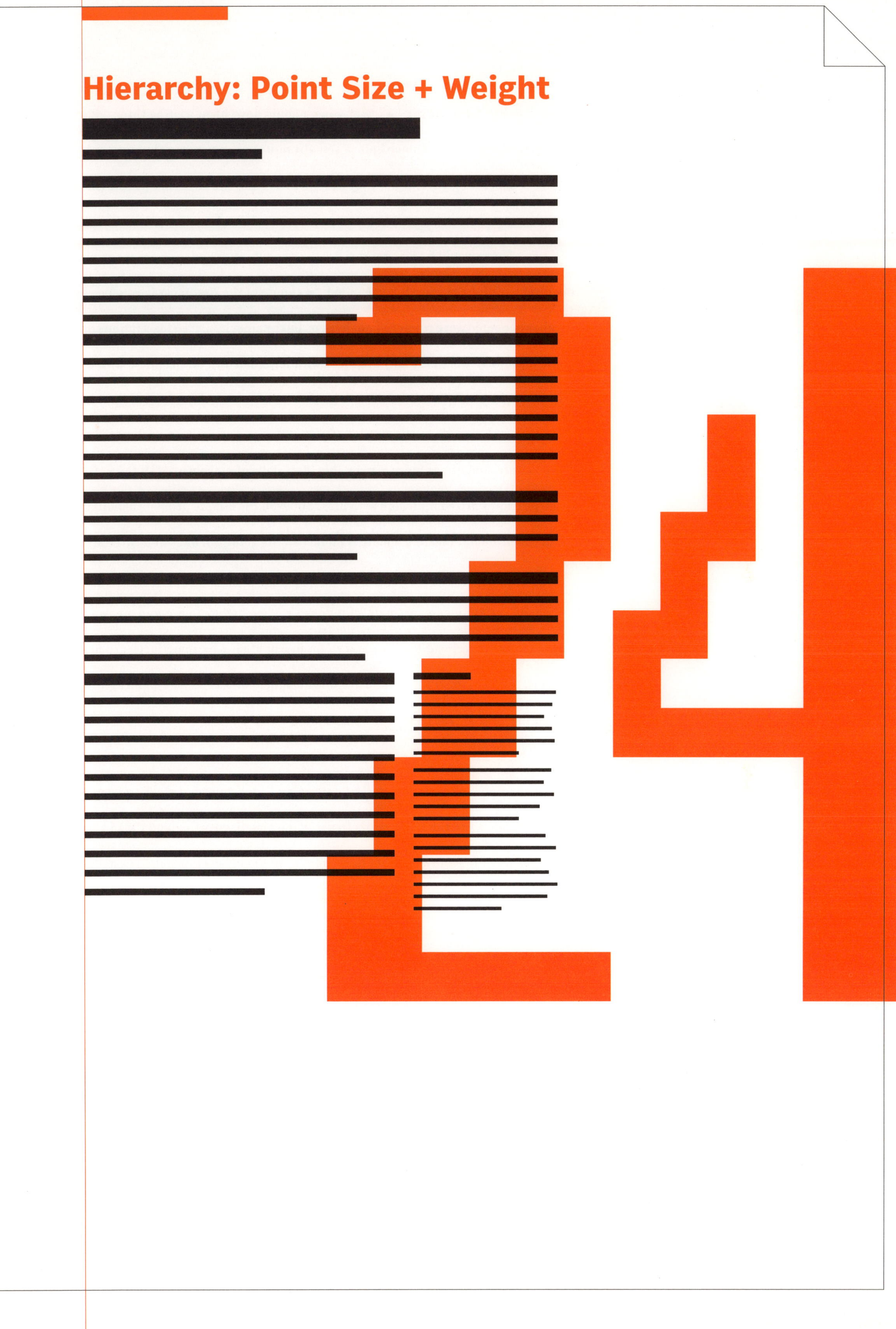

EXP
**24.1**

**This page**

1 The title is set in bold as a run-in head, with the graphic element used as the paragraph indicator set after it.

2 Leading on the footnotes is half the leading on the main text so that the thin rules between lines align perfectly with the rules of the text beside it.

**Opposite page**

3 The three columns of text and the notes column are clotheslined in four equal measures.

4 The break in the rule at the gutter between the third and fourth columns creates clear hierarchy and separation for the notes column. Without this small detail of an open space at the gutter, the rule would not function properly here.

**FF Cellini**
This Bodoni revival was designed by Albert Boton in the 1990s and updated in 2002. The structure of this face is similar to other revivals of its kind, but the lengthening of the ball terminals into teardrops is particularly notable.

**Adobe Garamond**
The original version of this face was designed by Claude Garamond (c. 1480–1561); this one was created by Robert Slimbach in 1989. Of the many versions of these typefaces, this is considered one of the most authentic to Garamond's original intentions. It embodies a classic, elegant French Renaissance style and provides excellent readability. More than 500 years after his death, the number of roman typefaces based on or derived from the work of Garamond is astounding. A truly timeless design.

EXPLORATION 24 Hierarchy: Point Size + Weight (typeset by Beth Wong) Title: 10pt FF Cellini Bold, tracking +50/1000 em Text: 8.5/22 FF Cellini, tracking +50/1000 em Footnotes: 6.5/11 FF Cellini, tracking +60/1000 em

1▸ **Type Builds Character** ■ Ever since people have been writing things down, they have had to consider their audience before actually putting pen to paper: letters would have to look different depending on whether they were to be read by mainly other people (in official documents or inscriptions), just one other person (in a letter), or only the writer (in a notebook or diary). There would be less room for guesswork if letter shapes were made more formal as the diversity of the readership expanded. ■ Some of the first messages to be read by a large number of people were rendered not by pens but by chisels.[1] Large inscriptions on monuments in ancient Rome were carefully planned, with letters drawn on the stone with a brush before they were chiseled.[2] Even if white-out had existed in those days, it would not have helped to remove mistakes made in stone. A bit of planning was also more important then, since stonemasons were sometimes more expendable than slabs of marble or granite. ■ Graphic design and typography are complicated activities, but even the simple projects benefit from thinking about the problem, forming a mental picture of the solution, and then carefully planning the steps between. ■ Scientists have not been content with just calling the human face "beautiful" if it meets certain ideals, or "ugly" if it doesn't. They had to go out and measure proportions of nose to jaw, forehead to chin, and so on to establish why some faces are more appealing than others.[3] ■ Typographers and graphic designers often choose typefaces for the very same reason they might fancy a person: They just like that person. For more scientifically-minded people, however, there are specific measurements, components, details, and proportions to describe various parts of a letter. While these won't tell you what makes a typeface good, they will at least give you the right words to use when you discuss the benefits of a particular face over another. You can say "I hate the x-height on Such-a-Gothic" or "These descenders just don't work for me" or "Please, may I see something with a smaller cap height?" and you'll know what you are talking about.

1) The official Roman alphabet, as seen on the Trajan Column in Rome, has never gone out of fashion. 2) When communications became more international, typefaces that were more universal were in demand. Today fraktur, gothic and similar styles are only used to evoke the feeling of a bygone era, for example on the banner of newspapers such as *The New York Times*. 3) Many digital typefaces evoke the timeless beauty of ancient inscriptions and early printing types. Trajan, designed by Carol Twombly in 1990, is a good example. ◂2

4

## TYPE BUILDS CHARACTER *Erik Spiekermann*

3▸ Ever since people have been writing things down, they have had to consider their audience before actually putting pen to paper: letters would have to look different depending on whether they were to be read by mainly other people (in official documents or inscriptions), just one other person (in a letter), or only the writer (in a notebook or diary). There would be less room for guesswork if letter shapes were made more formal as the diversity of the readership expanded.

Some of the first messages to be read by a large number of people were rendered not by pens but by chisels.[1] Large inscriptions on monuments in ancient Rome were carefully planned, with letters drawn on the stone with a brush before they were chiseled.[2] Even if white-out had existed in those days, it would not have helped to remove mistakes made in stone. A bit of planning was also more important then, since stonemasons were sometimes more expendable than slabs of marble or granite.

Graphic design and typography are complicated activities, but even the simple projects benefit from thinking about the problem, forming a mental picture of the solution, and then carefully planning the steps between.[3]

Typographers and graphic designers often choose typefaces for the very same reason they might fancy a person: They just like that person. For more scientifically-minded people, however, there are specific measurements, components, details, and proportions to describe various parts of a letter. While these won't tell you what makes a typeface good, they will at least give you the right words to use when you discuss the benefits of a particular face over another. You can say "I hate the x-height on Such-a-Gothic" or "These descenders just don't work for me" or "Please, may I see something with a smaller cap height?" and you'll know what you are talking about.

While metal letters could be made to any width and height, digital type has to conform to multiples of the smallest unit: the pixel. Every character has to be a certain number of pixels wide and high. This is not a problem when the letters are made up of 600 pixels per inch, as is the case with modern laser printers—those pixels are not discernible to our eyes, and we are happy to believe that we are looking at smooth curves instead of little squares fitted into tight grids.

On most screens, only 72 pixels make up one inch. We could see each and every one of them, if engineers hadn't already found ways around that. Computer screens, however, are not where we read most of our type these days. Smart phones, computers, and tablets all have high-resolutions screens, but microwave ovens, espresso makers, and all the other gadgets around us all still use small and modest displays. And the type unmistakably consists of bitmaps, which means that an 8-point letter is actually made up of eight pixels. If we allow six pixels above the baseline, including accents, and two below for descenders, that'll leave only three or four pixels for a lowercase character. In spite of these restrictions, there are hundreds of bitmap fonts, all different from one another by only a few pixels, but enough to prove that typographic variety cannot be suppressed by technological constraints.

**NOTES**

1 The official Roman alphabet, as seen on the Trajan Column in Rome, has never gone out of fashion.

2 When communications became more international, typefaces that were more universal were in demand. Today fraktur, gothic and similar styles are only used to evoke the feeling of a bygone era, for example on the banner of newspapers such as *The New York Times*.

3 Many digital typefaces evoke the timeless beauty of ancient inscriptions and early printing types. Trajan, designed by Carol Twombly in 1990, is a good example.

5+

EXPLORATION 24
HIERARCHY:
POINT SIZE + WEIGHT

TITLE: 7PT ADOBE GARAMOND BOLD, TRACKING +70/1000 EM

BYLINE: 7PT ADOBE GARAMOND ITALIC, TRACKING +10/1000 EM

TEXT: 7/12 ADOBE GARAMOND ROMAN, TRACKING +20/1000 EM

FOOTNOTES: 5.5/9.5 ADOBE GARAMOND ROMAN, TRACKING +20/1000 EM

**This page**

1 The title and byline are set in the same point size in two different weights. The whole line is force justified and the large space after the title helps the byline subordinate.

2 The footnotes are set the same way as the main text, with no returns between them. A simple double period that is baseline shifted upward serves as a graphic element between the text and the notes.

**Opposite page**

3 The byline is set as a run-in head. Even though it is second in the sequence, a byline may be set at a lower level of hierarchy than the body copy—depending on who the author is, of course.

4 The gutters between all the text blocks are the same width.

5 When an entire passage of text is set in italic, book or other titles within it (such as the newspaper title here) should be set in roman.

**Univers**
In the 1950s, Adrian Frutiger had the idea for a typeface of many weights and widths with identical x-heights and consistent ascender and descender lengths. Revolutionary at the time, it's now a type design standard. Arguably the most neutral, unadorned typeface ever created, the original had 21 weights that were numbered instead of named.

**Mønster**
Designed in 2014 by Sinder Bremnes, this delightful reverse-contrast headline font is full of big, bold, exaggerated letterforms. Although it may be "monstrous" in the best sense of the word, it's actually named after the Norwegian word for "pattern."

**FF Milo**
In 2000, Michael Abbink designed this face, named for a resilient grain, "to be a basic usable font like corn or grain is to any culture." A compact workhorse with low ascenders and descenders, its true italic has unusual little outstrokes at the ends of terminals to differentiate it from the roman.

1▸ **TYPE BUILDS CHARACTER** BY ERIK SPIEKERMANN

**Ever since people have been writing things down, they have had to consider their audience before actually putting pen to paper: letters would have to look different depending on whether they were to be read by mainly other people (in official documents or inscriptions), just one other person (in a letter), or only the writer (in a notebook or diary). There would be less room for guesswork if letter shapes were made more formal as the diversity of the readership expanded.** Some of the first messages to be read by a large number of people were rendered not by pens but by chisels.[1] Large inscriptions on monuments in ancient Rome were carefully planned, with letters drawn on the stone with a brush before they were chiseled.[2] Even if white-out had existed in those days, it would not have helped to remove mistakes made in stone. A bit of planning was also more important then, since stonemasons were sometimes more expendable than slabs of marble or granite. **Graphic design and typography are complicated activities, but even the simple projects benefit from thinking about the problem, forming a mental picture of the solution, and then carefully planning the steps between.** Scientists have not been content with just calling the human face "beautiful" if it meets certain ideals, or "ugly" if it doesn't. They had to go out and measure proportions of nose to jaw, forehead to chin, and so on to establish why some faces are more appealing than others.[3] **Typographers and graphic designers often choose typefaces for the very same reason they might fancy a person: They just like that person. For more scientifically-minded people, however, there are specific measurements, components, details, and proportions to describe various parts of a letter. While these won't tell you what makes a typeface good, they will at least give you the right words to use when you discuss the benefits of a particular face over another. You can say "I hate the x-height on Such-a-Gothic" or "These descenders just don't work for me" or "Please, may I see something with a smaller cap height?" and you'll know what you are talking about.**

2▸ ·· **1** The official Roman alphabet, as seen on the Trajan Column in Rome, has never gone out of fashion. **2** When communications became more international, typefaces that were more universal were in demand. Today Fraktur, Gothic and similar styles are only used to evoke the feeling of a bygone era, for example on the banner of newspapers such as *The New York Times*. **3** Many digital typefaces evoke the timeless beauty of ancient inscriptions and early printing types. Trajan, designed by Carol Twombly in 1990, is a good example.

Exploration 24
Hierarchy:
Point Size + Weight
(typeset by Priscilla Peña)

» Title
12pt Univers Bold Condensed
tracking +140/1000 em

» Byline
12pt Univers Condensed
tracking +110/1000 em

» First Paragraph
7/14 Univers Bold
tracking +20/1000 em

» Alternate Paragraphs
7/14 Univers Light
Tracking +20/1000 em

» Footnotes
5.5/12 Univers Light
tracking +20/1000 em

EXP **24.3**

# TYPE BUILDS CHAR ACTER

**BY ERIK SPIEKERMANN** ∻ Ever since people have been writing things down, they have had to consider their audience before actually putting pen to paper: letters would have to look different depending on whether they were to be read by mainly other people (in official documents or inscriptions), just one other person (in a letter), or only the writer (in a notebook or diary). There would be less room for guesswork if letter shapes were made more formal as the diversity of the readership expanded. ∻ Some of the first messages to be read by a large number of people were rendered not by pens but by chisels.[1] Large inscriptions on monuments in ancient Rome were carefully planned, with letters drawn on the stone with a brush before they were chiseled.[2] Even if white-out had existed in those days, it would not have helped to remove mistakes made in stone. A bit of planning was also more important then, since stonemasons were sometimes more expendable than slabs of marble or granite. ∻ Graphic design and typography are complicated activities, but even the simple projects benefit from thinking about the problem, forming a mental picture of the solution, and then carefully planning the steps between. ∻ Scientists have not been content with just calling the human face "beautiful" if it meets certain ideals, or "ugly" if it doesn't. They had to go out and measure proportions of nose to jaw, forehead to chin, and so on to establish why some faces are more appealing than others.[3] ∻ Typographers and graphic designers often choose typefaces for the very same reason they might fancy a person: They just like that person. For more scientifically-minded people, however, there are specific measurements, components, details, and proportions to describe various parts of a letter. While these won't tell you what makes a typeface good, they will at least give you the right words to use when you discuss the benefits of a particular face over another. You can say "I hate the x-height on Such-a-Gothic" or "These descenders just don't work for me" or "Please, may I see something with a smaller cap height?" and you'll know what you are talking about. ∻ While metal letters could be made to any width and height, digital type has to conform to multiples of the smallest unit: the pixel. Every character has to be a certain number of pixels wide and high. This is not a problem when the letters are made up of 600 pixels per inch, as is the case with modern laser printers—those pixels are not discernible to our eyes, and we are happy to believe that we are looking at smooth curves instead of little squares fitted into tight grids. ∻ On most screens, only 72 pixels make up one inch. We could see each and every one of them, if engineers hadn't already found ways around that. Computer screens, however, are not where we read most of our type these days. Smart phones, computers, and tablets all have high-resolutions screens, but microwave ovens, espresso makers, and all the other gadgets around us all still use small and modest displays. And the type unmistakably consists of bitmaps, which means that an 8-point letter is actually made up of eight pixels. If we allow six pixels above the baseline, including accents, and two below for descenders, that'll leave only three or four pixels for a lowercase character. ∻ Rhythm and contrast keep coming up when discussing good music and good typographic design. They are concepts that also apply to spoken language, as anyone who has had to sit through a monotonous lecture will attest; the same tone, volume and speed of speech will put even the most interested listener into dreamland. Every now and again the audience needs to be shaken, either by a change in voice or pitch, by a question being posed, or by the speaker talking very quietly and then suddenly shouting. An occasional joke also works, just as the use of a funny typeface can liven up a page. ∻ There's only one thing worse than a badly told joke, and that is a joke told twice. Whatever typographic device you come up with, don't let it turn into a gimmick. A well-coordinated range of fonts will give you the scope for contrast as well as rhythm, and will keep you secure in the bosom of a well-behaved family.

**1** *The official Roman alphabet, as seen on the Trajan Column in Rome, has never gone out of fashion.* **2** *When communications became more international, typefaces that were more universal were in demand. Today Fraktur, Gothic and similar styles are only used to evoke the feeling of a bygone era, for example on the banner of newspapers such as* The New York Times. **3** *Many digital typefaces evoke the timeless beauty of ancient inscriptions and early printing types. Trajan, designed by Carol Twombly in 1990, is a good example.*

EXPLORATION 24
*Hierarchy:*
*Point Size + Weight*
*(typeset by Fred Carriedo)*

*Title:*
*62pt, 44pt, 56pt, 48pt Mønster*
*no tracking*

*Byline:*
*7/14 FF Milo Bold*
*Tracking +100/1000 em*

*Text:*
*7/14 FF Milo Text*
*Tracking +55/1000 em*

*Graphic element:*
*9pt Mønster*

*Footnotes:*
*6/12 FF Milo Text Italic*
*Tracking +40/1000 em*

# Type Builds Character

*by Erik Spiekermann*

1▸ Ever since people have been writing things down, they have had to consider their audience before actually putting pen to paper: letters would have to look different depending on whether they were to be read by mainly other people (in official documents or inscriptions), just one other person (in a letter), or only the writer (in a notebook or diary). There would be less room for guesswork if letter shapes were made more formal as the diversity of the readership expanded.

Some of the first messages to be read by a large number of people were rendered not by pens but by chisels.[1] Large inscriptions on monuments in ancient Rome were carefully planned, with letters drawn on the stone with a brush before they were chiseled.[2] Even if white-out had existed in those days, it would not have helped to remove mistakes made in stone. A bit of planning was also more important then, since stonemasons were sometimes more expendable than slabs of marble or granite.

Graphic design and typography are complicated activities, but even the simple projects benefit from thinking about the problem, forming a mental picture of the solution, and then carefully planning the steps between. Scientists have not been content with just calling the human face "beautiful" if it meets certain ideals, or "ugly" if it doesn't. They had to go out and measure proportions of nose to jaw, forehead to chin, and so on to establish why some faces are more appealing than others.[3]

Rhythm and contrast keep coming up when discussing good music and good typographic design. They are concepts that also apply to spoken language, as anyone who has had to sit through a monotonous lecture will attest; the same tone, volume and speed of speech will put even the most interested listener into dreamland. Every now and again the audience needs to be shaken, either by a change in voice or pitch, by a question being posed, or by the speaker talking very quietly and then suddenly shouting. An occasional joke also works, just as the use of a funny typeface can liven up a page.

1 *The official Roman alphabet, as seen on the Trajan Column in Rome, has never gone out of fashion.*

2 *When communications became more international, typefaces that were more universal were in demand. Today Fraktur, Gothic and similar styles are only used to evoke the feeling of a bygone era, for example on the banner of newspapers such as* The New York Times.

3 *Many digital typefaces evoke the timeless beauty of ancient inscriptions and early printing types. Trajan, designed by Carol Twombly in 1990, is a good example.* ◂2

3▸ **EXP 24 ▪ Hierarchy: Point Size + Weight**

***Title*** 24pt FF Franziska Demibold, tracking +25/1000 em ▪ ***Byline*** 8/14 FF Franziska Book Italic, tracking +40/1000 em ▪ ***First Paragraph*** 12/18 FF Franziska Book, tracking +50/1000 em ▪ ***Text*** 8/14 FF Franziska Book, tracking +40/1000 em ▪ ***Footnotes*** 6/12 FF Franziska Book Italic, tracking +40/1000 em

EXPLORATION 24 • HIERARCHY: POINT SIZE + WEIGHT (TYPESET BY SHAWN HSU) TITLE: 12PT FF UNIT BLACK, TRACKING +100/1000 EM BYLINE: 7/22 FF UNIT ITALIC, TRACKING +300/1000 EM TEXT: 7/11 FF UNIT, TRACKING +30/1000 EM FOOTNOTES: 5.5/9.5 FF UNIT LIGHT, TRACKING +50/1000 EM

◂4

# TYPE BUILDS CHARACTER

*BY ERIK SPIEKERMANN*

◂5

Ever since people have been writing things down, they have had to consider their audience before actually putting pen to paper: letters would have to look different depending on whether they were to be read by mainly other people (in official documents or inscriptions), just one other person (in a letter), or only the writer (in a notebook or diary). There would be less room for guesswork if letter shapes were made more formal as the diversity of the readership expanded.

Some of the first messages to be read by a large number of people were rendered not by pens but by chisels.[1] Large inscriptions on monuments in ancient Rome were carefully planned, with letters drawn on the stone with a brush before they were chiseled.[2] Even if white-out had existed in those days, it would not have helped to remove mistakes made in stone. A bit of planning was also more important then, since stonemasons were sometimes more expendable than slabs of marble or granite.

Graphic design and typography are complicated activities, but even the simple projects benefit from thinking about the problem, forming a mental picture of the solution, and then carefully planning the steps between. Scientists have not been content with just calling the human face "beautiful" if it meets certain ideals, or "ugly" if it doesn't. They had to go out and measure proportions of nose to jaw, forehead to chin, and so on to establish why some faces are more appealing than others.[3]

Typographers and graphic designers often choose typefaces for the very same reason they might fancy a person: They just like that person. For more scientifically-minded people, however, there are specific measurements, components, details, and proportions to describe various parts of a letter. While these won't tell you what makes a typeface good, they will at least give you the right words to use when you discuss the benefits of a particular face over another. You can say "I hate the x-height on Such-a-Gothic" or "These descenders just don't work for me" or "Please, may I see something with a smaller cap height?" and you'll know what you are talking about.

Rhythm and contrast keep coming up when discussing good music and good typographic design. They are concepts that also apply to spoken language, as anyone who has had to sit through a monotonous lecture will attest; the same tone, volume and speed of speech will put even the most interested listener into dreamland. Every now and again the audience needs to be shaken, either by a change in voice or pitch, by a question being posed, or by the speaker talking very quietly and then suddenly shouting. An occasional joke also works, just as the use of a funny typeface can liven up a page.

◂6

1 → The official Roman alphabet, as seen on the Trajan Column in Rome, has never gone out of fashion.

2 → When communications became more international, typefaces that were more universal were in demand. Today fraktur, gothic and similar styles are only used to evoke the feeling of a bygone era, for example on the banner of newspapers such as *The New York Times*.

3 → Many digital typefaces evoke the timeless beauty of ancient inscriptions and early printing types. Trajan, designed by Carol Twombly in 1990, is a good example.

**Opposite page**

1 The first paragraph is set in a larger point size in a single column that is the width of the two columns below it.

2 Both columns and the vertical rule end at the same horizontal grid line.

3 A half-point rule is used to separate the colophon and to structure the other sections of the excerpt.

**This page**

4 The title is set vertically and reads from top to bottom, leading the eye toward the main text.

5 Leading under the byline is the same as the leading on the loosely linespaced paragraphs.

6 Footnotes are set vertically to echo the vertical title. Each note is set on a different measure to make it four lines deep. An arrow, from among the many available within the typeface, is used after the numbers instead of more typical punctuation.

**FF Franziska**

Jakob Runge's 2014 design carries many of the hallmarks associated with a 21st-century style of text serif: a relatively low stroke contrast with a dynamic form model, strong (almost slab) serifs, and a generous x-height. All these features make FF Franziska suitable for body type in magazines, in newspapers, and on the Web. Details such as the sliced rounds of tittles and terminals are revealed at large sizes.

**FF Unit**

The grown-up, no-nonsense sister of Erik Spiekermann's FF Meta, this straightforward face was designed by him with Christian Schwartz in 2003. Cooler than Meta, with squared curves and an upright posture, FF Unit is a sans suitable for more serious content.

# Page Layouts

Page layout is also called page composition. Most pages, whether in print or online, are designed using an underlying grid to structure the space. Very often the grid structure of a page is obvious by the fact that multiple elements align to each other at the same vertical or horizontal lines.

Designing a grid is a matter of deciding where there will be type and where there will be nothing (negative space) on the page. The negative spaces at the edges (margins) and the spaces in between text blocks (gutters) are key design decisions for any page design. Margins are typically larger than gutters so that text blocks group together.

The design of a page layout grid should be as complex as the content necessitates and not a single bit more complex than that. Too many lines on a grid is messy and disorienting, both for the designer and for the reader. Using the same underlying grid for a series of related pages (such as in a book or on a website) makes them look cohesive.

A page layout grid is highly recommended for almost all complex content because it provides structure, clarity, efficiency, economy, and continuity.

The following section catalogs all the page layouts for the Explorations shown in this book. Not only do these miniature pages provide a visual reference of the many possible ways to compose type on a page, the quarter-size drawings can be traced to practice thumbnail sketching or scaled up and used as templates. It has been said that “copying is how we learn,” so it might be educational to use them as a starting point for your own designs by inserting your own typesetting (or images) in place of the mock text blocks.

page 17: Indent

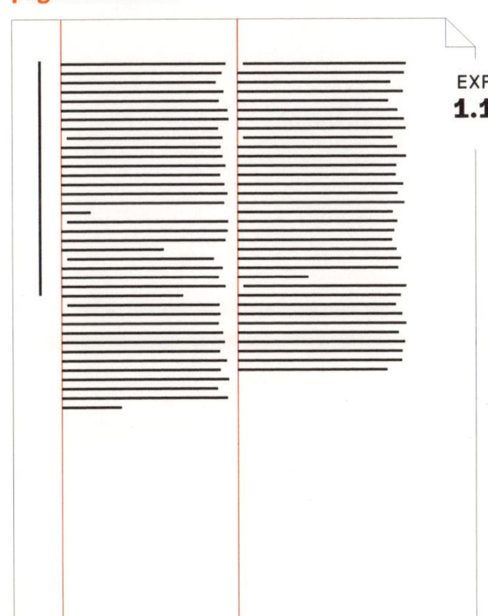


page 18: Indent

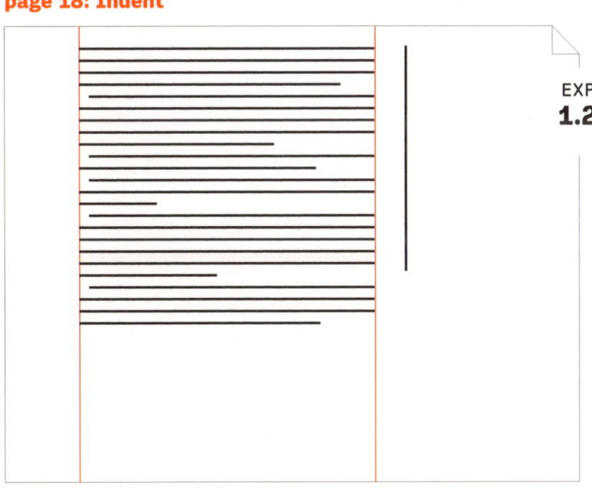


page 19: Indent

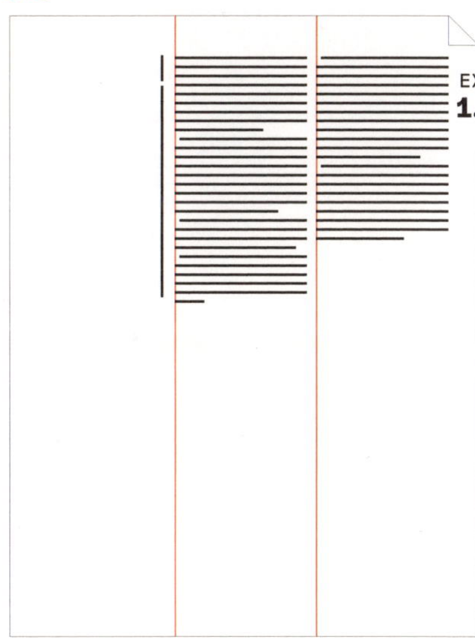


page 23: Exdent

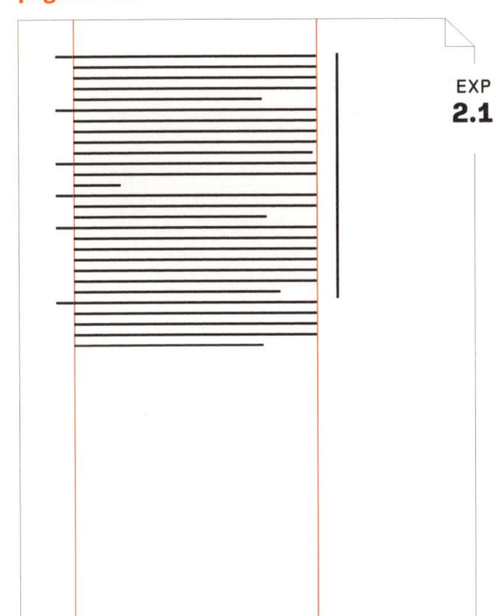


page 24: Exdent

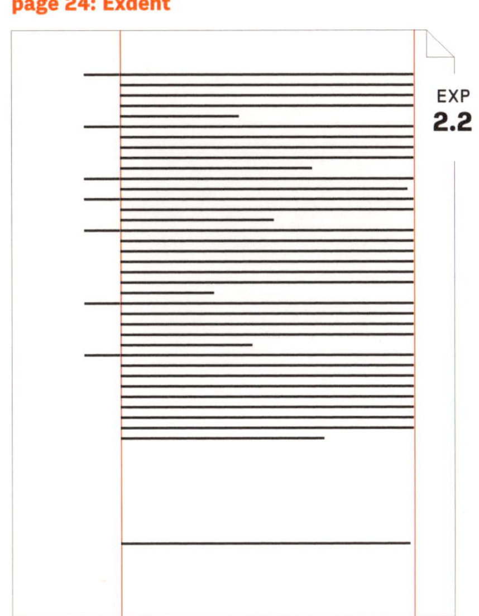


page 25: Exdent

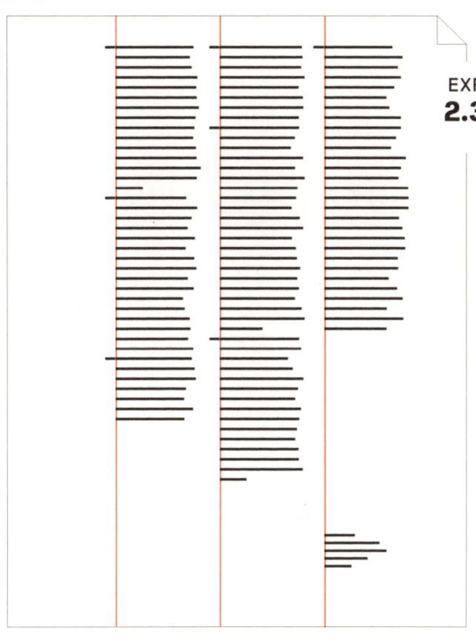


page 26: Exdent

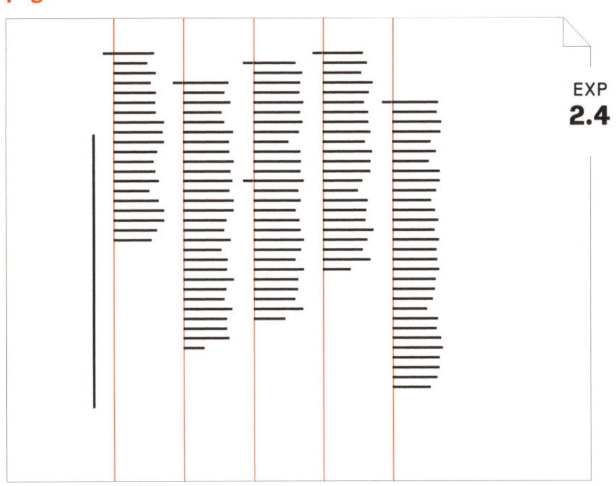


page 27: Exdent

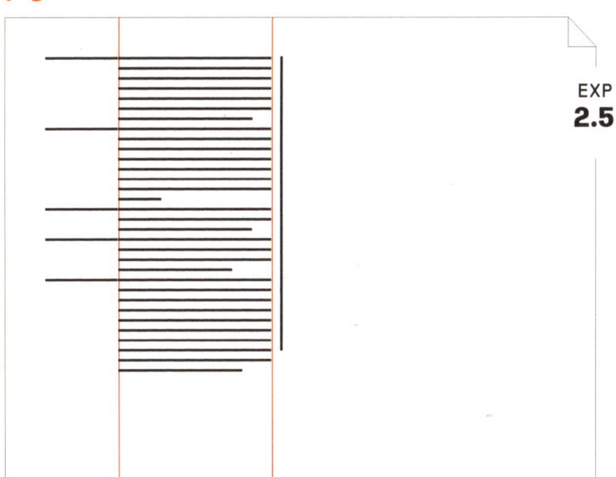

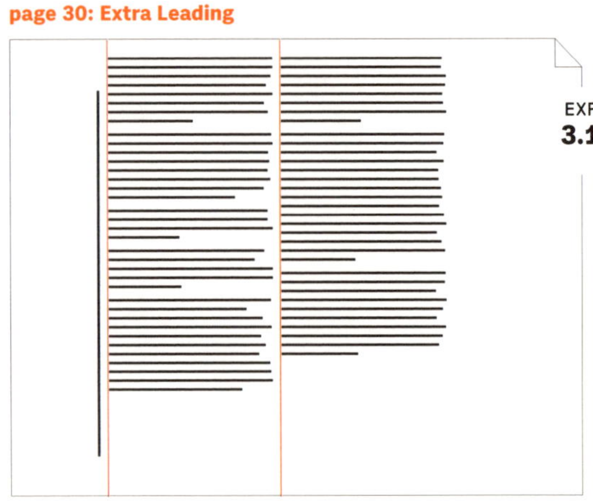


page 30: Extra Leading

page 31: Extra Leading

EXP
3.2

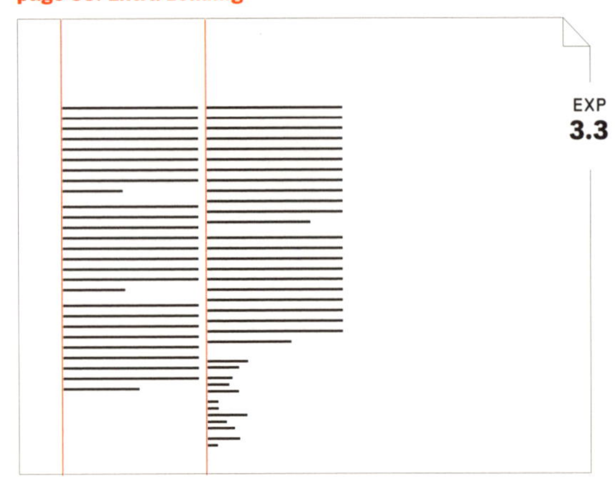


page 33: Extra Leading

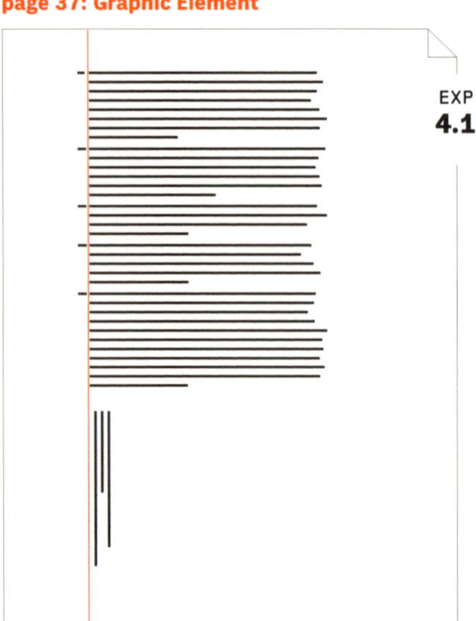


page 37: Graphic Element

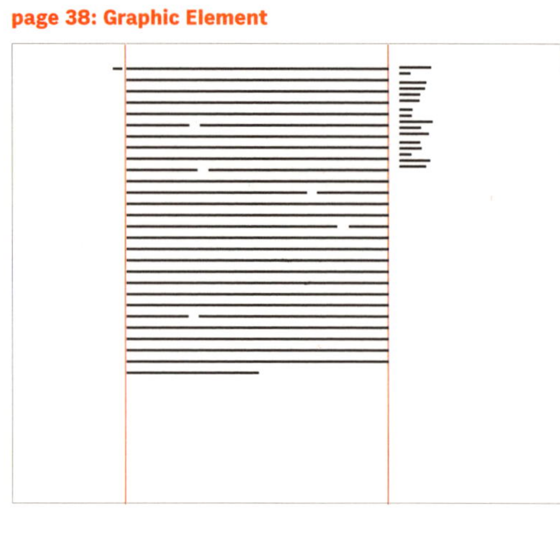

page 38: Graphic Element

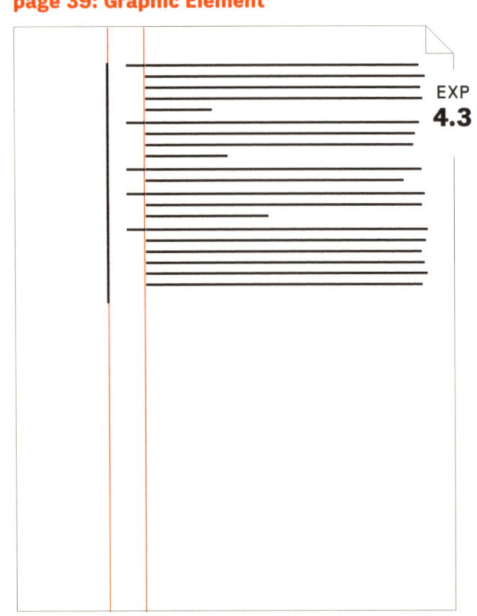


page 39: Graphic Element

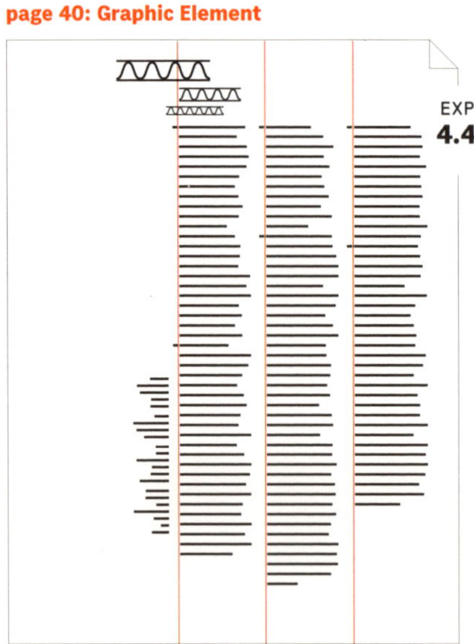


page 40: Graphic Element

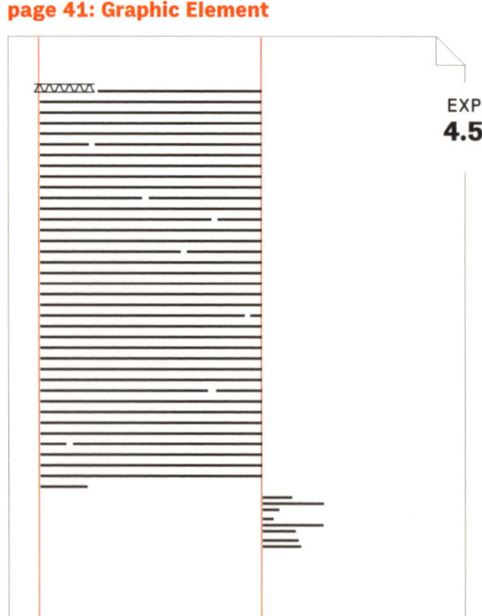


page 41: Graphic Element

page 44: Rule

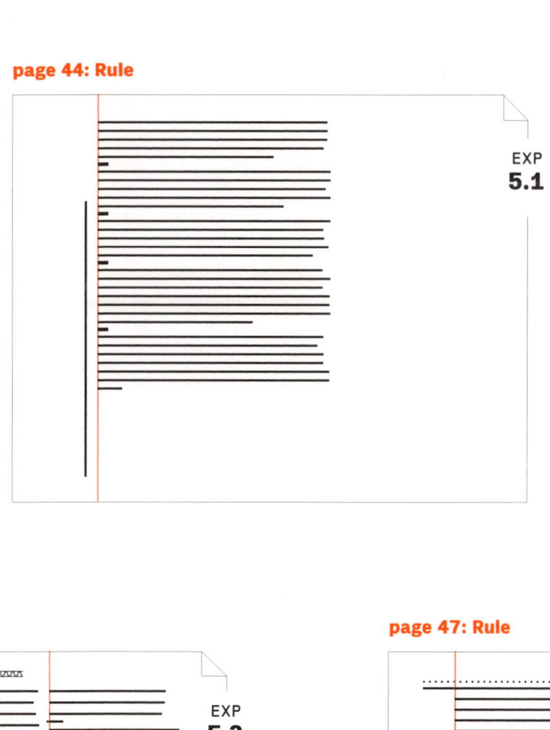


page 45: Rule

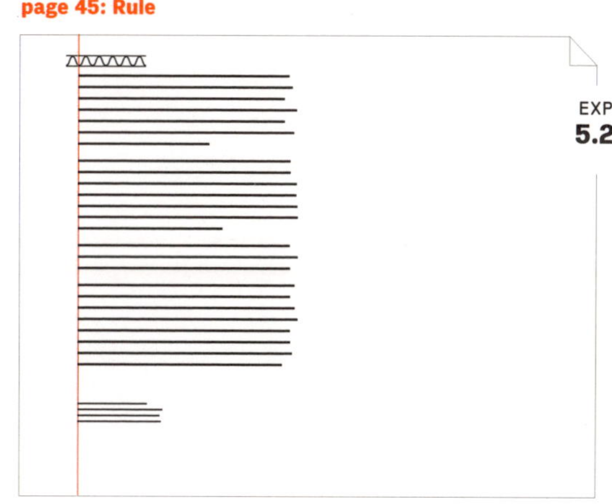


page 46: Rule

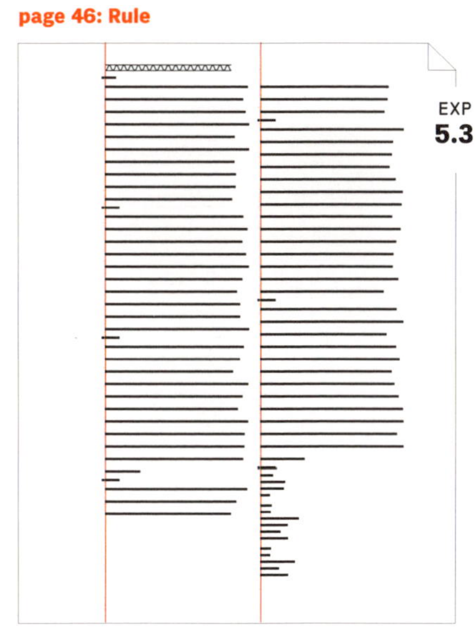


page 47: Rule

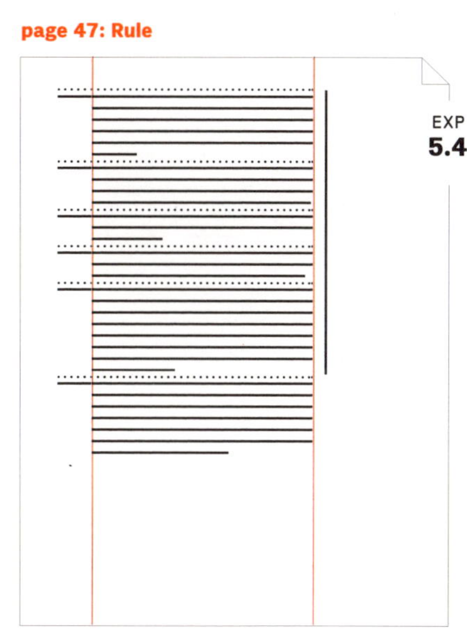


page 48: Rule

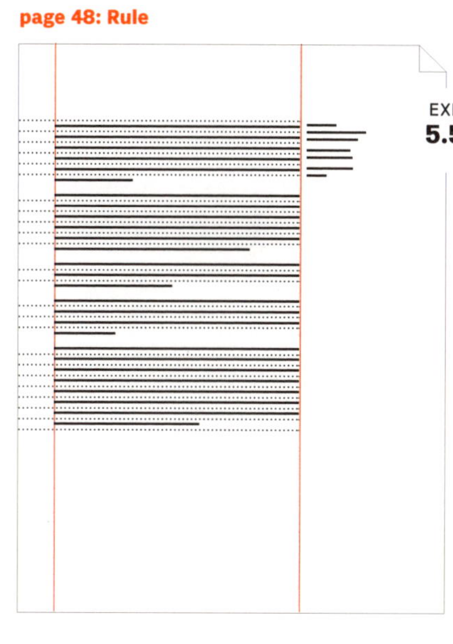


page 49: Rule

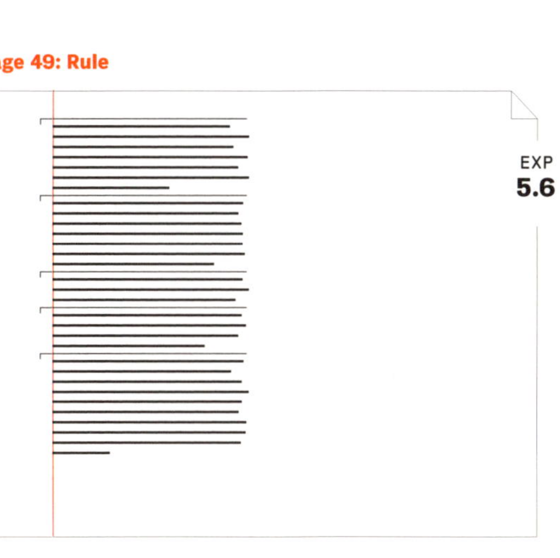


page 50: Rule

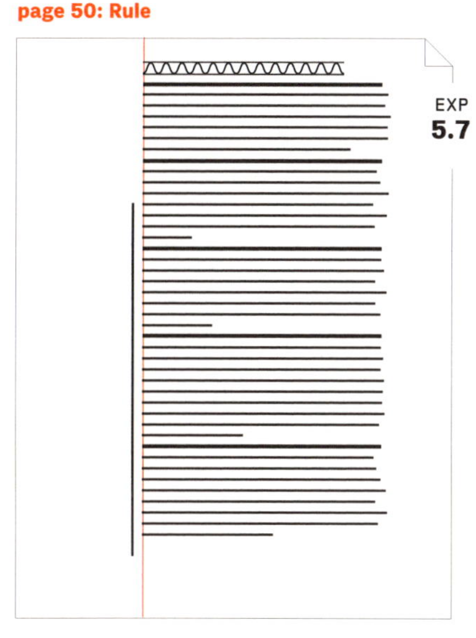


page 51: Rule

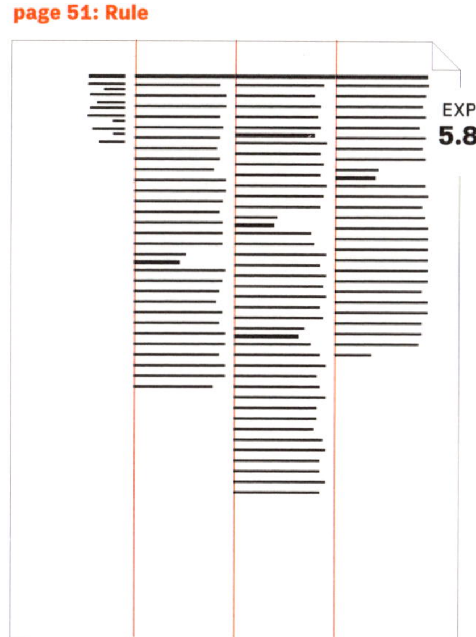

page 55: Initial Capital

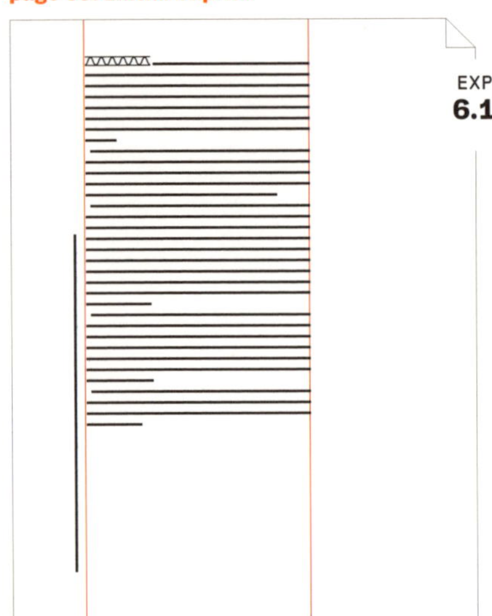


page 56: Initial Capital

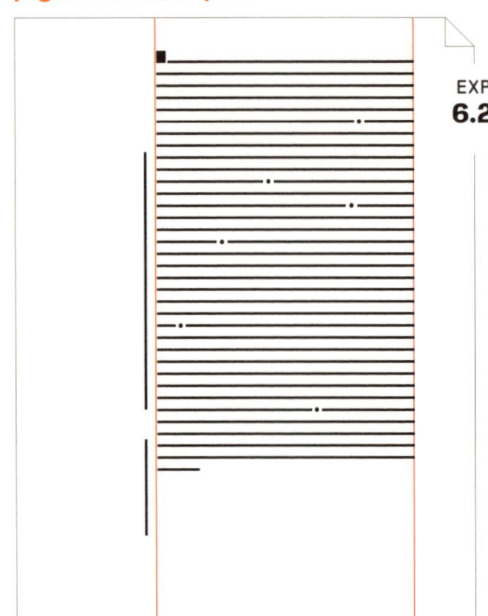


page 57: Initial Capital

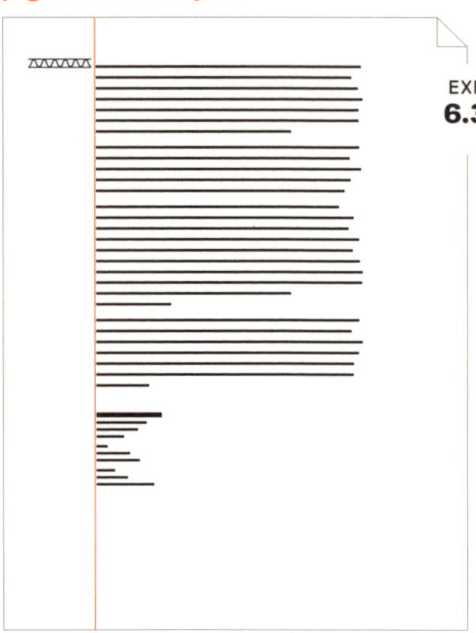


page 58: Initial Capital

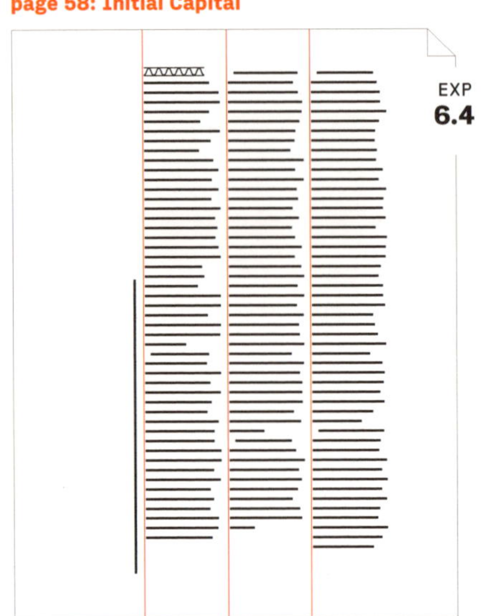


page 59: Initial Capital

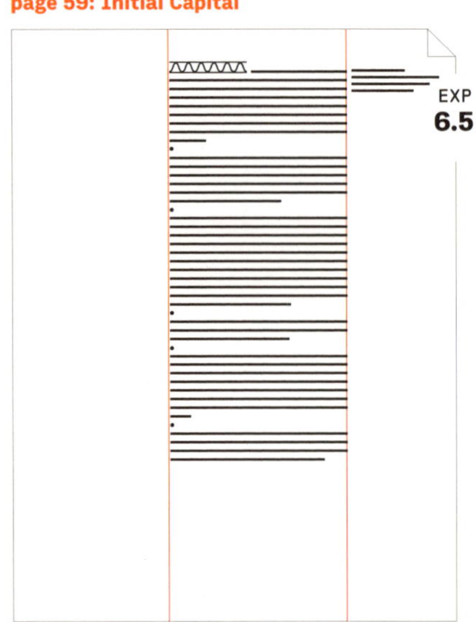


page 63: Drop Capital

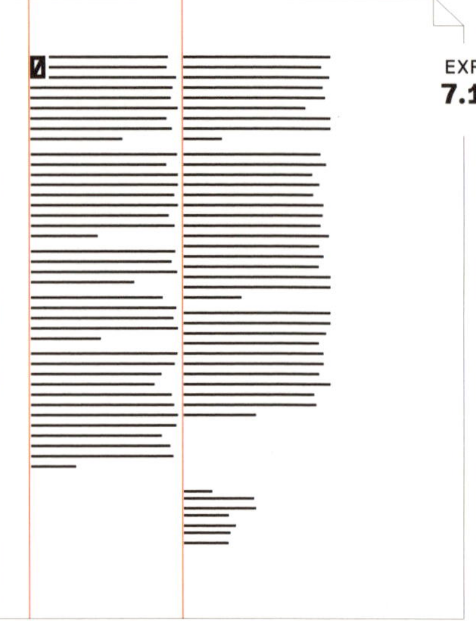


page 64: Drop Capital

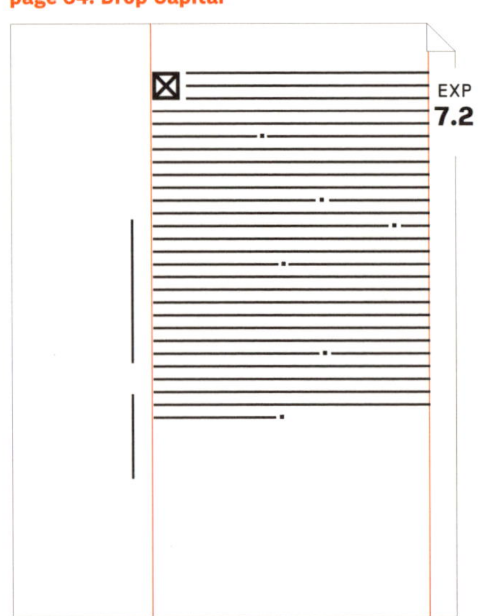


page 65: Drop Capital

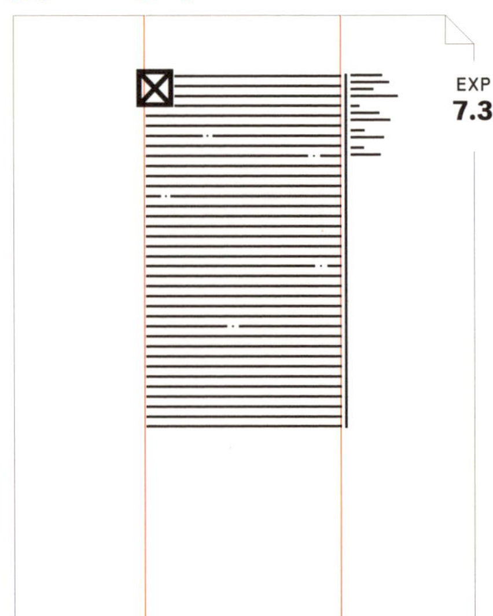

page 69: Flush Left

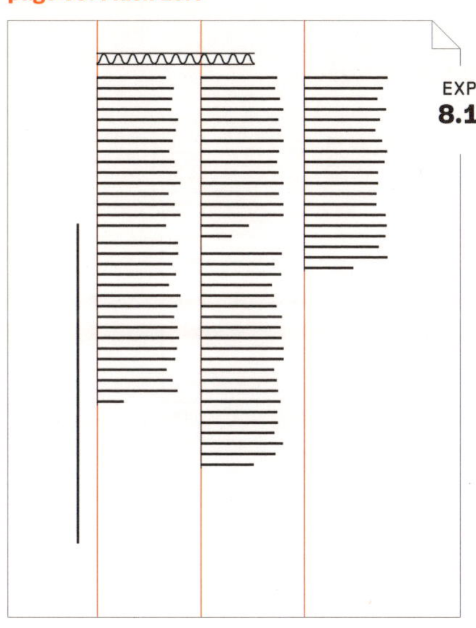


page 70: Flush Left

EXP
8.2

page 71: Flush Left

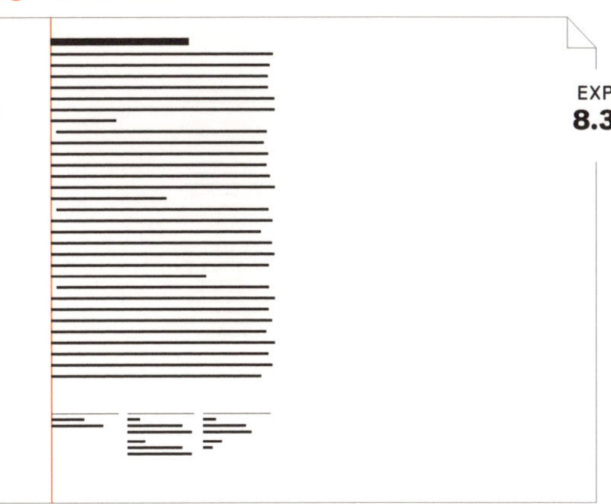


page 75: Justified

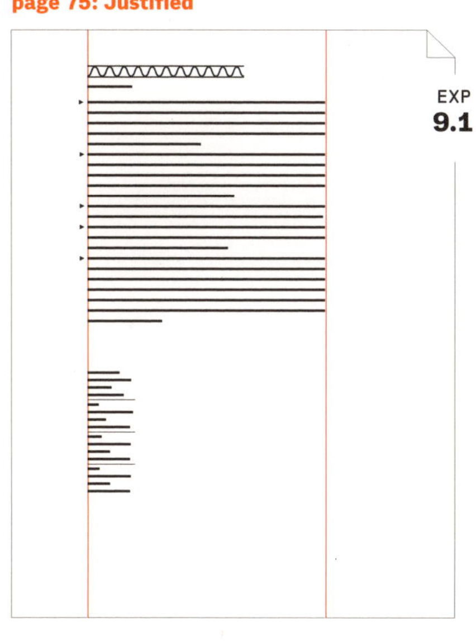


page 76: Justified

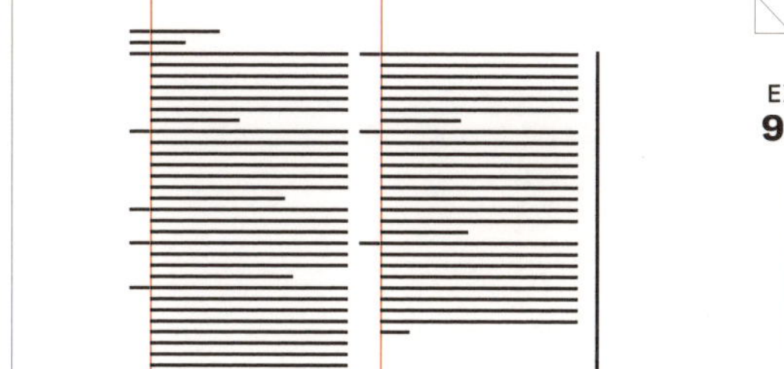


page 77: Justified

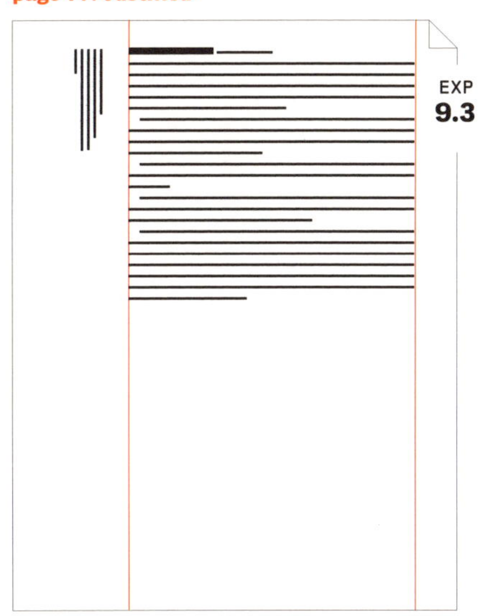


page 78: Justified

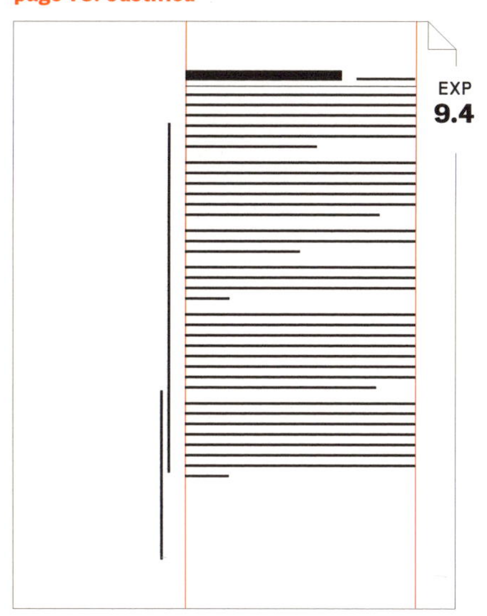


page 79: Justified

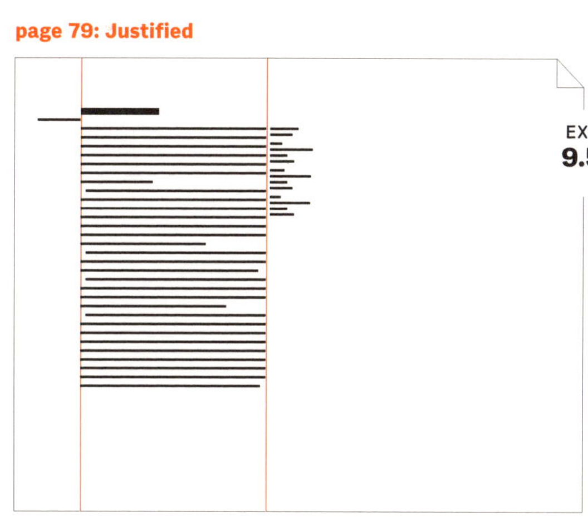

page 83: Flush Right

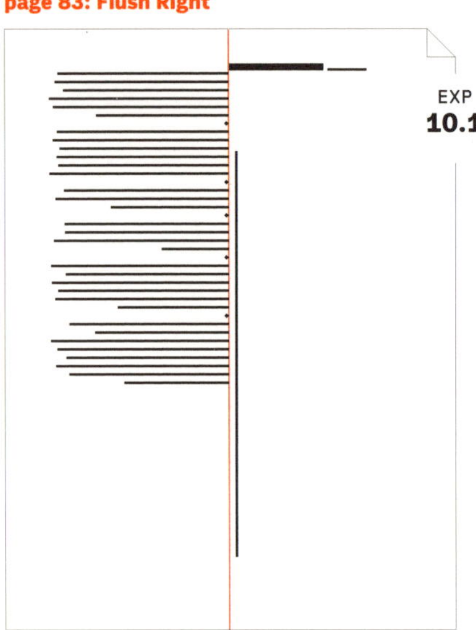


page 84: Flush Right

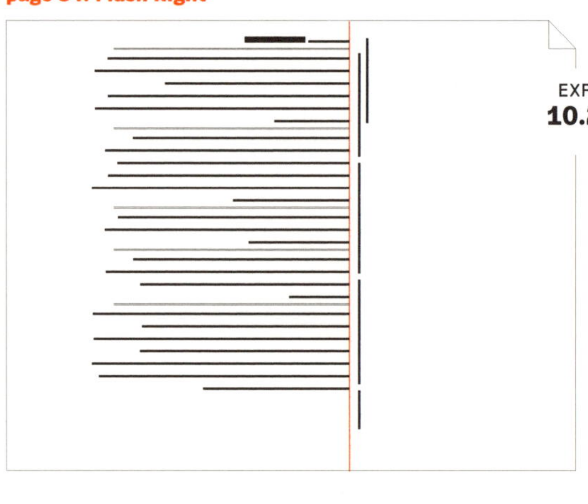


page 85: Flush Right

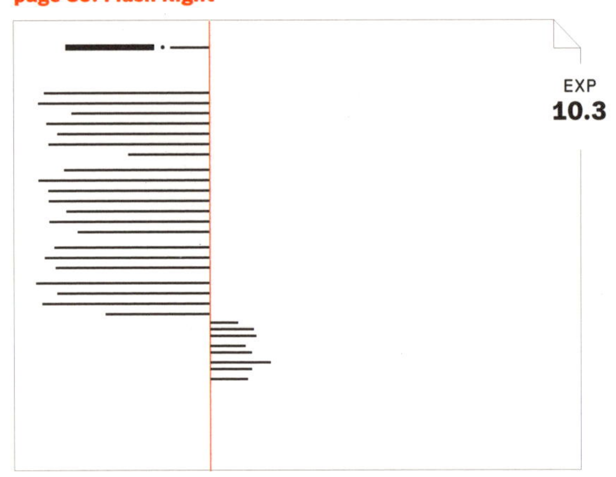


page 89: Centered

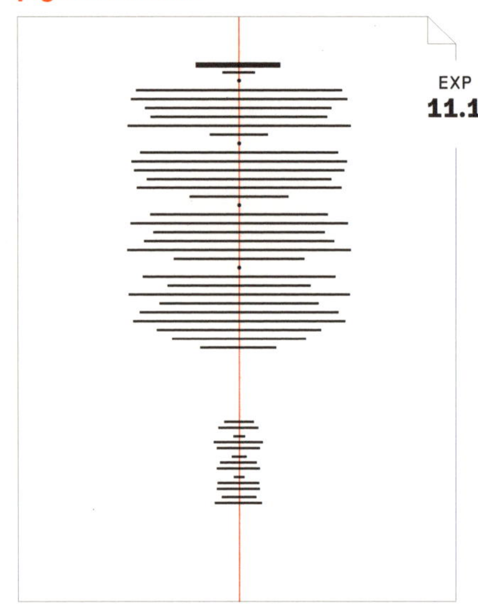


page 90: Centered

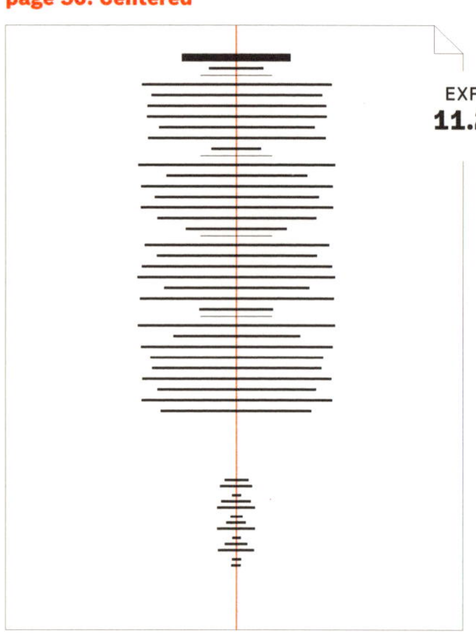


page 91: Centered

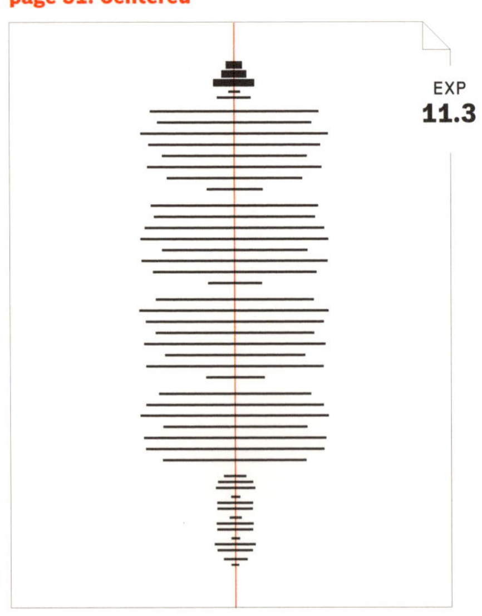


page 95: Capitals

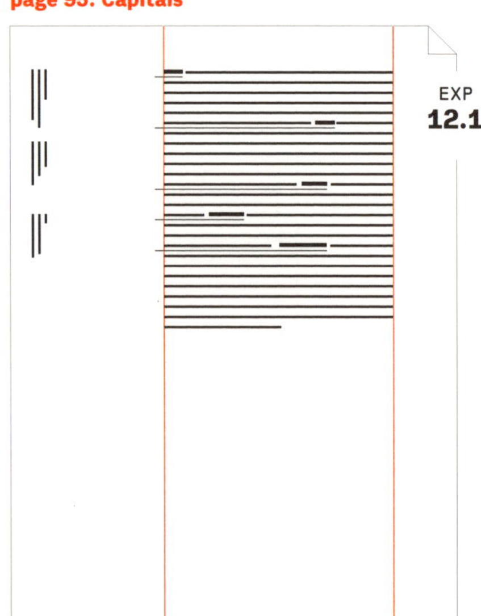


page 96: Capitals

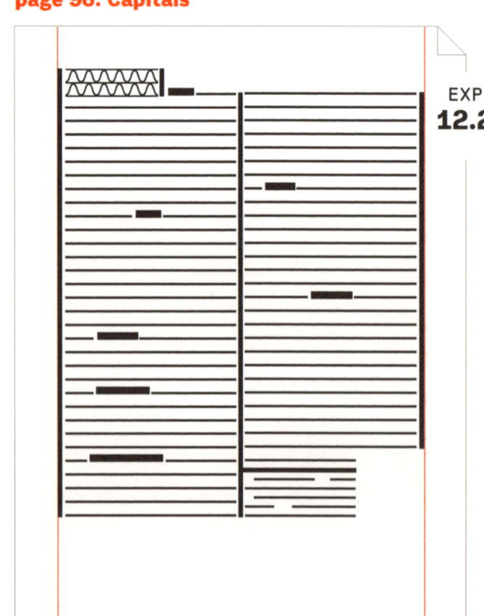

age 97: Capitals

EXP 12.3

page 98: Capitals

EXP 12.4

page 99: Capitals

EXP 12.5

age 102: Weight

EXP 13.1

page 103: Weight

EXP 13.2

page 104: Weight

EXP 13.3

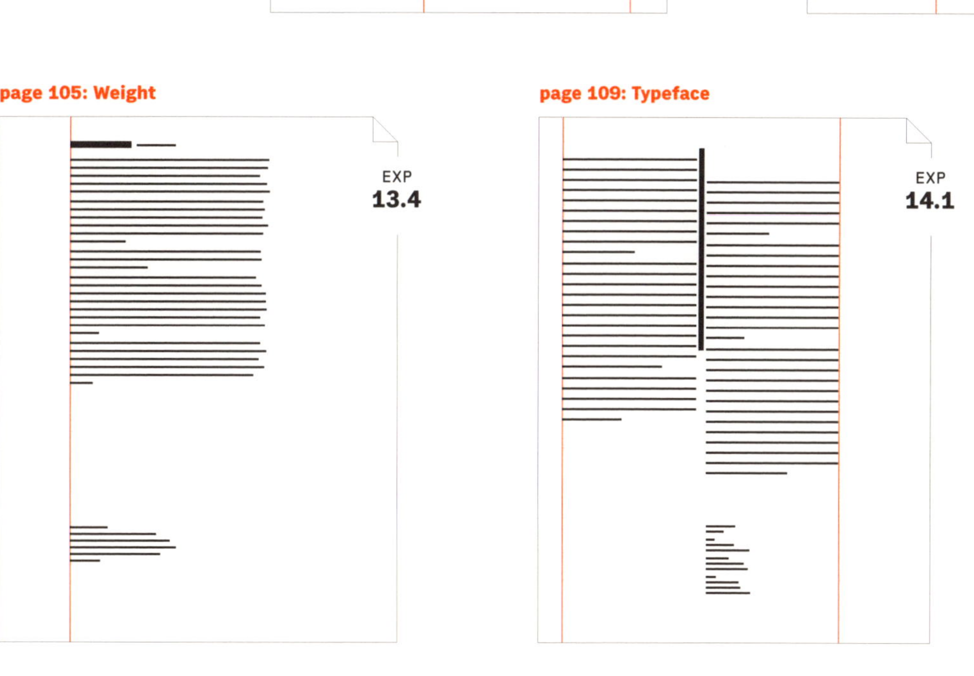

page 110: Typeface

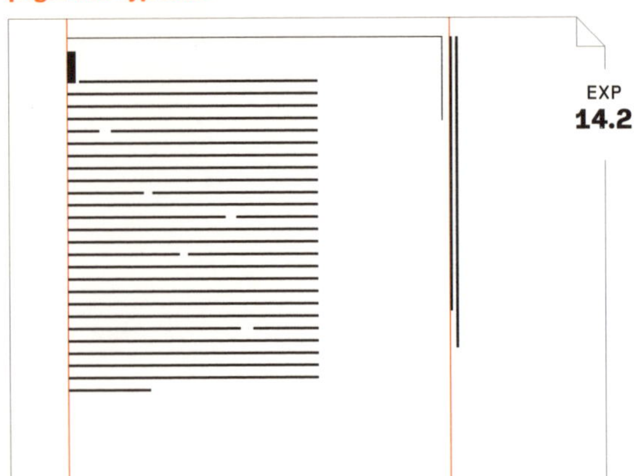


page 111: Typeface

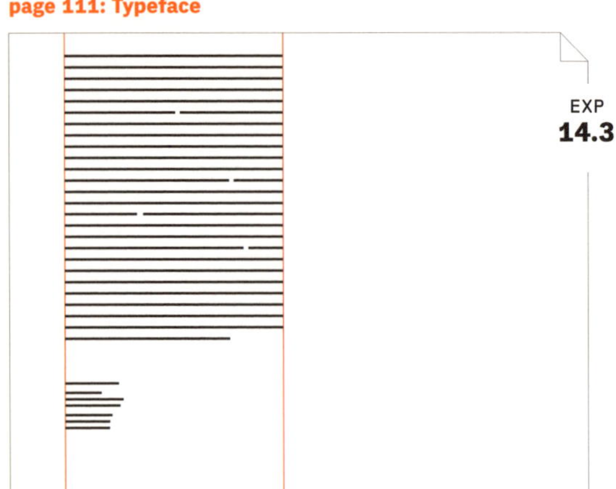


page 112: Typeface

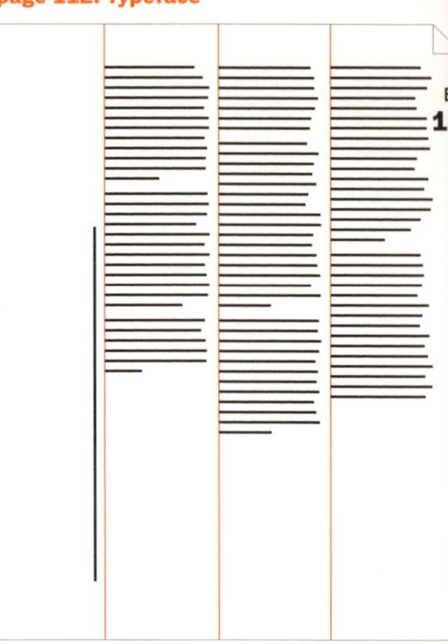

page 113: Typeface

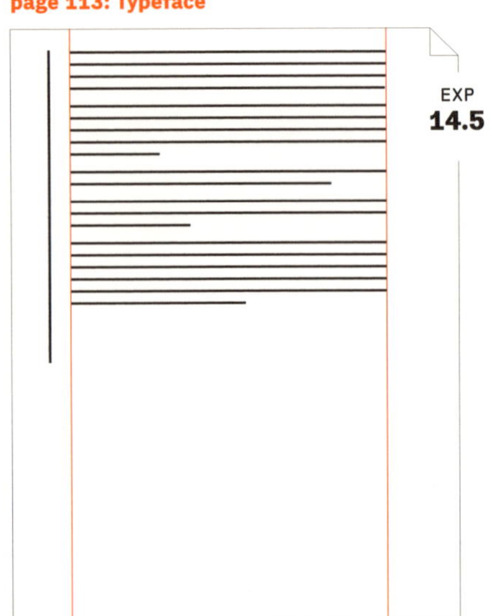


page 116: Point Size

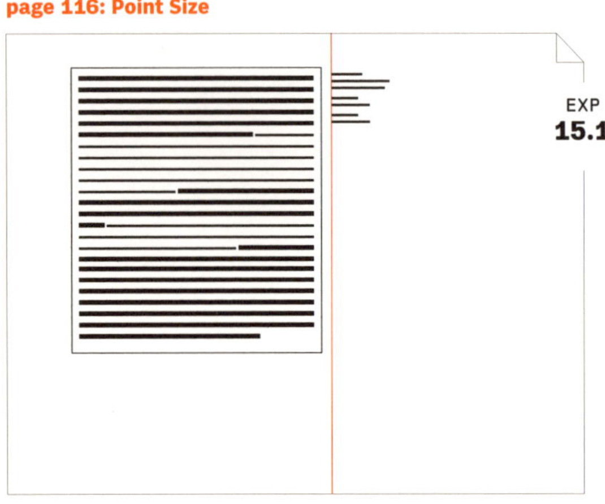


page 117: Point Size

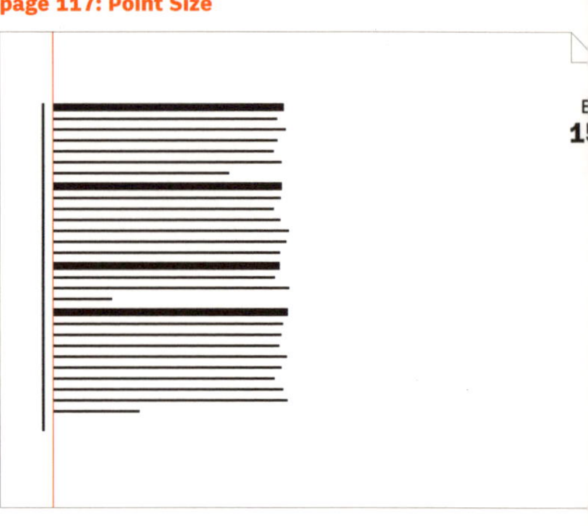

page 118: Point Size

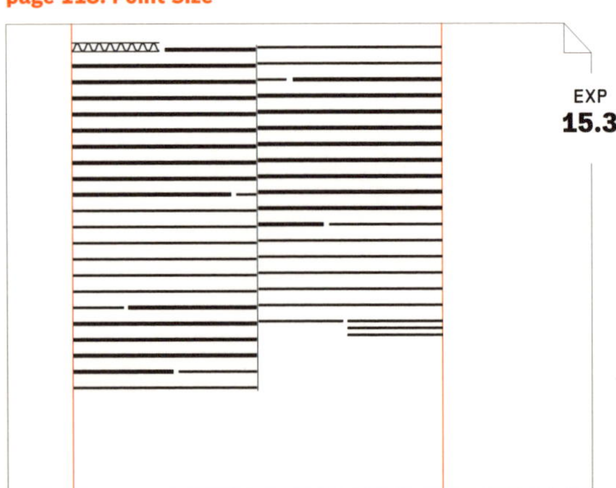


page 119: Point Size

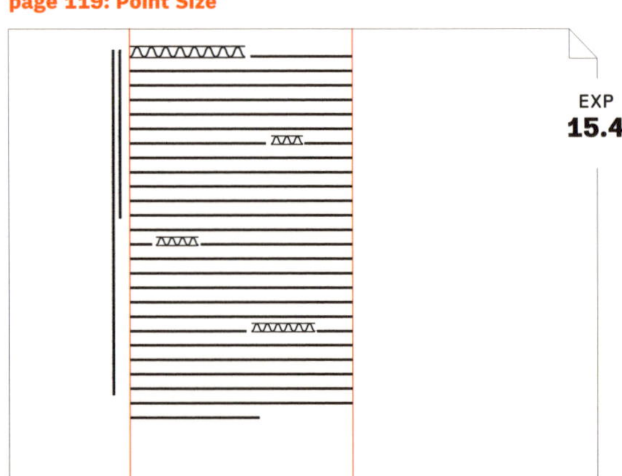

page 122: Leading

EXP
16.1

page 123: Leading

EXP
16.2

page 124: Leading

EXP
16.3

page 125: Leading

EXP
16.4

page 128: Tracking

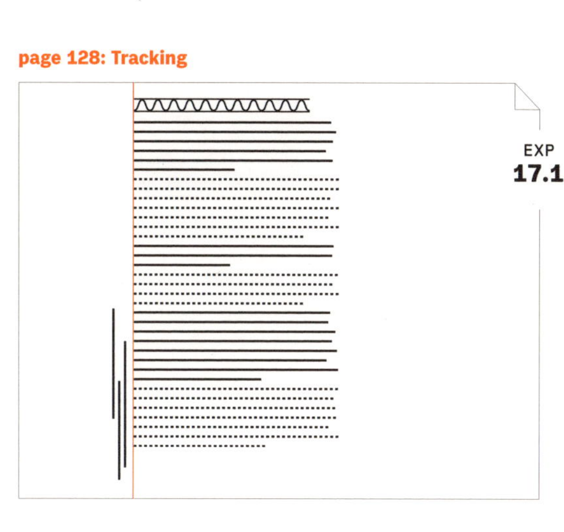

EXP
17.1

page 129: Tracking

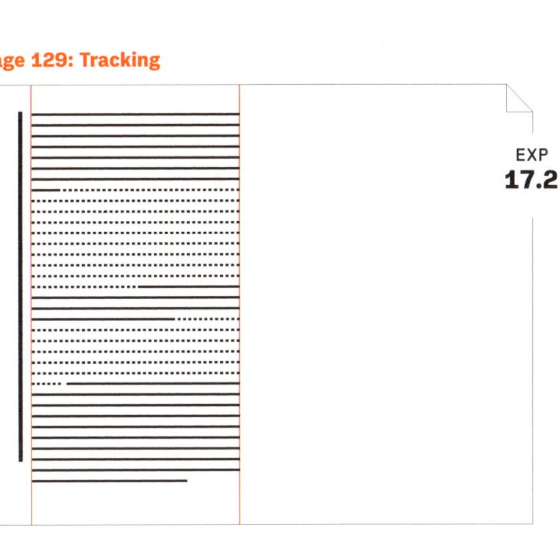

EXP
17.2

page 131: Tracking

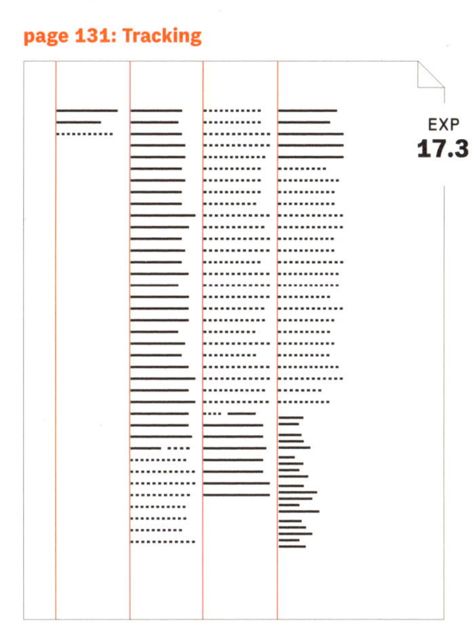

EXP
17.3

page 134: Margin

EXP
18.1

page 135: Margin

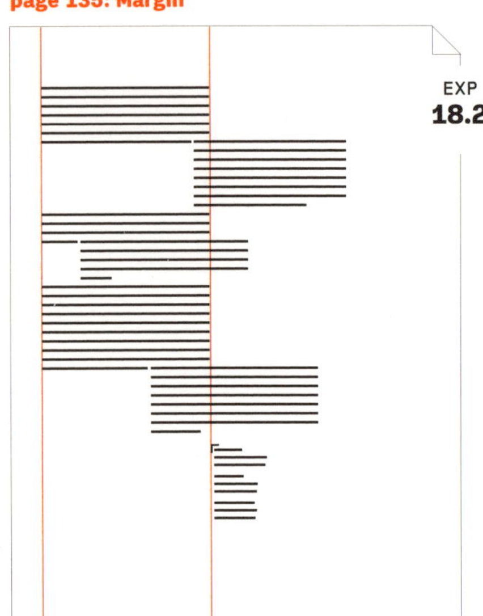


page 136: Margin

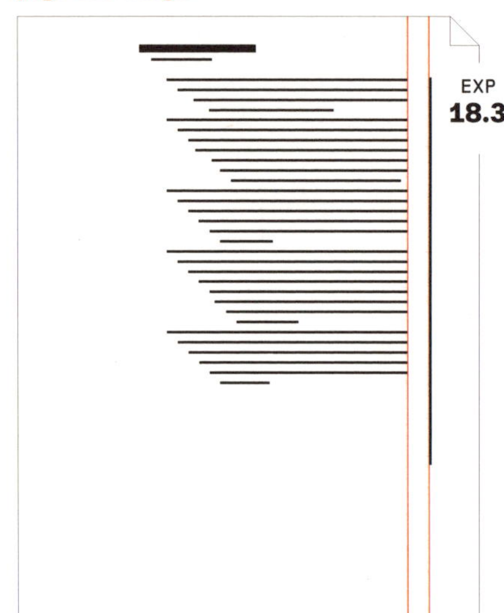


page 137: Margin

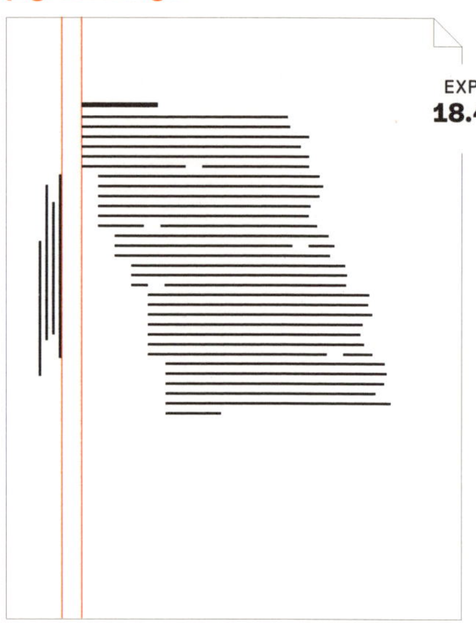


page 140: Column Width

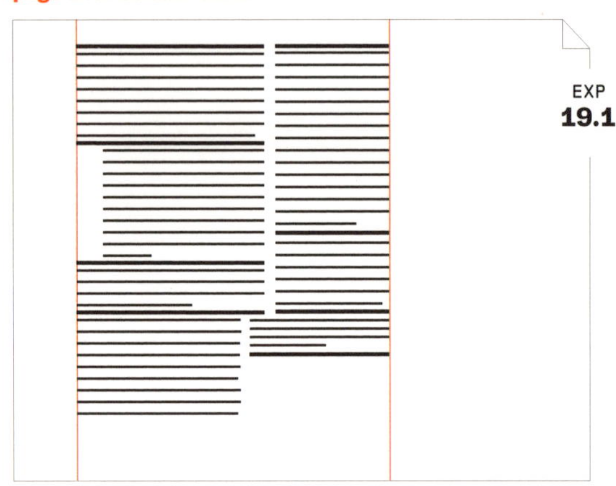


page 141: Column Width

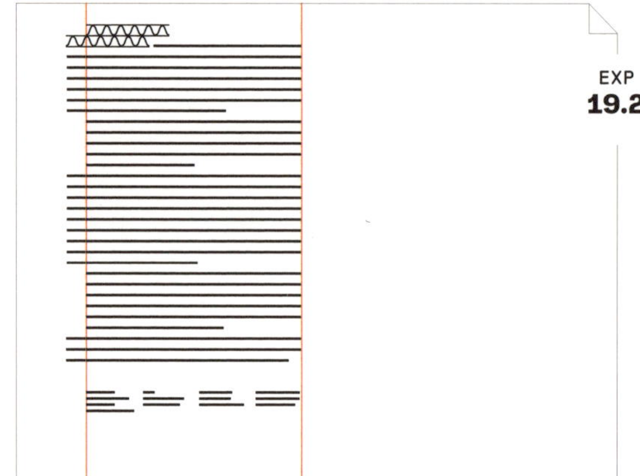


page 142: Column Width

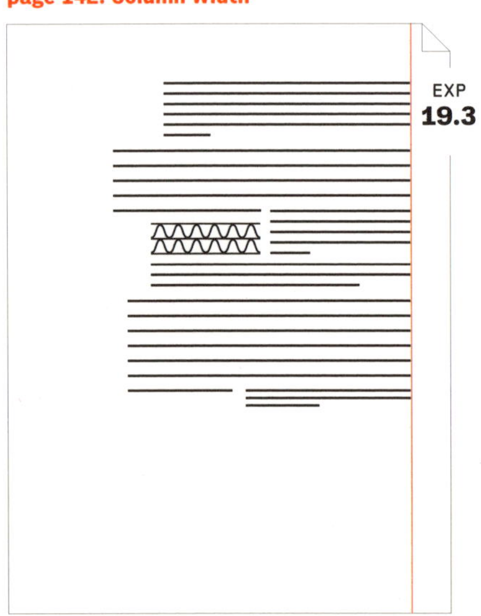


page 143: Column Width

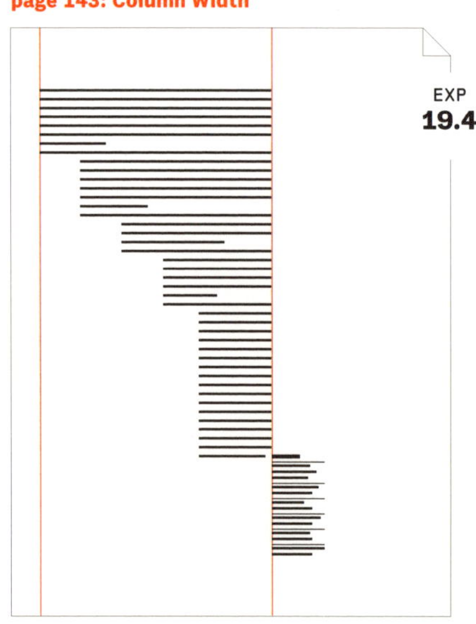


page 146: Interlock

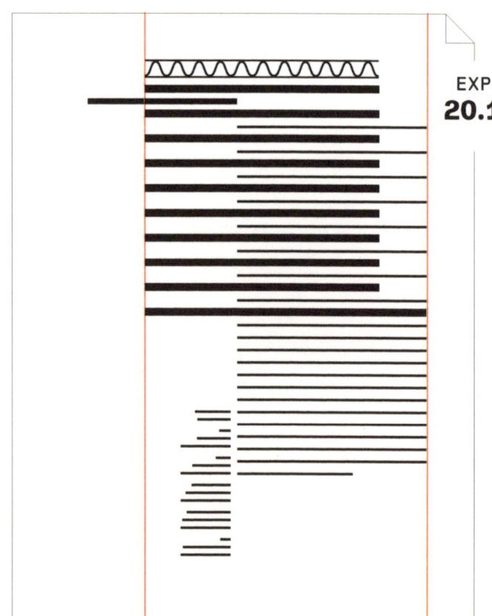

page 147: Interlock

page 148: Interlock

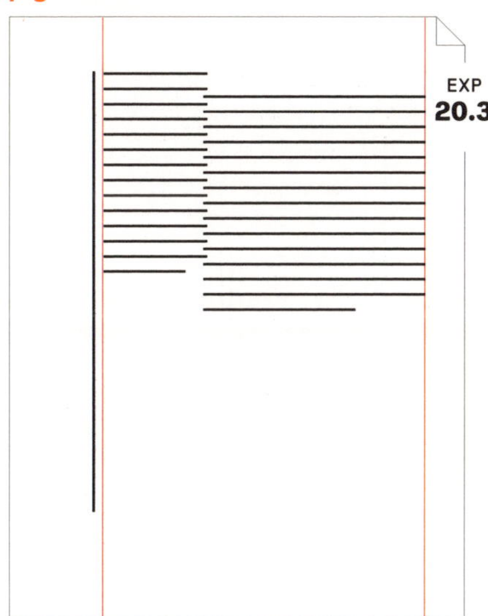


page 149: Interlock

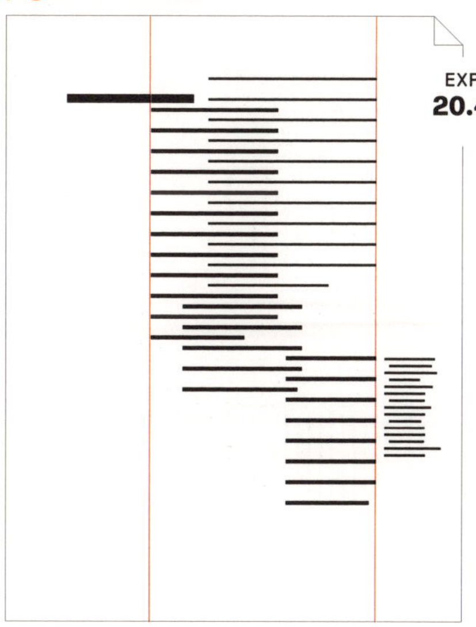


page 152: Overlap

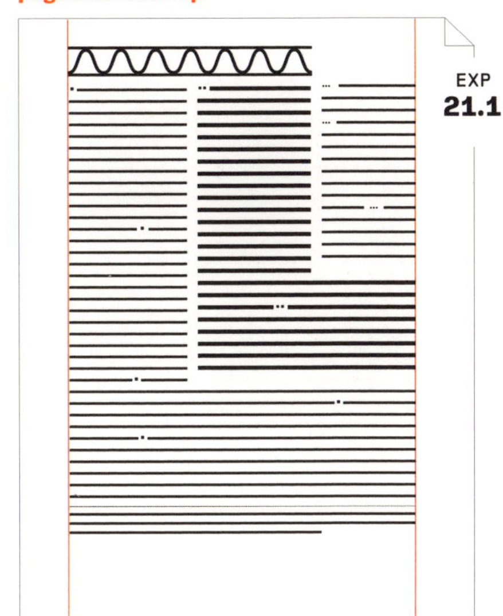


page 153: Overlap

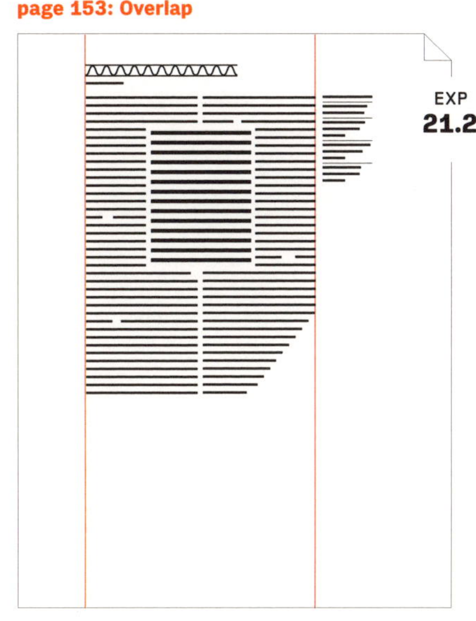


page 154: Overlap

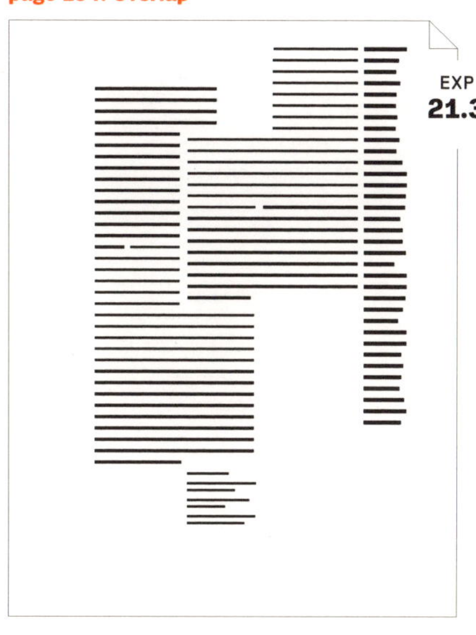


page 155: Overlap

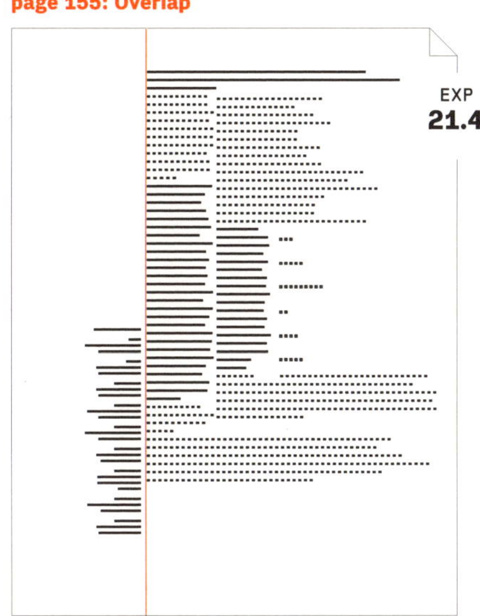


page 158: Direction

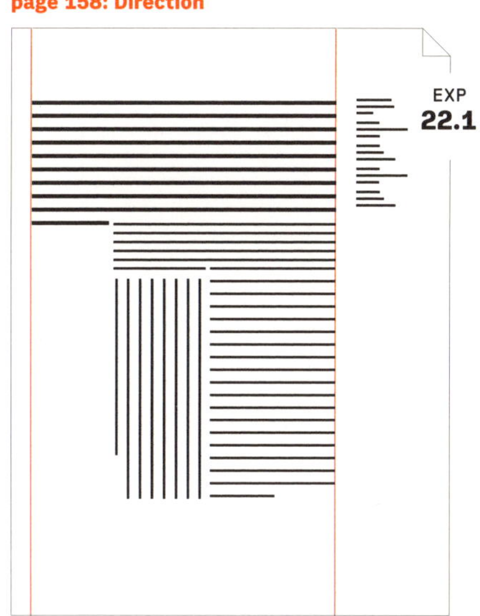

page 159: Direction

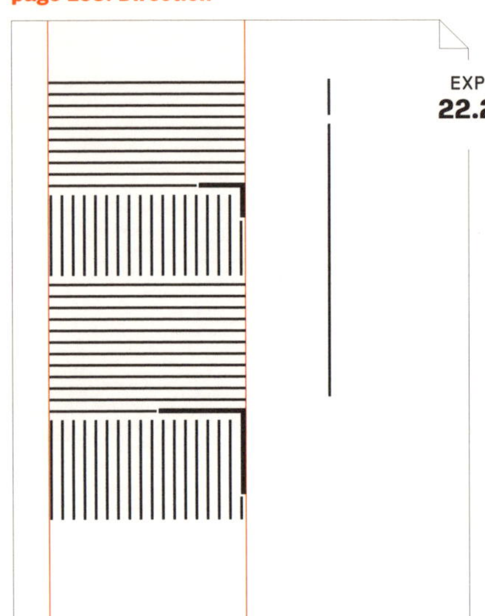


page 160: Direction

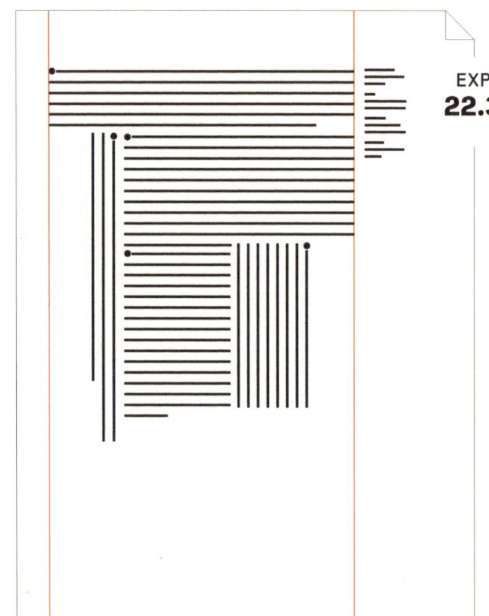


page 161: Direction

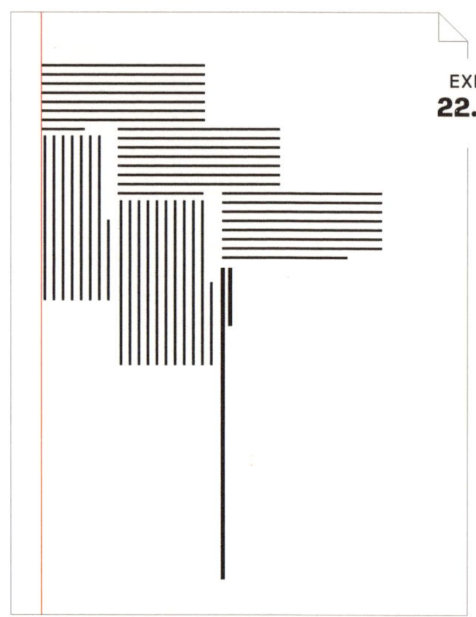


page 165: Hierarchy: Point Size

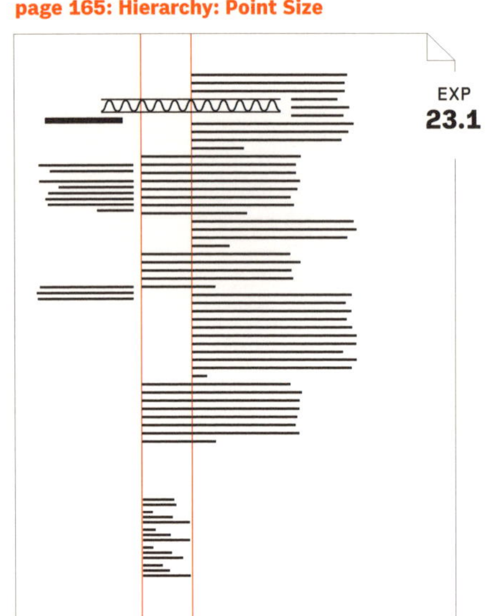


page 166: Hierarchy: Point Size

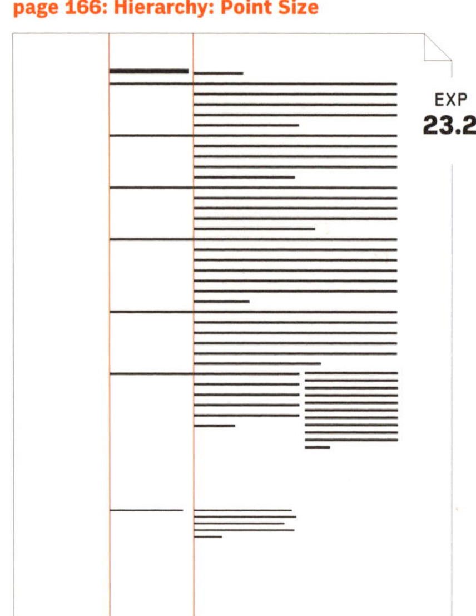


page 167: Hierarchy: Point Size

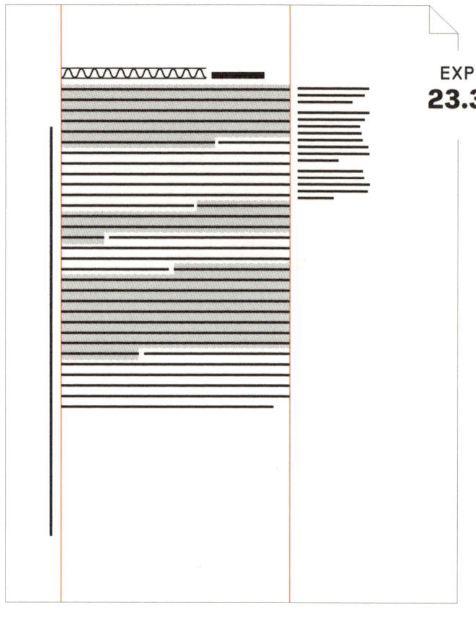


page 168: Hierarchy: Point Size

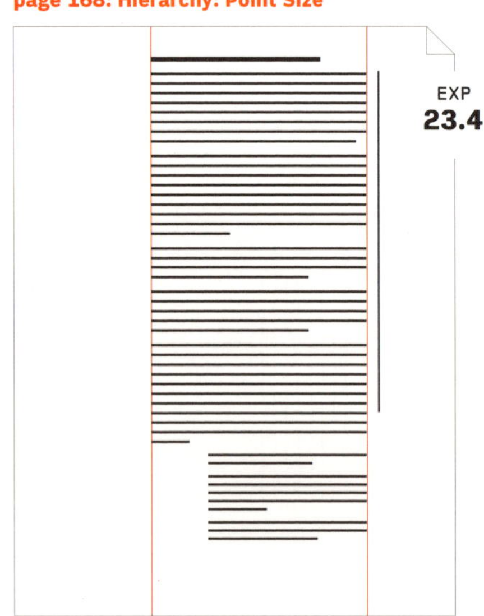


page 169: Hierarchy: Point Size

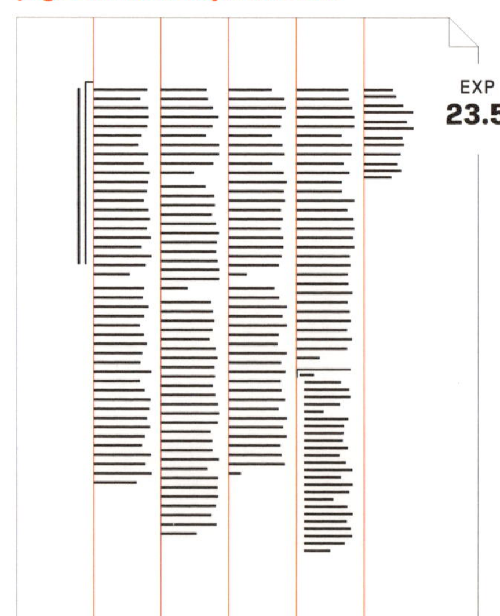

page 171: Hierarchy: Point Size

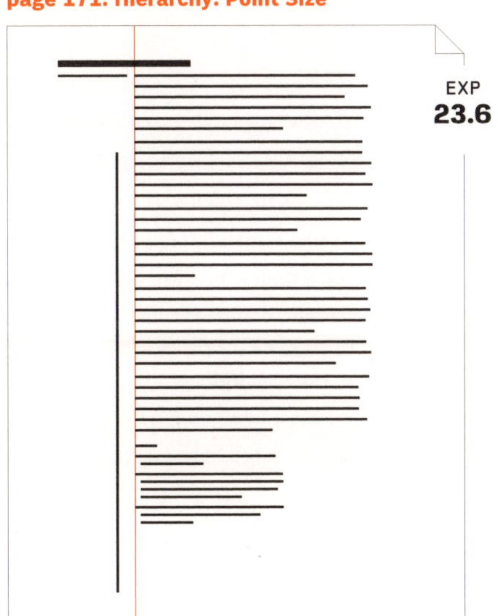


page 174: Hierarchy: Point Size + Weight

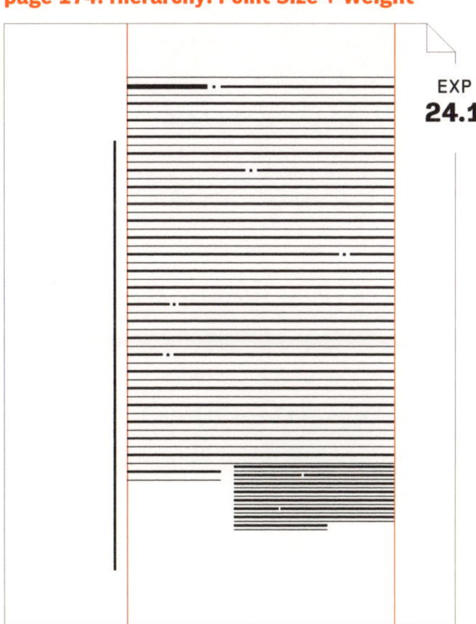


page 175: Hierarchy: Point Size + Weight

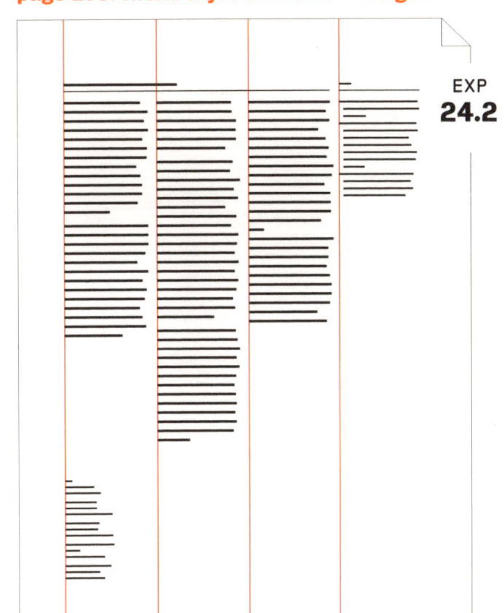


page 176: Hierarchy: Point Size + Weight

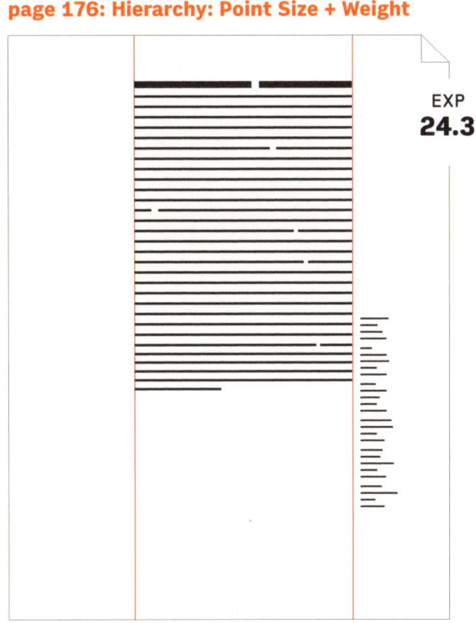


page 177: Hierarchy: Point Size + Weight

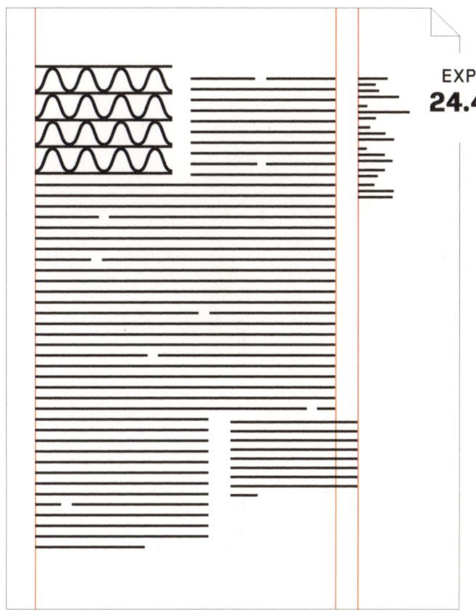


page 178: Hierarchy: Point Size + Weight

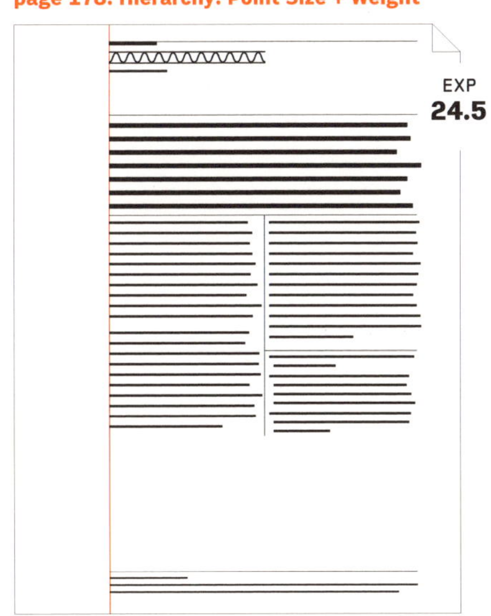


page 179: Hierarchy: Point Size + Weight

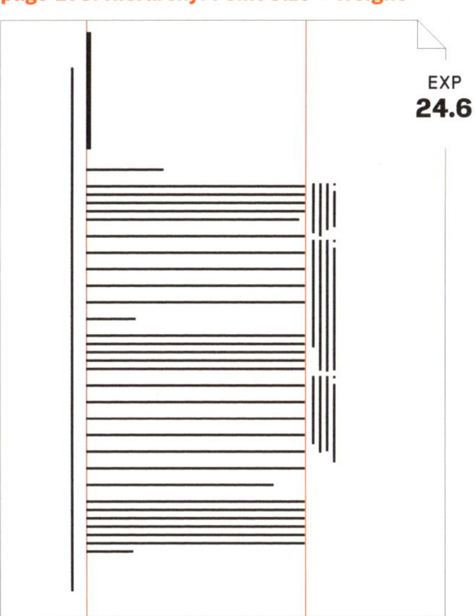

# Typeface Combinations

The following is a list of all the typefaces used together in this book. For each Exploration, the faces are listed in order of use. Some of these are tried-and-true combinations; others are ones that were discovered in the process of designing the pages.

Designing with two (or more) typefaces requires a bit of forethought and sensitivity. There is no shame in using one typeface at a time until you feel comfortable with the more complex task of using multiple fonts together. Although theoretically any two typefaces can be used together, it really depends on exactly how and why they are used; realistically, some faces just don't look very good together.

The possibilities for combining typefaces are endless; however, the basic guideline is to select (1) a serif face and a sans serif face that (2) have similar shapes. One way to discover typefaces with similar shapes is to look for ones designed by the same designer or created during the same historical era.

Note that type set in two different typefaces in the same point size may not look like it is the same size. Sometimes this works to your advantage. Other times, you will want the two faces to look like they are the same size because they need to express the same hierarchy. To make two typefaces look like they are the same size, make their x-heights match by using them at two different point sizes.

If you see a combination here that you like, but you don't have access to one or more of the typefaces, create a new combination by substituting one of the free or low-cost alternatives listed in the next section. For more information and to quickly search this list of combinations, visit *explorationsintypography.com/combos.*

**age 17**
.1
Aa *Aa*
**xploration**
F Meta Normal
**olophon**
F Meta Serif
Bold Italic

**age 18**
.2
Aa Aa
**xploration**
TC Mendoza
Roman Book
**olophon**
F Scala Sans Regular

**age 19**
.3
*Aa* Aa
**xploration**
MN Caecilia 56 Italic
**olophon**
eunesse Sans Regular

**age 23**
.1
Aa *Aa*
**xploration**
TC Officina Sans
**olophon**
haparral Italic

**age 24**
.2
Aa Aa
**xploration**
F QType
Condensed Book
**olophon**
ettler Bold

**page 25**
2.3
Aa **Aa** Aa
**Exploration**
FF BeoSans Hard R20
**Colophon**
FF Tisa Bold,
FF Tisa Regular

**page 26**
2.4
*Aa* Aa
**Exploration**
FF Engine Light Italic
**Colophon**
Cholla Unicase

**page 27**
2.5
Aa Aa
**Exploration**
FF Tibere Regular
**Colophon**
FF Pullman Inline

**page 30**
3.1
Aa AE
**Exploration**
FF OCR-F Light
**Colophon**
FF Beadmap Inline

**page 31**
3.2
Aa ***Aa***
**Exploration**
Bell Centennial Address
**Colophon**
Cooper Black Italic

**page 33**
3.3
Aa Aa
**Exploration**
FF Nuvo Medium
**Colophon**
FF Beowolf R20

**page 37**
4.1
Aa AB **Aa**
**Exploration**
FF Tronic Regular, FF Folk
**Colophon**
News Gothic Bold

**page 38**
4.2
Aa Aa
**Exploration**
FF Cube Light
**Colophon**
FF Dot Matrix Two Extended

**page 39**
4.3
Aa ***Aa***
**Exploration**
FF Zwo Semibold
**Colophon**
FF Tisa Bold Italic

**page 40**
4.4
Aa **Aa** Aa
**Exploration**
MVB Verdigris
**Colophon**
Ideal Sans Bold,
Ideal Sans Medium

**page 41**
4.5
Aa **Aa** Aa
**Exploration**
FF Netto Regular
**Colophon**
Cholla Slab Bold,
Cholla Slab Regular

**page 44**
5.1
Aa **Aa**
**Exploration**
Memphis Light
**Colophon**
Avenir Next Heavy

**page 45**
5.2
*Aa* Aa Aa
**Exploration**
FF Prater Script,
Base 9 Regular
**Colophon**
Base 12 Serif

**page 46**
5.3
Aa Aa ***Aa***
**Exploration**
Neutraface Text Demi,
Rufina Regular
**Colophon**
Rufina Bold Italic

**page 47**
5.4
*Aa* ***Aa***
**Exploration**
FF Enzo Medium Italic
**Colophon**
FF Page Serif
Demibold Italic

**page 48**
5.5
Aa **Aa** Aa
**Exploration**
FF Roice Regular
**Colophon**
FF Daxline Bold,
FF Daxline Regular

**page 49**
5.6
Aa **Aa**
**Exploration**
Spartan Book Classified
**Colophon**
Suburban Bold

**page 50**
5.7
Aa **Aa**
**Exploration**
Lingua, TXT101
**Colophon**
Container Regular

**page 51**
5.8
**Aa AB**
**Exploration**
FF Trixie Heavy
**Colophon**
FF Burokrat One

**page 55**
6.1
***Aa*** Aa *Aa*
**Exploration**
Matrix Script Bold,
FF Scala Sans Regular
**Colophon**
FF Scala Sans Italic

**page 56**
6.2
AB Aa *Aa*
**Exploration**
FF Scala Jewel, FF Scala
**Colophon**
FF Scala Sans Italic

**page 57**
6.3
Aa **Aa** Aa
**Exploration**
FF Absara Regular
**Colophon**
FF Absara Sans Bold,
FF Absara Sans Regular

**page 58**
**6.4**
Aa Aa Aa
**Exploration**
Cholla Unicase, Input Serif Condensed Regular
**Colophon**
FF Info Text Regular

**page 59**
**6.5**
Aa Aa
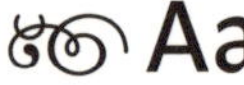
**Exploration**
Sabbath Black Heavy, Adobe Jenson, Dalliance Flourishes
**Colophon**
FF Legato Regular

**page 63**
**7.1**
AB Aa Aa
**Exploration**
Charlemagne Bold, Joanna Nova Italic
**Colophon**
Gill Sans Book

**page 64**
**7.2**
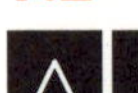
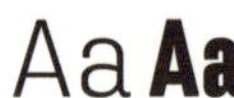
**Exploration**
FF Stealth Regular, FF Hydra Text Light
**Colophon**
FF Hydra Bold

**page 65**
**7.3**
Aa Aa Aa
**Exploration**
Goudy Text Regular, FF Parango Regular
**Colophon**
AW Conquerer Light

**page 69**
**8.1**
Aa Aa Aa
**Exploration**
FF Schulschrift B Linien Eins, FF Profile Light
**Colophon**
FF Profile Bold

**page 70**
**8.2**
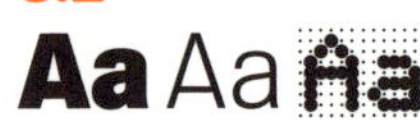
**Exploration**
FF Real Black, FF Real Light
**Colophon**
Foundry Flek Bold

**page 71**
**8.3**
Aa Aa Aa
**Exploration**
Tarzana Wide Bold Italic, Tarzana Wide Regular
**Colophon**
Cholla Slab Oblique

**page 75**
**9.1**
Aa Aa
**Exploration**
FF Letter Gothic Text Light
**Colophon**
Oblong Regular

**page 76**
**9.2**
Aa Aa Aa
**Exploration**
Fournier Regular, Fournier Italic
**Colophon**
FF Nexus Sans Regular

**page 77**
**9.3**
Aa Aa Aa
**Exploration**
Avenir 95 Black, Avenir 95 Black Oblique, Avenir 55 Roman
**Colophon**
Bodoni Old Face Regular

**page 78**
**9.4**
Aa Aa Aa
**Exploration**
FF DIN Black, FF DIN Regular
**Colophon**
FF Container

**page 79**
**9.5**
Aa Aa
**Exploration**
Lo-Res 12 Bold
**Colophon**
FF Cartonnage

**page 83**
**10.1**
Aa Aa
Aa
**Exploration**
Perpetua Bold, Perpetua Italic, Perpetua Regular, P22 Victorian Ornaments One
**Colophon**
FF Milo Regular Italic

**page 84**
**10.2**
Aa Aa
Aa
**Exploration**
FF Legato Demibold, FF Legato Light, FF Dingbats 2.0 Stars and Flowers
**Colophon**
FF Oneleigh Regular

**page 85**
**10.3**
Aa Aa Aa
**Exploration**
Centaur, Centaur Italic
**Colophon**
FF Absara Sans Thin

**page 89**
**11.1**
Aa Aa
AA
**Exploration**
Photina Ultra Bold, Photina Italic, Photina Regular, Maxime Ornaments
**Colophon**
FF Meta Small Caps

**page 90**
**11.2**
Aa Aa Aa
**Exploration**
Maiola Bold, Maiola Regular
**Colophon**
FF Quadraat Sans Italic

**page 91**
**11.3**
Aa Aa
Aa Aa
**Exploration**
FF Quadraat Bold, FF Quadraat Italic, FF Quadraat Regular
**Colophon**
FF Nuvo Regular

**page 95**
**12.1**
Aa Aa
Aa Aa
**Exploration**
Serifa 65 Bold, Serifa 45 Light
**Colophon**
Linotype Univers Basic Bold, Linotype Univers Basic Regular

**page 96**
**12.2**
AB Aa Aa
**Exploration**
Le Corbusier Regular, Fakt Medium
**Colophon**
Fakt Semicondensed Semibold

**page 97**
**12.3**
Aa Aa
Aa Aa
**Exploration**
Eidetic Neo Omni, Eidetic Neo Regular, FF Fago Extra Bold
**Colophon**
FF Fago Medium

**page 98**
**12.4**
AA Aa Aa
**Exploration**
Greta Text (small caps), Greta Text, FF Eureka Arrows
**Colophon**
Joanna Sans Nova

**page 99**
**12.5**
Aa Aa
Aa Aa
**Exploration**
Suomi Hand Script, FF Absara Sans Bold, FF Absara Sans Regular
**Colophon**
FF Absara Bold

**page 102**
**13.1**
Aa Aa Aa
**Exploration**
FF Sanuk Medium, FF Sanuk Light Italic
**Colophon**
FF Scala Bold

**page 103**
**13.2**
Aa Aa
Aa Aa
**Exploration**
Filosofia Italic, Filosofia Regular, FF Dingbats 2.0 Arrows
**Colophon**
FF Zine Sans Bold, FF Zine Sans Regular

**page 104**
**13.3**
Aa Aa Aa
**Exploration**
FF Fago Extra Bold, Chaparral Bold
**Colophon**
Chaparral Regular

**page 105**
**13.4**
Aa Aa Aa
**Exploration**
ITC Officina Serif Bold, ITC Officina Serif Bold Italic, ITC Officina Serif Book
**Colophon**
Syntax

**page 109**
**14.1**
Aa AA Aa
**Exploration**
FF Speak Regular, Democratica Regular
**Colophon**
FF Speak Bold

**page 110**
**14.2**
Aa Aa Aa Aa
**Exploration**
Modula Round Ribbed, FF Zine Serif Medium, FF Zine Sans Regular
**Colophon**
FF Zine Slab Medium Italic

**page 111**
**14.3**
Aa Aa Aa
**Exploration**
Neue Helvetica Medium, Clarendon Regular
**Colophon**
Neue Helvetica Heavy Condensed

**page 112**
**14.4**
Aa Aa Aa
**Exploration**
Myriad Regular, FF Atma Serif Book
**Colophon**
Matrix Script Bold

**page 113**
**14.5**
Aa Aa Aa
**Exploration**
FF Alega Normal, FF Alega Serif Normal
**Colophon**
Eboy Regular Beta

**page 116**
**15.1**
Aa Aa Aa
**Exploration**
FF Hertz, TXT101
**Colophon**
Eureka Sans Regular

**page 117**
**15.2**
Aa Aa
**Exploration**
FF Archian Night, FF Sub Vario Dry
**Colophon**
FF Sub Vario Dry

**page 118**
**15.3**
Aa Aa AA
**Exploration**
Bell Gothic Black, Bell Gothic Bold
**Colophon**
MrsEaves Small Caps

**page 119**
**15.4**
Aa ✤ Aa
**Exploration**
Baskerville Regular, FF Dingbats 2.0 Stars and Flowers
**Colophon**
Bell Centennial Name & Number

**page 122**
**16.1**
Aa Aa + Aa
**Exploration**
FF Antithesis Regular, FF Antithesis Italic, FF Antithesis Bold
**Colophon**
Hydra Bold

**page 123**
**16.2**
Aa Aa Aa
**Exploration**
Futura Black, FF Super Grotesk
**Colophon**
FF Super Grotesk Bold

**page 124**
**16.3**
Aa Aa
**Exploration**
FF Magda Clean Mono Regular
**Colophon**
FF Hydra Medium

**page 125**
**16.4**
Aa Aa Aa
**Exploration**
Eskapade Fraktur Black, FF Quadraat Sans Italic
**Colophon**
Joanna Medium Italic

**page 128**
**17.1**
Aa Aa Aa
**Exploration**
Fluidum Bold, FF Clan Thin
**Colophon**
Adelle Regular

**page 129**
**17.2**
Aa Aa
**Exploration**
FF Ticket Bold
**Colophon**
FF Gothic Min Condensed

**page 131**
**17.3**
Aa Aa
**Exploration**
OCR-B Medium
**Colophon**
Prestige Elite Regular

**page 134**
**18.1**
Aa Aa
∿∿ Aa Aa
**Exploration**
Doko Bold, Doko Book, Frutiger 55 Regular, Frutiger 56 Italic
**Colophon**
TXT101 Light, Doko Bold, Doko Book

**page 135**
**18.2**
Aa Aa Aa
**Exploration**
FF Meta Serif Book, FF Meta Serif Bold, FF Meta Black
**Colophon**
FF Meta Normal

**page 136**
**18.3**
Aa Aa Aa
AA Aa
**Exploration**
FF Kievit Bold, FF Kievit Italic, FF Kievit Regular
**Colophon**
FF Kievit Slab Bold, FF Kievit Slab Regular

**page 137**
**18.4**
Aa Aa Aa
**Exploration**
FF Nexus Sans Bold, FF Nexus Sans Regular, FF Nexus Mix Regular
**Colophon**
FF Nexus Typewriter Regular

**page 140**
**19.1**
Aa Aa
Aa Aa
**Exploration**
FF ThreeSix Regular, FF ThreeSix Medium
**Colophon**
Audimat Bold Italic, Audimat Regular

**page 141**
**19.2**
AB Aa Aa
**Exploration**
Sauna Small Caps, FF Clifford
**Colophon**
FF Clifford Italic

**page 142**
**19.3**
AB Aa Aa
**Exploration**
Iwan Stencil, FF Strada Regular
**Colophon**
Cholla Slab Bold

**page 143**

**19.4**

Aa Aa
Aa Aa

**Exploration**
FF Dax Wide Black, FF Dax Bold, FF Dax Regular, FF Dax Condensed Light
**Colophon**
Platelet

**page 146**

**20.1**

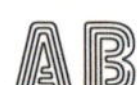

Aa Aa

**Exploration**
Ohm Bold, Locator Bold, Locator Regular
**Colophon**
Locator Bold, Locator Regular

**page 147**

**20.2**

Aa Aa Aa

**Exploration**
FF Typestar Black, FF Typestar Normal
**Colophon**
Brothers Regular

**page 148**

**20.3**

Aa Aa A+

**Exploration**
FF Seria Sans Bold, FF Seria Regular
**Colophon**
Exocet

**page 149**

**20.4**

Aa Aa Aa

**Exploration**
FF Max Fat Italic, FF Max Extra Light, FF Max Regular
**Colophon**
FF Alega Serif Light

**page 152**

**21.1**

Aa Aa
Aa Aa

**Exploration**
Harriet Display Black, Harriet Text Light, Harriet Text Medium Italic
**Colophon**
Benton Sans Condensed Bold

**page 153**

**21.2**

Aa Aa

**Exploration**
Sassoon Primary Regular, FF Cocon Regular
**Colophon**
Sassoon Primary Regular

**page 154**

**21.3**

Aa Aa Aa

**Exploration**
FF Plus Sans Extra Bold, Maxime Regular
**Colophon**
FF Plus Sans Extra Bold Italic

**page 155**

**21.4**

Aa Aa
Aa Aa

**Exploration**
FF Chambers Sans Black, FF Chambers Sans
**Colophon**
FF Chambers Sans Bold Italic, Folk Art Stitch

**page 158**

**22.1**

Aa Aa
Aa Aa

**Exploration**
TheMix Black, TheSans, TheSans Bold, TheSerif
**Colophon**
TheSerif

**page 159**

**22.2**

Aa AA

**Exploration**
FF Bau Regular
**Colophon**
Orator

**page 160**

**22.3**

Aa Aa ❶ ❷
Aa Aa

**Exploration**
Klavika Bold, Klavika Regular, FF Dingbats 2.0 Numbers
**Colophon**
PMN Caecilia 86 Heavy Italic, PMN Caecilia 56 Italic

**page 161**

**22.4**

Aa AB

**Exploration**
FF Good Condensed Book
**Colophon**
Unibody 8 Small Caps

**page 165**

**23.1**

Aa Aa

**Exploration**
FF Karbid Normal
**Colophon**
Base 12 Serif

**page 166**

**23.2**

Aa Aa

**Exploration**
Interstate Regular
**Colophon**
Calvert Regular

**page 167**

**23.3**

Aa Aa

**Exploration**
FF Balance Regular
**Colophon**
FF Celeste Bold Italic

**page 168**

**23.4**

Aa Aa

**Exploration**
OCR-A
**Colophon**
Akkurat

**page 169**

**23.5**

Aa Aa Aa

**Exploration**
FF Celeste
**Colophon**
FF Page Sans Demibold, FF Page Sans Light

**page 171**

**23.6**

Aa Aa Aa

**Exploration**
FF Avance, FF Mister K
**Colophon**
FF Kievit Italic

**page 173**

**24.1**

Aa Aa Aa

**Exploration**
FF Cellini Bold, FF Cellini Regular
**Colophon**
FF Cst Berlin West

**page 175**

**24.2**

Aa Aa Aa

**Exploration**
Adobe Garamond Bold, Adobe Garamond Roman
**Colophon**
FF Scala Sans Regular

**page 176**

**24.3**

Aa Aa
Aa Aa

**Exploration**
Linotype Univers Bold Condensed, Linotype Univers Condensed, Linotype Univers Bold, Linotype Univers Light
**Colophon**
FF Fago Office Serif

**page 177**

**24.4**

Aa Aa
Aa Aa

**Exploration**
Mønster, FF Milo Bold, FF Milo Text
**Colophon**
FF Avance Italic

**page 178**

**24.5**

Aa Aa
Aa Aa Aa

**Exploration**
FF Franziska Demibold, FF Franziska Book, FF Franziska Book Italic
**Colophon**
Lato Black, Lato Regular

page 179
24.6
Aa *Aa*
Aa Aa
**Exploration**
FF Unit Bold, FF Unit Regular Italic, FF Unit Regular, FF Unit Light
**Colophon**
FF Unit Rounded

pages 1–216
BOOK
**Aa** Aa *Aa*
**Heads**
Output Sans Black
**Text**
Output Sans Medium, Output Sans Medium Italic

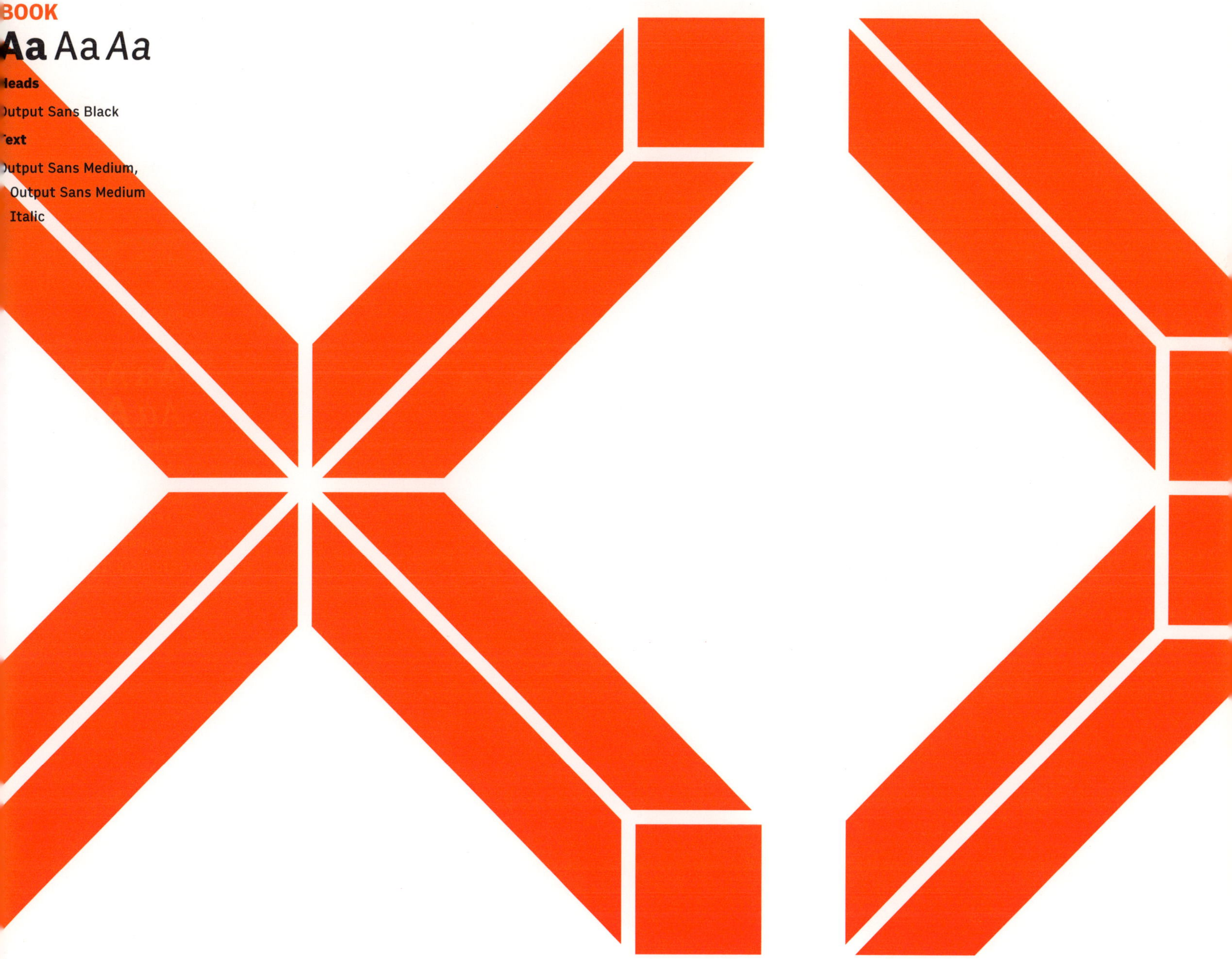

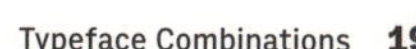

# Typefaces + Alternates

The following is a list of all the typefaces used in this book. Now that it's become easier to experiment with quality typefaces at a reasonable cost, each typeface is followed by a list of alternatives that will achieve a similar visual effect. While you always need to secure proper font licensing for commercial and professional work, many of the alternatives are totally free, free for a trial period, or free for educational use. They are available from the sources listed below (abbreviations in parentheses).

When using the alternative typefaces, remember that x-height, cap height, and sidebearings are all matters of design and will vary from typeface to typeface. Therefore, if you use an alternate, you may need to adjust the type specifications given in the colophon to produce similar results and ensure legibility. Use your own visual acuity and good judgment to decide.

**Apple** (OSX) Several fonts are included in the most recent Mac OS. *apple.com*

**Adobe Fonts** (AF) Many fonts are free via desktop sync with a Creative Cloud subscription. Formerly called Adobe Typekit. *fonts.adobe.com*

**Dalton Maag** (DM) Free trials. *daltonmaag.com*

**Dunwich Type** (DT) Free trials. *dunwichtype.com*

**Fatype** (FT) Free trials. *fatype.com*

**Fontspring** (FSP) Free trials for specific fonts. *fontspring.com/free*

**FutureFonts** (FUT) Discounts for experimental type designs in progress. Buy early, lock in at the cheapest rate, and get free updates. *futurefonts.xyz*

**Fontstand** (FST) Free trials for a short period, cheap rentals for a longer period. Students get €10 (approx. $US11) rental credit per year. *fontstand.com/students*

**Google Fonts** (GF) Free. *fonts.google.com* (Use SkyFonts for desktop sync. *skyfonts.com)*

**Grilli Type** (GT) Free trials. *grillitype.com*

**JTD Type** (JTD) Free trials. *jtdtype.com*

**Microsoft** (MS) Several fonts are included with Windows or the purchase of Office applications. *microsoft.com*

**Production Type** (PT) Free trials. *productiontype.com*

**Swiss Typeface** (ST) Free trials. *swisstypefaces.com*

**Typecuts** (TC) Students get 90% off. Contact Andrea Tinnes: *andrea@typecuts.com.* For a free trial of "PTL" fonts, contact Ole Schäfer: *info@primetype.com. typecuts.com*

**Typolar** (TY) Free for students; contact the foundry. *typolar.com*

**ages 57, 99**

AaBbCc

**F Absara**

avier Dupré, 2004

**lternatives**

haparral (AF)

reta (FST)

kolar (FST, AF)

**ages 57, 99, 85**

AaBbCc

**F Absara Sans**

avier Dupré, 2005

**lternatives**

kolar Sans (FST, AF)

alluna Sans (AF)

ederon Sans (FST)

**age 128**

AaBbCc

**delle**

eronika Burian,
José Scaglione, 2009

**lternatives**

MN Caecilia

exia (DM)

**age 168**

AaBbCc

**kkurat**

aurenz Brunner, 2004

**lternatives**

amber

oboto (GF)

an Francisco Compact
(OSX)

Veissenhof Grotesk

**age 113**

AaBbCc

**F Alega**

iegfried Rückel, 2002

**lternatives**

S Sinclair (FST)

urosoft (FST)

lone Rounded (FST)

enby Five (AF)

**pages 113, 149**

AaBbCc

**FF Alega Serif**

Siegfried Rückel, 2003

**Alternatives**

FF Sinclair (FST)

Eurosoft (FST)

Clone Rounded (FST)

Tenby Five (AF)

**page 122**

AaBbCc

**Antithesis**

Yanone (Jan Gerner), 2003

**Alternatives**

Doko (FST)

Capito (FUT)

Rumba (FST)

FF Suhmo

Kinesis (AF)

**pages 87, 117**

AaBbCc

**FF Archian**

György Szönyei, 1999

**Alternatives**

Ohm (FST)

Industry Inc (AF)

Bismuth (FST)

**page 112**

AaBbCc

**FF Atma Serif**

Alan Dague-Greene, 2001

**Alternatives**

FF Clifford (AF)

Walbaum 2010 (FST)

Baskerville Original (FST)

Abril (FST, AF)

Trianon (PT)

**page 140**

AaBbCc

**Audimat**

Jack Usine, 2014

**Alternatives**

Surogat (FST)

User Upright (FST)

Refrigerator Deluxe (FST)

**pages 171, 177**

AaBbCc

**FF Avance**

Evert Bloemsma, 2000

**Alternatives**

Galena

ITC Mendoza

Cicéro

FF Tisa (AF)

**pages 77, 44**

AaBbCc

**Avenir**

Adrian Frutiger, 1988

**Alternatives**

Objektiv (DM)

Soleil (FST, AF)

Museo Sans (AF)

Proxima Nova (FST, AF)

Sanomat Sans (FST)

## B

**page 167**

AaBbCc

**FF Balance**

Evert Bloemsma, 1993

**Alternatives**

FF Legato

Signo

Khang (FST)

**page 45**

AaBbCc

**Base 9**

Zuzana Licko, 1995

**Alternatives**

Battling (Nonpareille)

Guildford
(Red Rooster)

Telefon (FST)

Idealista (FST)

Houschka Rounded (AF)

**pages 45, 165**

AaBbCc

**Base 12 Serif**

Zuzana Licko, 1995

**Alternative**

Laski Slab (FST)

**pages 118, 119**

AaBbCc

**Baskerville**

John Baskerville, 1757

**Alternatives**

Libre Baskerville (GF)

Monotype Baskerville
(OSX)

Harriet (FST)

Ingeborg (FST)

Romain (ST)

**page 159**

AaBbCc

**FF Bau**

Christian Schwartz, 2002

**Alternatives**

IBM Plex Sans

Akzidenz-Grotesk

Equitan Sans (FST)

Trivia Grotesk (FST)

Lab Grotesque (FST)

Plan Grotesque (FST)

**page 30**

ABCD

**FF Beadmap**

David Crow, Ian Wright,
2002

**Alternatives**

Stag Dot (FST)

FindReplace (FST)

**pages 31, 35, 119**

AaBbCc

**Bell Centennial**

Matthew Carter, 1978

**Alternatives**

Trench Slab (FST)

Stag Sans (FST)

Stroudley (DM)

Flama (FST)

Lorimer No. 2 (DT)

**page 118**

AaBbCc

**Bell Gothic**

Chauncey H. Griffith, 1937

**Alternatives**

Griffith Gothic

Bell Centennial

Amplitude

Tang

**page 152**

AaBbCc

**Benton Sans**

Cyrus Highsmith,
Tobias Frere-Jones, 2000

**Alternatives**

Balto (FST)

Trade Gothic

News Gothic (AF)

Source Sans (GF)

**page 25**

AaBbCc

**FF BeoSans Hard**

Erik van Blokland,
Just van Rossum, 1992

**Alternatives**

Flex (FST)

Seravek (FST)

Comenia Sans (FST)

JAF Bernina Sans
(FST, AF)

**page 33**

AaBbCc

**FF Beowolf**

Erik van Blokland,
Just van Rossum, 1992

**Alternatives**

Preissig Antikva (FST)

Journal (FST)

Sastre

Plinc Whimsy (FST)

**page 77**

AaBbCc

**Bodoni Old Face**

Günter Gerhard Lange, 1983 (based on the work of Giambattista Bodoni, 1798)

**Alternatives**

Bodoni (AF)
Filosofia (FST)
Parmigiano (FST)
Caponi (FST)

**pages 139, 147**

AaBbCc

**Brothers**

John Downer, 1999

**Alternatives**

Council
Gin (AF)

**page 51**

ABCDE

**FF Burokrat**

Matthias Rawald, 1996

**Alternatives**

Gnuolane Grind (FSP)
FF Cartonnage

## C

**page 166**

AaBbCc

**Calvert**

Margaret Calvert, 1980

**Alternatives**

Trivia Slab (FST)
Memphis
Serifa

**page 79**

AaBbCc

**FF Cartonnage**

Yanek Iontef, 2003

**Alternatives**

Gnuolane Grind (FSP)
FF Burokrat

**pages 167, 169**

AaBbCc

**FF Celeste**

Chris Burke, 1994

**Alternatives**

Charlotte
Whitman
Athelas (FST, AF)

**page 173**

AaBbCc

**FF Cellini**

Albert Boton, 2003

**Alternatives**

Filosofia (FST)
Bodoni Old Face
Zahrah (FST)
Parmigiano (FST)

**page 85**

AaBbCc

**Centaur**

Bruce Rogers, 1914

**Alternatives**

Neacademia (FST)
Faunus (FST)

**page 155**

AaBbCc

**FF Chambers Sans**

Verena Gerlach, 2008

**Alternatives**

Lingua (FST)
FF Polymorph Base
Foundry Gridnik
Sirucanorm

**pages 23, 104**

AaBbCc

**Chaparral**

Carol Twombly, 2000

**Alternatives**

Tabac Slab (FST)
Brando (FST)
Mislab (FST, AF)
Dapifer (FST, AF)
FF Ernestine (AF)

**page 63**

ABCDE

**Charlemagne**

Carol Twombly, 1989

**Alternatives**

Trajan (AF)
Warnock (AF)
Capitolium 2 (FST)
Brioso (AF)

**page 56**

AaBbCc

**Cholla Sans**

Sibylle Hagmann, 1999

**Alternatives**

Capricorn
Fishmonger (FST)
Audimat

**pages 41, 71, 142**

AaBbCc

**Cholla Slab**

Sibylle Hagmann, 1999

**Alternatives**

Fishmonger (FST)
Ocre Serif (FST)

**pages 26, 58**

AaBbCc

**Cholla Unicase**

Sibylle Hagmann, 1999

**Alternatives**

Fishmonger (FST)
Magion (FST)
Torque (FST)

**page 128**

AaBbCc

**FF Clan**

Łukasz Dziedzic, 2007

**Alternatives**

FF Enzo (AF)
Taz
Camingo Dos (AF)
Dobra (FST)

**page 111**

AaBbCc

**New Clarendon**

R. Besley, 1845

**Alternatives**

Trivia Serif 10 (FST)
Farao (FST)
Ingeborg (FST)
Duplicate Ionic (FST)

**page 141**

AaBbCc

**FF Clifford**

Akira Kobayashi, 1999

**Alternatives**

Foundry Wilson
Farnham Text
Ingeborg (FST)
Baskerville Original (FST)

**page 153**

AaBbCc

**FF Cocon**

Evert Bloemsma, 2001

**Alternatives**

Congenial
FF Masala (AF)
Salsa (GF)

**page 65**

AaBbCc

**AW Conquerer**

Jean François Porchez, 2010

**Alternatives**

Gill Sans Nova
Mr Eaves (FST)

**pages 50, 76**

AaBbCc

**FF Container**

Stephan Müller, 1999

**Alternatives**

Foundry Fabriek
FF Oxide Stencil
Trim Stencil (FST)
Ironstrike Stencil (DT)
Industry Inc Stencil (AF)

**pages 31, 73**

AaBbCc

**Cooper Black**

Oswald Cooper, 1919

**Alternatives**

Hobeaux (FST)
Henriette (FST)

**page 173**

AaBbCc

**FF Cst Berlin West**

Verena Gerlach, Ole Schäfer, 2000

**Alternatives**

Metric
Zeppelin (FST)

**page 38**

AaBbCc

**FF Cube**

Jan Maack, 2008

**Alternatives**

Industry (AF)
Purista (FST)
Prometo (DM)

## D

**page 59**

**Dalliance Flourishes**

Frank Heine, 2000

**Alternatives**

ITC Bodoni Ornaments (OSX, older systems)
Hoefler Text Ornaments (OSX)
Adobe Wood Type Ornaments
Corundum Text Pi (FST)
Rufina Ornaments

**page 143**

AaBbCc

**FF Dax**

Hans Reichel, 1995

**Alternatives**

Diodrum (FST)
FF Daxline (AF)
Conto

**page 48**

AaBbCc

**FF Daxline**

Hans Reichel, 2005

**Alternatives**

FF Dax (AF)
Conto

**page 109**

AaBbCc

**Democratica**

Miles Newlyn, 1991

**Alternatives**

Mason (AF)
NewParis (ST)
Ambicase Modern
FF Disturbance

**page 78**

AaBbCc

**FF DIN**

Albert-Jan Pool, 1995

**Alternatives**

Simplon (ST)
Colfax (FST)
Flama (FST)
GT Pressura (GT)
Helsinki (FST)

**page 103**

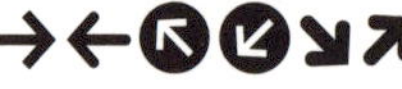

**FF Dingbats 2.0 Arrows**

Johannes Erler, Olaf Stein, Henning Skibbe, 2009

**Alternatives**

Greta Symbol (FST)
FF Eureka Arrows

**page 40**

**FF Dingbats 2.0 Circles and Crosses**

Johannes Erler, Olaf Stein, Henning Skibbe, 2009

**Alternatives**

TXT101
Zapf Dingbats (OSX)

ages 84, 119

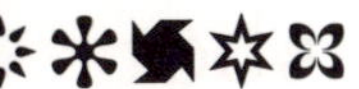

F Dingbats 2.0
tars and Flowers
ohannes Erler, Olaf Stein,
Henning Skibbe, 2009
**lternatives**
lypnopaedia (FST)
apf Dingbats (OSX)

age 134

AaBbCc

oko
ndrej Jób, 2011
**lternatives**
haparral (AF)
auna

age 38

AaBbCc

F Dot Matrix
tephan Müller, Cornel
Windlin, 1993
**lternatives**
exico Micro (FST)
oundry Flek

## E

age 113

AaBbCc

F Eboy
ai Vermehr, 1998
**lternative**
blong (FST)

age 97

AaBbCc

ideticNeo
odrigo Cavazos, 2000
**lternatives**
epone (FST)
Varnock (AF)
angBleu (ST)
reta (FST)
anto (FUT)

page 26

AaBbCc

FF Engine
Alex Scholing, 1995
**Alternatives**
Core Humanist Sans (FSP)
PTL Roletta Sans (TC)
Aniuk (FST)
Rooney Sans (AF)
Irma Text Round (FST)

page 47

AaBbCc

FF Enzo
Tobias Kvant, 2008
**Alternatives**
Duplicate Sans (FST)
PT Sans Caption
(GF, AF)
Encode Sans (GF, FSP)

pages 29, 125

AaBbCc

Eskapade Fraktur Black
Alisa Nowak, 2012
**Alternatives**
FF Broken Script
Hexenrunen (FST)
Gandur New (FST)

page 98

AaBbCc

FF Eureka
Peter Bil'ak, 1998
**Alternatives**
Chaparral
Pepone (FST)

page 98

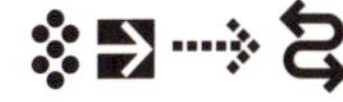

FF Eureka Arrows
Peter Bil'ak, 1998
**Alternatives**
Greta Symbol (FST)
FF Dingbats 2.0 Arrows

pages 98, 116

AaBbCc

FF Eureka Sans
Peter Bil'ak, 2000
**Alternatives**
Fedra Sans (FST)
Karmina Sans (FST)

page 148

ABCDEF

Exocet
Jonathan Barnbrook, 1991
**Alternative**
Priori Serif

## F

pages 97, 104

AaBbCc

FF Fago
Ole Schäfer, 2000
**Alternatives**
FF Meta (AF)
Lipa Agate (FST, AF)
Riga (FST)
Fedra Sans Alt (FST)

page 176

AaBbCc

FF Fago Office Serif
Ole Schäfer, 2000
**Alternatives**
Brix Slab (AF)
Mislab (AF)
Officina Serif

page 96

AaBbCc

Fakt
Thomas Thiemich, 2010
**Alternatives**
Neue Helvetica (OSX)
Acumin (AF)
Graphik (FST)
Volkart (FST)
Akzidenz-Grotesk
Suisse International (ST)

page 103

AaBbCc

Filosofia
Zuzana Licko, 2006
**Alternatives**
Caponi (FST)
URW Bodoni (AF)
Essonnes (JTD)
ITC Bodoni 72 (OSX)

pages 15, 70

AaBbCc

Foundry Flek
The Foundry, 2016
**Alternatives**
Stag Dot (FST)
FF Dot Matrix
Foundry Plek

pages 93, 128

AaBbCc

Fluidum
Aldo Novarese, 1951
**Alternatives**
Supernova Poster (FST)
Magasin
Butti
Primot
Xesy

page 37

AABBCC

FF Folk
Maurizio Osti, Jane
Patterson, 2003
(based on the work of
Ben Shahn, 1940)
**Alternatives**
Woodkit Print (FST)
Becker Gothics Egyptian
(DT)

page 155

AaBbCc

P22 Folk Art
Michael Want, 1997
**Alternatives**
Unibody 8
Lo-Res (FST, AF)
FindReplace (FST)

page 76

AaBbCc

Fournier
Pierre Simon Fournier,
c. 1742
**Alternatives**
Corundum (FST)
Athelas (FST, AF)
Source Serif (GF)
Adobe Caslon (AF)

page 178

AaBbCc

FF Franziska
Jakob Runge, 2014
**Alternatives**
Cardea (FST)
Alda (FST)
Aleksei (FT)

page 135

AaBbCc

Frutiger
Adrian Frutiger, 1976
**Alternatives**
Segoe (MS)
Myriad (AF)
FF Transit Print
JAF Bernino Sans
(FST, AF)

pages 123, 133

AaBbCc

Futura Black
Josef Albers
Paul Renner, 1926
**Alternatives**
Braggadocio
Reklame Stencil
Trim Stencil (FST)

## G

page 175

AaBbCc

Adobe Garamond
Robert Slimbach, 1989
(based on the work of
Claude Garamond,
c. 1540)
**Alternatives**
Garamond Premier (AF)
ATF Garamond (FST)
Nocturno (FST)
Adobe Caslon (AF)

page 63

AaBbCc

Gill Sans Nova
George Ryan, 2015
(based on the work of
Eric Gill, 1931)
**Alternatives**
Gill Sans (OS X)
Astoria Sans (AF)
Joanna Sans
Prenton (AF)
Mr Eaves XL Sans (FST)
P22 Underground (AF)

page 161

AaBbCc

FF Good
Łukasz Dziedzic, 2007
**Alternatives**
Typonine Sans (FST)
Knockout

page 129

AaBbCc

FF Gothic Min
Neville Brody, 1992
**Alternatives**
Capibara (FST)
FF QType

page 65

AaBbCc

Goudy Text
Frederic Goudy, 1928
**Alternatives**
Amador (AF)
Plagwitz (FST)
Moyenage (FST)

## H

pages 152, 157

AaBbCc

Harriet
Jackson Cavanaugh, 2012
**Alternatives**
Baskerville Original (FST)
Ingeborg (FST)
Miller
Iridium

**page 111**

AaBbCc

**Neue Helvetica**

Linotype, 1983
(based on the work of
Max Meidinger, 1957)

**Alternatives**

Neue Haas Grotesk
Nimbus Sans (AF)
Suisse Int'l (ST)
Aktiv Grotesk (DM)
Acumin (AF)
Nitti Grotesk (FST)

**pages 43, 116**

AaBbCc

**FF Hertz**

Jens Kutilek, 2015

**Alternatives**

Ibis
RePublic (FST)
Utopia Caption (AF)
Trianon Caption (PT)
Parmigiano Piccolo (FST)

**pages 64, 122, 124**

AaBbCc

**FF Hydra Text**

Silvio Napoleone, 2004

**Alternatives**

Tablet Gothic (FST, AF)
Godfrey (FST)
Maple (FST)
Chivo (GF)

## I

**page 40**

AaBbCc

**Ideal Sans**

Jonathan Hoefler, 2011

**Alternatives**

Mundo Sans
Prenton (AF)
Cronos (AF)
Anselm Sans (FST)

**page 58**

AaBbCc

**Input Serif Condensed**

David Jonathan Ross, 2014

**Alternatives**

FF Typestar
Defender (FST)
Cordale (DM)

**page 58**

AaBbCc

**FF Info Text**

Ole Schäfer, Erik
Spiekermann, 1996

**Alternatives**

Fira Sans (GF)
FF Unit

**page 166**

AaBbCc

**Interstate**

Tobias Frere-Jones, 1994

**Alternatives**

Overpass
Mission Gothic
Proxima Nova
(FST, AF)
Sweet Sans (FST)

**page 142**

AaBbCc

**Iwan Stencil**

Klaus Sutter, 2008
(based on the work of
Jan Tschichold, 1929)

**Alternatives**

Compass Stencil
FF Flightcase
Futura Black

**page 59**

AaBbCc

**Adobe Jenson**

Robert Slimbach, 1996
(based on the work of
Nicolas Jenson, c. 1470)

**Alternatives**

Arno (AF)
Calluna (AF)
GT Sectra (GT)
Maiola (FST)

**page 19**

AaBbCc

**Jeunesse Sans**

Johannes Birkenbach,
1993

**Alternatives**

Mr Eaves (FST)
Sweet Sans (FST)

**pages 63, 125**

AaBbCc

**Joanna Nova**

Ben Jones, 2015
(based on the work of
Eric Gill, 1937)

**Alternatives**

Whitman
Perpetua

**page 165**

AaBbCc

**FF Karbid**

Verena Gerlach, 1999

**Alternatives**

Juvenis (FST)
Komet
Congenial
Buendia (FST)

**page 24**

AaBbCc

**Kettler**

Eric Olson, 2002

**Alternatives**

Pennsylvania
ITC Officina Serif
Tesla Slab
Monospace (FST)
User (FST)

**pages 136, 171**

AaBbCc

**FF Kievit**

Michael Abbink, 2001

**Alternatives**

Flex (FST)
Stella (FST)
Nota (FST)
Seravek (FST)
Comenia Sans (FST)

**page 136**

AaBbCc

**FF Kievit Slab**

Michael Abbink,
Paul van der Laan 2013

**Alternatives**

PMN Caecilia
Charlie (FST)
Adelle (FST, AF)
FF Nexus Mix
TheSerif

**page 160**

AaBbCc

**Klavika**

Eric Olson, 2004

**Alternatives**

Camingo Dos (AF)
Botanika (FST)

**page 178**

AaBbCc

**Lato**

Łukasz Dziedzic, 2011

**Alternatives**

Seravek (FST)
Linotype Aroma No. 2
Stella (FST)
Cronos (AF)

**pages 96, 101**

AaBbCc

**Le Corbusier**

Nico Schweizer,
Philippe Desarzens, 1999

**Alternatives**

Jeanneret NF
FF Flightcase
Bodoni Stencil
Bodoni Classic Stencil
Parmigiano Stencil (FST)
Stencil (AF)

**pages 59, 81, 84**

AaBbCc

**FF Legato**

Evert Bloemsma, 2004

**Alternatives**

Duplicate Sans (FST)
Candara (MS, OSX)
Winco (FST)
Echo (FST)

**page 75**

AaBbCc

**FF Letter Gothic Text**

Albert Pinggera, 1996

**Alternatives**

Queue (FST)
Katarine (FST)
Ronnia (FST, AF)

**pages 50, 107**

AaBbCc

**Lingua**

Eric Olsen, 2003

**Alternatives**

Fig
FF Chambers Sans
Foundry Gridnik
Bs Mandrax
Materia

**page 146**

AaBbCc

**Locator**

Eric Olsen, 2003

**Alternatives**

Global (FST)
Museo Sans (AF)
Montserrat (GF)
Myriad (AF)

**pages 79, 173**

AaBbCc

**Lo-Res**

Zuzana Licko, 2001

**Alternatives**

FF SubVario
FF SubMono
Pexico (FST)
Tephra (DM)

## M

**page 124**

AaBbCc

**FF Magda Clean Mono**

Cornel Windlin, 1995

**Alternatives**

Valentine
Kettler (FST)
Remi (FST)
Covik Sans Mono (FUT)

**page 90**

AaBbCc

**Maiola**

Veronika Burian, 2005

**Alternatives**

Adobe Jenson
Arno (AF)
Calluna (AF)
GT Sectra (GT)

**pages 55, 112, 121**

*AaBbCc*

**Matrix Script**

Zuzana Licko, 1986

**Alternatives**

Jeanne Moderno
Italic (AF)
Abril Italic (FST)
Acta Italic (FST)

**page 149**

AaBbCc

**FF Max**

Morten Olsen, 2003

**Alternatives**

Burlingame
Carnas
Neo Sans

**pages 154**

AaBbCc

**Maxime**

Éric de Berranger, 1999

**Alternatives**

Capito (FUT)
ITC Mendoza
Skolar (FST, AF)
Aleksei (FT)
GT Sectra (GT)
Fedra Serif A (FST)

page 89

**Maxime Ornaments**
Éric de Berranger, 1999
**Alternatives**
ITC Bodoni Ornaments (OSX)
Hoefler Text Ornaments (OSX)
Wood Type Ornaments
Corundum Text Pi (FST)

page 44
AaBbCc
**Memphis**
Rudolf Wolf, 1929
**Alternatives**
Stymie
Rockwell
Sanchez Slab

page 18
AaBbCc
**ITC Mendoza**
Jose Mendoza y Almeida, 1991
**Alternatives**
Maxime
Skolar (FST,AF)
Aleksei (Fatype)
GT Sectra (GT)
Fedra Serif A (FST)

pages 17, 89, 135
AaBbCc
**FF Meta**
Erik Spiekermann, 1991.
**Alternatives**
Fira Sans (GF)
Karmina (FST)
Riga (FST)
Gloriola (FST)

pages 17, 135
AaBbCc
**FF Meta Serif**
Christian Schwartz, Erik Spiekermann, Kris Sowersby, 2007
**Alternatives**
Karmina (FST, AF)
Cambria (MS)
Aleksei (FT)

pages 83, 177
AaBbCc
**FF Milo**
Michael Abbink, 2006
**Alternatives**
Greta Sans (FST)
Kohinoor (FST)
Bliss
Libertad

pages 145, 171
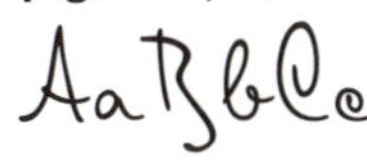
**FF Mister K**
Julia Sysmäläinen, 2008
**Alternatives**
Rosaline (FST)
Lakeside (FST)
Suomi Hand Script

pages 110, 115
AaBbCcDd
**Modula Ribbed**
Zuzana Licko, 1985
**Alternatives**
Senator (AF)
Jesus Loves You

pages 61, 177
AaBbCc
**Mønster**
Sindre Bremnes, 2014
**Alternatives**
Bigfish (AF)
Fatboy (AF)
Cottonwood (AF)
HWT Tuscan Extended (AF)

page 112
AaBbCc
**Myriad**
Carol Twombly, 1991
**Alternatives**
Frutiger
JAF Bernino Sans (FST, AF)
Setimo (DM)
Suisse Sign (ST)
Corbel (MS)
Gemeli (PT)

## N

page 41
AaBbCc
**FF Netto**
Daniel Utz, 2008
**Alternatives**
Clone Rounded (FST)
Bryant (FST)
GT Pressura (GT)
Proxima Nova Soft (FST, AF)

page 41
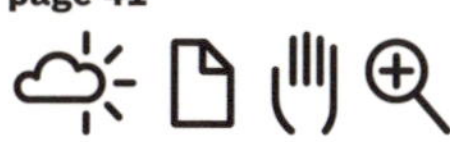
**FF Netto Icons**
Daniel Utz, 2008
**Alternatives**
Greta Symbol (FST)
FF Dingbests
Allumi Dingbats

page 46
AaBbCc
**Neutraface Text**
Christian Schwartz, 2002
**Alternatives**
Telefon (FST)
Brandon Grotesque (AF)
FF Bauer Grotesk
Avenir

page 37
AaBbCc
**News Gothic**
Morris Fuller Benton, 1908
**Alternatives**
Trade Gothic
Franklin Gothic

page 137
AaBbCc
**FF Nexus Mix**
Martin Majoor, 2004
**Alternatives**
TheSerif
FF Scala
Lumin (FST)
Tabac Slab (FST)
Trivia Slab (FST)

pages 76, 137
AaBbCc
**FF Nexus Sans**
Martin Majoor, 2004
**Alternatives**
TheSans
FF Scala Sans
Lumin Sans
Tabac Sans
Trivia Sans

pages 127, 137
AaBbCc
**FF Nexus Typewriter**
Martin Majoor, 2004
**Alternative**
FF Letter Gothic Text

pages 33, 91
AaBbCc
**FF Nuvo**
Siegfried Rückel, 2008
**Alternatives**
Katarine (FST)
Irma Text Round (FST)

## O

page 75
AaBbCcDd
**Oblong**
Zuzana Licko, Rudy VanderLans, 1988
**Alternatives**
Hammertone (FST)
Box Gothic
Indoo BT
P22 DeStijl

page 168
AaBbCc
**OCR-A**
Adrian Frutiger, 1968
**AAlternatives**
Typestar OCR
OCR-B (AF)

page 131
AaBbCc
**OCR-B**
Adrian Frutiger, 1968
**Alternatives**
FF Typestar OCR
OCR-A (AF)
The Future Mono (FUT)

page 30
AaBbCc
**FF OCR-F**
Albert-Jan Pool, 1995
**Alternatives**
OCR-B (AF)
Suisse International Mono (ST)
Nitti (FST)

page 105
AaBbCc
**ITC Officina Serif**
Erik Spiekermann, 1989
**Alternatives**
Slabo (GF)
Adelle (FST, AF)
Charlie (FST)
Mislab (FST, AF)

page 23
AaBbCc
**ITC Officina Sans**
Erik Spiekermann, 1989
**Alternatives**
Katarine (FST)
Ronnia (FST)
Lipa Agate (FST)

pages 67, 146
AABBCC
**Ohm**
Tal Leming, 2009
**Alternatives**
Eclectic Crumpany NF
Varvid

page 84
AaBbCc
**FF Oneleigh**
Nick Shinn, 1999
**Alternatives**
Centaur
Finura (FST)
Neacademia (FST)

page 159
AABBCC
**Orator**
John Scheppler, 1962
**Alternatives**
FF Typestar
1403 Vintage Mono
ITC Officina
Trim Mono (FST)

pages 1–216
AaBbCc
**Output Sans**
David Jonathan Ross, 2016
**Alternatives**
IBM Plex Sans
JAF Bernina Sans (AF)
Kohinoor (FST)
San Francisco (OSX)

## P

page 83

**P22 Victorian Ornaments**
Richard Kegler, Christina Torre, Amy Greenan, 2000
**Alternatives**
Maxime Ornaments
Rufina Ornaments

page 169
AaBbCc
**FF Page Sans**
Albert Boton, 2003
**Alternatives**
Cora (FST)
Darby Sans (FST)

page 47
AaBbCc
**FF Page Serif**
Albert Boton, 2003
**Alternatives**
Matrix (FST)
Karmina (FST)

page 65

AaBbCc

**FF Parango**

Xavier Dupré, 2001

**Alternatives**

Adobe Jenson (AF)

Alegreya (G)

Arno (AF)

Garamond Premier (AF)

page 83

AaBbCc

**Perpetua**

Eric Gill, 1928

**Alternatives**

Romain BP (ST)

Capitolium 2 (FST)

SangBleu (ST)

Thema (FST)

page 89

AaBbCc

**Photina**

Jose Mendoza y Almeida, 1972

**Alternatives**

Lavigne (FST)

Marlene Grande (FST)

Kepler (AF)

Greta (FST)

Abril (FST, AF)

page 143

AaBbCc

**Platelet**

Conor Magnat, 1993

**Alternatives**

Base 9 Sans (FST)

Base 12 Sans (FST)

page 154

AaBbCc

**FF Plus Sans**

Jürgen Huber, 2003

**Alternatives**

Foundry Form Sans

Karmina Sans (FST, AF)

FF Unit

Bosis

pages 19, 160

AaBbCc

**PMN Caecilia**

Peter Matthias Noordzij, 1990

**Alternatives**

Charlie (FST)

Lexia (DM)

Laski Slab (FST)

Trivia Slab (FST)

page 45

AaBbCc

**FF Prater Script**

Steffen Sauerteig and Henning Wagenbreth, 2000

**Alternatives**

FF Prater Sans

FF Prater Serif

Wisdom Script

Grand Hotel (GF)

FF Kosmik

Enfantine (PT)

page 131

AaBbCc

**Prestige Elite**

Clayton Smith, 1953

**Alternatives**

Pitch

FF Elementa

Courier

page 69

AaBbCc

**FF Profile**

Martin Wenzel, 1999

**Alternatives**

Flex (FST)

Andulka Sans (FST)

Cronos (AF)

page 27

ABCDE

**FF Pullman Inline**

Johannes Erler, 1997

**Alternatives**

Feisar Express (FST)

Changeling Neo Inline (FST)

Diversa Inline (FST)

Zico Display Inline (FST)

## Q

pages 90, 91

AaBbCc

**FF Quadraat**

Fred Smeijers, 1997

**Alternatives**

Capitolium News 2 (FST)

Lava (FST)

Arno (AF)

page 125

AaBbCc

**FF Quadraat Sans**

Fred Smeijers, 1997

**Alternatives**

Proza

DTL Documenta Sans

Cronos (AF)

Preto Sans

page 24

ABbCc

**FF QType**

Achaz Reuss, 2007

**Alternatives**

Purista (FST)

Changeling Neo (FST, AF)

Stratum 1 (FST)

Industry (AF)

## R

page 48

AaBbCc

**FF Roice**

Alex Scholing, 2003

**Alternatives**

Core Humanist Sans (FSP)

PTL Roletta Sans (TC)

Aniuk (FST)

Rooney Sans (AF)

Irma Text Round (FST)

page 46

AaBbCc

**Rufina**

Martin Sommaruga, 2014

**Alternatives**

Lavigne (FST)

Kepler (AF)

Fayon

## S

page 59

AaBbCc

**Sabbath Black**

Miles Newlyn, 1992

**Alternatives**

Cabazon (AF)

Plinc Hanover (FST)

FF Brokenscript (AF)

St Croce (FST)

page 102

AaBbCc

**FF Sanuk**

Xavier Dupré, 2006

**Alternatives**

Camingo Dos (AF)

Klavika (FST)

Botanika (FST)

page 153

AaBbCc

**Sassoon Primary**

Rosemary Sassoon and Adrian Williams, 1995

**Alternatives**

Fabula

Kite One (GF)

Tekton (AF)

Taffy

Blueprint

page 141

AaBbCc

**Sauna**

Underware, 2002

**Alternatives**

Aniuk (FST)

Doko (FST)

FF Masala (AF)

Core Humanist Sans (FSP)

pages 56, 102

AaBbCc

**FF Scala**

Martin Majoor, 1990

**Alternatives**

Chaparral (AF)

Diogenes (FST)

Tyfa Antiqua (FST)

pages 56, 151

ABC123

**FF Scala Jewel**

Martin Majoor, 1990

**Alternatives**

Diversa Floral (FST)

Plinc Quaint (FST)

Plinc Trillium (FST)

Braga (FST)

Oskar Inline (FST)

History (FST)

pages 18, 55, 175

AaBbCc

**FF Scala Sans**

Martin Majoor, 1999

**Alternatives**

Calluna Sans (AF)

Comenia Sans (FST)

Stella (FST)

page 69

AaBbCc

**FF Schulschrift**

Just van Rossum, 1991

**Alternatives**

Learning Curve (AF)

Line (FST)

Plinc Circle (FST)

Giddyup (AF)

Segoe Script (MS)

page 148

AaBbCc

**FF Seria**

Martin Majoor, 2000

**Alternatives**

FF Nexus Serif

FF Scala

RTF Stern (AF)

page 148

AaBbCc

**FF Seria Sans**

Martin Majoor, 2000

**Alternatives**

FF Nexus Sans

FF Scala Sans

Berling Nova Sans

Nota (FST)

pages 65, 95, 148

AaBbCc

**Serifa**

Adrian Frutiger, 1968

**Alternatives**

Adelle (FST, AF)

Lexia (DM)

Irma Text Slab (FST)

Produkt (FST)

RePublic (FST)

page 49

AaBbCc

**Spartan Classified**

American Typefounders, c. 1935

**Alternatives**

U8 (FT)

GT Walsheim (GT)

Proxima Nova (FST, AF)

page 109

AaBbCc

**FF Speak**

Jan Maack, 2007

**Alternatives**

Tondo (DM)

Clone Rounded (FST)

Core Humanist Sans (FSP)

Proxima Nova Soft (FST, AF)

FF Netto (AF)

page 64

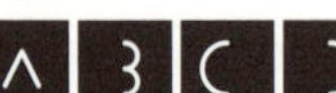

**FF Stealth**

Malcolm Garrett, 1995

**Alternatives**

Woodkit (FST)

Ladislav (FST)

Estilo (FST)

History (FST)

Euclid Flex (ST)

**page 142**

AaBbCc

**FF Strada**

Albert Pinggera, 2002

**Alternatives**

Calibri (MS)

Foco (DM)

FS Pimlico (FST)

Alto

Orenga

**pages 21, 49**

AaBbCc

**Suburban**

Rudy VanderLans, 1993

**Alternative**

Modula Round Sans (FST)

**page 117**

AaBbCc

**FF SubVario**

Kai Vermehr, 1998

**Alternatives**

FF SubMono

Pexico (FST)

Tephra (DM)

Lo-Res (FST, AF)

**page 99**

AaBbCc

**Suomi Hand Script**

Tomi Haaparanta, 2010

**Alternatives**

Felt Tip Roman (FST)

Capucine (FST)

FF Erikrighthand

Zemke Hand

**page 123**

AaBbCc

**FF Super Grotesk**

Svend Smital, 1999

**Alternatives**

Drescher Grotesk

Futura (OSX)

GT Eesti (GT)

Uni Grotesk (FST)

FF Bauer Grotesk

**page 105**

AaBbCc

**Syntax**

Hans Eduard Meier, 1968

**Alternatives**

Cronos (AF)

Nota (FST)

Mr Eaves Sans (FST)

Triplex Sans (FST)

## T

**page 71**

AaBbCc

**Tarzana Wide**

Zuzana Licko, 1998

**Alternatives**

Pluto

Buendia (FST)

FF Basic Gothic (AF)

**page 158**

AaBbCc

**TheMix**

Luc(as) de Groot, 1994

**Alternatives**

Echo (FST)

Charlie (FST)

FF Kievit

FF Nexus Sans

**page 158**

AaBbCc

**TheSans**

Luc(as) de Groot, 1994

**Alternatives**

FF Kievit

FF Nexus Sans

Echo (FST)

**page 158**

AaBbCc

**TheSerif**

Luc(as) de Groot, 1994

**Alternatives**

FF Kievit Slab

FF Nexus Mix

Charlie (FST)

**page 140**

AaBbCc

**FF ThreeSix**

Paul McNeil and Hamish Muir, 2012

**Alternatives**

Foundry Fabriek

FF Dot Matrix

Technomat (FST)

**page 27**

AaBbCc

**FF Tibere**

Albert Boton, 2003

**Alternatives**

Capitolium 2 (FST)

Coranto 2 (FST)

Arno (AF)

**pages 63, 129**

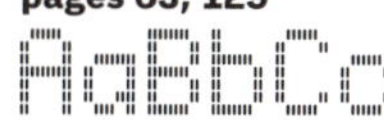

**FF Ticket**

Daniel Fritz, 2000

**Alternatives**

FF Luggagetag Two

Filament

UNDA Vertical

**pages 25, 39**

AaBbCc

**FF Tisa**

Mitja Miklavcic, 2008

**Alternatives**

FF Avance

Galena

ITC Mendoza

Cicéro

**page 51**

AaBbCc

**FF Trixie**

Erik van Blokland, 1991

**Alternatives**

Chandler 42 (AF)

John Doe (AF)

Nitti Typewriter (FST)

Publico Text Mono (FST)

**pages 37, 163**

AaBbCc

**FF Tronic**

Hyun Cho, 2003

**Alternatives**

Technomat (FST)

Pexico (FST)

Tephra

**pages 116, 134**

**TXT101**

Carolina de Bartolo, 2013

**Alternatives**

The Written Word

Puzzler (FST)

Simple Ribbon

**page 147**

AaBbCc

**FF Typestar**

Steffen Sauerteig, 1999

**Alternatives**

ITC Officina Sans

T-Star

Letter Gothic (AF)

Katarine (FST)

## U

**page 161**

**Unibody 8**

Underware, 2003

**Alternatives**

Pexico (FST)

Lo-Res (FST, AF)

**page 179**

AaBbCc

**FF Unit**

Erik Spiekermann and Christian Schwartz, 2008

**Alternatives**

ITC Officina Sans

FF Info Text

**page 179**

AaBbCc

**FF Unit Rounded**

Erik Spiekermann and Christian Schwartz, 2008

**Alternatives**

Pilcrow Soft (FST)

Stag Sans Round (FST)

**pages 95, 176**

AaBbCc

**Univers**

Adrian Frutiger, 1957

**Alternatives**

Neue Helvetica

Benton Sans

**page 70**

AaBbCc

**FF Utility**

Lukas Schneider, 2008

**Alternatives**

Geogrotesque

URW Topic

## V

**page 40**

AaBbCc

**MVB Verdigris**

Mark Van Bronkhorst, 2003

**Alternatives**

Zenon (FST)

Garamond Premier (AF)

Sabon Next

ITC Galliard

Custodia

Arno (AF)

## Z

**pages 103, 110**

AaBbCc

**FF Zine Sans**

Ole Schäfer, 2001

**Alternatives**

Fedra Sans (FST)

Greta Sans (FST)

**page 110**

AaBbCc

**FF Zine Serif**

Ole Schäfer, 2001

**AAlternatives**

Quercus Ten (FST)

Tribunal (FST)

**page 110**

AaBbCc

**FF Zine Slab**

Ole Schäfer, 2001

**Alternatives**

FF Kievit Slab

Lumin (FST)

**page 39**

AaBbCc

**FF Zwo**

Jörg Hemker, 2002

**Alternatives**

Setimo (DM)

JAF Facit (FST, AF)

Gemeli (FST, PT)

# Glossary

## A

**alphabet** writing system wherein one character stands for each sound in the language.

**ampersand** ligature for the word "and" from the Latin "et."

**ascender** part of a letter that extends above the meanline.

**autohyphenation** hyphenation created by software; compare manual hyphenation.

## B

**baseline** imaginary line that letterforms sit on in lines of text.

**bitmapped** showing the squared-off forms of pixels.

**body** main part of a text; also body copy.

**bold** heavier weight of a typeface.

**bracket** transitional curved area between stroke and serif.

**byline** credit line, often beginning with the word "by."

## C

**cap height** distance from baseline to capline.

**capitals** uppercase characters.

**capline** imaginary line at the top of capital letters.

**centered** set ragged on both right and left edges.

**character** letter, punctuation mark, or figure.

**clotheslining** aligning multiple columns along the same top baseline and varying the depths of each.

**colophon** typographic and/or print production specifications, usually listed at the end of a publication.

**column** vertical division of a page.

**composition** arrangement of visual elements on the page; layout.

**contrast** difference in stroke width within a letterform; also called stroke modulation.

## D

**descender** part of a letter than extends below the baseline.

**dingbat** nonalphanumeric mark or ornament.

**display type** type set in large sizes, usually for heads; compare text type.

**drop capital** large letter at the beginning of a text that is inset two or more lines into the first paragraph.

## E

**em** relative measure equal to the point size of the type.

**em dash** longest dash, used for a break in thought in a sentence or a credit line at the end of a text.

**en** relative measure equal to half an em.

**en dash** used in place of the words "to" or "through;" half the width of an em dash.

**exdent** paragraph indication where the first lines of each paragraph are shifted to the left; also called hanging indent or outdent.

## F

**family** set of typefaces with coordinated forms and characteristics.

**fixed width** each character having the same width; also called monospaced.

**fleuron** decorative character, usually in the shape of a leaf or flower.

**floriated** decorated with flowers and/or leaves.

**flush** aligned.

**font** used interchangeably with the word "typeface" today; its original meaning was a single point size and weight in a specific typeface.

**footnote** information at the end of a text referenced within the main text.

## G

**glyph** character; form of a letter.

**graphic element** non-alphanumeric mark; examples include a bullet, pilcrow, or arrow.

**grid** imaginary lines defining boundaries on a page.

**gutter** space between columns.

## H

**head** title; text that is uppermost in hierarchy.

**hierarchy** order of importance.

**horsey** large and clunky; inelegant.

**hyphen** shortest of the horizontal punctuation marks; used only for hyphenation.

## I

**indent** paragraph indication where the first line of each paragraph is shifted to the right by a small amount, usually 1 or 2 ems.

**initial cap** capital letter at the beginning of a text that is set in a larger point size.

**italic** slanted weight of a typeface; true italic letterforms are not based on their roman counterparts.

## J

**justified** flush on both the left and right sides of the text block.

## K

**kerning** adjustment of the space between two characters; compare tracking.

## L

**leading** distance measured in points from baseline to baseline; linespace.

**legibility** used interchangeably with "readability," its true meaning is the degree to which an individual letterform can be easily read; compare readability.

**ligature** two characters joined into one.

**linespace** distance measured in points from baseline to baseline; leading.

**lining figures** numbers that are based on the cap height.

**lowercase** minuscule forms of letters; colloquially called smalls.

## M

**margin** space from the edge of the page to the type or printing.

**meanline** imaginary line across the top of lowercase letterforms.

**measure** column width or line length.

**monospaced** each character having the same width; see fixed width.

## N

**negative leading** when leading is set less than point size.

## O

**oblique** slanted weight of a typeface based on the roman.

**Oldstyle figures** numbers that are designed based on the x-height plus ascenders and descenders; also called text figures.

**optical sizes** type designs with subtle variations for use in a range of point sizes; also called size-specific.

**orphan** last line of a paragraph alone at the top of a column.

## P

**paragraph** group of related sentences in a text.

**paragraph indication** way of differentiating groups of related sentences within a text.

**pig bristles** excessive punctuation, typically at ends of three or more lines of text in a row.

**pilcrow** classic symbol for a new paragraph.

**point size** measure of type size in points.

**punctuation** analphabetic marks used to organize a text.

## R

**ragged** not flush.

**readability** degree to which a body of text can be easily read; compare legibility.

**recto** originally the front side of a sheet of papyrus; today the right-hand page in a book; compare verso.

**reverse contrast** stroke modulations opposite of normal, heavier in the horizontals than in the verticals; also called inverse stress.

**revival** typeface designs derived from an earlier classic design.

**rivers** when word space is optically greater than linespace, whether or not these large word spaces line up vertically; a manifestation of uneven "color" and therefore to be avoided.

## S

**sans serif** typefaces without serifs.

**script** typefaces based on handwriting.

**serif** small stroke at the terminal of a main stroke.

**set solid** when point size is set equal to leading.

**setting** short for "typesetting."

**small capitals** set of capital letterforms the size of the x-height.

**soft return** line break that is not a paragraph break.

**subhead** head that is lower in hierarchy than one or more heads above it.

## T

**terminal** ending of a stroke in a letterform, a key distinguishing feature in a typeface design.

**text figures** numbers that are based on the x-height plus ascenders and descenders; also called Oldstyle figures.

**text type** type set in small sizes, usually set between 7 and 10 points, and intended for continu-ous reading.

**tittle** dot on letters i and j; any small diacritical mark.

**tracking** letterspacing; overall amount of space between letters on a passage of text; compare kerning.

**two-letter hyphenation** when only two letters precede or follow a hyphen; to be avoided for aesthetic reasons.

**typeface** complete group of characters designed to work as a set; today, used interchangeably with the word "font," although technically they do not share the same meaning.

**typesetting** practice of composing type on a page.

**typographer** person who designs typefaces or who sets type.

**typographic color** overall texture of a body of text; even "color" is your highest typographic priority.

**typography** art and craft of setting type.

## U

**u/lc** common abbreviation for upper- and lowercase; also abbreviated u&lc.

**underline** line used underneath a text to provide emphasis or differentiation.

**uppercase** capital letterforms.

## V

**vernacular** commonplace, ordinary or everyday.

**verso** originally the back side of a sheet of papyrus; today the left-hand page in a book; compare recto.

## W

**weight** varieties of related character sets within a typeface; text faces typically contain roman (regular), bold, and italic versions at minimum.

**widow** single word or a very short line at the end of a paragraph; also the first line of a new paragraph alone at the bottom of a column.

**word space** space between words.

## X

**x-height** distance from the baseline to the meanline; varies in size and ratio to cap height from face to face.

# Acknowledgments

Most days it seems like I work all alone in my studio. When I put together my thoughts for these acknowledgments, it becomes clear how many outstanding people I've had the pleasure to work with. Thank you! I could not have done it without you. I feel lucky to have had all of you become a part of my work and a part of my life.

With utmost appreciation to my professors at Carnegie Mellon University (where it all began): Dan Boyarski, Todd Cavalier, Joann Maier, Karen Moyer, Suzanne Slavick, and Mary Weidner. Your brilliant instruction transformed my way of seeing, and then my entire life thereafter.

To all the design students I've had the privilege to share knowledge with, thank you for your kind attention. I am honored by your willingness to listen, learn, and practice at my direction. This book is inspired by your creativity and enthusiasm.

Great thanks to my new coauthor in this edition, Stephen Coles, for his excellent and earnest writing of the typeface descriptions and the alternates. You have made invaluable contributions to the world of typography, and I am delighted to have your work in this second edition.

To David Jonathan Ross for his lovely typeface Output Sans, and his gracious permission to use it in this volume.

For recognizing the potential of this project in its infancy, I offer my sincerest gratitude to the legendary designer Erik Spiekermann. I am eternally in your debt for your support of this project. Thank you for your friendship and kindness.

For her help with the page layout section and other important new design elements in this edition, I am grateful to my friend and former student Chiharu Tanaka. Thank you for always being on my team!

To my dear old friends from CMU: Robert Bollinger, Maria Carluccio, Harold Hambrose, Mona Kim, and David Yu. (With a special shoutout to Robert for his generosity—and his puns.) I would not be the designer nor the person I am today without all you guys. #BFFs

For bold votes of confidence in the very early days of this project, many thanks to my fellow typophiles, Rod Cavazos and Joachim Müller-Lancé.

For the opportunity to teach so many students over the years, I thank the leaders of the Graphic Design department at Academy of Art University, Mary Scott and Phil Hamlett. I'm also grateful to all my fellow Academy of Art typography instructors, particularly those who have used the book in their classes: David Hake, Andrew Loesel, John Nettleton, and Nita Ybarra.

Many thanks to the typography teachers and students from other colleges and universities who used the first edition of this book in their classes. I enjoyed seeing the resulting work and getting your feedback. It's my hope that you will find added value in this revised edition.

Several sample Explorations were kindly re-created by former students based on the exceptional work they had done in my class. For these beautiful pages, I thank Matt Cacciola, Fred Carriedo, Candice Cheung, Gloria Hiek, Shawn Hsu, Vincent Lo, Priscilla Peña, Chiharu Tanaka, Anne Tsuei, and Beth Wong.

A number of colleagues, collaborators, friends, and former students gave me encouragement and support for the first edition or for this one. My thanks to Troy Alders, Augustus Ang, Meghan Arnold, Hal Belmont, Laura Belmont, Daniel Burgess, Gregory Cadars, Fred Carriedo, Jackson Cavanaugh, Whitney Clark, David Cole, Theresa dela Cruz, Dan Emery, Erik Gomez, Nigel Glover, Jonathan Graziani, Allan Haley, Anthony Jagoda, Nick Johnson, Anis Jun, Charles Malonzo, Ugla Marekowa, Christopher Morlan, Christina Palaia, Priscilla Peña, Michael Pieracci, Rich Prahm, Addy Procter, David Jonathan Ross, Brian Singer, Jennifer Sterling, Jeff Towner, Susan Verba, Matt Wakeman, Christine Wallis, Robert Woehrle, and Beth Wong. Know that even the smallest words of reassurance make a big difference. Thank you all!

And, finally, with much pride and love to my late father, Dominick, and my mother, Evelyn. Together you showed me the meaning of dedication, the value of teaching by example, and the importance of doing things for others. And for an endless supply of wisdom and unconditional love, I thank the rest of the incredible members of my too-numerous-to-mention extended family. Whatever success I enjoy in my life is shared with each and every one of you. ♥

# urther Reading

*he Anatomy of Type: A Graphic Guide to 100 Typefaces*
y Stephen Coles

*he Elements of Typographic Style*
y Robert Bringhurst

*side Paragraphs: Typographic Fundamentals*
y Cyrus Highsmith

*odern Typography*
y Robin Kinross

*he New Typography*
y Jan Tschichold

*top Stealing Sheep and Find Out How Type Works*
y Erik Spiekermann

*hinking with Type*
y Ellen Lupton

*ypographic Design: Form and Communication*
y by Rob Carter, Philip B. Meggs, Ben Day, Sandra Maxa,
nd Mark Sanders

*he Typographic Desk Reference*
y Theo Rosendorf

*ypographie: A Manual of Design*
y Emil Ruder

*ypography: Macro and Microaesthetics*
y Willi Kunz

*ypography: My Way to Typography*
y Wolfgang Weingart

*ypography for Lawyers*
y Matthew Butterick
See also the more general information in Mr. Butterick's online book,
*ractical Typography* at *http://practicaltypography.com.*)

# About the Authors

**Carolina de Bartolo** is a designer, author, educator, and publisher. The first edition of her typography textbook, *Explorations in Typography: Mastering the Art of Fine Typesetting,* and its digital companions were recognized with several design awards.

A graduate of the School of Design at Carnegie Mellon University, Carolina is a systems thinker who also revels in details. She began her career designing statements and forms at Siegel & Gale in New York City and later worked on the Citibank banking machine user-interface design team at Two Twelve Associates. During her tenure as design history chairperson at AIGA San Francisco, she founded the chapter's library. She has been an MFA thesis adviser and has taught all levels of typography as well as design history at Academy of Art University in San Francisco since 2000.

**Stephen Coles** is an Editorial Director & Associate Curator at Letterform Archive in San Francisco. He publishes *Fonts In Use* (fontsinuse.com) and *Typographica* (typographica.org), and he wrote the book, *The Anatomy of Type.* Stephen was formerly a creative director at FontShop and a member of the FontFont TypeBoard.

**Erik Spiekermann** is an art historian, information architect, type designer, and the author of *Stop Stealing Sheep and Find Out How Type Works.* Two of his typefaces, FF Meta and ITC Officina, are considered to be modern classics. He founded MetaDesign (1979) and FontShop (1988). He is behind the design of well-known brands such as Audi, Bosch, VW, German Railways, and Heidelberg Printing, among others; information systems for Berlin Transit and Düsseldorf Airport; and publications like *The Economist.* He designed exclusive typefaces for corporations such as Deutsche Bahn, Bosch, ZDF (German TV), Cisco, Mozilla, and many others.

Erik is Honorary Professor at the University of the Arts in Bremen and in 2003 received the Gerrit Noordzij Award from the Royal Academy in The Hague. In 2006 he was awarded an honorary doctorship from Pasadena Art Center. He was made an Honorary Royal Designer for Industry by the RSA in Britain in 2007 and Ambassador for the European Year of Creativity and Innovation by the European Union for 2009. In 2011 he received the German National Design Award for Lifetime Achievement as well as the TDC Medal and a Lifetime Award from the German Art Directors Club.

He is frequently asked to contribute to books and magazines on topics from visual language to bicycles (he owns 13 of them).

Erik was managing partner and creative director of Edenspiekermann with offices in Berlin, Amsterdam, and San Francisco until June 2014, when he moved from that position to the supervisory board. He now runs an experimental letterpress workshop in Berlin. Erik splits his time between Berlin and San Francisco.

# Index

**“Each problem that I solved became a rule, which served afterwards to solve other problems.”**

—René Descartes